PRAISE FOR *NO RIGHT TO WIN*

A UNIQUE APPROACH TO THE STUDY OF A MAJOR HISTORICAL EVENT…

"No Right to Win is a unique approach to the study of a major historical event. It virtually places the reader in attendance at a major gathering of Battle of Midway veterans—a veterans' seminar that never ends. The experience is almost like engaging in conversation with the men of Midway themselves, resulting in a great deal of fresh, interesting information about the most important sea battle of the twentieth century, and especially about those who fought and won it."

—Vice Admiral William D. Houser, USN (Retired), Deputy Chief of Naval Operations (Air Warfare), 1972-1976

A MILESTONE IN MIDWAY HISTORY…

"No Right to Win represents not only a milestone in Midway history, but naval historiography as well. The access of World War II veterans, students, and enthusiasts to one another on the Internet affords a case study in how history is being preserved in the information age. Altogether an absorbing study!"

—Barrett Tillman, author of *Clash of the Carriers* and *Wildcat: the F4F in World War II*

THE STORY BEHIND THE STORY…

"For a decade the Battle of Midway Roundtable has delved deeply into the pivotal 1942 naval action that set the United States on the path to victory in the war against Japan. Actual participants of the battle, relating their experiences and sharing their special expertise, interact in a unique way in this popular Internet forum with historians, enthusiasts, and each other to the great benefit of preserving history. In his excellent and entertaining new book *No Right to Win: a Continuing Dialogue with Veterans of the Battle of Midway*, Ronald Russell has distilled the very best of the exchanges in the Midway Roundtable that he moderates. By examining key facets of the battle and testing controversial theories, he reveals many hitherto unknown facts, offers incisive insights into its many complex aspects and mysteries, and also tells the "story behind the story." *No Right to Win* will appeal not only to Midway specialists but to all readers who want to know more about one of the most important and dramatic battles in world history."

—John B. Lundstrom, author of *The First Team, The First Team and the Guadalcanal Campaign,* and *Black Shoe Carrier Admiral: Frank Jack Fletcher at Coral Sea, Midway and Guadalcanal*

No Right To Win

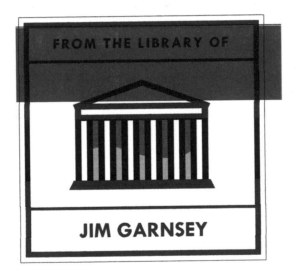

Near Midway, June 4, 1942: Fighter pilot Tom Cheek's second aerial kill of the day flashes past his Grumman Wildcat as he spots another Zero to his left, about to attack the vulnerable TBD Devastators of Torpedo Squadron Three. Below, Ensign Wesley Osmus bails out of his stricken TBD as it spirals toward the water. (From an original painting by John Greaves, www.johngreavesart.com)

No Right To Win

A Continuing Dialogue with Veterans of the Battle of Midway

Ronald W. Russell

iUniverse, Inc.

New York Lincoln Shanghai

No Right To Win

A Continuing Dialogue with Veterans of the Battle of Midway

Copyright © 2006 by Ronald W. Russell

iUniverse books may be ordered through booksellers or by contacting:

iUniverse
2021 Pine Lake Road, Suite 100
Lincoln, NE 68512
www.iuniverse.com
1-800-Authors (1-800-288-4677)

ISBN-13: 978-0-595-40511-4 (pbk)
ISBN-13: 978-0-595-84878-2 (ebk)
ISBN-10: 0-595-40511-8 (pbk)
ISBN-10: 0-595-84878-8 (ebk)

Printed in the United States of America

To the codebreakers who had the vision…
To the Marines who had to hold…
To the seamen who had to defend, endure, and survive…
And to the aviators who had the courage…

To all of the victors of Midway whose vision, resolve, spirit, and courage dramatically changed the course of a war

CONTENTS

▼

List of Illustrations

Introduction

Inscribed on the walls of the beautiful World War II Memorial in Washington, D.C. are many stirring quotes arising from the war, or from renowned works about the war. On the memorial's south wall, in the Pacific Theater section, one of them proclaims "They had no right to win. Yet they did, and in doing so they changed the course of a war." Those two brief sentences from Walter Lord's foreword in *Incredible Victory* sum up the Battle of Midway with profound conciseness.

In June of 1942, one of the most powerful war fleets the world had ever known descended upon the tiny atoll of Midway, about 1100 miles northwest of Hawaii. The Japanese intent was to lure the U.S. Navy's few remaining aircraft carriers and scant supporting vessels into the open where they would suffer a decisive defeat, forcing the Americans to sue for peace and thus bring World War II in the Pacific to a quick end on Japanese terms. The vast armada of aircraft carriers, battleships, cruisers, destroyers, and submarines that the Imperial Japanese Navy was bringing to the fight seemed far more than adequate for the task. The Americans would be hopelessly outclassed and outgunned. There could be only one possible result.

But it didn't happen that way. Through an amazing combination of skill, courage, and especially luck, the U.S. not only prevailed at Midway but delivered to the enemy a devastating setback that halted all Japanese expansion in the Pacific. That unexpected development significantly affected the rest of the war in all theaters, as you'll find explained in Appendix B.

This book, though, is not just another account of the Battle of Midway, for that story has been told many times. Rather, this is a book about the men who fought and won the "Incredible Victory," the veterans of the battle themselves. It is the story of a very unique group of Midway airmen, sailors, and Marines; men who have volunteered to share their knowledge and experiences of twentieth century history through the use of twenty-first century methods, and to do so on a continuing, almost daily basis. They are the veteran members of the *Battle of Midway Roundtable*, a stalwart corps of octogenarian ex-warriors, ably using computer gadgetry that most of their Greatest Generation contemporaries eschew. Through their active participation on the Internet-based Roundtable, aided by the generous support of noted military authors and historians, hundreds of men and women around the world, of all ages and backgrounds, have gained an extensive body of knowledge of the Battle of Midway. To the extent possible, that knowledge has been imparted to these pages.

From its humble, accidental beginning in 1997 to its respected position today as a living resource on the most crucial naval engagement in American history, the Battle of Midway Roundtable has continuously maintained the interest of veterans, students, hobbyists, historians, authors, screenwriters, military professionals, and myriad others for many years. It has served its members as a convenient electronic meeting hall where the victors of Midway seem, as if by magic, to always be present and willing to share their personal memories of the battle.

Their accounts of the Battle of Midway and the understandings that we can derive from them are contained within the following chapters. Some of it may be familiar to you, but most readers will encounter at least a few surprises, and perhaps even a revelation or two that are rather stunning.

For those who have only a minimal awareness of the battle—why and how it was fought and the impact it had on the rest of the Second World War and beyond—I recommend that you first read Appendix B, which explains its key aspects and their importance. Knowing those basic facts will equip you to understand and perhaps better appreciate what you'll find on the following pages.

Ronald W. Russell
July 25, 2006

Author's Acknowledgements

My first and most obvious acknowledgement must go to all those wonderful veterans on the Battle of Midway Roundtable who so willingly and often eloquently shared their tales of the battle over a period of many years. This book is *their* story, and without their generosity in answering endless questions of every stripe—frequently the same questions, over and over—you would be reading something else right now. (You'll find them all conveniently listed in Appendix A.)

Except for a few passages duly noted, every veteran story, anecdote, or quote on these pages has appeared in some form in the message traffic and newsletters of the Battle of Midway Roundtable or on its Internet site. However, since the organization cranked out something like *seven thousand* individual e-mail messages plus over three hundred newsletter pages during its first eight years, I occasionally found it convenient to borrow from the works of members who had previously published some of the Roundtable's best veteran tales. That seemed a logical alternative to endless digging through megabytes of old computer files stored in a daunting jumble of formats and indexing methods. Thus, it is with deep gratitude that I acknowledge the kind cooperation of Australian archivist James Bowen, curator of the Pacific War Historical Society, a unique resource focused on the battles of the Coral Sea and Midway, and Canadian commercial artist John Greaves, whose web site includes several Midway veteran stories illustrated by his original artwork. This book's frontispiece showcases an example of John's talent, and he also assisted with its front cover design.

Several other Roundtable members were crucial to the successful completion of this project. My initial salute naturally goes to William H. Price, the Roundtable's founder and energetic captain during its first five years. Next, I must thank attorney Allen M. Peisner for legal coaching and extensive editing services. This book is a far superior product thanks to Allen's wide-ranging contributions. Special thanks also go to naval aviation author Barrett Tillman for proofreading the manuscript and offering many important suggestions for improvement. I'm also indebted to John Lundstrom, Robert Cressman, Jon Parshall, Alvin Kernan, and Stanford Linzey for their willingness to share their knowledge and experience as the authors of published works on the Battle of Midway. Bill K. Vickrey provided an abundance of detail from his personal Battle of Midway archives (unrivaled anywhere outside of the Navy Department, if there), and Bernard Cavalcante at the U.S. Naval Historical Center in Washington was an able accomplice in ferreting out data on many Midway veterans (and as you'll see in Chapter 15, a few *alleged* Midway veterans).

Sincere thanks also go to Bowen P. Weisheit, the author *The Last Flight of Ensign C. Markland Kelly, Junior, USNR*, for the use of a key diagram from his book; to Dr. James D'Angelo and the International Midway Memorial Foundation for permission to quote from their exclusive interview with VB-6 skipper Richard Best; to Tom Evans and the family of Torpedo Squadron 8 pilot Ensign William Evans for the use of the latter's poignant personal letters sent home prior to his death at Midway; to *The Daily Gazette* of Schenectady, New York for permission to include their article on a bogus Midway veteran in Appendix E; and to Ben Lanterman (photographer) and Kent Walters (aircraft owner) for the original cover photo. Kent's fine flying scale SBD Dauntless is an authentic 1:6.7 model of the plane flown at Midway by Bombing Squadron Six pilot Ensign George Goldsmith.

To anyone, anywhere who should be mentioned here and isn't—and there most likely are a few—I claim the constraints of advancing age and humbly beg your forgiveness. The fact that your name doesn't show up on these pages does not mean that your participation on the Roundtable and/or help with this book are not deeply appreciated.

Glossary

The following is a list of abbreviations, acronyms, and special terms used in this book. Each definition is appropriate for the Battle of Midway era and in some cases will not be consistent with modern usage.

1/c, 2/c, 3/c	First, second, and third class; enlisted naval rank designators
1MC	"Number 1 Master Caller," a ship's PA or general announcing system
AA	anti-aircraft. Also AAA or "triple-A," anti-aircraft artillery
Adm.	admiral; four-star rank, equivalent to a U.S. Army full general
AMM	Aviation Machinist's Mate; enlisted specialty, aircraft mechanic
AOM	Aviation Ordnanceman; enlisted specialty, aircraft weapons
ARM	Aviation Radioman; enlisted specialty, radio operators and R/Gs
ASW	anti-submarine warfare
BB	battleship
BOM	the Battle of Midway
BOMRT	the Battle of Midway Roundtable
CA	heavy cruiser
CAP	Chief Aviation Pilot; an enlisted pilot (see NAP). Also…
CAP	combat air patrol; fighter defenses over a task force
Capt.	Captain; naval rank equivalent to an army colonel. Also…
Captain	the commanding officer of a USN ship or station, regardless of rank
CarDiv	carrier division; two or more aircraft carriers and supporting ships
Cdr.	commander, naval officer, equivalent to an army lieutenant colonel
CEAG	Commander, *Enterprise* Air Group (Lt. Cdr. C. Wade McClusky)
CHAG	Commander, *Hornet* Air Group (Cdr. Stanhope C. Ring)

CHC	Chaplains Corps of the U.S. Navy
Chief	Chief Petty Officer, naval rank equiv. to an army sgt. first class
CINCPAC	Commander-in-Chief, Pacific Fleet (Adm. Nimitz)
CIU	Combat Intelligence Unit, Pearl Harbor ("Station HYPO")
CL	light cruiser
CO	commanding officer
ComInt	communications intelligence
CruDiv	cruiser division; two or more cruisers and supporting ships
CV	aircraft carrier
CVL	light aircraft carrier
CWO	Chief Warrant Officer; a commissioned WO
CYAG	Commander, *Yorktown* Air Group (Lt. Cdr. Oscar Pederson)
DD	destroyer
DesRon	destroyer squadron; a grouping of destroyers or destroyer divisions
Dog	hand-operated clamp that secures a watertight door or hatch
Ens.	Ensign; USN rank equivalent to an army second lieutenant. Also…
Ensign	the national flag
F	Fireman; non-rated sailor in an engineering department
F4F	Grumman "Wildcat" fighter
FRUMEL	post-BOM name for the ComInt command in Australia
FRUPAC	post-BOM name for the ComInt command in Hawaii
GQ	general quarters; battle stations aboard a warship
Head	shipboard lavatory; toilets
HYPO	(also Station HYPO) unofficial name for CIU and FRUPAC.
IJN	Imperial Japanese Navy (**-S** = IJN ship)
Kate	IJN Type 97 torpedo bomber and carrier-born land bomber
KIA	killed in action
Kido Butai	Japanese carrier task force (a.k.a. *Mobile Force, First Air Fleet*, and *First Carrier Striking Force*)
LSO	landing signal officer; guides aircraft to a landing on the flight deck
Lt.	Lieutenant; USN officer, equivalent to an army captain
Lt. Cdr.	Lieutenant Commander; USN officer, equiv. to an army major
Lt.(jg)	Lieutenant, Jr. Grade; USN officer, equiv. to an army first lieutenant
MACH	Warrant Machinist; the rank of many USN warrant officer pilots

MAG	Marine Air Group. MAG-22 was VMF-221 plus VMSB-241 on Midway.
MIA	missing in action
Nagumo Report	Vice Adm. Nagumo's after-action report for *Kido Butai* at Midway
NAP	Naval Aviation Pilot; the rating for an enlisted pilot
NAS	naval air station
ONI	the Office of Naval Intelligence, Washington, D.C.
OP-20-G	ComInt branch of the U.S. Naval Communications Directorate
PBY	Consolidated "Catalina" seaplane, patrol bomber
Petty Officer	(PO) navy non-commissioned officer, equiv. to army corporals/sergeants
R/G	radioman-gunner (aircrew)
Rear Adm.	Rear Admiral; two star rank, equivalent to an army major general
RM	Radioman; enlisted specialty, shipboard communications
SBD	Douglas "Dauntless" dive bomber
Scuttlebutt	sailors' slang for a rumor or unsubstantiated information
Sea	Seaman; non-rated enlisted sailor. See also **F**—Fireman.
Sickbay	medical treatment facility at a shore station or aboard ship
SigInt	signal intelligence (same as ComInt)
Snafu	World War II slang: "situation normal, all fouled up"
SOC	Scout, Observation, Curtiss (small seaplane carried on cruisers)
TBD	Douglas "Devastator" torpedo bomber
TBF	Grumman "Avenger" torpedo bomber
USMC	United States Marine Corps (**-R** = Marine Corps Reserve)
USN	United States Navy (**-R** = Naval Reserve)
Val	IJN Type 99 dive bomber
VB-3	Bombing Squadron 3, USS *Yorktown*
VB-6	Bombing Squadron 6, USS *Enterprise*
VB-8	Bombing Squadron 8, USS *Hornet*
VF-3, VF-3/42	composite fighter squadron aboard USS *Yorktown*
VF-6	Fighting Squadron 6, USS *Enterprise*
VF-8	Fighting Squadron 8, USS *Hornet*
Vice Adm.	Vice Admiral; three star rank, equiv. to an army lieutenant general
VMF-221	Marine Fighting Squadron 221, Midway
VMSB-241	Marine Scouting-Bombing Squadron 241, Midway

VP	patrol squadron (PBYs at the BOM)
VS-2	Scouting Squadron 2, USS *Lexington* (at the Coral Sea)
VS-5	Scouting Squadron 5, USS *Yorktown* (VB-5 renamed)
VS-6	Scouting Squadron 6, USS *Enterprise*
VS-8	Scouting Squadron 8, USS *Hornet*
VT-3	Torpedo Squadron 3, USS *Yorktown*
VT-6	Torpedo Squadron 6, USS *Enterprise*
VT-8	Torpedo Squadron 8, USS *Hornet*
WO	Warrant Officer; a technical specialist above the enlisted ranks
XO	executive officer; the second in command of a ship/squadron/station
Y	Yeoman; enlisted admin specialist, i.e., ship or squadron clerk
Zero	Japanese A6M Type 0 fighter (U.S. code name "Zeke")

CHAPTER 1

▼

ON LINE WITH THE
GREATEST GENERATION

The Biggest Show on Earth

Lieutenant Howard P. Ady, Jr. U.S. Navy, was a PBY Catalina patrol bomber pilot during the Battle of Midway (BOM). His squadron was based on the atoll itself, and along with PBYs from other squadrons, Ady and his crew were tasked with searching for the Japanese fleet that communications intelligence experts knew to be heading their way. If the enemy could capture and hold Midway, the Hawaiian islands and especially Pearl Harbor itself would be threatened. That would severely hinder the Americans' ability to prosecute the war into the western Pacific and could potentially disrupt the vital lifeline to Australia and General MacArthur's Southwest Pacific command. Quite simply, the Japanese had to be stopped, defeated, and turned back at Midway, but first they had to be found.

By luck of the draw, Ady's aircraft was assigned one of the few search sectors in which the Japanese fleet was most likely to be spotted. And so it came to be: the enemy carriers finally appeared as Thursday morning, the fourth of June, 1942 began to dawn. Ady's radioman electrified those listening on the island and aboard the ships of the U.S. task forces with the message:

TWO CARRIERS AND MAIN BODY OF SHIPS
CARRIERS IN FRONT
COURSE 135 SPEED 25

As Ady himself would later explain, it was "like watching a curtain rise on the Biggest Show on Earth."[1]

The Battle of Midway was thusly joined, and the course of World War II in the Pacific was about to undergo a fundamental change.

*   *   *   *

The Civil War Around a Table

William H. Price was only twelve years old when he first encountered anything related to the Battle of Midway. Like nearly all young boys, he liked to play "army" with his buddies, and in 1943 there was much to fire the imagination. The Second World War dominated news broadcasts on the radio and the newsreels at the Saturday matinee.

The North Carolina youngster and his friends became particularly fascinated with naval air combat when they saw the detailed dioramas by Normal Bel Geddes in *Life* magazine. The dioramas' initial appearance in *Life* depicted scenes from the Battle of the Coral Sea, the first ever carrier-to-carrier combat. But young Bill's interest really escalated a few months later when the magazine featured Geddes' more expansive dioramas on the Battle of Midway. The realistic views of diving aircraft, majestic ships, and bomb and torpedo strikes throwing mountains of water into the air were a feast for the young boy's mind, creating strong memories that he retained for decades.[2]

But other than Samuel Eliot Morison's *History of United States Naval Operations in World War II*, there wasn't much of substance about the Battle of Midway to be found in general market publications in the years immediately after the war, although Price always read anything that came along. Finally, in 1967, Walter Lord produced his Midway best seller, *Incredible Victory,* which at that time was the most comprehensive report of the battle available to the public. Price read it cover to cover, then read it again.

However, the Battle of Midway was a minor element in Price's life at that time. After graduating from college in 1952, he went to work in Washington, D.C. for the Armed Forces Security Agency, which later became the National Security Agency (NSA). He was interested in the science of cryptology, which became the foundation for his career. Initially assigned to decoding work, he would occasionally dabble in traffic analysis, the art of extracting meaningful information from an adversary's radio messages without decoding them. While that was simply an indicator of his keen interest in his job, it got him into trouble with his superiors who expected him to keep his nose to the codebreaking grindstone while on their clock.

But that didn't deter him from an abiding interest in all aspects of his work. He gradually perfected both his decoding and traffic analysis skills, and also began to work with the early generation computer systems that the government employed in the 1950s. The latter eventually became Price's prime responsibility, and over the years he developed a number of information management systems that enabled his group to rapidly correlate and analyze the daily influx of data from the agency's many field operatives.

He left the NSA for a tour in Vietnam as a civilian contractor with the Agency for International Development. Upon returning to the United States he commenced a new career with the State Department, specializing in the development of computerized resources for managing the data and information that arrived daily from American embassies and consulates around the world. It was during those early years at the State Department that he acquired a new avocation: American history.

While Price enjoyed reading about the Battle of Midway and related topics, history in general was not something that had particularly interested him. But that began to change in the late 1960s when he became aware of a number of State Department coworkers involved in something called "The District of Columbia Civil War Roundtable." The group met for dinner twice per month for in-depth discussions on assorted battles and issues of the Civil War, and they sometimes took field trips to nearby historic sites. Price had previously visited the battlefield at Gettysburg, and hence had a passing knowledge of that pivotal conflict that had been the turning point in the war. He decided to join the D.C. Roundtable and eventually became an enthusiastic member.

But he didn't lose his fascination for the Battle of Midway. That memory remained in the back of his mind, and it was sharply rejuvenated by the 1976 movie *Midway*, the first post-war motion picture to focus exclusively on the battle. His interest piqued further with the 1982 publication of *Miracle at Midway* by Gordon W. Prange, which complemented *Incredible Victory* and became a best seller in its own right.

The advent of the Internet in subsequent years enabled Price to employ his computer skills in seeking out Midway-related information (a tedious task in the days before on-line search engines). He began composing notes and amassing a collection of books and media articles on the subject, and he constructed a unique and meticulously detailed chronological outline of the battle based on the timeline in Prange's book and the official Japanese after-action report of the battle.

A Familiar Name

Midway remained a private fascination for the next several years; something that held Price's interest during idle hours at home. But that dramatically changed one day in 1997 when he received a routine telephone call at work from another government employee who identified himself as Howard Ady.

Price did a classic double-take on hearing that name in his telephone receiver. "Wait a minute," he said. "You're Howard Ady?"

"That's right," said the voice. "Have we met before?"

"No," Price replied. The voice was too youthful to be a World War II veteran. "But tell me…by any chance, are you related to the Howard Ady who flew a PBY patrol plane at the Battle of Midway in 1942? The one who initially discovered the Japanese carrier force?"

"Sure," said the voice. "That's my dad."

Another double-take. "That *is* your dad? He's, uh, still alive?"

"Yeah. He lives in Arizona, in a retirement home. We talk on the phone now and then and exchange e-mail a lot."

"E-mail? Your dad does e-mail?"

"Oh yeah, all the time. He's quite good at it."

Price thought that over for a few seconds. "Mr. Ady, we definitely need to get acquainted. I'd like to talk with you about your dad. Do you think I could meet him?"

"Well, sure, he visits me here every now and then. But tell me, do you do e-mail at home? You could meet him by e-mail at first."

"Yes, I do e-mail at home. I certainly do," Price replied. "What's your dad's ID?"

At that instant he realized that he might be on to something very new and potentially very interesting.

Coming On Board

Bill Price sent his first e-mail message to the elder Howard Ady in October of 1997. Ady was delighted to hear from him and responded quickly. He met with Price during a visit to Washington, and the two commenced a casual e-mail exchange focusing on the Battle of Midway. Price wanted to know all of the details concerning Ady's flight on the first morning of the battle and the critical role his PBY aircraft played in the discovery of the Japanese carrier force. Ady was happy to oblige.

Price had been a frequent visitor to a couple of Midway-related Internet sites, particularly that of Christopher T. Hawkinson, who was at least as fervent and painstaking in researching the battle as Price. By 1997 Hawkinson had arguably amassed the web's most comprehensive collection of BOM narratives, data, images, and references in one place. Another Internet resource that captured Price's interest was the Imperial Japanese Navy (IJN) site operated by Jonathan B. Parshall, a business analyst in Minneapolis. Parshall had acquired a fascination for the IJN's ships as a youngster, which he augmented during a year spent in Japan after college. He decided to develop a web site devoted solely to the Japanese navy of World War II, since no one else had done so. He didn't think such a narrowly-focused resource would attract much attention more than a half century after the IJN had ceased to exist, but that was not the case. He quickly found that many shared his attraction for the former enemy's navy, and the popularity of his site rapidly grew.

Bill Price was among the earliest fans of Parshall's efforts, and it occurred to him that both Parshall and Hawkinson would be interested in his e-mail exchanges with Howard Ady. He began including them as "CC" (informational) addressees on his messages, and got positive responses from both. Hawkinson suggested that Price should consider inviting others interested in Midway to join the discussion. In effect, it could be a sort of e-mail circular. Hawkinson could post Price's e-mail address on his web site, and anyone wanting to join the circular could simply let him know. Price agreed.

One of the first to respond was Bill K. Vickrey, a retired insurance company manager in North Carolina. While Jon Parshall and Chris Hawkinson had the most impressive IJN and BOM data repositories available on the Internet, Bill Vickrey had possibly the most comprehensive collection of references on the battle to be found anywhere else. He became interested in the BOM before the war was even over, as a U.S. Navy pharmacist's mate (medical corpsman) assigned to the 13th Naval District in Seattle, Washington. The USS *Enterprise* (CV-6) arrived in port one day in 1945, and Vickrey became acquainted with several of the ship's company while tending to them in the naval station dispensary. The *Enterprise* men were proud of their ship's twenty-two battle stars, and none of those stars shown more brightly in their minds than the one earned at the Battle of Midway. Vickrey listened with interest and admiration to their tales of the great battle, and he remembered them in the years that followed..

After the war Vickrey began a long career as an insurance company agent, broker, and executive. The growth of his business required him to travel extensively across the nation, which afforded ample opportunity to meet with friends and relatives just about anywhere. One day, remembering his fascination for the Battle of Midway, he decided to see if he could find some of the main participants and perhaps meet with them for a discussion about the battle. An easy resource was the U.S. Naval Academy at Annapolis, which maintained contact information on each of its graduates. It was a simple matter to look up a few of the principal players from the battle and introduce himself by phone; a comfortable notion for salesman Vickrey, who had to be outgoing and friendly with any stranger in order to make a living.

Engaging the Men of Midway

One of Vickrey's first calls was to Lt. Cdr. Richard H. Best, U.S. Navy (Retired). Vickrey knew that Best was a genuine hero of the battle and a largely unheralded one. He had been the commander of a squadron of SBD dive bombers from the *Enterprise,* part of the air group led by Lt. Cdr. C. Wade McClusky that successfully bombed two of the four Japanese carriers assaulting Midway. According to Best, McClusky made a tactical error in forming his planes for their dives, with the result that the entire group of thirty-one bombers was set to attack only one of the enemy ships. Best instantly perceived what was about to happen and quickly ad-libbed an adjustment that managed to direct three of the planes toward a second carrier. Through skill and a lot of luck, one or perhaps two of the bombs from Best's trio struck the ship squarely and the third was a damaging near miss, knocking the enemy vessel and its highly dangerous air group out of the war.[3]

Best and Vickrey hit it off from the start, and Vickrey was particularly proud to call Dick Best one of his closest friends. That relationship brought him contact with a great many more Midway veterans, for Best was happy to introduce Vickrey, either in person or via e-mail, to a number of his squadron-mates from the battle as well as others from that era.

Thus when Vickrey noticed the invitation on Chris Hawkinson's web site to join a new e-mail circular focusing on the Battle of Midway, he not only brought himself aboard but in time referred several veterans of the battle who were delighted to have a chance to exchange views among compatriots with whom, in some cases, they'd had no contact for over fifty years. By the end of its first year, then, Bill Price's informal little discussion group had a small but solid corps of

Midway veterans and other interested parties exchanging e-mail with each other nearly every day.

The Battle of Midway Around a Table

The group rapidly grew in numbers as the word spread. By the end of the second year Price was forwarding e-mail to nearly two hundred recipients, including several in Canada, Europe, Australia, and New Zealand. The volume of traffic (e-mail messages) expanded with the growth in membership, with the result that in that second year Price was on the keyboard each and every day, seven days per week, sometimes handling and sending along five, ten, or even fifteen messages per day. The single day record, set one day in 2001, was twenty-two messages!

Now retired, Price was astonished at the monster he'd created, but he now had time available for the task and loved every minute of it. He found it fascinating that all those old vets—generally in their late seventies at least, and some in their mid eighties—were amazingly competent with computers. It was the Greatest Generation, *on line*. Who would have ever dreamed it?

Such an expansive group had to have a name, Price reasoned, and it didn't take long for him to think of a suitable choice. Remembering his old District of Columbia Civil War Roundtable gang in the State Department, he started calling his e-mail circular "The Battle of Midway Roundtable" (BOMRT). He thought it especially appropriate in this case, since a tenet of King Arthur's mythical roundtable was that everyone was equal: the king and his knights all sat equally around the table; no one was at its head. So it was with the BOMRT: retired Navy captains and admirals exchanged friendly, informative missives with former corporals and petty officers, with young students seeking information for school history projects, and even with ship and aircraft hobbyists wanting to get the last possible detail right on their flying scale models. It became a wonderfully homogenous group and Bill Price's full time job in retirement.

CHAPTER 2

▼

CHANGES OF COMMAND

The Roundtable Turns

My association with the BOMRT began during its third year, when I was researching the Battle of Midway for a novel that I had in mind. My own naval career plus employment as a technical writer had motivated me to write a book focused on the great battle, a fascination since my teenage years that rivaled Price's.

I thought I'd start my tale aboard Howard Ady's patrol plane, but I really didn't know a whole lot about PBYs. Some detail about the aircraft's configuration and equipment was necessary for the story, so I started searching the Internet for PBY information. I found some truly great resources, but one site especially caught my attention: Chris Hawkinson's. He had posted a wealth of information that I could use in my story, but I also spotted his notice about Bill Price's Midway e-mail circular. *Why not*, I thought. Perhaps I could get some useful input for my novel from that group, whoever they were. I sent an introductory message to Price and was added to his roster in June of 2000.

For the next two years I participated on the Roundtable as one of its 200-plus international members, receiving and digesting Bill Price's daily e-mail output and occasionally offering a contribution of my own. I found the first-hand accounts by actual veterans of the battle—Marines on the atoll, sailors on the ships, pilots and gunners in the planes, and codebreaking wizards who purloined the enemy's secrets—to be a never-ending fascination.

Then, in late September of 2002, Bill Price mysteriously went silent. Nothing was received from him for nearly two weeks; a phenomenal occurrence considering that he'd never missed more than one day of Roundtable output in nearly five years. Something was clearly wrong. Finally, a few members received a message from his daughter stating that Bill had undergone a surgical procedure that didn't turn out well. In brief, he was facing a very long recuperation from a serious malady that would sap his strength and energy for unknown weeks or months. There would be no more BOMRT traffic from Bill Price for the foreseeable future.

That message was eventually forwarded to me. I felt both sympathy for Price and disappointment that a unique historical resource had come to a premature end. I wondered if another member would want to bring it back to life, and if not, I'd consider attempting it myself. After several days with no further word from anyone, I contacted as many Roundtable participants as possible to see if they'd like me to carry on in Bill's stead. The responses were totally supportive. The members around the world didn't want the BOMRT to end any more than I did.

And so it began. It was now *me* shackled to my computer for at least an hour each and every day, receiving, editing, and forwarding all manner of e-mail traffic to and from an increasing roster of members. In time it became two hours every day. As more new members came aboard bringing a steadily increasing traffic load, it eventually became evident that managing the association through the forwarding of individual e-mail messages to nearly 250 recipients seven days a week simply could not continue. After only eighteen months at the helm, I decided that a major change in the nature and operation of the Roundtable was an unavoidable necessity.

Thus, on the first of May in 2004, the BOMRT transitioned from a daily e-mail exchange to the publication of a more conventional weekly periodical, *The Roundtable Forum*. Distribution of the *Forum* was still accomplished by e-mail, but I began to enhance it with a variety of Internet-linked features that made it more like an electronic magazine. I was attempting to emulate the style and appeal of professional publications such as the U.S. Naval Institute's popular *Naval History* journal, but with our own very unique content: a continuing dialogue with a large number of veterans of the Battle of Midway. As I write these words more than two years later, the new members keep coming.

*   *   *   *

DeLo and the Admiral

Without the active participation of over fifty actual veterans of the Battle of Midway, the BOMRT would be little different than any other informal history discussion group. But in our case, discussion of history is aided and supported by the very men who helped make the history itself. It is their first-person input to our *Roundtable Forum* articles and Internet pages that sustains a level of interest and value that can't be found elsewhere.

One of the first Midway-era veterans to come aboard was, ironically, not actually a veteran of the Battle of Midway. But Captain Frank L. DeLorenzo, U.S. Navy (Retired), had contributed one small component to the eventual victory by transporting its mastermind out to Pearl Harbor in order to take command of the shattered Pacific Fleet. "DeLo," as he came to be known on the Roundtable, was one of the pilots of a four-engine PB2Y seaplane carrying Admiral Chester Nimitz to Hawaii in December 1941. He remembers the flight well:

> I was privileged to be one of the pilots who flew Admiral Nimitz from San Diego to Pearl Harbor on Christmas Day, 1941, a little over two weeks after the attack on Pearl Harbor. He was to relieve Admiral Husband Kimmel as CINCPAC and take over the badly wounded Pacific Fleet. We took off from San Diego in the early evening of December 24th in a PB2Y-2 Coronado, a four-engine seaplane and a big brother of the PBY Catalina. My log book shows the flight took 17.2 hours.
>
> We reached Pearl Harbor about mid morning on Christmas day. Upon arriving over the harbor, we invited Admiral Nimitz up to the flight deck in order to observe the damage and destruction, and he eagerly accepted. We made wide circles over Pearl Harbor and Hickham Field. He was seated in the left hand pilot's seat for purposes of this observation and he just kept shaking his head and clucking his tongue. God only knows what was going through his mind, but if it was anything like what we were thinking at the time, it would have been *those dirty bastards! Somehow, some way, we are going to make them pay!*
>
> We were looking at the crumpled hulks of our proud Pacific Fleet battleships. We saw skeletons of what were once hangars, and flight lines filled with junk that used to be military aircraft. The carnage was sickening. And with all of that on his mind, what was the admiral's demeanor as he disembarked to take on this great responsibility? He took the time to shake the hand of every member of the crew, to thank us for a comfortable flight, and to apologize for

having taken us from our families on Christmas Day. What a giant of a man! What a great leader to take over the Pacific Fleet! I felt proud that we were able to bring the right man to the right place at the right time.[1]

DeLo was well acquainted with Howard Ady. The two first met in Yokosuka, Japan after the war when DeLo was executive officer of USS *Kearsarge* (CV-33) and Ady was operations officer aboard USS *Hornet* (CV-12). They spent considerable time together in connection with *Hornet* relieving *Kearsarge* on station with the Seventh Fleet.

They renewed their acquaintance in retirement when Bill Vickrey, who had known DeLo for some years, told him about Bill Price's little e-mail circular and who he might find there, such as Ady. Thus, DeLo joined the Roundtable in its first year, actively contributing to the group's knowledge of seaplane and amphibious air operations in the early stages of the war. As of this writing, at age ninety-plus, he is one of two nonagenarians on the Roundtable and is still going strong.

While DeLo wasn't present at the Battle of Midway, it does seem that we can rightly call him a combat veteran of Midway. He sent the following message to the Roundtable in 2002, in which he was praising the book *Marines At Midway*, by Robert Heinl:

> For a long but great historic tale of the Marines at Midway, get Heinl's book or download it from the Internet. It covers the birth of the base, the preparations for the Battle of Midway, and the battle itself. It is accurate and fascinating.
>
> As an aside and most interesting to me, in Appendix II, "Midway Chronology," there is an entry that says "Jan 25, 1942: Midway shelled by Japanese submarine I-173." My flight logbook shows that I flew to Midway on January 25, 1942, and an entry shows "shelled by Jap submarine."

CHAPTER 3

▼

HIT 'EM WHERE THEY AIN'T

Kicking Japan's Front Door

While the BOMRT is focused primarily on the Battle of Midway, the participants have often found merit in the analysis of events that occurred both before and after the battle; generally encompassing the war in the Pacific from Pearl Harbor to the Battle of the Santa Cruz Islands during the Guadalcanal campaign. Essential preconditions and circumstances led up to the climax at Midway, and understanding them is an integral part of understanding the battle itself. Even more important, it had such a far reaching impact on subsequent history that frequent discussion of such later events is inevitable.

Two of Midway's important preconditions were the daring Doolittle raid against the Japanese mainland in April of 1942, and the Battle of the Coral Sea in the following month. Lieutenant Colonel Jimmy Doolittle's bold strike caused Admiral Isoroku Yamamoto, commander-in-chief of the Combined Fleet of the Imperial Japanese Navy, to forge ahead with his plan for a proposed Midway operation. But in the Coral Sea, the IJN fleet carriers *Shokaku* and *Zuikaku* sustained enough damage to keep them home when Yamamoto and his fleet sailed for Midway, a critical factor in the ultimate American victory.

The Roundtable's roster includes men who sailed with the Doolittle task force and others who fought in the Coral Sea. Among them were flight deck seaman Otis Kight, dive bomber pilot Clayton Fisher, fighter pilot Tom Cheek, cruiser gunnery officer William Houser, gunfire controlman Bernard Cotton, and torpedo squadron seaman George Bernstein.[1] The six shared their recollections of the Doolittle mission with the Roundtable in 2003, and as we had come to expect long before, their tales in many cases included interesting anecdotes that never made it into the history books.

Kight, now a retired lieutenant commander, quickly became renown on the Roundtable for his eloquence and sharp wit. Here he gives a short, colorful analysis of the Doolittle mission:

> At that early stage of the war, about all we had were straws to grab. Someone in his wisdom looked into past history and discovered the tactic of "hit 'em where they ain't." Japan didn't use very much of its military to guard the homeland. Like our own modern teenagers, they felt they were bulletproof and immortal. Their homeland was in no danger, ever. They had won every major campaign. They thought they were invincible. And all of a sudden, while they were out running rampant, someone comes along and kicks in their front door. They were violated! And in essence, that brought about the Battle of Midway.
>
> No, Jimmy Doolittle's raid was no saturation bombing like the Eighth Air Force, but it put a kink in the Japanese high command's reasoning and planning that was only straightened out on the deck of the USS *Missouri* in 1945.

*   *   *   *

Doolittle Leads the Way

While Kight has perhaps been the champion of wit on the Roundtable, the prize for both quantity and quality of input has to go to Commander Clayton Fisher, USN (Retired). An SBD dive bomber pilot in Bombing Squadron 8 (VB-8) during the entire operational life of the carrier USS *Hornet* (CV-8), Fisher has contributed immensely to our knowledge of the nitty-gritty details of life in an SBD cockpit. He also gets credit for a wealth of interesting tales and anecdotes about the trials and tribulations of naval pilot training (first as a student and later as an instructor) and about life aboard a carrier during both mundane as well as terrifying times. Also, he has been a major source of information and valuable analysis when questions of detail arise about the Battle of Midway, particularly with regard to the controversial flight of the *Hornet's* air group on the first day of the battle, about which much more will be said in succeeding chapters.

Jimmy Doolittle's B-25s were carried toward Japan by a task force consisting of the *Hornet*, with all sixteen of the Army bombers loaded on its flight deck, the carrier USS *Enterprise* (CV-6), along to provide protective air cover for the ships, and a number of supporting vessels. Here, Fisher gives his recollections on the morning of the launch:

> Don Adams, Roy Gee, and myself, all VB-8 pilots, were aboard the *Hornet* on April 18, 1942 and witnessed the launch of the B-25s. Most of the *Hornet* pilots shared their staterooms with a B-25 aircrew officer. We added a cot for the additional bed space in our rooms. Those Army airmen seemed to be more worried about making a carrier takeoff than they did about their almost suicidal mission. But I didn't think they had to worry, at least not about the takeoff. In February I was aboard the *Hornet* in Norfolk when we launched two B-25s as a test. Those planes got off the deck easier than our own Navy aircraft.
>
> I watched Doolittle's launch on the morning of April 18th. We had heavy seas and the *Hornet* was pitching quite heavily. As the old salts would say, we took some "green water" over the flight deck when the bow pitched down. I was watching from the forward starboard catwalk along the flight deck and got rather wet from the spray.
>
> The weather was clear but with a high overcast, and we had a very strong wind that caused the ship to pitch heavily. We had water and salt spray going down the flight deck through the launch area. A sailor working as a plane spotter was blown into a propeller as he was trying to guide an aircraft to the launch spot. He lost an arm at the shoulder.
>
> The task force wanted to get within 440 miles from Japan to launch, but we were sighted by a small picket boat early that morning. The *Enterprise* dive bombers and fighters tried to sink it, and I believe a cruiser also helped. The *Hornet* passed through the debris of the sunken boat. I saw a wooden crate and a body.
>
> We had left our destroyer escorts back at a rendezvous point because they could not keep up with the larger ships for the final run-in to the planned launch point due to heavy sea conditions. Anyway, it had to be assumed the picket ship had reported our position, and so the order was given to send the B-25s off as soon as possible, even though we were still about 660 miles from Japan. That extra distance was a critical concern with regard to the Army planes being able to make it to friendly territory in China.
>
> Jimmy Doolittle was the first to go. It was a great takeoff; no problem. One B-25 did make a bad takeoff, though. The pilot held the nose up so high that he was dragging his tail skid. He ballooned up, almost stalled out, cleared the flight deck, and then we lost sight of him as the bow pitched up. I thought he'd crashed, but we finally saw him very low over the water. His props were blowing salt spray off the surface!
>
> As soon as the B-25s were launched, all the *Hornet's* fighters were brought up from the hanger deck in case we were attacked by long range Japanese air-

craft. It had not been a good feeling when all of our own planes were confined below due to the crowd of Army bombers on the flight deck!

Elusive Pickets

When the Japanese picket boat was sighted, the task force attempted to quickly destroy it before it could transmit a radio warning to the Japanese mainland. The cruiser USS *Nashville* began a bombardment from its main six-inch battery and the *Enterprise* launched a flight of fighters and dive bombers. One of the fighter pilots was Tom F. Cheek, who would eventually retire from the Navy as a commander and who would also become one of the Roundtable's essential resources for matters of detail concerning fighter operations during the early months of the war. Here is Cheek's description of the events of that day, and note that he and his *Enterprise* shipmates initially had only speculation to tell them exactly where their ships were going and what they were going to do when they got there.

> To add a bit more to the speculation, on the morning the *Hornet* joined up with *Enterprise* I was towing a gunnery target. As I flew over the *Hornet*, I looked down and saw those B-25s packed on the flight deck. Needless to say, I spent the next three and a half hours wondering about our destination. Tokyo wasn't even considered.
>
> On the morning of April 18th, I was spotted for launch on the *Enterprise* and watched the first three B-25s take off from the *Hornet*, then I took off. The picket boat was being strafed by the division I was with: Warrant Officer Bayers, AMM2/c Packard, AMM1/c Sumral, and myself. On my last pass I was aiming at the after cabin engine spaces when I saw two objects flying through the air from the after deck. At first I thought they were fish boxes, like the Washington trollers use for packing their catch. Then I saw that the objects had arms and legs. Fifty caliber ricochet had apparently picked them up.

*   *   *   *

The Wrath of Miles Browning

There was an unconfirmed story aboard the *Enterprise* about the task force's chief of staff, Captain Miles Browning, becoming irate at the fighter pilots for strafing the picket boat while it was allegedly showing a white surrender flag (this was obviously very early in the war when some Americans had illusions about the

Japanese surrendering in the face of a superior force). Other observers reported that the "surrender flag" was actually a clothes line full of laundry. Cheek confirmed the story in this message to Bill Price.

> Bill, you said that you did not know if the story was true about Browning chewing out Warrant Officer Bayers for strafing the boat with white flags flying. Every word is true. I was standing alongside Mr. Bayers, wondering what the hell was going on. Browning was wild-eyed and looked like he was about to foam at the mouth. But here's what really had happened: Bayers was leading a division made up of APs [enlisted and warrant officer pilots]: himself, Packard, Sumral, and me. Shortly after takeoff from the *Enterprise*, we were vectored out to a large cloud, then to another one, and another one. We looked over a lot of cloud mass but never sighted a target. Returning to the task force, I was surprised when I saw Bayers peal off and dive, followed by Packard and Sumral. I then saw the picket boat. I didn't see any white flags, but I did see a machine gun firing from the port wing of the bridge and a heavier, slow firing gun on the bow. Sumral took out the gun as I followed him in. We made two passes each with four 'fifties. The boat bobbed like a cork in the heavy seas, up and down like a yoyo; there was a sheen of oil on the water around it. The *Nashville* was still firing.

*   *   *   *

Cruiser Broadsides

Aboard the cruiser USS *Nashville* (CL-43) was a young gunnery department officer, Ensign William D. Houser. He'd reported aboard in January, at the start of a long and highly distinguished career that would eventually see him testing jet fighters, commanding a carrier task force during the Cold War, and retiring as a vice admiral, after which his wealth of experience would become invaluable when he became a frequent and generous contributor to the Roundtable. Another of the group's prolific writers and key source of information about the life for an enlisted man aboard those early carriers was Bernard Cotton, a gunfire controlman on the *Hornet*. He completed his own distinguished naval career, retiring as a Chief Fire Control Technician and later undertaking a long career as a systems engineering consultant for various Defense Department contractors.

During the lengthy discussion of the Doolittle mission on the Roundtable, an interesting exchange developed between Cheek, Houser, and Cotton as to the effectiveness of the *Nashville's* bombardment of the picket boat. The cruiser did fire hundreds of large caliber projectiles at the little craft, with little or no result. Admiral Houser gave us the following report:

> Fire was opened immediately, at excessive range, the objective being to silence radio transmissions in the event the sampan [picket boat] had not yet sent a warning to Tokyo. It was bouncing up and down from the rough seas, with our projectiles passing over and under. Because the ammo on board was armor piercing and designed to go through steel, the hits on the sampan merely made six inch holes. There were no survivors to recover when we went by the first sampan although a few hours later we sank another one and brought five or six survivors aboard as POWs.

Bernie Cotton then added his own, slightly different eyewitness account from his vantage point high on the Hornet's superstructure:

> That day was completely overcast with very heavy winds and very heavy seas. The flight deck control officer had to time the pitching of the ship as to when he would give the "go" sign to each of the B-25s, such that the bow would be on the upswing as the plane took off. As a further indicator of the seas that day, the cruiser *Nashville* took the patrol boat under fire. One minute the Japanese vessel was on the crest of a wave and the next minute it disappeared. As a result, you could witness the fall of the *Nashville's* shot either going over the boat or falling short. I believe she expended hundreds of six-inch rounds before the splashes finally went from white (indicating a miss) to black, which indicated a hit.

But Cheek followed that report with his own observation:

> Sorry to say, but I can't help wondering about the *Nashville's* hits, as I recall they never even ruffled the laundry on the ship we were strafing.

Bernie Cotton continued:

> The Japanese boat was actually firing back at the Nashville, a very pathetic scene. The range was approximately 12,000 yards and their fall of shot was about one third of the range to cruiser.
>
> Incidentally, when the picket boat was first sighted, two SBDs from the Enterprise on ASW patrol dumped their depth charges and were attacking with their thirty caliber machine guns when one of them took a hit from the boat. The SBD was smoking pretty good as it went by us and headed back to the Big E.

So maybe the *Nashville* got a couple of rounds on (or through) the picket boat and maybe it didn't, but discussion of it kept our Doolittle veterans on the Roundtable in a friendly little debate for several days, more than sixty years after the fact.

*   *   *   *

Hang On!

There was great consternation in the radio rooms of the task force ships as the radiomen heard strong transmissions from the picket, obviously sending a dreaded warning to the mainland. Japanese records after the war would reveal that no action was taken because the picket failed to confirm its initial report. But at the time the Americans assumed that they had lost all measure of surprise, which brought the decision to launch the Army bombers at extreme range. Helping to do so was George Bernstein, an enlisted member of Torpedo Squadron 8 (VT-8), which would later be immortalized at the Battle of Midway. On the morning of April 18th, Bernstein, who would eventually retire from the Navy as a lieutenant, was part of the flight deck crew preparing the B-25s for launch. Here is his recollection:

> I was assigned to the flight deck, pushing planes. GQ sounded prematurely when the Japanese boat was sighted, and we had to prepare for an immediate launch. I was put on the nose wheel bar of the first plane (Doolittle's) and every other one after that. It sure was windy! We had to literally drop to the deck and hang on with our fingers in the tie-down fittings when the B-25s revved up. I had a line attached to myself and to other men on the team to keep us from blowing in towards the props.

If you watch the Navy's film footage of the B-25 launch from the *Hornet's* flight deck (i.e., the opening scene of the 1976 movie *Midway*) you can see the flight deck crewman dropping prone and hanging on for dear life when each plane lurches forward, as Bernstein describes above. His narrative brings a grim reminder of Clay Fisher watching a plane handler lose an arm at the shoulder.

Tom Cheek ended the Doolittle discussion on the Roundtable with a rather dramatic revelation that, so far as I could determine, has not previously come to light in any of the familiar histories of World War II:

Making contact with the picket ships upset a lot more than Doolittle's intended takeoff point. One of our ready room briefings included the surprising news that, after launching Doolittle at the planned four hundred mile mark, the task force was to have set a course toward southern Japan to bomb the coal mines on Kyushu! I've often wondered what the result of that would have been!

*   *   *   *

Carriers vs. Carriers

In May 1942, the Japanese sent a strong force to capture Port Moresby, on the southern coast of New Guinea, just across the Coral Sea from northern Australia. Had they succeeded, the threat to Australia itself would have been especially grave. While a general invasion of the entire continent was probably beyond Japan's logistic resources, their control of southern New Guinea and the Coral Sea would have tempted them to neutralize or even seize a few key points on Australia's north coast, effectively isolating MacArthur and ultimately denying the U.S. Navy its vital submarine bases in western Australia. Japanese control of even a small piece of the Aussies' homeland would have doubtless caused the quick return of their army from north Africa at a time when Rommel's Afrika Corps was still threatening the Suez canal. Thus, control of Port Moresby was crucial to the Allied cause for multiple reasons.

Its fate was decided on May 7-8, 1942 in the Coral Sea, with the first-ever clash between opposing carrier forces and their air groups. The Japanese brought two of their best fleet carriers, *Zuikaku* and *Shokaku* to the fight (both veterans of the Pearl Harbor attack), along with the light carrier *Shoho* and an invasion fleet to take Port Moresby. Opposing them were the American carriers *Lexington* (CV-2) and *Yorktown* (CV-5). In the ensuing air-sea struggle, *Shoho* was sunk, *Shokaku* was heavily damaged and *Zuikaku* suffered serious losses in planes, although the ship itself wasn't hit. Both surviving CVs retired, though, and the Japanese commander canceled the Port Moresby invasion.

As a result, the Battle of the Coral Sea was a strategic victory for the Americans, but it was a painfully expensive one: the *Lexington* was sunk, along with an oiler and a destroyer, and the *Yorktown* suffered major damage. While that may appear as a tactical draw (two large CVs out of action on each side), the U.S. Navy could not afford to wage an even fight with the Japanese. Continuing to swap a carrier for a carrier at that stage of the war would have left the enemy in control of the Pacific in a matter of months.

*   *   *   *

Filming the Battle

Aboard the *Yorktown* in the Coral Sea were many sailors and airmen, both officer and enlisted, who would ultimately become active participants on the BOMRT. A key member of the group was William G. Roy, then a second class photographer's mate, who became known for his many combat photos of shipboard action that found their way into the national archives and into virtually every book written about the Battle of Midway. Roy gave the Roundtable his recollections of the Battle of the Coral Sea in this report:

> I served on the bridge of the USS *Yorktown*, with the permission of Captain Elliott Buckmaster, to photograph the action during the battle of the Coral Sea, May 7-8, 1942. This was the first battle fought between opposing American and Japanese aircraft carriers. What impressed me foremost was the skill and expert seamanship of Captain Buckmaster, giving orders from the open bridge and sighting Japanese dive bombers and torpedo aircraft from the wings of the bridge. During the enemy's dive bomber attacks, he would see their bombs coming down and shout orders for "hard to starboard!" or "hard to port!" The bombs would explode alongside *Yorktown* and throw shrapnel into the side of the ship and water up to and over the bridge level. With great skill, Captain Buckmaster combed the wakes of eight torpedoes by taking them "bow on" as each white, foamy wake came shimmering toward the ship. Our flight deck would lay over and roll back repeatedly as the *Yorktown* went into a hard turn at thirty-five knots. The ship's wake was boiling into a large, white curve as she turned.
>
> I did my job with the camera but stayed well clear of the captain. When a Zero fighter came in strafing our bow, I saw the flight deck splintering and just knew that when the pilot pulled up, his bullets were going to hit the bridge. I ducked, but a chief petty officer standing on the port side of the bridge got hit in his left shoulder and was knocked down. Bullets ricocheted all around the bridge.
>
> The Battle of the Coral Sea effectively stopped the Japanese objective of blocking American forces from supplying Australia. And the most important lesson learned in the battle was that the American striking force was no longer built around our battleships. The fight in the Coral Sea proved that the aircraft carrier was the ship we would depend upon for future battles in the Pacific.

*   *   *   *

Red Circles on the Wings

Peter Newberg was an electrician's mate (EM3/c) on the *Yorktown* at the Coral Sea, and happened to be a witness to one of the more bizarre episodes to occur in that or any naval battle. Here are his recollections of the incident as he related to the Roundtable in 2005:

On board the *Yorktown*, 7 May 1942 in the Coral Sea, about 1800 hours: it was an eventful day. The *Lexington* and *Yorktown* air groups attacked and sank the Japanese carrier *Shoho* that morning. In addition, two more enemy carriers with strong support had been located within striking distance. All aircraft had been recovered and air operations, for the moment, had been secured for the night. We understood that the Japanese knew where we were.

I was a newly made electrician's mate assigned to a flight deck repair party for general quarters (battle stations). Tension shot up all over topside when a group (four or five as I recall) of unidentified aircraft appeared, port side amidships, flying parallel and reverse to our course, just out of gunnery range. One of them began signaling by blinker light. I distinctly recall shouted comments from the signal bridge: "we can't make it out!"

Both *Lexington* and *Yorktown* launched fighters immediately. By that time it was pitch dark and we were faced with a night recovery, something that the *Yorktown* had never done, at least as long as I had been aboard. In any event, I found myself watching our fighters by the blue of their exhausts when some additional exhausts of a slightly different color and shape appeared in our landing circle. Orders were radioed to our pilots to turn on their running lights, which they did, leaving the other exhausts in the dark. But only for a moment, after which the strangers lit up and again, as with their exhausts, they looked somewhat different.

In the meantime, the LSO was having major problems trying to take our guys aboard in the dark. The only visible light on the ship was the dim landing light illuminating his position port side aft. When I looked to see what was going on, he was trying to raise an oncoming airplane that continued to come in too low. In the last few seconds, when the pilot was about to plow into the stern under the flight deck, he poured the coal to his engine and pulled up and off to port. The signal light flicked briefly on red circles painted on his wings. Then, as is often said, "all hell broke loose!" The next plane in the landing circle was fired on by the destroyer in plane guard position about 1000 yards aft. Seeing this, *Yorktown* began firing all automatic weapons at this unfortunate airplane as he flew down the starboard side. It happened to be one of our fighters.

Thoroughly shot up but still barely flying, that F4F burped and snorted its way around the landing circle and came aboard in a crash landing with one angry, wounded pilot. After this, all other aircraft, ours and theirs, disappeared. To my knowledge they were never rescued by either side.

One of our lost pilots that night was an Australian by birth. Someone in his family once asked me what I might be able to tell them about that night. It seems that one of our pilots had told them that he was shot down by friendly fire from the *Yorktown*. You might imagine how pleased I was to tell them that the report was not true. By the way, the *Lexington* flooded their flight deck with lights and landed their returning aircraft with no problems.

*   *   *   *

To War in a SOC

One of the U.S. Navy's supporting vessels that would see action in both the Coral Sea and Midway battles was the cruiser USS *Portland* (CA-33). The fast heavy cruisers were the principal escort ships to the carriers, each sporting a large caliber main battery, an assortment of antiaircraft weapons, and its own small air group consisting of catapult-launched Curtiss scout seaplanes, or SOCs, for search and rescue missions and for antisubmarine patrol. One of the *Portland's* SOC pilots was Ralph V. Wilhelm, who would ultimately command three Navy squadrons during a twenty-year USN career, after which he became a manager with the Honeywell corporation. He came aboard the BOMRT during its first year upon Frank DeLorenzo's recommendation.

Wilhelm had maintained a daily personal log until the Navy banned such diaries in August 1942, and it has served as an especially valuable historical resource on the Roundtable. Here are his log notes covering the Battle of the Coral Sea:

We had reveille at 0500, ate breakfast, and then went to GQ. Today [May 8, 1942] was the most exciting day I have ever had in my life! The carriers *Yorktown* and *Lexington* sent out scouts at dawn, but we on *Portland* were not to launch until told to do so. A short time later, we were ordered to send out one plane for inner air patrol. I took it and was launched at 0730. At 0930, while flying around on patrol, I saw all the planes taking off from our two carriers and I then knew that our scouts had made contact. They departed at 0940, about 100 planes, and headed on course 045. Our ships kept steaming south, so I knew that we were not intending to make surface contact with the enemy fleet. Since I was on inner air patrol my radio frequency was on the warning net and nothing interesting ever comes over it. I had Kilgore, my radioman-gunner, change to the fighter director frequency and we heard our planes attacking "bogeys." At about 1100 the carriers launched all their fighters and scouts to act as a torpedo defense patrol. After that the force was at thirty knots steaming south for five minutes, then west for the same amount of time, then south again, etc. I was not sure what was going on.

The ship was supposed to recover me at 1100, therefore, I stayed close over the force to detect their recall. At 1117 I was at 1200 feet over one of our DDs, on the starboard quarter of the formation, when it all started! At first I saw flashes of gunfire from the AA guns of the carrier, then from all ships in the force. The sky was a solid blanket of anti-aircraft bursts a few seconds later, all between 1000 and 3000 feet altitude. Then I saw Japanese planes diving on the force from everywhere. I was being fired upon by our anti-aircraft guns along with the Japs, so to get out of the way I dove for the water and headed out the starboard beam of the force at about fifty feet over the white-caps! A short distance to my left were two Japanese torpedo planes, and above me at about a thousand feet were three of their dive bombers. We were all headed in the same direction. I was making 120 knots, and they were going about 200 knots. I then test-fired my fixed gun and Kilgore fired his free gun. We were pleased that both guns were in good order! I then dropped my two one hundred pound bombs to give me more maneuverability in case I was attacked. One of their torpedo planes turned around and went back strafing the ships. The other four climbed into the clouds and were gone. As we were flying out the beam away from the ships, the AA guns were firing at the Jap planes and also at me! They were firing at all planes in sight, and I could see the splashes in the water behind me. Never did my plane feel so slow as it did then!

A couple minutes after the raid started, the *Lexington* was hit hard and flame and smoke shot up all around it. I thought sure that she would sink right away. Planes were everywhere, diving and fighting. It lasted about seventeen minutes and then it was all over. I came back to the ship, making sure that I gave the correct recognition signals, and was recovered at 1225. I counted fourteen ships on my return, so I knew that we hadn't lost any. The attack was centered on the two carriers and the other ships were only strafed. No one was injured on our ship and we were only hit with a few pieces of falling shrapnel. I inquired why the ship didn't let me know that an attack was imminent since the Jap planes were tracked in on radar from 68 miles out, but, they claimed they had forgotten!

Our planes must have attacked the Jap ships at the same time because they returned about an hour after the attack on us. The enemy force was supposed to have consisted of two CVs, a few CAs and some DDs. Our guys badly damaged one CV and possibly damaged a second. They attacked us with about fifty planes, quite a number of which were shot down. Our F4Fs and SBDs claim to have shot down about ten planes, and our AA got about the same number. A Jap four-engine patrol bomber was also shot down just before the attack. It smoked all the way down.

After our planes were all recovered, except for those lost, we steamed south at twenty-five knots. We knew *Lexington* and possibly *Yorktown* were hit, but we didn't know how badly. At 1700 the *Lex* sent out a visual message that she was on fire below decks and that it was not under control. At that point, she started smoking badly and did so all afternoon, even though making good speed. We started preparing a boat to take some men over to help fight the fire, but it was so bad that she slowed to a stop at 1730 and her captain gave the order to abandon ship. The DDs went in close to pick up the survivors, then distributed them around to the cruisers. By 1930 we had 400 *Lexington* people on board, twenty-five of whom were officers.

There were many terrific explosions on the *Lex* before she went down, and then at about 2000, as she was flaming merrily, a very large explosion occurred. She threw parts of her hulk all over the sky and then sank to be no more. Prior to this, a DD put two torpedoes into her in order to expedite her sinking because the fire could be seen for miles and might have attracted the enemy. The survivors said that of the 2900 personnel on board, about 2500 survived. They claimed that three torpedoes as well as two bombs hit her. A fire was started down in the bottom of the ship and they could not get down there to extinguish it.

I am sleeping on a transom in the wardroom tonight because an Ensign McDonald of the *Lex's* Bombing Squadron 2 is using my bunk. He was shot in the shoulder by Zero fighter, then bounced over the side and crashed in the water upon landing. He was picked up by a DD and transferred to our ship. Of the 400 people we received, only about forty are injured, but most of those are burned very badly.[2]

In a separate report, Wilhelm told the Roundtable that the *Portland* received another 400 *Lexington* survivors on May 10th, making his cruiser "a very crowded ship!" The *Portland* arrived in the Tonga Islands on May 15th, where it transferred its 800 men from the *Lexington* to the armed transport *Barnett* for return to the U.S.

*   *   *   *

Lessons Learned and Ignored

Analysis of Midway and related battles is a principal activity on the Round-table, and we have been exceptionally fortunate to include on our roster one who is an acknowledged expert at such. Donald M. "Mac" Showers commenced his naval career in 1941, and one of his first assignments was as an analyst with Commander Joseph Rochefort's cryptology experts in Pearl Harbor, the group that ultimately broke the Japanese naval code and thus made victory at Midway possible. For the next thirty years Showers continued a highly distinguished career in naval intelligence, retiring in 1971 as a rear admiral. He continued working for the Central Intelligence Agency as a civilian analyst for another dozen years. In the following report, he gave the Roundtable his impressions of the impact of the Battle of the Coral Sea:

> Bear in mind that Coral Sea was the U.S. Navy's first sea battle against a significant Japanese force in World War II. It was the first battle where opposing surface forces never sighted each other; all combat was by aircraft. It was the beginning of a quick learn for us! Before World War II we were prepared to fight a battleship war with carriers providing air cover. The Japanese attack on Pearl Harbor took us out of that mode overnight. Thereafter we used carriers only because we had them; the BBs were not available. And it worked magnificently.
>
> We suddenly found ourselves in a carrier war and we adapted to it as rapidly as we could. But the Japanese had the upper hand because they had planned and prepared for just that, and we had to learn it by default with antiquated aircraft and largely untrained pilots. We came out lucky in the Coral Sea, and we certainly did score a strategic victory. With very little time to prepare, the same thing happened at Midway except that there we were lucky enough to score a tactical as well as a truly important strategic victory.
>
> Coral Sea was a more significant victory for Australia than the U.S. Ever since the end of World War II, Australia has celebrated the Coral Sea anniversary much like we do with our annual commemorations of the Battle of Midway. When I speak about these events, I always link Coral Sea and Midway with equal significance; Coral Sea being the salvation of Australia, and Midway the same for the U.S. It's a matter of national pride to each country.

Imperial Japanese Navy expert Jon Parshall provided the Roundtable with the following insight on the Battle of the Coral Sea, underscoring how vital its outcome was to the eventual victory at Midway:

> Coral Sea very clearly was a defeat for the IJN, although they themselves did not regard it as such at the time. Part of the reason is that the consequences of the battle were not immediately apparent. But the battle was a three-fold defeat for the Japanese. First, in denying Port Moresby to them, it deprived their forces of a valuable geographic position that would have been of great use in threatening Australia. Second, of course, it deprived them of Carrier Division Five (*Shokaku* and *Zuikaku*) during the battle of Midway, which they fully intended to use. The presence of CarDiv 5 at Midway almost undoubtedly would have tipped the odds decisively in Yamamoto's favor during that battle.

Third, and less obvious, the Japanese high command didn't seem to *learn* anything from their setback in the Coral Sea. A perceptive observer would have divined that the days of easy pickings in the Pacific were over. The Japanese could no longer run the same sort of shoestring operations that had secured their initial zone of operations for them. In other words, speed and boldness by themselves weren't good enough any more. Massive force was becoming more important. That CarDiv 5, whose mass was marginal to the task given it in the Coral Sea, had been handed an unexpected setback should have gotten senior Japanese heads working; something like "hey, that Midway operation we're about to do is also using some pretty marginal formations. Perhaps we ought to tweak the plan."

None of that occurred. That was due in part to the fact that CarDiv 5 didn't make it back to port until almost the time Admiral Nagumo was due to sortie for Midway. There was little opportunity to absorb lessons learned, although the impression one gets is that even if CarDiv 5's commander had been waving his hands and saying, "hey, guys, you need to hear this," Admirals Yamamoto and Ugaki weren't listening in any case.

CHAPTER 4

▼

THE CODEBREAKERS

A Critical Advantage

The "Miracle at Midway" was actually the result of several miracles, or at least of several crucial and often improbable occurrences that had to happen in a specific sequence to give the defenders any chance for victory. There can be little doubt that the first of those is the remarkable success of the U.S. Navy's communications intelligence (ComInt) teams in intercepting and decoding Japanese radio messages, thus providing the American side with a critical advantage.

The principal force behind that success was Commander Joseph J. Rochefort, who headed up the Fourteenth Naval District's communications intelligence office in Hawaii. Officially labeled "Combat Intelligence Unit, Pearl Harbor" (CIU) before and during the Battle of Midway, the command later evolved into the Fleet Radio Unit, Pacific (FRUPAC). Over the years it has also been widely and unofficially referred to as "Station HYPO," or simply "HYPO," from the phonetic alphabet term for the letter "H."[1] Rochefort and his CIU team worked closely with Admiral Nimitz' CINCPAC staff, funneling their intercepts and analyses directly to those who had to act upon them. The quantity and quality of intelligence data supplied to Nimitz by Rochefort was unsurpassed by ComInt operations in the U.S. and elsewhere in the Pacific Theater. Indeed, as will be seen later, OP-20-G (the radio intelligence branch at naval communications headquarters in Washington) was far more of a hindrance than a help to Nimitz in the decisive final few weeks before the battle.[2]

But there were other ComInt units in the Pacific that also contributed magnificently to our strategic victory in the Coral Sea as well as to our total victory at

Midway. Chief among them were the U.S. Navy operators and analysts in Australia who staffed a counterpart to Commander Rochefort's operation in Hawaii. Generally referred to as "Melbourne" or "Belconnen" during the BOM era, the group largely consisted of refugees from Corregidor, where they had ably operated "Station CAST" (CAST being "C" in the phonetic alphabet, for Corregidor).[3] With Lieutenant Rudolph Fabian in charge, the Melbourne team performed the same interception, decryption, and analysis functions as the CIU in Hawaii, with both activities sharing data between themselves and with OP-20-G via a common secure radio link that they called the "COMB" (Combined) net.[4]

Breaking JN-25

It is beyond the scope of this brief chapter to adequately convey the remarkable accomplishments of the codebreaking wizards led by Rochefort and Fabian. Suffice to say that by the time the Battle of the Coral Sea was looming, they had jointly managed to crack enough of the enemy's naval code, dubbed JN-25, to predict the intent and makeup of the Port Moresby assault force. By the time Japanese bombers were winging their way toward Midway in June, Rochefort and company were reading substantial portions of the enemy's radio traffic almost as reliably as the Japanese radiomen themselves.

To get some level of appreciation for how astounding that accomplishment was, here's a short description of how Japanese radio signals were first intercepted at a radio receiving site, then decoded by the cryptology specialists at Pearl Harbor or Melbourne. The first requirement, of course, was to manually copy the Japanese signals as they were being sent, no simple task for Americans accustomed to a twenty-six letter English alphabet and its Morse code equivalent. Japanese was not only radically different from English, but its "Morse" version presented an additional daunting task for U.S. Navy radiomen.

Philip H. Jacobsen was one of those radiomen, assigned to the intercept station on Oahu in 1942. A retired lieutenant commander who'd had a long career in communications intelligence, he joined the BOMRT in its third year and quickly became known as a valued resource on matters of detail concerning ComInt technology and practices as they existed at the time of the Battle of Midway. Here he describes some of the training he had to undergo to become a Japanese intercept operator:

> At first, we were introduced to Japanese phonetic printing, *Katakana*, often shortened to just *Kana*. We knew the Morse Code equivalents for 26 of the 48

Kana telegraphic characters. In addition to learning the 48 *Kana* characters in their [visual] form, we had to learn almost 22 new telegraphic code combinations to be able to copy the entire Japanese telegraphic code. It was required that we copy *Katakana* at 18 words per minute by pencil before we could start copying the Japanese telegraphic code on the special 48 key RIP-5 typewriter. It used the Romanized version of the Japanese alphabet, called *Romaji*.

In addition, we were instructed on Japanese naval communications procedure, message formats, operating signals, [and] operator idiosyncrasies.[5]

Once a good copy of a Japanese radio signal was produced by intercept operators like Jacobsen, it was delivered to the decoding section in order to determine its meaning, and that's where the real wizardry of ComInt came into play. The following simplified explanation of the Japanese navy's encoding system illustrates the difficulty of the task. First, (1) selected words and phrases of the Japanese language were codified into a master list of five-digit numeric code groups. Then, (2) to prepare a message for transmission, the numeric code group for each word or phrase in the message was altered by adding the value of a five-digit cipher (or "additive") from a second list. Finally, (3) the sums of the code groups and their corresponding additives comprised the message that was transmitted on the air. For example, here's how the Japanese phrase *higashi no kaze ame* ("east wind rain") might have been prepared for transmission:

(1) First encryption: HIGASHI NO = 10236, KAZE = 56703, AME = 37038, which gives the code group string "10236 56703 37038."

(2) A sequence of three JN-25 ciphers are then selected, such as "45038 11234 62851."

(3) Second encryption: The JN-25 ciphers are added to the three original code groups that stand for the desired text:

$$10236 \quad 56703 \quad 37038$$
$$\underline{45038 \quad 11234 \quad 62851}$$
$$55264 \quad 67937 \quad 99889$$

Note that they used *non-carrying* addition: in the first column above, 6 + 8 = 4, not 14.

Thus, the string to be transmitted on the air in this example is "55264 67937 99889." That's what Rochefort and Fabian's radio intercept operators would hear in their headphones, type out, and deliver to the cryptanalysts, who seemingly by magic could discern that "55264 67937 99889" meant "east wind rain" in English! Now expand that process into a multi-page, complex battle plan specifying ships, squadrons, task groups, logistics, dates, times, and locations, and you begin to get a small grasp of the amazing achievement that the ComInt teams at Pearl Harbor and Melbourne pulled off in delivering Yamamoto's entire battle plan to CINCPAC before the first shot was fired at Midway.[6]

"Attack…Midway"

Exactly how that happened was a subject of much discussion and more than a little debate on the Roundtable. At issue was the purported discovery of Yamamoto's Midway operation order by Yeoman 2/c William Tremblay, a U.S. Navy enlisted man working at the Melbourne center. Here's the story as related by Bill Price in a short article prepared for the Roundtable in 2002:

> This is the story of why the U.S. won the Battle of Midway. It's not something that you'll find in any one book or other reference because I've compiled it from a variety of sources, all very credible.
>
> On the evening of May 20, 1942, U.S. Navy Ensign Ralph Cook was called from his hotel in Melbourne, Australia to come to the series of apartments that housed a portion of the communications intelligence teams of both the Australian and U.S. navies. Ensign Cook went to the garages where his team's IBM equipment was located in order to solve a problem concerning a recovered Japanese code book. The job completed, he decided to get a cup of coffee at one of the apartments. While relaxing with his coffee, he noticed a sudden burst of excitement coming from the area of the deciphering group.
>
> Japanese JN-25 radio messages consisted of words and phrases that were coded into five-digit numeric groups, then encrypted by adding a five-digit cipher to each of the original groups in the message. The result was a seemingly random string of five-digit numbers. However, if you possessed the sequential cipher table and knew at which point in the table the originator had commenced the encoding process, the message could be reduced to its unencrypted form by subtracting out the correct cipher from each five-digit group in the intercepted message. If you also knew the meaning of the underlying five-digit numeric code groups, it was possible to read most or sometimes all of many such messages.
>
> Yeoman 2/c Bill Tremblay was one of Melbourne's deciphering specialists. By first identifying the group that gave the starting point in the JN-25 cipher table, he could proceed to tediously subtract out the appropriate ciphers, leaving the unencrypted numeric codes of the original message. He would then pass the message to the translating group for breaking the codes into Japanese text, and then into English.

Cipher stripping was a monotonous, continuous grind of number crunching. To help relieve the boredom, Tremblay had memorized the translated meaning of some of the underlying code groups. He had been near the end of his twelve-hour shift that evening, and having completed work on all of the available "good" intercepts—those that seemed to have been copied clearly and completely—he decided to work on some of the "crap traffic," or intercepts that were incomplete or garbled, and had more or less been put aside as unlikely to produce readable intelligence.

The excitement noted by Ensign Cook arose when Tremblay recognized the code groups for "attack" and the geographic indicator "AF" in the same message. "AF" was known to be the Japanese designation for Midway. Tremblay rushed the message to his chief petty officer, who awoke the duty officer, Lieutenant Gil Richardson. Richardson took one look at the message and immediately passed it to his translating group for priority attention. The team worked on the garbled portions as best they could, restarting numerous times with a re-positioned cipher table, but only succeeded in recovering a few additional code groups from the lengthy message.

Recognizing the message's importance as an apparent Japanese attack plan for Midway, Melbourne sent it via the COMB net to the Combat Intelligence Unit at Pearl Harbor (HYPO) and to OP-20-G in Washington, D.C. OP-20-G did not have a copy of the original intercept, but HYPO searched through their traffic and found a copy that was also garbled. Alva "Red" Lasswell, a Marine linguist at HYPO, led an intensive translation effort for the numeric groups that were not yet decoded, separating the message into small pieces and working each piece separately. The Melbourne team continued work on the message at the same time, forwarding partial translations to HYPO as soon as they were revealed. HYPO then brought the message to the attention of Admiral Nimitz.

Lasswell also coordinated his efforts with Rosie Mason in OP-20-G, but Mason had doubts about the meaning of "AF," which he related to Joseph Redman, who was Director, Naval Communications. Redman agreed with Mason and reported his misgivings to Admiral Earnest King, Commander-in-Chief of the U.S. Fleet. King cautioned Admiral Nimitz in Hawaii about the identification of "AF," warning him that others were concerned it actually referred to Hawaii itself or perhaps even the west coast. King ordered Nimitz to be very careful in his planning to meet the Japanese threat.

Despite the pressure from Washington, Nimitz believed the intelligence being passed to him from Commander Joseph Rochefort and his team at HYPO, who began to struggle with the problem of convincing OP-20-G that "AF" was Midway. One of Rochefort's staff, Jasper Holmes, remembered the water purification equipment that had been installed on the atoll when he was an engineer in Honolulu. He suggested to Rochefort that Midway could transmit a "bait" message in the clear, reporting a problem with its water plant. Rochefort agreed, and instructions were sent to Midway via cable. Shortly thereafter, a plain text radio message went out from Midway to Pearl, stating that their water distillation equipment had broken down and to rush a repair crew. A Japanese intercept station on Wake Island took the bait and sent a message to Tokyo reporting that "AF is running short of water."

HYPO intercepted and decoded the Wake Island transmission, but Rochefort took no immediate action because it would appear to be self-serving. However, Melbourne had intercepted the same message and quickly sent copies to HYPO and OP-20-G. Washington was finally convinced.

Differing Recollections

Price had learned of Tremblay's find through a close personal acquaintance with Cook, whom he met while working at NSA. Cook was the military personnel officer there in the mid 1950s, and went on to command the Naval Security Group during the Vietnam War. He retired from the Navy as a rear admiral in 1971. His recollection of the details of Tremblay's discovery seemed quite clear and detailed to Price, who happened to have an especially high regard for the veterans of the Corregidor/Melbourne ComInt team. It was the Corregidor group, for example, that had initially determined that "AF" was the Japanese geographic designation for Midway as early as March 1942.[7]

The problem with the Tremblay story, as related by Cook via Price, is that it is unsubstantiated by any known documentation arising from Melbourne, HYPO, OP-20-G, or anywhere else. There is simply no historical record of Melbourne ever finding the Japanese plan for Midway, and in fact, there does seem to be authoritative evidence that HYPO found it themselves six days before the May 20th date mentioned by Cook.[8] Admiral Showers articulated his doubts about the Tremblay story in a message to Bill Price after the above article appeared on the Roundtable:

> I'm sorry, but I can't share your enthusiasm for this Melbourne report. It is fascinating reading and totally understandable from the Australian point of view, but it is not an accurate account of how radio intelligence supported Admiral Nimitz. I'll continue to do my best to keep the record straight.

Of course, "the record" as understood by Showers and Jacobsen was that the Japanese op-order for Midway was first discovered at HYPO, and it was further development of that intelligence that enabled Rochefort to hand CINCPAC virtually all of Yamamoto's battle plan before the battle commenced. While there was never any claim that Melbourne's contribution to the effort was anything less than exemplary (Showers made a point of explaining that HYPO, Melbourne, and OP-20-G all worked together in a joint effort), Price was alone on the

Roundtable in supporting the notion that Tremblay had discovered anything not found and exploited elsewhere.

An interesting wrinkle to this discussion was the fact that Tremblay himself was a member of the Roundtable at the time. A retired Navy lieutenant, he lived in a remote area of Missouri and joined the group in 2001 upon the invitation of one of our members who visited him at Price's urging. Tremblay was found to be a quiet, pleasant, unassuming man who had no particular inclination to expound on the matter of what he had or hadn't accomplished with regard to the Battle of Midway. It simply was not an important issue with him. Regrettably, he passed away a few months later before anyone could engage him in extensive discussions about his time at Corregidor and Melbourne.

The matter was mostly closed in 2004 when Price provided a further description of his understanding concerning Tremblay's find:

> The message Bill Tremblay happened to identify was the May 20th message from Admiral Yamamoto to all of his fleet commanders prescribing the routes and attack times for Midway. This is the message that HYPO advised Admiral Nimitz to act upon, and the one that caused Nimitz to sortie three carriers toward Midway.

While that would seem to indicate that both HYPO and Melbourne had, in succession, found two separate elements of the Japanese battle plan, there still was nothing in the voluminous records from HYPO that any such information had arrived on the COMB net from Melbourne or anywhere else on May 20th.[9]

In the end, it's reasonable to conclude that what may have actually happened was nothing more than that alluded to by Admiral Showers above: the intercept operators and analysts at both HYPO and Melbourne worked together as a unified team in order to produce one output for CINCPAC. Tremblay's specific discovery could have duplicated one that was also copied and decoded in Hawaii; thus, when its report arrived on the COMB net, the HYPO staff would have recognized it as information they already possessed and filed it without action. Or, the Melbourne report might have contained one or two elements not successfully recovered by HYPO, with the result that it contributed some level of enhancement to the quality of the final report.[10] In either case, the fact that some elements came from Melbourne and that others came from HYPO was not important to the historical record. The only thing that really mattered was the product itself that was delivered to Admiral Nimitz.

∗   ∗   ∗   ∗

"AF" Needs Water

One of the more interesting and somewhat legendary episodes of the Battle of Midway concerns the so-called "water ruse," an insidious scheme to get the Japanese to reveal their secret geographic code for Midway. Their radio messages didn't contain familiar names for the islands and nations in the Pacific. Instead, they adopted a cryptic code list for all of them, and learning the meaning of each designator on the list was almost as tedious as decrypting JN-25 itself. According to the popular view in most history books, the Americans suspected that the symbol "AF" was the enemy's designation for Midway, but they had to confirm it in order to determine if the Japanese attack was really coming where they thought it was instead of to Hawaii, the Panama Canal, or even the west coast of the United States (I'll have more on that popular view in Chapter 12).

As Bill Price related above, Rochefort baited the Japanese by sending a request to Midway's garrison (via undersea cable, obviating any enemy interception) to transmit an unencrypted report that their water distillation plant had failed and that they only had a two-week supply of fresh water left. That was duly done, and a short time later the Japanese listening post on Wake Island was heard to report to Tokyo that "AF sent the following radio message: quote, at present time we have only enough water for two weeks. Please supply us immediately. Unquote." That ended all speculation concerning the meaning of "AF" and the target of the coming Japanese attack.[11]

Admiral Showers told the Roundtable in 2003 how the water-ruse plot came about:

> Jasper Holmes [HYPO section chief] was the originator of the "AF" water deception. I was personally present when the conversation between Rochefort and Holmes occurred, and I heard Holmes lay out the proposition. Rochefort accepted it, forwarded it to Edwin Layton [CINCPAC intelligence officer], who obtained approval by Nimitz, and we were off and running.
>
> Washington's attempt to target the IJN fleet somewhere other than Midway was based on their belief that Midway was too insignificant for such a large force. Their candidates were Oahu (Pearl Harbor) or a U.S. west coast target. Army headquarters advocated that the target would be the Panama Canal. I have heard that late in May, as Nimitz was continuing preparations to defend Midway, Admiral King [USN commander-in-chief] sent him a personal message forbidding him to deploy his limited fleet against such a supe-

rior IJN force unless he could prove with certainty that "AF" was Midway. This demand filtered down from Nimitz to Layton to Rochefort. It was then that Rochefort came to Holmes' desk, next to mine, and said, "Jasper, we've got to come up with a way to prove to Washington that 'AF' is Midway." Holmes then laid out his plan, to which Rochefort replied, "Very good, Jasper. Very good." That was high praise from Rochefort.

I witnessed this entire event, and it is as vivid in my memory as if it only happened yesterday.

After the above report by Admiral Showers appeared on the Roundtable, we were all surprised to get the following message a short time later from Walt Grist, a retired U.S. Marine master sergeant who had been on Midway at the time:

> For the record, we *did* have a breakdown of our water system in May 1942. We were restricted from taking showers except with salt water! If you didn't have salt water soap, it was useless to try to take a shower. So we went into the lagoon to swim and bathe. All of the fresh water we had was limited to cooking and medical use. A ship would come in on occasion, and if they had extra water they would offload it to our water towers or trailers. But we still had to take salt water showers!

Ironically, the Japanese had fallen for a concocted ruse that was essentially factual!

*   *   *   *

Japan's Friends in Washington

As far as Rochefort and Layton were concerned, the water-ruse exercise was totally unnecessary. They were already convinced that "AF" was Midway, and Admiral Nimitz believed them. The only doubters were at OP-20-G in Washington, whose officer in charge at the time, Commander John R. Redman, had an ongoing feud with Rochefort and anyone else who didn't go along with his views of ComInt matters, regardless how far off the mark they might be. Redman had a strong ally in his own brother and immediate superior, Captain Joseph R. Redman, Director, Naval Communications. Together the Redmans conspired to disparage Rochefort and the accomplishments of his CIU at every opportunity. While the Pearl Harbor team was delivering volumes of critical detail on enemy operations and intentions to CINCPAC, the Redmans in each case either disagreed with the CIU's conclusions, or when they turned out to be inarguably correct, John Redman would claim that the intelligence had been developed by his own OP-20-G team. Unfortunately, it was the Redmans' twisted version of reality that reached the ears of Admiral King.

That abysmal state of affairs led to one of the worst blunders in resource management ever perpetrated by the U.S. Navy. Shortly after the Battle of Midway, Commander Joseph J. Rochefort, who as an expert Japanese linguist and cryptologist was one of America's most formidable weapons against a then-powerful enemy, was transferred out of HYPO and out of ComInt altogether, a move that had been orchestrated entirely by the Redmans. Moreover, in an act of jealous pique that defies all reason, they managed to block the awarding of any medals to Rochefort for his vital contribution to the victory at Midway. He had been recommended for a Distinguished Service Medal (DSM) by his boss in the Fourteenth Naval District, Rear Admiral David W. Bagley ("Com 14"), as reported to the Roundtable in 2001 by naval aviation author and historian John Lundstrom:

> While doing some research for my new book about Admiral Fletcher, I found the following message on microfilm in the CINCPAC Secret & Confidential message file: Confidential Message 261918 of August 1942, Com 14 to Vice OPNAV, info CINCPAC: "For especially meritorious conduct in performance of his duties, my serial 01645 of 8 June recommended J. J. Rochefort, Comdr USN for appropriate award. In view of OPNAV 191705, Commandant desires resubmit recommendation. Services as officer in charge radio intelligence this district considered particularly outstanding and contributed materially to successes of Coral Sea and Midway actions. Specifically recommended for Distinguished Service Medal."

Stephen Budiansky, an author and respected authority on ComInt matters, followed that with this message to the Roundtable:

> The story of how the recommendation from the 14th Naval District for Rochefort's DSM was sidetracked is well known. Nimitz enthusiastically forwarded to Admiral King the recommendation from Com 14, although Rochefort himself tried to have it all dropped, insisting that putting him in for a medal would only "make trouble." On 20 June 1942, John Redman sent a memo to the vice chief of naval operations denigrating Rochefort and asserting that ComInt in "combat areas" could not be expected to handle anything more than "routine work" to keep abreast of "minor changes" in cryptographic systems. Simultaneously, his brother Joseph Redman, by that time Director of Naval Communications, wrote a memo declaring that Rochefort was not qualified to be in charge of Station HYPO and ought to be replaced by "a senior officer trained in radio intelligence rather than one whose background is in the Japanese language." On June 22, King accepted the advice of

his chief of staff who, clearly on the basis of the Redmans' lobbying, advised denying the medal, stating that Rochefort had "merely efficiently used the tools previously prepared for his use" and that "equal credit is due" to Washington for "correct evaluation of enemy intentions."

That blatant distortion was allowed to stand, and Rochefort languished in unimportant assignments for the rest of his career. He retired in 1953 as a captain and passed away in 1976.

Final Recognition for a Hero of Midway

Those who worked for and with Rochefort in the CIU never forgot the gross injustice perpetrated against a genuine hero of World War II by the vindictive Redmans. In 1986, after a campaign led by Admiral Showers, President Reagan and Navy Secretary John Lehman posthumously awarded the DSM to Captain Rochefort. Admiral Showers explained how it came about:

COM14 recommended Rochefort for the DSM and Nimitz endorsed it, but it was killed in Washington in 1942. In 1958, Jasper Holmes visited Admiral Nimitz, who was then retired in California, and told him the full and detailed story, which Nimitz had not realized before. Nimitz then wrote a two page hand-written letter to the Secretary of the Navy appealing for a reopening of the case. SECNAV replied that WWII awards had been closed and nothing could be done. In about 1982, Edwin Layton commenced work on his book, *And I Was There*, which became possible because World War II ComInt files had then been declassified and put in the National Archives. When I learned of that from Layton, I used those declassified materials to reopen the case. I had help from the Naval Security Group, the Office of Naval Intelligence, and a number of historians. We made a good case, and I wrote the DSM citation.

The issue of Rochefort's DSM had been one of Layton's two main objectives in writing his book (the other being to vindicate Admiral Kimmel with regard to the Pearl Harbor attack), and I knew that Jasper Holmes had also long wished to get it done. It took three years to get it approved over a pretty rocky road, but SECNAV finally did so in the Fall of 1985, just as the Layton book was being published. Holmes was seriously ill in a nursing home by that time, but I called him to relay the news, and his gratified comment was, "Mac, this is a promise fulfilled." He died soon thereafter.

The Navy wanted to mail the award to the Rochefort children, but I sidetracked that idea. Through my White House friends, I got President Reagan to make the presentation in the White House at the end of May 1986. The Naval Security Group paid for the Rochefort families to come to Washington for the presentation, and it made the front page of the New York Times.

Mark Twain at HYPO

Oddly, Rochefort was the subject of what many consider a further injustice, in connection with the Hollywood movie *Midway* that was released in 1976, the year he died. His part in the film was played by actor Hal Holbrook, who had been acclaimed for his folksy portrayal of Mark Twain in stage and television productions. Unfortunately, Holbrook's version of Rochefort did not personify a naval officer with a professional demeanor and sharp military bearing, as those who knew Rochefort have described him. Phil Jacobsen offered the Roundtable this comment:

> We were given an indoctrination into the basement activities of the Combat Intelligence Unit. Commander Rochefort could be seen wearing his famous maroon smoking jacket and slippers, sifting through the various files on desktops. However, this was due to the air conditioning and the hard cement floor. Whenever Rochefort left those spaces, he was always very properly attired and presented a fine military appearance. Also, his language was articulate and quite proper, not as Hal Holbrook portrayed him in the movie.

Admiral Showers had worked directly with Rochefort at the CIU and knew his on-the-job appearance and mannerisms as well as anyone. Here is his reaction to Hal Holbrook's portrayal:

> The impersonation of Cdr. Joseph J. Rochefort in the 1976 *Midway* movie could not have been more completely opposite his true personality. The mustachioed, cigar-smoking, loud-mouth, red-neck type portrayed by Hal Holbrook was totally out of character. Joe Rochefort was clean-shaven, occasionally smoked a pipe at his desk, was quiet-mannered and soft-spoken; a gentleman in all respects.
>
> He also was *not* an eccentric, as indicated in the movie in many instances. In the basement where we worked, it was cold and damp due to overly effective, non-dehumidifying air conditioning. Everyone who spent hours on end in that environment had to add clothing for comfort. Rochefort wore a burgundy corduroy smoking jacket and lined bedroom slippers only when on duty in HYPO spaces.

Noted military author Barrett Tillman gave the Roundtable this more succinct version: "It was Holbrook playing Mark Twain playing Rochefort! An appalling performance!"

*   *   *   *

"We've Broken the Japanese Code!"

One of the most vital elements of ComInt is security. Many would place it at the top of the list, for if security is compromised—that is, if the enemy finds out that you've broken their codes—then they'll quickly change their encryption system. The result is a sudden, critical lapse in communications intelligence, and that can lead to a misreading of the enemy's intentions and capabilities. When that happens, battles that should have been won can be lost, and men who should have survived invariably die. Thus, keeping from the enemy any knowledge that you might be able to read their communications is of paramount importance. In general, the feeling has always been that the ComInt wizardry pulled off by Commander Rochefort and his counterparts had been a well-maintained secret prior to the Battle of Midway.

Consequently, it was a bit of a surprise on the Roundtable to receive the following letter from Frank DeLorenzo:

> In December 1941, I was in Patrol Squadron 13 flying four-engine Coronado PB2Y seaplanes out of San Diego. On Christmas Eve I was one of the pilots in the crew that flew Admiral Nimitz from San Diego to Pearl Harbor in order for him to take command of the Pacific Fleet. We arrived at mid-morning on Christmas Day.
>
> We remained in the Oahu area flying search and patrol flights until mid-February when we initiated logistic flights from Oahu to Sydney, Australia via Palmyra Island, Canton Island, Suva, and Auckland, New Zealand. On these flights and also when on Oahu at Pearl Harbor as well as Kaneohe Bay, I recall hearing stories that we had broken the Japanese code. I heard this tale from numerous people who always recited it with glee and excitement. It seemed to be common knowledge among U.S. military personnel.
>
> My question for the Midway Roundtable: how good is my memory? Are there any others of you out there who can support my recollections, either in person or with documentation?
>
> And if my recollections are correct—and I firmly believe that they are— were we not extremely fortunate that this information did not filter its way back to the Japanese?

Of course, this subject was on Admiral Showers' home turf, and he was quick to respond:

I never heard the rumors reported by DeLo, but I might have been the last to hear them since I was inside the shop doing the work. I cannot refute that there may have been such talk, but it certainly should not have happened. If it was a common thing, I'd think that Naval Intelligence (the district intelligence office) would have investigated them, and I never heard of that either.

During World War II, communications to ships at sea were sent regularly on the fleet broadcast, a multi-frequency HF [short wave] radio broadcast which could be copied by all ships, including submarines. All sorts and classifications of information was sent this way. Ships could copy it all if they wished, but they could only decode and read those messages for which they held the crypto gear or the system key. There was a great number and wide variety of those.

The systems in which highly classified intelligence was sent were held only among the major commands, usually flag officers [admirals]. Only they could read such messages. After the Battle of the Coral Sea, the *Lexington's* flag communications officer had access to this traffic because he had his crypto gear with him and he was using it, contrary to regulations. (His naval career didn't fare well after that.)

On June 7, 1942, the Chicago Tribune published a story written by a Mr. Johnston, who had been on board *Lexington* when she was sunk in the Coral Sea. While its survivors were on a transport returning to San Francisco, Johnston befriended the *Lex* communications officer, who told him the story of breaking the Japanese code, thus enabling Admiral Nimitz to join the Battle of Midway. He printed nearly all the details contained in Admiral Yamamoto's op-order, which we had read. The comm officer was not supposed to know about this, but he'd rescued his crypto gear from the *Lex* and continued to read the intelligence reports while on the transport.

Fortunately, the ship was keeping radio silence, so Johnston couldn't file a story while at sea, but he did so as soon as he reached San Francisco. The Tribune published it. All hell broke loose in Washington, and FDR wanted to get the Tribune's publisher hung for a treasonous act during wartime. But saner heads prevailed. The Navy convinced FDR not to press a case because far more would have been revealed in open court than had already been published. True as the story was, it was never acknowledged, and no legal action was ever taken.

The bottom line, however, is that in those days, without rapid communications, CNN, satellites, etc., the Japanese *never* learned of the compromise. They didn't subscribe to the Chicago Tribune and had no other source of info. (They were pretty sad in their own intelligence collection.) We told the Japanese about the incident in our interviews with senior officers after the war, and they admitted they had never heard of it. But the facts as published, even though never acknowledged officially, could certainly have given rise to the talk that DeLo remembers. However, this would have been after the middle of 1942, and I gather his recollections appear to have occurred in an earlier period. I cannot explain that.

Alvin Kernan, a veteran of the USS *Enterprise* at Midway, is another of our Roundtable members who remembered hearing the codebreaking rumors prior to the battle. The following passage is found in *Crossing the Line*, his published wartime memoirs:

> ...as we approached Pearl...the rumor mill began to whisper a fantastic story. The Japanese fleet, it was said, was about to attack Midway Island, with a diversionary move on the Aleutians, and we, having broken their code, were going to lie off Midway and surprise them...Modern historians of the war still assume that secrecy on this critical matter was carefully maintained, that our success at Midway resulted from it, but I can testify that the deepest Navy secret—that we had broken the Japanese code and were reading their messages—was widely known among the enlisted men, and the proposed strategy and tactics for the coming battle learnedly and gravely discussed by the "admirals of the lower deck."[12]

After the above quote appeared in an issue of *The Roundtable Forum*, Kernan amplified it with the following:

> Serious questions about my statements in *Crossing the Line* were raised by people who were enough concerned to take the time to write long and detailed letters. Here is one:
> "I am troubled most by your comments on page 47 about enlisted personnel knowing all about the Japanese coming to attack Midway, and details of how the Navy planned to fight the battle. And that enlisted personnel knew all about our having cracked the Japanese JN-25 code. Until Halsey brought *Enterprise* into Pearl harbor [just before the battle of Midway] he knew nothing about the Japanese coming to Midway. No communication of that kind had been sent to *Enterprise*. Fletcher, on *Yorktown*, likewise knew nothing about it. No such communication had been sent to *Yorktown*. And as for how the Navy was going to fight, Nimitz asked Spruance where he would place his carriers. He selected NE of Midway, and Nimitz approved...No communication of where Spruance would place his carriers could have reached *Enterprise* when she was steaming fast to get back to Pearl Harbor. That decision was yet to be made."
> I wrote a long letter back telling him that my memory was firm on this particular point, because I remembered not only being told all about the code and the plan before the *Enterprise* came into Pearl Harbor, prior to going out to Midway, but that I also remembered realizing as the battle developed how accurate the scuttlebutt had been, which gave me a double lock on the memory. Then came a letter from another old shipmate (Dan Vanderhoof, ACOM) on the *Enterprise*, backing up my own experience:

"An intelligence officer who wrote you that the scuttlebutt about Midway a month before the battle was untrue simply did not know what he was talking about. Just before leaving Pearl Harbor, I chanced to meet on Ford Island an old friend from Olympia. His name was Bill Phillips and he was then flying rear seat in a TBD attached to VT-3 on the *Yorktown*. The gist of the conversation was the upcoming battle in the Midway, Johntson Island area. So much for the best kept secret of the war. You were 100% correct. Of course, Bill did not make it. I've thought many times since that every rear seat man, as well as the pilots who flew in the Battle of Midway in TBDs were sacrificial lambs. It certainly turned out that way."

"Bill Phillips" in Kernan's above letter would have been ARM3/c William Phillips, a Torpedo Squadron 3 (VT-3) radioman-gunner who indeed was lost during the morning battle of June 4, 1942. The writer of the first letter in Kernan's message (the intelligence officer) would appear to have presented inarguable facts that would have obviated all foreknowledge about the coming battle, at least aboard the *Enterprise* before it arrived at Pearl. Yet, Kernan's recollections added to those of DeLo above suggested that it happened nonetheless, even though they are only hearsay.

But the next letter to arrive was quite a bit more than just hearsay. Dan Kaseberg had been a yeoman (squadron clerk) with VT-3 aboard the *Yorktown*, and he managed to come up with a sixty-three year old document that spoke volumes about a general foreknowledge of the enemy's plan:

Here's my two cents on "did we or did we not know" that the Japanese code was broken. As I recall, when we of VT-3 were ordered to board the Mighty "Y," we were told that we were headed for a decisive naval battle with overwhelming Japanese forces, and to lose there could result in our needing to operate from the west coast of the U.S., a huge setback. In my memory we were informed that the Japanese code had been broken and then they proceeded to give us a list of the enemy's forces and our own. I have a copy on oil soaked onionskin paper, which I found in my pocket after leaving the *Yorktown* on 4 June 1942.

I cannot say that all units listed on the paper were involved and I know the PBY squadron numbers are wrong, but bear in mind that it was written *before* the battle. We thought that the code had been broken, especially when we were given this list of their forces. Here is the list:

- Our designation: Task Force 17. Flagship: USS *Yorktown* (CV-5) with the flag of Admiral Jack Fletcher. Included in this force, cruisers *Astoria* and *Portland*, along with Destroyers *Morris, Anderson, Hammann, Hughes,* and *Russell*.

- Task Force 16: Under the Flag of Admiral Spruance, included the carriers *Enterprise* (CV-6) and *Hornet* (CV-8), cruisers *Minneapolis*, *New Orleans*, *Atlanta*, *Vincennes*, *Pensacola*, and *Northampton*, and ten destroyers.

- Task Force 11: This was comprised of the carrier *Saratoga* (CV-3), cruisers *Chester* and *San Diego*, and six destroyers.

- The submarines *Dolphin*, *Gato*, *Cuttlefish*, *Grenadier*, *Gudgeon*, *Cachalot*, *Flying Fish*, *Tambor*, *Trout*, *Grayling*, *Nautilus*, and *Grouper*, along with Patrol Squadrons VP-284, VP-290, VP-345 and VP-350.

- The Japanese vessels known to be involved, prior to June 4, 1942: Striking Force: Carriers *Kaga*, *Akagi*, *Soryu*, *Hiryu*, plus one unknown CV. Support: 4 *Kirishima* [class] BB, 2 *Tone* CA, 4 *Mogami* CA, and DESRON 2 & 4. Train: 2 *Mizuho* AK, 1 *Atago* CA, 1 *Tarao* CV, 2 *Myoko* CA, 1 *Chitose* VP, 1 *Chiyoda* VR, 4 *Kaikawa* AV.

These pages were difficult for me to read due in part to the age of the document, and this was from a copy I had made. The original documents are on oil-soaked onion skin paper. I hope I have read them correctly, and have not misspelled the names of any ship.

Kaseberg posted a photo of his artifact on a personal web site for all to see.[13] Thus, it would seem that documentary evidence existed to prove that our ComInt secrets had leaked, apparently rather freely. But was that really the case? Admiral Showers responded with an explanation of how common knowledge of Japanese intentions could easily have spread among the sailors of the fleet and even on Midway *without* any sort of actual leak:

> I must comment on Dan Kaseberg's interesting commentary in *Forum* #31. His sentence states, "we *thought* (emphasis mine) that the codes had been broken, especially when we were given a list of their forces." That was a good guess, but far different than being *told*. There could have been a number of other sources for that detail. Speculation, even when correct, can never replace fact.
>
> It may be useful to give the Roundtable Admiral Nimitz' reason for doing what he did, and the security considerations that supported that action. The complete story on the Japanese Midway force was provided to the commanders of the U.S. task forces in an ULTRA [communications intelligence] summary sent out by Commander Layton [CINCPAC intelligence officer]. Admiral Nimitz was a strong advocate of his fighting forces being told what they were about to encounter. He made a trip to Midway and told the troops there that they were about to be attacked, and he then reinforced the island defenses to provide maximum capability to defend.[14]

Following that, a non-ULTRA message was sent to the fleet providing our forces the details of what they were about to confront, as a means of preparing them for the seriousness of the situation. Would anyone involved have been satisfied with less? Admiral Nimitz was a leader, not a bystander! His purpose was to instill maximum confidence in the ability of the U.S. forces involved to accomplish their mission successfully. I argue that, as a leader, he was totally correct.

Speculation as to the source of the information is certainly appropriate, but speculation will never replace knowledge, and it didn't in this case. Moreover, there was no known compromise to the enemy. Hence, it makes no sense to me to say that, in effect, "we knew it all the time."

To summarize Admiral Showers' point, we did indeed learn of the Japanese attack plan through codebreaking, and CINCPAC did indeed fully inform the fleet about what they were going to face, as Dan Kaseberg discovered. But neither CINCPAC nor anyone else ever divulged *where* that vital information came from. Codebreaking was an obvious, logical guess, but to those outside of the ComInt teams and Admiral Nimitz' staff, that's all it was.

As for Midway itself, expectations of a major clash there would certainly have developed as far back as May 2nd, when Nimitz visited the atoll and asked its commanders what they needed to resist a Japanese amphibious assault. Speculation would have spread far and wide when those assets started arriving in force over the next few weeks, all without anyone revealing anything about codebreaking.

CHAPTER 5

▼

DEFENDING THE ATOLL

The First Battle of Midway

The fact that the Battle of Midway occurred in June of 1942 is well known, but what may be less familiar is that there were actually *two* battles of Midway. Of course, the "Incredible Victory" was the more famous of the two, but the other one was no less crucial to the U.S. Marines who happened to be there at the time.

Corporal John V. Gardner was one of those Marines, as a field communications specialist with the 6th Marine Defense Battalion. He joined the Corps in 1940 and served on Midway from August 1941 through November 1942. He had stateside assignments until May 1945 when he shipped out to Hawaii in advance of the invasion of Japan planned for November. With the end of the war in September, he was sent to China and served until 1947, after which he returned to civilian life. He was introduced to the Roundtable in its first year by Bill Vickrey, and has been one of our principal resources for information about life on the atoll before and during the great battle.

Midway's first taste of war occurred on the night of December 7, 1941, but general awareness of what happened there has been overshadowed by the calamitous events at Pearl Harbor on that date. Here, Gardner tells us of the "first battle of Midway," in a letter forwarded to the Roundtable in 2002:

> Friday, December 5, 1941, was a special day on Midway. That was the day that the Pan American Clipper was to stop overnight while en route to Wake, Guam, and Hong Kong. It was eagerly awaited, for the Clipper would most likely be bringing us mail.

It was unusual for me to be assigned to the security guard detail, since I was a field telephone man attached to C Battery, five-inch artillery. We communications personnel had daily duties for checking communications at the gun batteries. But on December 5th our battery was scheduled for guard duty on the island, and with several men unavailable in sickbay, I was ordered to stand guard.

Life on Midway was generally very informal, except for the raising of the colors each morning, which was totally formal in military fashion. Lieutenant George Cannon was the Officer of the Day. The colors were raised, and Lieutenant Cannon then stood before the guard detachment to read the orders of the day. The announcements that morning were very unusual, for they included a message from CINCPAC (Commander in Chief, Pacific) that read, "MAINTAIN A VIGOROUS ALERT. JAPANESE FLEET MANEUVERING YOUR AREA."[1]

Over the years I have frequently thought about that particular day, December 5th, on Midway Island. I suppose Lieutenant Cannon's message wasn't frightening because we were young back then and didn't know any better. But I've told this story to many others over the past forty-five years, and have often pondered that message. I've wondered what Captain Simard, or Battalion Commander Shannon would have done had unidentified ships appeared on the horizon. The fact is that there's little that we could have done if faced by more than two enemy vessels intent upon an attack. I assume that Wake Island and Guam received the same warning message.

I had the 1600 to 2000 watch on the 5th, and got to see the Philippine Clipper arrive at about 1700, then move toward its moorage near the Navy dock. It was interesting to observe a few passengers disembark from the plane, then ride to the Pan American Hotel in a "woody" model 1940 Ford station wagon.

On Saturday morning, December 6th, I had the 0400-0800 watch on the dock. The passengers arrived from the hotel and were carried to the Clipper by a small vessel. After the huge seaplane's engines warmed up, it taxied out into the lagoon and gracefully lifted off the water, headed westward toward Wake Island.

The Sunday morning attack on Pearl Harbor sent us to full alert. All guns were manned. Camouflage was improved. Ready ammo boxes were filled. Major O'Neil came to our battery and gave us a pep talk, of sorts. He declared that our training days were over. We were at war, and word was coming in that we had lost at least one battleship at Pearl Harbor, the USS *Arizona*.

At 2125 that evening, Midway was attacked by two Japanese destroyers. Several hundred rounds were fired at the island, causing fairly severe damage. We lost one PBY near the hangar, but the worst hit was a 4.7-inch round that went through a ventilation port in the solid concrete electric power house, badly wounding Lieutenant Cannon and three enlisted men. Our batteries vigorously returned the fire, getting hits on both destroyers and raising smoke on one of them. They broke off toward the west and over the horizon in darkness.

The Philippine Clipper that had departed Midway the previous day was caught up in the Japanese attack on Wake Island. The aircraft's captain had decided to return to Midway, and the plane arrived at about the time we were under attack from the destroyers. The captain reported by radio that he could see the vessels smoking and possibly burning a few miles southwest of us. Our gun batteries were alerted that the Clipper was arriving and going to attempt a night landing in the lagoon, something that hadn't previously been tried. All flight operations by the Clippers were carried out during the daylight hours, but this was a dire emergency.

Even though all batteries had been alerted to the arrival of the Clipper, one of our nervous Marines fired on her. I heard that she suffered 16 holes in her thin aluminum skin, but there was no serious damage. After taking on fuel, the aircraft taxied into the lagoon in preparation for a night takeoff, hoping to miss the dangerous coral heads that could have destroyed her in seconds. (Earlier, a PBY attempting to take off in darkness had done just that! It struck a coral head and sank in the shallow water.) The Clipper took off successfully and flew on to Hawaii.

Lieutenant George Cannon and two enlisted men died of their wounds received during the Japanese bombardment. Cannon commanded a machine gun squad. Two of his gunners raked the decks of the attacking destroyers. After the Japanese shell hit the power house, he continued to direct fire despite his wounds, until he lost consciousness and died. He was posthumously awarded the Congressional Medal of Honor, and now lies at the Punch Bowl Cemetery on Oahu.

PFC Donald J. Drake was another 6th Marine Defense Battalion veteran who experienced that first battle. He left Midway in 1943, served briefly on Guadalcanal, then landed in the second wave on Okinawa in 1945. After the war he went to college on the G.I. Bill, became an attorney, and returned to active duty as a Navy JAG officer. He retired as a lieutenant commander in 1971 and joined the Roundtable in 2002. He related his recollections of the first battle of Midway in the following letter.

Regarding the powerhouse on Sand Island, where Lt. George Cannon was killed on the night of 7 December 1941: the powerhouse was a large concrete structure, said to be "bombproof." The walls were reinforced concrete, four feet thick. It had a double roof with a "concussion deck" between the two roofs. The lower roof was one foot of steel reinforced concrete and the upper roof was also four feet thick. The space between the two roofs was about ten feet in height. Around the walls of the concussion deck there were large openings about five feet wide, extending from floor to ceiling about every ten feet.

The purpose of that configuration was to cause any bomb which should penetrate the upper roof to explode when it hit the lower roof and the concussion would escape through the openings. Lt. Cannon had a machine gun command post with a telephone switchboard on the concussion deck between the two roofs.

At about 2130 on the night of December 7th, two Japanese destroyers made a firing run from south to north along the west end of Sand Island, walking their fire from west to east down the island. During that attack the powerhouse, the seaplane hangar, and the Pan American direction finders on the west end of Frigate Point were hit and the hanger was burned. About twenty minutes or so later, the two destroyers were cruising from west to east along the reef on the south side of Frigate Point (the west end of Sand Island) when they were illuminated by my searchlight. They immediately commenced firing again, but all of their fire at that time was directed at the light. Our guns began returning fire, but as soon as the destroyers hit the searchlight they ceased fire, laid a smoke screen and retreated to the south.

✳   ✳   ✳   ✳

"Take Your Post, Marine!"

The Roundtable's most detailed narration of life in the Corps and of the defense of the atoll during the main battle comes from Edgar R. Fox, who served six years with the Marines followed by a nineteen-year career in the U.S. Army Signal Corps. He found the Roundtable during its first year through an Internet search that landed him on Chris Hawkinson's web site. Here is Ed's story:

> Volunteering for the Corps on 1 June 1941 in Omaha, Nebraska, I had not the slightest conception as to what lay ahead for me. I had been motivated to enlist by the attack on the American gunboat *Panay* in the Yangtze River in 1937. Helping my parents recover from the Great Depression by leaving home was also in the back of my mind.
>
> I was also a member of the National Guard at the time. The Guard was very lax on qualifications—be able to walk, breathe, and say "yes, sir"—all for the sum of $21.00 per month. I was even promised thirty days *vacation* each year. How could one complain with benefits like that during the Depression?
>
> In Omaha, the recruiting sergeant presented me with a train ticket for travel to the San Diego Marine Corps Training Station. I was even sent "Pullman style," with first class meals and sleeping quarters. Now that was living! But I was greeted at the train station in San Diego by one mean-looking gunnery sergeant. After forming the bewildered "boots" into a makeshift formation, the gunny asked, "anyone in the ranks with prior service?" That's when I

learned my first lesson: *don't ever volunteer!* Gunny had me come front and center and informed me that I was to be the platoon guide. "Do you know what a guide is supposed to do, boot?"

That's when I made my second mistake. "I think so," I replied. We all then found out the meaning of "drop and ten!" What a beginning!

We slept in ten-man pyramid tents with wood decking and canvas cots. Close order drill was the primary subject, along with organized calisthenics with arms. Our weapon (not a *gun* or *rifle*) was a 1903 bolt action Springfield. We learned the parts and care of our weapon, which was our sleeping partner on many a night. The food was superior to what most of us ever had at home. Also, many recruits did additional duty in the mess hall for an extra $5.00 per month.

Physical training was primarily associated with learning your General Orders by heart. Woe be to the person who by the second week didn't know his G/Os, I being among the unlucky ones! My punishment was to string cigarette butts on a spool of thread by a certain time. Even with friends helping me smoke packs of cigarettes (at 5 cents a pack), I did not make the deadline. For that failure, I had to fill my back pack with wet sand and wear it for twenty-eight hours. I still know my General Orders.

The drill instructors ("DIs") pushed us hard. Training platoons were very competitive in everything. Our platoon had to be *the best*, or else. One morning our gunny marched us to the brig. One squad at a time entered this fearful establishment. We sat in a cell and had the door slammed and locked. Each squad spent ten minutes in there and listened to a lecture on "P & P," which was a Marine's term for a brig diet of bread and water. That was what was going to happen to us if our platoon failed in any way in winning top honors at the end of the three month training period.

We were taught the basics: map reading, how to box a compass, work together to achieve a goal, become proficient on the '03 Springfield, .45 caliber pistol, .30 caliber machine-gun, grenades, bayonets, and hand-to-hand combat.

There were times in the middle of the night when the DI would wake us up and order us to pack up for an extended time in the "boonies." The first week you were taught what was to be in your pack, and the gunny's wrath would be all over you if you failed to have the complete requirements within. At the end of the march some three to fours hours later, we would be told to "prepare for inspection." The standard procedure was to empty your pack and lay the contents out on your poncho, identical to the picture in the manual. One poor soul named Helms had newspaper in his pack, nothing else. When the Gunny came by for inspection not one word was said to him. The DI just went on as if Helms was not there. When we were told to pack up and prepare to march back to our tents, our route took us to the brig. Helms was told to fall out and report to the turnkey. His weapon and bayonet were taken from him in front of the platoon. The expression on his face was all about dread. He was led into the brig and locked in a cell. We then came into the brig one at a time, told Helms goodbye, and left. Helms got P&P that night and the next morning. Gunny brought him back the next day just before noon lunch. Helms spoke about his time in the pokey, of lost sleep, and "sweep & swab" all night long.

Training was severe. Sometimes we thought combat would be easier than three months under this gunny, but had it not been for our gunnery sergeant's dedication to us, which we did not realize at the time, I and many others would not be here today.

The last day we were in full greens—spit and polish. All the training platoons passed in review before the VIPs on the reviewing stand, and *our platoon* was the color guard. As we formed up that morning, Gunny called me front and center and asked, "Marine, do you know the duties of a guidon bearer?" My reply was, "yes, Gunny, I do!" He then placed the guidon in my hands and said, "take your post, Marine." In my life to date, there were many times I felt proud of my accomplishments, but this honor, as the gunny ordered me to be the platoon's guide to pass in review, was without a doubt the proudest moment that I can recall.

By the way, Helms graduated with honors and was later recommended for Officer Candidate School.

Digging In on Midway

When I arrived on Midway early in January 1942, I had been in the Marine Corps for six months. Like others, I was green, untested, and so cocky that I wondered why we needed so many of us (fifty-six) to defeat the Japanese.

The day we disembarked onto Midway's Sand Island, we were shelled by a submarine. The projectiles did not land near our location, confirming to us boots that those Japanese couldn't hit a barn wall if they were inside the barn. I was to learn later how foolish that notion was.

We practiced extensively on how best to repel an invading force. At the same time we spent long days and into the evening constructing barbed wire lines with concertina wire. We also constructed demolition devices. These were wooden boxes about two feet square packed with nails, spikes, and many pounds of dynamite, with an impact detonator located on the island side of the mine. One could fire his weapon at the bulls eye painted on the box to detonate the device. In theory, this was a good morale booster for us, but as the days went on the heat played havoc with the dynamite compound. We learned that it was best not to walk between the device and the surf, for the clumsy gooney birds (Midway's famous albatrosses) often would crash into one of these motion-sensitive mines.

With only one year in the Corps, I was not in any position to know what lay ahead. We prepared for an attack, but us lowly "grunts" had such a swaggering attitude that we were more concerned about our beer ration at the time. Call it blind, dumb, or bravado if you will; we were just inexperienced at warfare. The only times we had come under fire since Pearl Harbor was when Japanese submarines would surface at dusk and fire a few rounds. They were on the horizon. Not one of those rounds ever came close to our bunker.

Many of us were cross-trained on almost every weapon on the island, including the four tanks. Not that we would be proficient on those weapons, but we could operate the tank and load the 7-inch naval guns, the 3-inch anti-aircraft (AA) guns, the 40 mm. Bofors AA dual mounts, and the .50 caliber Browning machine guns. The 40 mm. AA guns could also be depressed for use against an amphibious landing.

If there were any secondary positions inland, my team was not informed. Fall back and retreat was not in our training manual. Nor did we train for such an event. Our order of battle was "deny the enemy the ground in front of you."

My machine gun (MG) bunker was dug almost to the water line on the southeastern tip of Sand Island. If the Japanese had invaded Midway, as they planned to, my MG bunker would have been directly in the path of their assault waves. During high tides it became rather moist inside the bunker. We had a coral sand deck. Our gear and shoes were never stored on the deck. The bulkhead (or wall) was lined with sandbags. I believe the overhead was of oak, similar to railroad ties. The exterior had a waterproof covering, then a neat layer of sandbags covered with some eight to nine feet of coral sand. Foliage was transplanted on the top. The front and rear of this mound was also heaped with coral sand sloping off some twenty feet or more.

There were two rooms inside the bunker. One was very small with a low overhead. It had the two-tiered double bunks, an equally small table, four ammo boxes for chairs, and one single light bulb of very low wattage. The second room housed the .30 caliber Browning water-cooled 1917 model machine gun. I think this room was about six feet square. The MG was mounted on a tripod that was sandbagged on a ledge. We had an excellent view of the beach, the barbed wire, and reef through the port. We had our gun lined up on the barbed wire, the theory being that the enemy would gang up on the wire and you would then have your target. There were similar barbed wire lines on either side of our bunker, but those lines were for the MG bunkers on our right and left to cover. Those bunkers were located 200 yards away. The overall plan was that the field of fire of each MG would overlap the adjacent gun on the left or right.

At the rear of the MG bunker we had a round, sandbagged, five-foot deep hole with a mono mount for a .30 caliber Browning automatic rifle, or "BAR." Its magazine held twenty rounds, and it was my selection for a personal weapon. I also carried a .45 caliber pistol. This position was intended for use against aircraft.

When not on alert, we ate in the mess hall, got fresh showers, clean clothes, and clean heads (toilets). On alert, hot food would be brought near our position. On "red alert," our famous C-rations would have to do. A slit trench was the norm for calls of nature, but sometimes we would scrounge wood from the night stores and build our own outhouse. The trouble with the outhouse was keeping it hidden. Japanese submarines had a nasty habit of surfacing at twilight and firing off several quick rounds at the island before diving. Their aim wasn't good, but we weren't going to give the Japanese our outhouse for a target. No Marine was going to be caught in a makeshift outhouse on the beach while under fire from off shore! We made one that collapsed until it was needed.

We had a searchlight battery close to our MG bunker. It was a dangerous companion when under fire from the sea. A Japanese submarine surfaced off the southern coast of Sand Island on February 8, 1942 and began firing at the island. A five-inch battery began returning fire, and our nearby searchlight battery lit up to probe for the submarine. A searchlight draws fire like a moth to candlelight. We ran like hell for cover!

As the southeastern tip of Sand Island was close to the reef, it was deemed the point the enemy might select to infiltrate for reconnaissance. Because of this potential, my area of beach patrol and the area on each flank was often inspected at night by the Officer of the Day (OOD), mainly to see if we grunts were paying attention to our Special Orders. I had a fear that some overeager OOD might surprise me by approaching from my rear, let alone the enemy. I worried about the OOD more than the enemy (I could always shoot the enemy). I devised a tactic that would alert me somewhat, if one did try to cross my path or approach from my rear. I would gather a branch of foliage and drag it behind me as I walked my patrol. On my return, I would be able to see tracks left on the beach if the OOD had come down to check on me. Once I found him hiding in the inland shrubbery. He hadn't spotted me, so I snuck up on him, stuck the muzzle of my BAR against his butt and shouted in a loud voice, "Who goes there?" That officer never challenged my ability again.

Condition Red!

The day the Japanese attacked Midway will never leave my memory. At one hour before sunrise all personnel on the island went to Condition Red, a normal routine every morning. Word had been passed down that the IJN was close and that an assault on the island was imminent. During the battle I was to remain stationed at my machine-gun position on the southeastern tip of Sand Island. Our sole job was to deny the enemy any foothold. I had a .30 caliber water-cooled machine-gun, a .30 caliber BAR, a .45 cal. pistol, fifty hand grenades, and two rolls of toilet paper. We joked about the TP. We figured that if we expended all our munitions we'd sure as hell need the TP!

As we ate our cold breakfast, the sirens began to sound. The IJN had been sighted! Now it was a waiting game. I do not remember the exact time, but the sirens sounded again. Word was passed that the Japanese were coming and to take cover. AA fire could be heard, then the bombs. The attack lasted only a few minutes. The nearby AA guns ceased firing. I then went topside to get a view of the island, and observed the north end in smoke and flames.

I awaited our returning planes that morning, but hardly any of our Midway-based aircraft returned. So many flew off that day to deny the enemy access to the island and to protect me, many never to return. To this day, I have the highest respect for those men. They did not know me, nor I them. What they did was the job they were trained to do. They gave the ultimate sacrifice, and I have often wondered if I could have been that brave.

Our Midway defenses may have looked great on paper, but the issue would have been in doubt if we'd been invaded. At the time I was untried, untested, too young, and too cocky to realize the consequences of combat. Iwo Jima taught me how foolish I had been at Midway. Had the IJN begun to shell us, my position would not have held up. Even a near miss would have brought the coral sand down in front of the port, blinding us for sure. Had the enemy gained the island, where would we go? We would stay and fight, doing what we had been trained for. We would have held the ground we were assigned to protect at a terrible loss. I just pray that I would have been as brave as the Navy and Marine airmen who attacked the carriers that day and did not return.

After Midway, I trained as a forward observer for artillery and air support with the 5th Marine Division. I was in the third wave at Iwo Jima and called in several emergency barrages from a battleship. I experienced then what a naval bombardment can do. If the tables had been turned at Midway, we would have been hurting![2]

*   *   *   *

Air Attack

For the most part, the familiar references on the Battle of Midway tell us that the Japanese began their assault with a devastating air attack on the two islands, then go into great detail about the subsequent air-sea struggle between the opposing fleets. We are told a good deal about the heroism of the atoll's U.S. Marine airmen in mostly obsolete aircraft, and the fact that Midway's fuel tanks were bombed, resulting in a black column of smoke that could be seen for many miles. But we generally don't find much about the actual defense put up by the Marines on the ground. I brought that to the attention of the Roundtable in 2004 with this inquiry:

Here's a question for our Marines and naval personnel who were present on the atoll during the Japanese air raid on the morning of June 4th: the fact that the enemy carried out an aggressive attack that caused major damage has been well documented, but less clear is what success the defenders on the ground had in knocking down any of the attackers.

The Japanese, of course, claimed that nothing was lost to ground fire. The John Ford movie clip seems to suggest that at least one aircraft was downed on the island, but as we know, some of those sequences were filmed elsewhere.

The various reference books are a bit vague on this subject, so I'm wondering what our guys who were there really saw. Did you actually observe any of the attackers going down? Was there any wreckage on one of the two islands or nearby? How effective was the Marine AA fire, and that of the PT boats and other small craft in the lagoon? Please give us a description of what you actually saw during or after the raid.

Walt Grist, a mechanic with Marine Scouting-Bombing Squadron 241 on Eastern Island, came in with the first reply:

I had a ringside seat across the runway opposite the tetrahedron that was at the intersection of the two runways running west to east on Eastern Island. There was also a .50 caliber water-cooled machine gun alongside, manned by men from the VMSB-241 ground crew. A Zero flew down the runway about 40 feet altitude and all guns trained on him. The impact area was about thirty yards past the north-south runway that the fighters used. The plane was demolished and everybody tried to get a piece of it. The pilot was buried in the late afternoon, and as far as I know he is still there. There were several planes shot down over the island that VMF-221 [the Marine fighter squadron] led in, and they impacted on Sand Island or in the Lagoon. Others had to ditch away from the atoll. I don't know just how many went down on the island or in the lagoon. I personally only saw the one go down on Eastern Island.

John Gardner had the next response:

Several of the attackers were shot down, four or five or so. I know of one that was right in the middle of Sand Island. I went over there when the attack ended and John Ford was shooting movie film. I may be one of the two guys in one of his well-known pictures.

Gardner is referring to Hollywood movie producer and director John Ford (most famous at that time for his 1939 classic *Stagecoach*) who was also a commander in the Naval Reserve. He was called up at the outset of the war and tasked with making a film record of some of its key events. Admiral Nimitz sent him to Midway with a Navy photographer's mate on May 25, 1942 without telling him why or what to expect when he got there. He soon found out, and his color documentary of the Japanese air attack on June 4th has long been one of the most famous and enduring cinematic records of the war.

✳   ✳   ✳   ✳

In the Trenches with John Ford

Don Drake had an interesting anecdote about John Ford on Midway in this 2005 letter to the Roundtable:

> In late May 1942 I was serving in Searchlight Section 5, G Battery, 6th Defense Battalion at Midway. There were eight of us living in a plywood shack surrounded by sandbags, on the concussion deck between the two roofs of the Sand Island powerhouse. A week or so before the BOM, we were joined by Commander John Ford and a photographer's mate named Jackie. We expected that we would see little of them when the bombing started, but that was not the case. They quickly assimilated into our small group and we taught them some salty Marine Corps language, which they adopted into their own vocabulary. During idle time awaiting the arrival of the Japanese, Commander Ford spent a considerable amount of time repeatedly playing our small collection of eight phonograph records.
>
> On the morning of June 4th, both Commander Ford and Jackie were busily filming the action. Ford had a Kodak Cine home movie camera and Jackie used a professional model movie camera. The seaplane hangar, about a long block east of us, was hit by one or more bombs. The laundry across the street to our west was hit, and two bombs hit between the laundry and our control station tower, about 20 or so feet southwest of the laundry. The powerhouse was not hit except for shrapnel from the bombs and perhaps some machine gun fire from strafing.
>
> After the Japanese planes left, several of us were gathered on the roof of the powerhouse and I noticed that Ford had a small red spot, about the size of a quarter on his upper arm, just below the shoulder, which was oozing blood. He had apparently been hit by shrapnel or, more likely, by a piece of concrete that had been chipped from the building by shrapnel. He had been so intent on taking pictures that he had not noticed it and, when I called it to his attention, he said something to the effect of "My God, I've been hit!" He later stopped by the sickbay where a Band-Aid was applied.
>
> Our visitors remained with us for a week or so after the battle, although they were invited to stay with the island commander. One night, Commander

Ford invited a lieutenant commander, who was a USN artist and a long-time friend of his to our troop shelter. He produced a box of cigars and, through a haze of cigar smoke, they regaled us with stories about Hollywood parties, Paris, stars, and starlets.

They left for Pearl Harbor early one morning on a PBY. About a week later we received a box of 100 phonograph records! I am certain that I can speak for all of us that we enjoyed their visit.

*   *   *   *

Surviving the Amphibious Assault

Ed Fox, in his fine narration above of life on Midway before and during the battle, expressed an opinion that was more or less universally held by everyone there at the time: if the Japanese had managed to pull off their planned naval bombardment and invasion, the defenders "would have been hurting." This subject was discussed in depth on the Roundtable on two occasions. In the first, early in 2003, the consensus from the veterans who served on the atoll was essentially that related by Fox: they would have fought bravely, but they really didn't feel they stood much of a chance. John Gardner explained it like this:

> Our survival was unlikely because of the tremendous firepower the IJN had coming in to bombard: many battleships, cruisers, etc. With that kind of firepower, far more than took Wake Island, Midway atoll would have been decimated. A few men always survive, but the gun batteries like our three inch and five inch would most likely have been destroyed. Consider too, our island air power was gone by noon on the first day. With no air cover, IJN carrier planes would have controlled the skies. When any defensive gun battery uncovered [from concealment], it would have been rapidly destroyed by bombs and strafing. The 6th Defense Battalion (Reinforced) was something just over 3000 men. Most likely half or more would have been dead or wounded. I am realistic in telling you this. I doubt very much that we could have held. By the time an enemy landing was under way, most likely the *Enterprise* or *Hornet* would have been gone. I think Admiral Spruance would have had to run for it to the east and leave us Marines and sailors on the ground to do the best that we could, but it wouldn't have been enough. I, like other Midway atoll vets, have thought a million times how lucky we were.

Underwhelming Force

The subject came up again late the following year, and our Marine veterans restated their feelings along familiar lines: they simply could not have held against the firepower of all those Japanese battleships and cruisers. But this time the discussion included the participation of a couple of qualified experts on the subjects of amphibious operations in general and the capabilities of the Japanese navy's Midway invasion force in particular. IJN researcher and author Jon Parshall injected an entirely new line of thinking with this letter to the Roundtable:

> Everyone has been assuming that the IJN could simply sit back and bombard the islands at their leisure for days and then go in. If the Japanese had had that much flexibility, then the situation would indeed have been dire for the Marines. But the tides weren't going to let them do that. That's why Yamamoto wouldn't let the operation date slip, even after two of his carriers were crippled at Coral Sea.
>
> There is absolutely no indication from Japanese sources that they would have modified their plans to land at low tide. Everything I have seen indicates that they were going to do a quick bombardment, then assault the atoll directly from the southern approaches. The primary sources and the official Japanese War History (*Senshi Sosho*) all say that the 7th of June is when the landings were to happen, period [June 6th Midway time].
>
> So figure that their navy has about four hours to get the job done. Remember that the Japanese had no aerial reconnaissance of the islands, and thus had no idea where the Marines' defensive facilities were located. Their best, most recent maps of the islands had been hand-drawn on the morning of June 4th, and thus were located aboard the Japanese carriers. I've seen them on microfilm in the actual carrier air group action reports. But there was no way to get that information to Admiral Kurita's four cruisers that were tasked with the shore bombardment mission.

Parshall's statement above illustrated a key point that is rarely considered in discussing the proposed Japanese invasion of the atoll. It is well known that Admiral Yamamoto's forces committed to the Midway operation included what appeared to be an overwhelming bombardment capability: eleven battleships, sixteen cruisers, and fifty-four destroyers. But what is less known and rarely considered is that the Japanese operations order called for only *four cruisers* to shell the islands ahead of the amphibious landings. The rest of the cruisers, all of the battleships, and all of the destroyers were assigned other tasks, the most important of which, in Yamamoto's vision, was to lie in wait for the American ships that would sortie from Pearl Harbor after Midway had been taken. And the Japanese were notoriously inflexible in deviating from an op-order, no matter what unforeseen circumstances upset their plans.

Parshall continued:

> Basically, then, the cruisers were going to show up at dawn and fire as best they could at whoever or whatever they could see. Most likely, they were simply going to generally lob shells for four hours and hope for the best. Then the barges were going to be loaded, and Col. Ichiki's troops would head for the beaches. If the Marines chose to withhold their fire until the barges grounded on the reef, it would have been very difficult for the IJN warships to even see, let alone destroy those weapons beforehand. Certainly, many of the Marines' heavy infantry weapons (MGs) would have survived, because there was no reason for them to be shooting at naval vessels in any case. Col. Shannon's stated battle plan was to "wreck 'em on the reef," and I take him at his word. His Marines would have hunkered down and withheld their fire until soft targets materialized.
>
> Note, too, that the Japanese had no formal doctrine for naval gunfire support, and there's nothing to suggest that they would have done it very well while making it up on the fly. If any of the Marines' seven-inch guns were operable and started shooting back (and odds are that they would have), that's going to have the effect of keeping the Japanese cruisers farther offshore than they'd want to be for delivering an effective bombardment.
>
> It is clear from actions like D-Day in Normandy that the most effective gunfire support was typically from destroyers' five-inch guns delivered at very close range to the beaches, 1500 yards or less. There's no evidence to suggest that the Japanese would have taken their vessels that close in, certainly not the cruisers. Furthermore, none of my research has uncovered any mention that the normal ammunition loadout for Kurita's cruisers, the main gunfire support vessels, had been modified. That means that the vast majority of their eight-inch ammo was likely to be armor piercing, which was useless for shore bombardment. Even modest slit trenches will dramatically increase the odds of survival against artillery, and the Marines certainly had plenty of those in addition to reinforced bunkers. The net result is that it's unlikely a four hour bombardment would have significantly degraded the islands' defensives.
>
> The IJN's air superiority might have helped their cause, but recall that the strike on June 4th with 108 aircraft had caused only a dozen killed in action on the atoll out of a garrison of over 2500 men. Also, the Japanese had suffered prohibitive casualties in CarDiv 2's Type 97 (Kate) squadrons due to heavy AA fire. In other words, another strike or two from the IJN carriers was not going to tip the balance decisively in favor of the Japanese. They might have degraded American defenses somewhat, but there's no way they would have wiped them out. In fact, there was never a single case during the entire Pacific war where air support or naval bombardment so impaired the defensive capabilities of the Japanese that the Americans were able to just wade ashore

and take an objective. It simply doesn't work that way. No matter how heavy the bombardment, some defenders, and usually more of them than you want, live to fight back.

The bottom line is that when assessing the probable outcome of the planned assault, you need to ask yourself this basic question: who would you rather be, a Marine enduring a four-hour bombardment in a trench with a BAR, or one of Col. Ichiki's men, clutching a rifle, wading through more than 200 yards of chest-high surf onto a beach covered with barbed wire and mines while taking fire from the guy with the BAR?

An Amphibious Catastrophe

In addition to our Midway veterans and others who served in that era, the Roundtable's roster has included a large number of other Navy and Marine Corps officers—regular, reserve, and retired—who are of later generations and who served in later wars or campaigns. One of those was Captain Will D. O'Neil, USNR (Retired), who had specialized in amphibious warfare during a portion of his naval career that began in 1960. Captain O'Neil provided us with important insight into the critical flaws in the IJN's Midway invasion plans that Jon Parshall first suggested above. With the following message to the Roundtable, he started many of us thinking about the possibility that an enemy invasion of the atoll might have actually failed, even without the presence of American carriers:

I was involved in amphibious operational planning and execution in my naval career, and I studied World War II amphib operations for insight. One that I looked at was the proposed Japanese landing on Midway, which I concluded could only have ended in a bloody catastrophe for the Japanese. I occasionally referred to it in talks to my officers as a good example of almost everything one could possibly do wrong in an assault.

Thus I was quite surprised to find in *The Roundtable Forum* that some believe the Japanese could surely have taken the islands had their forces not been turned back. I'm convinced that the assault, had it taken place, was almost certain to fail and was destined to be the most intense (in terms of casualties per yard of front per unit of time) amphibious catastrophe ever.

A lot of attention has been focused on the pounding envisioned prior to the assault. It seems as if some are imagining an intense, multi-day effort comparable to what our forces delivered against targets like Iwo Jima. In fact, the Japanese had neither the intention nor the resources for any such thing. Their plan was first to neutralize Midway as an airbase through air attacks. They had anticipated accomplishing that with their strike on June 4th, but that left a lot undone. It would probably have taken repeated strikes with the expenditure of a great deal of available ordnance before the job was complete. There would have been little left for attacks on the defensive installations.

Moreover, the Japanese had virtually no intelligence on Midway, not even the number of defending troops. Since the Marines had taken some trouble with camouflage and tone-down, their defense installations (as contrasted with the airfield and administrative structures) would have been nearly impossible to locate.

Four heavy cruisers had been loaded out as a bombardment force.[3] According to Japanese amphibious doctrine, those would have closed the islands before dawn on the morning of the assault and commenced firing at first light, at the same time the assault waves reached the reef. The point was to catch the defenders by surprise. They seem to have been unaware that the Marines had multiple radars that were reasonably efficient at detecting and tracking surface targets. They certainly would have had no difficulty in seeing cruisers or a large group of assault craft. The radars could also provide accurate range for fire control. Thus the ships would have found themselves taken under accurate fire by shore batteries the moment they themselves opened fire, if not before, and they would also have faced attacks by Midway's PT boats. Some of the other major factors I see include:

- The assault forces had little if any superiority in numbers over the Marines. In part, that was because the Japanese did not understand the extent to which the Midway garrison had been built up from its pre-war strength of 750 defenders. Our WWII experience showed that anything less than a 3:1 superiority was extremely risky.

- There was no rehearsal for the landing and, indeed, the Japanese army and naval landing forces committed to the operation had never worked together at all. Our doctrine and experience would say that that in itself was a certain recipe for disaster. There are always major glitches buried in an invasion plan. If you don't expose them in a rehearsal, you get to discover them in the course of the assault.

- The Japanese counted on getting to the reef before being detected, operating under cover of darkness. In fact, the Marines' radar would have made it possible to vector the PTs in for an attack and then follow up with fire from the shore batteries. That very likely would have inflicted significant casualties before the assault ever reached the line of departure, as well as sowing much confusion.

- The Japanese had a reasonably sound fire support doctrine. Suppressive fires were supposed to be continued until the troops reached the beach, followed by selective support fires directed at strong points. Initially those were to be directed by spotters in seaplanes, shifting to fires called from the beach as soon as communications were set up. That was bound to fall apart at Midway. First of all, the cruisers were going to find themselves tied up for some time in duels with the shore batteries. If and when they managed to suppress those, they would find that the floatplanes were not effective in locating targets ashore and directing fire against them. (That is certainly what our own forces found time and again.) Finally, their usual procedures for shore-to-ship communications were not going to work because they depended on finding a sanctuary for a bulky transmitter and a naval comms party, and there was no place for that.

- With a reef that stands well above the water by several feet at all states of the tide, plus underwater obstacles and mines, and with no amtracks on the Japanese side, they would have had to wade ashore. If the Marines manned their guns and held to their fire plan, a great many of the invaders would have died in the water or on the wire. And those that did get ashore would have nothing with them but small arms. That, in turn, would have meant very heavy casualties in digging the Marines out of their holes. Assuming that the Marines did not break (as the Japanese expected they would) then it was a matter of attrition on both sides; there simply is no room for maneuver on such small islands. The Japanese would have suffered multiple casualties for every one they inflicted, and since they had no overall superiority in numbers, they would certainly have run out of troops before they had gotten very far. Once the attackers are significantly outnumbered by the defenders, the end comes very quickly.

- The Marines had mobile reserves of infantry and armor prepared to counterattack any penetrations of the defenses. The armor was light, but the Japanese had no way to get at the defenders' weapons ashore.

- Finally, the Japanese were in for a very long day. They would have hit the reef at first light, 0625, and darkness did not fall until 2111, over fifteen hours later. No reserves were available and there never would have been a time when the way was clear for resupply or bringing in heavy gear. Thus they had to last for sixteen hours before they'd even get a chance to use their superiority in night fighting. Given the circumstances, it seems very unlikely that they would have had anyone capable of fighting by then.

The Bombardment That Never Was

The above treatises by Parshall and O'Neil were initially resisted by those of us entrenched in the traditional view that Midway's defenders, no matter how brave and determined, could not have prevailed against the huge force that the Japanese committed to Midway. Objections raised generally fell along the following lines: (1) was Cruiser Division 7—the four heavy cruisers assigned to support the amphibious invasion—really incapable of an effective bombardment? (2)

Wouldn't control of the air give the Japanese all of the advantage they needed to neutralize the Marines' gun emplacements? (3) The Japanese overwhelmed Wake Island with a far smaller force. Couldn't they expect to do the same at Midway with a much bigger one?

Parshall countered the first two points with this response:

> *Effectiveness of the Japanese cruisers:* nothing that I have read points to any special ammo loadout for the cruisers. I simply don't think it's credible to say that, in light of a lack of evidence to the contrary, we should simply assume that the Japanese were deviating from their normal operating practices. Their cruisers normally carried large numbers of armor piercing (AP) shells because that's what one needs to fight surface battles. Indeed, we have evidence that even for special bombardment missions, the Japanese still carried normal ammunition loadouts. For the bombardment of Henderson Field on Guadal-canal in October 1942, their two BBs (battleships) fired a grand total of 104 Type 3 special incendiary shells, 189 rounds of Type 0 high explosive (HE) ammo, 55 sub-caliber 12-inch rounds of an unknown type, and 625 14-inch AP rounds. Setting aside the 55 sub-caliber shots, what you see is 293 rounds out of 918 fired that were HE or incendiary, whereas the remaining 625 rounds were AP, of very limited utility against soft targets. That suggests that the two BBs, even for a designated shore bombardment mission, were carrying about 20 percent HE or Type 3, which compares very closely with typical loadouts that call for about 20 to 25 percent HE shells.
>
> It would appear, then, that the IJN didn't make a practice of loading spe-cial ammo for specific mission profiles; they went with what they had. As a result, until I see Japanese sources saying otherwise, I'm not buying into the notion that Cruiser Division 7's ammo allocation was anything different than normal combat loading. Note, too, that standard IJN gunfire support doctrine emphasized surprise, rather than heavy bombardment, which was to be avoided as much as possible. Firing during the landing was begun only when specifically requested by the commander of the ground forces. Therefore, I don't think the Marines were going to be on the receiving end of a very heavy bombardment at all. Furthermore, if doctrine called for fire to be directed by liaisons operating ashore, that lessens the chance of good gunfire being called in, because liaison personnel probably weren't going to reach the beach alive.
>
> *Japanese control of the air:* The Japanese would have had the ability to launch several more strikes against Midway, assuming they had won on June 4th. They probably would have been able to attack twice more on the 5th. However, conjecture must be based on an assessment of how they performed on the 4th, and the answer is that they weren't all that effective. Yes, they knocked out some barracks, fuel tanks, and the like, but their effect on the actual defenses of Midway was practically nil, and it cost them eleven planes. Other aircraft were written off as losses after they landed. That doesn't bode

well for continuing air operations against Midway. First off, it says that Japanese accuracy on their bombing attacks wasn't very good. They didn't have a good feel for the exact location of American defensive installations, and they readily acknowledged that flak was intense and accurate. That same flak would have still been there on June 5th and 6th, and the Japanese would have faced increasing attrition as their air groups weakened. And even supposing the Japanese won the naval battle by sinking or driving off the American carriers, their air groups would have likely taken heavy losses in doing so, meaning that any further attacks on Midway would have been made by depleted air groups that had demonstrated, even at full strength, that they couldn't put Midway out of business.

Then, for the third point, Captain O'Neil weighed in with a convincing argument that Midway was a far more difficult target for the Japanese than Wake Island:

> It will be recalled that the first attempt at Wake, on December 11, 1941, was a bloody fiasco for the attackers, after which they retired to their base to think things over. When they returned twelve days later, it was in considerably more force and with a determination to prevail or die in the attempt. And the position of the defenders on Wake was desperate. In terms of land extent, Wake is larger than the two Midway islands, and there were only about 400 troops to defend it. Wake has about 16,000 yards of practicable seaward beaches and a land area of about 8.5 million square yards, so there was no possibility of a real defense, especially as the Marines could not shift from one side to the other while under attack. With so small a force, the Wake defenders could not prevent the attackers from gaining a beachhead at an undefended point. Once they were ashore, the numerical advantage of the attackers was telling.
>
> But at Midway, (a) the attackers would have had no numerical advantage, (b) the defenders had fair prospects of inflicting attrition before the assault, (c) the defenders had good prospects of inflicting *very serious* attrition during the assault itself, and (d) the defenders had the strength to mount counterattacks on any survivors. The defenders at Midway had eight times as many troops per yard of beach and five times as many per acre as those at Wake.

It's a very rare thing when you can change the mind of war veterans who are in their eighties and nineties. Decades of reminiscing on strongly-held memories tends to form iron-clad opinions that senior citizens will seldom surrender or even suffer much in the way of debate. Yet, the foregoing in-depth analyses by O'Neil and Parshall on Midway's defenses and the Japanese op-plan in June 1942 seem to have had exactly that effect on the Roundtable's Midway Marines.

Ed Fox explained it best, in a telephone conversation with me after the final commentary on this topic appeared in *The Roundtable Forum*. "I've been under the impression for sixty-two years that we Marines had virtually no chance of surviving a Japanese amphibious assault," Fox said. "I've changed my mind. Whenever I read Captain O'Neil's *Forum* articles on this subject, I feel better and better."

CHAPTER 6

▼

ABOARD THE CARRIERS

Yorktown's Ad Hoc Air Group

Of the three U.S. aircraft carriers at the Battle of Midway, the USS *Yorktown* (CV-5), flagship of Task Force 17, is of special interest for a number of reasons. The most compelling of those, perhaps, is the fact that the ship was able to participate in the battle at all. Because of severe damage sustained at the Battle of the Coral Sea in May, Admiral Nimitz was told that repairs at the Pearl Harbor shipyard would take up to ninety days. He gave them just seventy-two hours to get the carrier minimally ready for action, and in yet another miracle of Midway, they actually got it done.

Another interesting peculiarity about CV-5 at the Battle of Midway was its air group. The *Yorktown* squadrons, especially Scouting Squadron 5 (VS-5) had been severely stressed in the Battle of the Coral Sea only four weeks previously. The ship's airmen could not be expected meet the challenges of another major battle so soon without more planes and a lot of help. Therefore, in order to muster up a full-strength air group for the Midway operation, replacement pilots and even two whole squadrons were brought aboard from the USS *Saratoga* (CV-3) while that carrier was completing stateside repairs. The *Saratoga's* Bombing Squadron 3 (VB-3) replaced VS-5 while its Torpedo Squadron 3 (VT-3) replaced VT-5.

That was rather straightforward, but the confusion starts when you look at *Yorktown's* new scouting and fighter squadrons. For reasons apparently best known to themselves, CINCPAC's staff decided that it would be too awkward to have two bombing squadrons on board *Yorktown* at the same time, VB-3 from

Saratoga and *Yorktown's* own VB-5. Therefore, since the battle-worn VS-5 had been sent ashore, it was directed that VB-5 (for which there was no replacement) would remain on board and be redesignated "VS-5" for the Midway operation, much to the displeasure of VB-5's pilots and enlisted personnel.

Even more discontent was heard among the men of *Yorktown's* fighter squadron, VF-42. *Yorktown* was getting the new F4F-4 Wildcat fighter, replacing the F4F-3s it flew at Coral Sea, and the ship's pilots had never seen, much less flown the significantly different "dash four" model. But Lieutenant Commander John S. Thach, of *Saratoga's* VF-3, had exactly the F4F-4 experience required for the *Yorktown*. His squadron, though, was suffering from a lack of pilots, so the decision was made to flesh out VF-3 by having it absorb VF-42 en masse: pilots, aircrew, maintenance personnel, and all related equipment and spare parts. The Yorktowners riled against what they deemed a backwards decision, but it was to no avail. Thach was skipper of "VF-3" and that's what the combined squadron officially came to be known on the Navy's roster and in most history books. The fact that sixteen of the new squadron's twenty-eight pilots and all of its enlisted men were from VF-42 was not considered important at the time.[1]

VF-42's veterans never surrendered their old name, and an annual VF-42 squadron reunion is still held to this day. As one might expect, when some of those vets started logging into the Battle of Midway Roundtable, they all steadfastly identified themselves as having served with "VF-42, USS *Yorktown*" during the battle. One of them who joined us in 2001 was William F. Surgi, who had been an aircraft mechanic with the squadron. Bill Surgi was one of the most vocal of those striving to retain his squadron's identity in the historical record, as evidenced by this letter to the Roundtable:

> Regarding recognition of the air group that operated from CV-5, the squadrons supporting them were the old air group of the *Yorktown*. I am bringing this up to enlighten all that only the aircrews from *Saratoga's* squadrons were aboard, while the *Yorktown* enlisted personnel from VF-42, VS-5, VB-5, and VT-5 did their aircraft maintenance.
>
> My statement is this: who was it that kept those planes in the air? It was the butt-bustin' crews of VF-42, VS-5, VB-5, and VT-5!

Surgi went on to provide us with a detailed organization structure for the squadron, emphasizing VF-42's role:

> Here is the *Yorktown's* Air Group in its proper setting. Clip this out and paste it over the *Yorktown* section of your Midway order of battle:

- Commanding Officer: Capt. Elliot Buckmaster

- Executive Officer: Cdr. Dixie Keifer

- Commander, *Yorktown* Air Group (CYAG): Lt. Cdr. Oscar Pederson

- VF-3: Lt. Cdr. John S. Thach, 11 pilots, 11 F4F-4 Wildcats

- VF-42: Lt.(jg) William N. Leonard, 19 pilots, 19 F4F-4 Wildcats

- VB-3: 18 SBD-3 Dauntless (aircrew only—aircraft maintained by VS-5 personnel)

- VS-5: 18 SBD Dauntless, + 8 Saratoga pilots (actually VB-5 flying as VS-5)

- VT-3: 13 TBD-1 Devastator (aircrew only plus one mechanic and one yeoman—aircraft maintained by VT-5 personnel)

Having been there, I would like to point out that what has been identified as the units operating on CV-5 is not a true picture. The remainder of *Saratoga's* air group sitting at NAS Kaneohe was not at Midway. The *Yorktown's* old air group was, for the most part, still intact on board. My own squadron, VF-42, was still together after Midway at the USMC airfield at Ewa until decommissioned on 22 June 1942. Bill Leonard signed my orders to CASU-2 on that date.

Surgi's enthusiasm for identifying VF-42 as the "real" fighter squadron aboard *Yorktown* at the BOM is understandable due to the "VF-3" label applied to all of the squadron's pilots in most references. Some historians have implied that VF-42's pilots were officially transferred to VF-3 for the Midway operation, but that is incorrect. Under the emergency conditions then extant, no one bothered with such formalities. The *Yorktown's* fighter pilots simply reported to Lieutenant Commander Thach without official orders. Lieutenant (j.g.) Leonard did serve as Thach's executive officer (XO) in the combined squadron, but that was a circumstance born of necessity when VF-3's actual executive officer was killed in a tragic landing accident just as the ship was heading out to Midway.

The VF3-VF42 relationship was nicely explained to the Roundtable by Rear Admiral Leonard, as written for him by his son Rich Leonard:

Regarding VF-42 and VF-3: there weren't any written orders assigning the sixteen VF-42 pilots to VF-3. Dad reports that he was called into *Yorktown* air group commander Pete Pedersen's office and told that VF-42 CO Charlie Fenton and XO Vince McCormack were staying behind at Ewa Marine Corps Air Station and that he (Dad) was to take the rest of the squadron's pilots over to Kaneohe Naval Air Station and report to Jimmy Thach. Dad was the senior of the lot with the exalted rank of Lt.(jg) So, they all hopped into an available Sikorsky JRS and flew over to Kaneohe.

Of course, all the maintenance folks belonged to the squadron, not the ship's company, and were all on the books as being in VF-42. To give you an idea of their attachment to their own squadron, after VF-3 XO Don Lovelace was killed, the next senior pilot was Dad. Just as the squadron CO's plane was #1, the custom was for the XO's plane to be numbered half way through the numeric sequence, in this case #13, as the XO would lead the fourth division. They quickly pulled Dad's #25 aside and painted "13" over his #25 to denote his becoming the new XO. Dad says it just happened; no one told them to do it, but as Bill Surgi once told me, "one of ours was the new XO and needed the right number on his plane." Johnny Adams was Dad's wingman and his plane got the same treatment, going from #26 to #14.

It's interesting that when Thach reported the results of air-to-air action after the battle, he was careful to note whether a pilot was VF-3 or VF-42.[2]

*   *   *   *

Pushing Planes

Otis Kight was also with VF-42 aboard the *Yorktown*, serving as what he fondly refers to as a "plane pusher" in the squadron. One of his primary duties as a non-rated seaman was to literally push aircraft into position on the flight deck by hand (this was before the days of tractors, or "mules" like those used on modern carriers and at airports).

As mentioned in Chapter 3, Kight has entertained the Roundtable over the years with some of its most interesting and sometimes witty contributions. Here are his recollections of life aboard an American carrier at the start of World War II:

> All of us on the *Yorktown* in '42 were of the Great Depression era. Life and death were accepted as parts of ongoing history, without heart bypasses, miracle drugs, hip replacements, and similar things that we take as normal now. People got sick—they died. People who lived past sixty-five were "old people." Death did not have the horror or shock it does to the last two or three generations. If America had another war in which we lost two thousand troops in five hours, the country would have a cow! Between Pearl Harbor and Tarawa we lost twice that many and didn't even draw in a deep breath.
>
> I joined the U.S. Navy on my seventeenth birthday, 29 July 1941, one month after graduating from high school. I was shipped from Atlanta to Macon, sworn in, and on a train to boot camp at Norfolk before I knew I was

a sailor. I only remember two basic lessons from boot camp. (1) Our drill instructor said it years before George C. Scott did in the movie *Patton*: "you ain't going out there to die for your country. You're gonna make some SOB Jap or German die for his country!" And (2) from a turret captain who had pulled the triggers on the eight inchers (his quote I can still hear as clear as Memorex): "Kight, there's two things you don't lose in this man's Navy. And the other one's your sense of humor!" As I performed the classic Jack Benny double-take with my mouth wide open, he replied, "and when you find out what the first one is, you got the job of Chief of Naval Operations in the bag!" I never did make CNO, but I've had a laughingly great career.

In the exams at the end of boot camp, I aced the radio test and scored above ninety on the mechanic's test. The guy at the assignment desk figured I got the answers from somewhere, so he marked me for "deck," which turned out to be my lucky day since my group was assigned to aviation squadrons. They needed us "boots" for mess cooking, compartment cleaning, and as plane pushers. I was assigned to Fighting Squadron 42 aboard USS *Yorktown*, then somewhere east of the Panama Canal.

Seaman Kight was then repeatedly shuttled aboard one ship after another in vain attempts to catch up with the *Yorktown*. His adventures during this time would amount to another chapter in this book. Instead, suffice to say that after a five-week odyssey, he finally wound up back at Norfolk—on Saturday, the 6th of December, 1941. Kight continues:

Not having been paid for five weeks, I stayed in the barracks that night. It was Sunday morning breakfast, standing by to transfer to my squadron, "dinner" (lunch to the unlearned), and listening to Glenn Miller on the radio. When the news about Pearl Harbor came, I had to teach most of the guys there where it was and what it meant. My uncle had been aboard the battleship *Utah* back in the 1920s, and he told me all about Pearl. An hour or so later we were on the way to the piers and the *Yorktown*. I was assigned a berthing space, which was the mess hall. You could hang your hammock after 2100 (9:00 PM), and could sleep in until 0515. At 0530 the boatswain would relieve one end of your hammock lashing if you were still in it.

There was a billet on *Yorktown* for a radio striker (apprentice), and one slot for a plane pusher. I had a full seabag, including tennis shoes, and some others didn't. So I wound up as the third guy in the number ten plane pusher crew. After working for hours doing that, I had "volunteer" tours in the bakery, parachute loft, and laundry.

My specific assigned task was to move aircraft around the flight and hangar decks. Ten of us were a crew. There was no slack when we were at GQ (general quarters). When the aircraft were all out, we were assigned secondary tasks. Mine was as an ammunition booster for the Marine detachment manning the water-cooled .50 caliber machine guns mounted on the starboard forward catwalk. I got into the forward magazines, right below the flight deck, pulled out a magazine can, about sixty pounds, and toted it about fifteen feet aft down the catwalk to the guns. They took it from there. The gunners on that battery could dump ammo faster than a two-year old could get rid of breakfast.

When two of our pilots shot down a Japanese Kawanishi flying boat off Jaluit in one of our first air actions, I didn't have any remorse that over half a dozen good Japanese aviators had died, just the thought that one of our pilots had when he reported over the radio, "we just shot his ass off!" Like my drill instructor had said, the enemy died for his country.

I made Seaman First Class (Sea1/c) in April 1942 due to having a Navy-type jackknife on me at the right time. The warrant officer who somewhat controlled the plane pusher mob mustered all of us one slack day and stated, "everyone with a pocket knife, one step forward." Me and another guy out of about fifty stepped out. "You two are now rated Seaman First." That was his way to ensure we all carried knives. In those days aircraft were secured to the flight deck with "nine thread," a very rugged manila rope line. If it was wet and stressed, the securing knots wouldn't release easily. Ergo, the term "rope wrench" was coined, and all those of adult responsibility carried one, officially labeled as "knife, pocket, folding." (Earlier in life I'd known it as a Boy Scout knife.)

Daily Life on the Yorktown

I'm occasionally asked about the hardships experienced at that time, i.e. food, living conditions, clothing, shipboard work, etc. My usual response goes something like this. Those of you who are audiophile purists never had the joy of bringing in a program from The Grand Ole Opry on your crystal set, with static, wavering volume, and white noise. We had never heard of Dolby and Bose back then, so we didn't know what we were missing. We also had not heard of air conditioning, freeze drying, shelf-stored milk, teflon, Nomex, and underway replenishment by helicopter. It was an age of accepting tincture of iodine, belladonna, and Octagon soap. If it didn't use vacuum tubes or have a grease fitting, we didn't really accept or trust it. "R & R" wasn't in our language. The chief said, "take it off, fix it, put it back on." Today it's "remove and replace with a new one!"

The South Pacific was romantic, but only in the musical. Berthing compartments had a temperature of 95-110 degrees F. in the afternoon, and cooled off to 85 by reveille the next morning. Oh yeah, this was also before the popularity of deodorants. So most of us would take one blanket (for padding) and head for the bomb nets. These were nets under the flight deck for the crew to dive into during an air attack. They were made of corrosion resistant metal with about a two inch square grid. Always a cool breeze when under way.

We in the Air Department had it made. We could see daylight *all* day, and most of the time, starlight too. A work day was from two hours before dawn to three hours after sunset. The "black gang" (in the engineering departments) had temps of 110-130 F., with shifts of four hours on and two off during their entire work day! That was the way it was; it wasn't questioned, just accepted and cussed.

Creature comfort consisted of all cotton clothing in the tropics. The ship's laundry was most efficient, but a person needed at least four sets of dungarees with underwear to change if one could stand his own stink. So most of us would take a shower (all salt water except a ten to fifteen-second rinse off) with our underwear on and with salt water soap. One reason for the underwear/shower routine was the notorious effect of sending anything to the laundry. Large amounts never came back. Especially socks and underwear. All clothing was stenciled with the owner's name which was visible on the dungarees, but not on socks or skivvies (underwear) when worn by some pilferer. So we kept three sets of skivvies. The good part of hot berthing compartments was that the wet skivvies dried in about an hour. We on the plane pusher crews also wore tennis shoes which got washed about every week. We found out that 100-octane gas and engine oil was a good remedy for athlete's foot, although that never got mentioned in the New England Journal of Medicine.

The heat question really never came up as a civil liberties issue for me. After enjoying sixteen summers fairly close to Atlanta, where the temperature rarely dropped below ninety degrees by sunrise, I had it made aboard ship! The most brutal weather conditions were in the North Atlantic in winter time. I still have both big toes numb from frostbite just working on the flight deck of the *Wasp* on a two day trip from Norfolk to Bermuda in November, 1941. As the saying still goes, "it's easier to wipe off sweat than goosebumps!"

The Sweet Smell of Death

During the Battle of the Coral Sea, I remember having a feeling for the first time that there were people out there that meant ill to my ship. The resultant attitude was *you're not going to hurt my ship*, as I went back under the flight deck for another can of .50 caliber. The Japanese bomb that near-missed on the starboard bow came about twelve to fifteen feet from me, clipping a wire cable in the middle strand on the catwalk guard rails.

We worked all the rest of the day, spotting aircraft, respotting them, looking up for dive bombers and along the horizon for the torpedo planes. Finally, after dusk and dark, we were secured, sent below for our cold salt water shower with a fresh rinse, and then to relieve the damage control parties sorting out the bomb damage on the number two and three decks. Up to the time of Coral Sea, I had only read in Hemingway's novels about "the sweet smell of death." The damage area was a disaster, and I realized then what the "sweet smell of death" really was. There were parts and particles; some ship, some shipmate. The bomb landed in a compartment used to stow arresting cable components, and particles of arresting cable had limited the bomb blast. We sorted out pieces of the ship, put pieces of the crew in body bags, and put the other trash in garbage cans until the compartment was clear enough to use shovels, then fire hoses, then Cresol (a creosote disinfectant) and swabs. And always, the "sweet smell of death." And the thought crossed my mind then and many more times later, *where is my number?* There was sadness and respect for the dead, but not the wholesale celebration this present generation embraces. We gave them a military burial at sea and went on with the business of war.

As far as fear or terror, no! There was none of it anywhere I could see or hear, just a pure dedication to fight the enemy with all that we had; to survive with our ship.

The Coral Sea Battle served me well. It was "Combat 101" that let me know what to really expect at Midway. I am still amazed and thrilled every morning when I see light through square cornered windows. My thoughts are "I won again." And when it's time to vote, on any level, I secretly vote about five hundred times, for all those who gave their all so I can vote. I thank each and all of you who read this, for remembering. And I thank those who sacrificed everything so that we could be among those who remember. Those who are remembered are not gone.[3]

∗   ∗   ∗   ∗

Aboard the Enterprise

Over the years, the Roundtable has attracted the membership of men and women of all ages and backgrounds and from many diverse walks of life, and that's even true of the Battle of Midway veterans on its roster. One of the more interesting of them is Alvin Kernan, who served with Torpedo Squadron 6 (VT-6) on the USS *Enterprise* during the battle. On first glance, Kernan may not seem all that unusual—he did have an exciting wartime career in naval aviation, earning a Navy Cross, a Distinguished Flying Cross, and five Air Medals from inside the turret of a TBF Avenger torpedo bomber. But several of our Roundtable members had similarly intensive combat experiences during the war—what makes Kernan a bit unusual is his subsequent civilian career: he became a professor of Shakespearian literature at Princeton University.

When you think of a university professor who specializes in the humanities—Shakespeare, at that—you rarely visualize someone who started adulthood by engaging in vicious aerial gunnery duels with Japanese fighters and otherwise living the stressful, profane, hazardous life of an enlisted sailor on three World War II aircraft carriers, one of which was sunk while he was aboard. Such is the case with Kernan, though, who has authored three books related to his wartime experiences. In one of them, *The Unknown Battle of Midway*, he gives us a very insightful look into the persona of the typical U.S. Navy sailor at the start of the war:

> In the early days of the war almost all enlisted men were from blue collar, low or lower middle class homes. We would have denied that we were an underclass, there wasn't such a thing in America, we thought, conveniently forgetting that blacks and Asians were allowed to serve in the Navy only as officers' cooks and mess attendants. Our teeth were terrible from Depression neglect, we had not always graduated from high school, none had gone to college, our complexions tended to acne, and we were for the most part foul-mouthed and drunkenly rowdy when on liberty. We certainly didn't look like heroes. With no understanding of social class, I used to wonder in the shower or the crowded compartment when everyone was dressing why so many of us were skinny, bepimpled, sallow, short, and hairy. We bragged, however, about what we would do when we got liberty in Honolulu again, about the cars we had driven and girls we had known in civilian life. You had to wonder sometimes why any of us had joined the Navy, so good were the lives we described at home. In truth we were a very ordinary group of young men, some new recruits, others petty officers with years of service and training behind them, all volunteers, all regular Navy, USN...[4]

Dodging Bullets

While *The Unknown Battle of Midway* is essentially a historical treatise focused primarily on the saga of the U.S. torpedo squadrons during the battle, Kernan's *Crossing the Line* is autobiographical; his personal memoirs of the entire war. The following excerpt provides an interesting glimpse of life aboard the *Enterprise* as it prepares to leave Pearl Harbor for Midway. He is describing some of his various duties as an aviation ordnanceman in VT-6:

> The time in port was short and filled with all-hands details provisioning the ship, refilling the magazines, getting stores and fuel aboard. The bright floodlights burned all night, as one lighter after another came alongside, while workmen from the yard installed new guns and equipment. But no one complained, for once, and excitement shone in the men's eyes. By the late morning of May 28, lighters sill alongside, we were under way, steaming out of that deep and narrow channel that leads south out the great harbor at Pearl to the

open Pacific Ocean. Though we were unaware of it, at the same time (May 29 Japanese time), Isoroku Yamamoto on his flagship *Yamato*, the largest ship in the world—seventy thousand tons, nine 18.1-inch guns—was leading the Japanese fleet out of Yashiro-jima through the Bungo Channel on the way to Midway, twenty-five hundred miles to the east. The *Yorktown* was being patched up in the dry dock at Pearl and would follow in a few days…

Once underway, we continued belting machine-gun ammunition obsessively, like some rite of war, piling up huge mounds of ammunition ready for use in the planes. We also piled up an enormous amount of trash that had to be burned…at night when the smoke would not give away the position of the ship to submarines or scout planes…The trash contained bullets here and there, missed in the sorting, and after these lay in the hot fire for a time, they exploded. Since they had no firm backing when they exploded, the bullets lacked the force to go through the insulated steel sides of the furnace, but if by chance one came through the door of the incinerator when it was open, it would maim anyone it hit. The job required two sailors, dressed only in skivvies in the boiling heat that was filled with the stale smell of trash, flames lighting the small space weirdly. One man opened the door of the furnace and then slammed it closed instantly once a shovelful of trash had gone in. The other sailor, me, threw a shovel load in the furnace then quickly dropped to the deck to avoid any rounds that might have cooked off since the last shovelful was thrown in. The pops were loud and frequent, and eight hours of shovel-drop-pop from sunset to sunrise jangled the nerves. But the danger was less, much less, than the frustration of being occupied with trash disposal while going into what we all knew would be one of the great naval battles of all time.[5]

✳   ✳   ✳   ✳

Brothers on the Hornet

Several months before Americans learned of the terrible tragedy of the Sullivans—five brothers serving on the same ship, all killed at the same time during the Guadalcanal campaign—there was another set of brothers serving on the USS *Hornet*. Fire controlman Bernie Cotton was accompanied aboard the ship by his brother, Francis X. Cotton (known to all as "FX"), an aviation ordnanceman in Torpedo Squadron 8 (VT-8). FX was the bombardier in one of the squadron's TBD Devastator torpedo bombers. In the following letter to the Roundtable, Bernie describes the dreaded feeling he had watching VT-8's planes take off and then fail to return after the bitter battle on the morning of June 4th.

At the Battle of Midway, the order was given to launch aircraft. The first to launch were the F4Fs, then the SBDs, and finally the TBDs. I thought FX was in Waldron's plane as they took off. We stayed at GQ all that day. We watched as the Japs attacked the *Yorktown*, which was about eight miles from us. She did not seem to be hurt too bad, but could not recover her aircraft, which then diverted to both the *Enterprise* and the *Hornet*.

When we secured from GQ that evening, none of the TBDs had returned. My gun director officer kept consoling me, saying that they probably landed on Midway. As I made my way down the island I passed the squadron armory...*and there was FX sitting on a workbench, reading a comic book!* I could have shot him!

Bernie hadn't considered at the time that the TBD bombardier doesn't fly on torpedo missions, so his day-long worry about his brother's fate had been for naught.

The two remained together on the *Hornet* until it was lost at the Battle of the Santa Cruz Islands in October 1942. They then went their separate ways, with Bernie ultimately retiring from the Navy as a Chief Fire Controlman and FX as a lieutenant. Both eventually became members of the Roundtable, with Bernie providing frequent personal insight on the brief life of the *Hornet*. FX, for his part, gave us one of the more amusing anecdotes about the Midway era, which you'll find in Chapter 14.

*   *   *   *

Tragedy on the Flight Deck

But in general, there was precious little amusement to be found anywhere on the first day of the battle. At virtually every quarter it was war of the most vicious kind, full of horrors deliberately inflicted as well as accidentally caused. One of the accidents occurred aboard the *Hornet* as some of the shot-up F4Fs from the *Yorktown's* fighter squadron sought a clear deck in lieu of their own damaged ship.

Tom Cheek's wingman that morning was Ensign Dan Sheedy, and as you'll see in the next chapter, Tom owed his life to Sheedy, who was badly wounded in dogfights with Japanese Zeros. Several of the *Yorktown* F4Fs had critical battle damage; Sheedy's instruments were shot out and one side of his landing gear was partially lowered. Worse, when his plane hit the deck hard, the other wheel collapsed, slewing the aircraft to starboard and pointing its nose at the *Hornet's* island. The jolt also caused the fighter's six .50 caliber machine guns to fire a brief burst, spraying the island and killing three Marines, a VB-8 crewman, and Lieutenant Royal R. Ingersoll, the son of Atlantic Fleet commander Admiral Royal E. Ingersoll.[6] Clay Fisher was in the VB-8 ready room at the time and has this recollection:

> I remember the incident well. George Ellenberg, a fellow VB-8 pilot, and I were in the ready room when George asked me if I wanted to go out on the *Hornet's* island catwalk and watch the dogfights over the *Yorktown* through his binoculars. I was tired from the long morning flight and expected to fly again later, so I begged off. Then, shortly after George left the ready room, we heard a fighter's guns firing. A few minutes later one of our squadron crewmen came into the ready room, very excited and carrying a bloody pair of binoculars. He told us "Mister Ellenberg was just killed on the catwalk!"
>
> After the VT-8 losses, this was another terrible blow. But a few minutes later, Ellenberg came stumbling into the ready room with blood all over his face, shirt, and hands. He looked awful, but he mainly had a laceration on his forehead that wasn't too serious (head wounds always bled profusely). He had been hit by a piece of metal knocked off the island by the fighter's guns.
>
> This incident was a huge shock to all of us on the ship. I heard that the decision was made to bury the victims at sea from the fantail that night because of the effect on the morale of the crew. Also, no one knew what was going to happen the next day. Chaplain Harp and a group of pharmacist's mates accomplished the burial. I heard it was a real tough job getting the bodies through the passageways and onto the fantail.
>
> I've often wondered if I'd have gotten hit (or worse) if I'd elected to go with George when he first asked.

✳   ✳   ✳   ✳

Bandsmen to War

As horrible as the Sheedy accident aboard *Hornet* was, it didn't begin to compare to the ongoing agony on the *Yorktown*. The two air attacks on June 4th and the submarine attack on June 6th killed fifty-four of the ship's company and wounded a great many more. Another thirty-two in the air group were lost in the attacks against the Japanese fleet on the 4th.[7]

Aboard the *Yorktown* was a twenty-one year old member of the ship's band, Musician 1/c Stanford Linzey, who later in life became a member of the U.S. Navy Chaplain Corps, retiring in 1974 as a captain. Chaplain Linzey joined the Roundtable's cadre of *Yorktown* veterans in 2001, adding his unique, faith-based perspective on life and death aboard the carrier at Coral Sea and Midway. He has also been very active in annual commemorations of the Battle of Midway as well as other events centered around World War II veterans, frequently delivering the invocation for such gatherings. In the following excerpts from his book, *God Was At Midway*, Chaplain Linzey describes his battle station experiences aboard the *Yorktown* and his harrowing escape from the ship before it sank.

During battle, the ship's band does not sit on the deck in concert formation playing "Nearer My God to Thee" while the ship goes down, though that possibility may be nearer than one thinks. Bandsmen have various duties in times of battle. Some work as medical corpsmen and stretcher bearers, working with the ship's doctor. Others, such as I, were telephone talkers at various repair parties...I was the telephone talker for Repair Party 4, located on the third deck amidships in the galley compartment.[8] It was my job to report messages from the officer at Central Battle Station, in the bowels of the ship, to my repair party officer, Warrant Officer B. M. McKensie. I also had to relay his messages and replies back to Central Station.

Repair parties are located throughout the ship to assess and repair damage to the ship in their localities so that they can keep the ship afloat and steaming. They fight fires, shore up bulkheads, patch holes, keep firefighting equipment operating, keep electrical systems operable, and the like. Doctors and medical corpsmen in the area take care of the wounded.

Prior to the battle [of Coral Sea], I thought the task would be nearly impossible, because I had to remember frame numbers and hatch numbers plus other commands back and forth. No mistakes were allowed. However, once the battle began, I was surprised at how easily it came after all the training and practice.

During a battle, the men lie or sit on deck. If they were to stand up, they could break their necks on the overheads if the ship were to lurch violently due to explosions. It seemed the British had this experience and passed it on to us.

As the battle developed, we were lying down on the third deck, which was right at water level and a prime target for torpedo strikes. I had the headphones on. All of a sudden I heard the man on the bridge announce over the phones, "enemy aircraft approaching, 100 miles." A short time later the voice said, "enemy aircraft approaching, 50 miles." Then he said, "stand by for torpedo attack."

At once a strange feeling or sensation came over me, a strange awareness of reality. It seemed like an eerie consciousness of the moment of truth. I wondered if this could be real. Up to this moment, we had played war. We had rehearsed battle plans...but now, at any moment, the decks could explode beneath me...

As I lay on the deck in advance of the impending event, I tried to imagine what it would be like. In my mind's eye I could see the planes approaching. How would it feel to be blown to bits? In a split second, I could be in eternity. How would that feel? Where is eternity?

Death Below Decks

The bombers came, and the bombs dropped. There were six near misses. Some explosions pierced the side of the ship in several places, and some dented the skin of the hull below the waterline.

Then—WHAM!

A direct hit on the flight deck ripped through the thick metal like it was paper, throwing us about our compartment and sending shrapnel flying through our steel bulkhead. The bomb tore through to five decks below and exploded. It had gone through the compartment where the Marines lived and continued down through Repair Party 5, the group just forward of Repair Party 4, where I was located.

This was an armor-piercing shell…it left a gaping hole in the third deck, the one we were on, just forward of us in the next compartment. We were separated from the blast only by one bulkhead (steel wall) and a watertight door, and it was punctured by the steel debris that had crashed through it…

Most of Repair Party 5 was wiped out, and the dead were laid out on the mess decks to await burial at sea…Planking was placed over the hole in the compartment so we could walk back and forth to carry out our duties. The pungent smell of burnt flesh, sweet and nauseous, was sickening. Every time we had to go through the compartment we had to cover our mouths and noses to avoid breathing it, for it was penetrating and repulsive.

Abandon Ship!

The *Yorktown* was grievously wounded in the Coral Sea, but Linzey and his shipmates faced a greater peril the following month at Midway. The carrier was critically damaged by bombs, then two aerial torpedoes slammed into the hull. *Yorktown* quickly tilted over to a twenty-seven degree list. Fearing that it might capsize, Captain Buckmaster ordered the crew off the ship. In the following passage from his book, Linzey describes his escape from the doomed vessel.

There in the galley compartment on the third deck, we knew that to have any chance of survival we would have to climb up the sloping deck, work our way to the bulkhead hatch that now was aslant in the overhead, and repeat the procedure for the decks above. Our great fear was that at any moment the listing ship might capsize or sink three miles to the bottom of the sea.

Frightened as we might have been, there was no panic. Our naval training took over, and in the galley compartment, we got in line to climb up the slippery, leaning deck. We took off our shoes to get better footing for our climb and began our ascent. We knew this part of the ship so well we could have located the hatch even without the battle lanterns, but when the first men hesitated, we knew that something was wrong.

The watertight hatch to the second deck was warped shut by the explosions! However, in the center of each watertight hatch there was a scuttle, a small circular quick-acting hatch that could be opened by the turn of a wheel. To our great relief, the first man got it open, and the rest of us climbed up through the manhole, each in turn, one at a time…

We repeated the procedure to arrive at the next level and eventually came out onto the hangar deck…my initial joy at seeing daylight was immediately dampened as I gazed in amazement at the sight of the devastation. I saw twisted metal, gaping holes in the steel hangar deck as if a great finger had plucked holes in it, and debris scattered everywhere…Amid all this, men were going up, around, and over the debris, and over the side to abandon the derelict ship. The wounded were being dragged across the slippery decks in stretchers, and some were simply picked up and carried bodily…

Like all the others, I took off all my clothes down to my skivvies so as not to be weighted down. Someone threw me a Mae West life jacket, and I gratefully put it on…Determined to leave the ship and go down one of the lines into the sea, I moved closer to the upper edge of the hangar deck. All lines were filled, but eventually I found a place and grasped the two-inch line. I lowered myself down the side of the ship and into the waiting oil-covered water…Oil gushing from the fuel tanks had covered the water with several inches of thick ooze. The water was warm and oily, and we were about three miles from the nearest land, *straight down below us!*[9]

*   *   *   *

All Hands to Battle Stations!

Chaplain Linzey reported that he spent "hours" in the water, being rescued by the destroyer USS *Balch* just as his strength was about gone. His tale of escape from the doomed carrier and eventual rescue was typical of those of several other *Yorktown* veterans on the Roundtable, each of whom related his personal experience for us.

One of those was Commander Tom Cheek, whom we first met in Chapter 3 as an *Enterprise* fighter pilot during the Doolittle mission. Cheek flew from the *Yorktown* at Midway as a member of "Fighting 3," the merged F4F squadron led by Lieutenant Commander Thach. In later years, he wrote a detailed description of his harrowing flight on the morning of June 4th, 1942, followed by a gripping narrative of the attacks upon the *Yorktown* that followed. He shared the document with the Roundtable in 2003.

Unlike his wingman Sheedy, Cheek had managed to get his Grumman fighter back to the *Yorktown* before battle damage halted further flight operations. That meant that Cheek, having survived a deadly encounter with Zeros over the Japanese fleet, had to face death three more times that day; from the enemy dive bombing attack, then the torpedo attack, and finally another desperate ordeal as he was forced to abandon the stricken vessel. The story begins in the squadron ready room, where Thach has just instructed each of his fighter pilots to prepare a written report of the morning air battle:

> As I sat staring at the sheet of paper, trying to arrange my whirling thoughts, a dull, stinging sensation drew my eyes to the arch of my left foot. A piece of the shoe leather the size of a half-dollar was missing, exposing a pink spot of raw flesh. When did that happen? Gazing down at the wound, it was there, it was a fact, but my mind refused to bring it into reality. The combat report forgotten, I was still wondering at the wound when the 1MC jarred my mind back to the present with, "ALL HANDS TO BATTLE STATIONS! ENEMY AIRCRAFT, PORT QUARTER, DISTANCE THIRTY-FIVE MILES!"
>
> There was an immediate rush by all hands out of the ready room onto the flight deck. All eyes were focused to the northwest where spiraling streaks of black smoke across the sky marked falling aircraft. Our combat air patrol had evidently intercepted the intruders. As we watched, we wondered—were the falling black streaks enemy aircraft or ours?
>
> The incoming attack of eighteen dive bombers and six Zeros were from the carrier *Hiryu*. Hidden by a rain squall, she had escaped detection when our dive bombers attacked the Japanese First Carrier Striking Force. As *Yorktown's* five inch guns began to add black puffs of AA into the path of the approaching attack, Thach appeared. "Get back in the ready room!" he ordered. "You cost Uncle Sam too much money to be out here!" Back in the ready room we sat tense, listening as the tempo of the antiaircraft fire outside rose in waves of sound. The bark of the five-inch guns signaled the approach of each attacker, followed in sequence by the *pump-pump* of the 1.1-inch mounts, the chattering 20 millimeters, and finally the rattle of the .30 and .50 caliber machine guns as the enemy approached his drop point.

Struck by Three Bombs

As the sound of the AA fire became a constant roar, we were suddenly jolted by an explosion in the after part of the ship. It was immediately followed by a second, then a third, this time closer and more severe. I gripped the arm of my chair tighter and settled deeper into the cushioned seat. Suddenly, there was silence. As we waited, choking black fumes flooded into the ready room. The after hatch opening into the interior island structure had been left open, and sooty black smoke boiled up through the ladder wells from the decks below. Again the ready room rapidly emptied. Gasping and teary eyed, we looked around in the fresh air on the open flight deck. The ship lay dead in the water while its screening cruisers and destroyers churned in a protective circle around her. Within minutes we were joined by coughing, soot-blackened, engineers from the engine and fire room spaces. The last bomb had penetrated the flight deck at an angle, penetrated the stack where it exploded, blasting back down the uptakes, snuffing out the boiler fires and flooding the spaces with choking smoke and fumes.

On the after flight deck, where a bomb had exploded on contact at deck level, repair crews were rapidly repairing a gaping hole in the deck with sheets of boiler plate. The bomb blast had sent shrapnel ripping through the gun crews and other exposed personnel. Around and in the deck-level 1.1-inch gun battery, first aid teams were removing and checking bodies for signs of life. There were none living. Curiosity drew me in that direction; I wandered aft and entered a mind-shocking area. Approaching the after end of the island structure, a bloody splotch on the gray painted side of the superstructure caught my eye; it brought to mind a child's drawing of a "gingerbread man." On the deck below lay a mass of bloody flesh encased in shredded denim.

"I bent down to pick up another can of ammo, something knocked me flat, and when I stood up, there he was!" The strident voice came from a group gathered near the port edge of the flight deck abreast the point of the bomb's impact. All but the speaker were quietly looking down into the 20 millimeter gun battery on the catwalk below, where a headless gunner still manned his gun, held in place by the gun mount shoulder straps.

Only five dive bombers and three Zeros survived the attack to return to the *Hiryu*, but they'd left the *Yorktown* dead in the water and without power. By 1400, though, repair parties had the ship underway again. A low cheer sounded through the ship as the first vibration of the churning propellers traveled through the hull. We began building up speed to nineteen knots.

Yorktown Suffers a Second Attack

The respite was not long however; radar had detected a second attack approaching from the west. Again all hands scrambled to man their battle stations. We had barely settled into our seats in the ready room when a frantic command sounded from the speaker system, "FIGHTER PILOTS, MAN YOUR PLANES!" Fumbling with my flight gear and plotting board, elbowing my way through the crowd blocking the hatch, I found myself one of the last to leave the ready room. On the flight deck, engines were starting as I made my way aft. I found that each fighter already had a pilot in it. Finally, just past the island structure I spotted a Grumman unoccupied and scrambled into its cockpit. Buckled in and with a thumbs up from a mechanic, I flipped the starter switch. The engine coughed twice and died. As the five inch batteries opened up, I was ready to try to start the engine for a third time when a mechanic climbed up on the wing and yelled, "no gas!" With the 1.1-inch gun tubs just above me joining the blasting five inch, I decided the ready room was a safer place to be.

The room was filling up with flight deck personnel as I made my way to a seat facing the inboard bulkhead and sat down between Ensigns Evans and Eppler. After viewing the carnage that the shrapnel from the bomb blast had worked on the exposed gun crews, flight deck workers now needed little urging to seek shelter. This time with all hatches dogged down tight, we sat tense and listened as the attack developed. For the first few minutes it seemed a replay of the bombing attack; the roaring of the AA batteries, the ship rattling as if it was trying to shake itself apart. Then came an explosion that lifted us up out of our seats. Although I was separated from the chair a mere fraction of an inch, there was the impression that I'd risen high in the air. The entire ship twisted and whipped in a motion like a terrier shaking a rat. As I sensed my body descending, the compartment lights went out, but not before I realized that Evans and I had each gripped the other's hand. In the blackness we had scarcely settled back into our seats when a second explosion sent us skyward again.

There was immediate confusion. The ship heeled sharply to port, chairs and men slid down the tilting deck, and those of us in the front tier of seats found our legs pinned to the inboard bulkhead by the weight of the furniture and bodies in back. Again the guns went silent. The only sounds in the compartment were those of squirming bodies and heavy breathing. Then, the sound of voices and curses in the dark as those nearest the exits attempted to open the hatches.

Above all that, a steady voice queried, "anybody got a flashlight?" The weak beam of a small light revealed the after hatch twisted and hopelessly jammed. Hammering from outside the forward hatch turned the flashlight's beam in its direction; the handles of the hatch's locking dogs were unmoving. The sound of hammering stopped, then started anew. Low "ahs" and the rasp of exhaled breathing sounded through the compartment as one by one the dog handles moved to the open position. As the hatch swung open and light flooded into the compartment, a rapid, yet orderly exit began by those nearest the open doorway. Pressure on our legs lessened as men behind us freed themselves of the jumbled seats and joined the exodus. Pulling our legs free, we followed the others out to the fresh air and low sunlight of the flight deck.

Over the Side

The ship listed steeply to the port side. Looking out across the flight deck, instead of viewing a distant horizon, one gazed directly into the gray-blue sea. Walking was difficult. Many an unwary sailor stepping on a slick spot found himself sitting instead of standing. There was an unusual quiet. Men spoke in muted tones and tensed, startled as a brass shell casing falling from above rang like a cracked bell as it struck the wooden deck. At long intervals the ship would roll slowly to port, a few degrees at the most, yet each roll to port seemingly increased the angle of list in that direction. Scanning the faces of those around me, it was obvious the thought of capsizing was on everyone's mind. There was no outcry, only a low murmur of voices rippled across the deck when, from the ship's speakers a quavering voice commanded, "ALL HANDS, ABANDON SHIP!"

We had been under attack by ten torpedo bombers and six fighters from the *Hiryu*. Only half of that group returned to their carrier, and again *Yorktown* lay dead in the water with two torpedo hits on the port side and in danger of capsizing. Days later we would learn that at 1705, *Hiryu* was attacked by dive bombers from *Enterprise*. Four one-thousand-pound bomb hits amidships left the carrier a flaming hulk and not long to remain afloat. The First Carrier Striking Force was no longer an effective force. Also, at the close of the day, 2200 names would be erased from the muster rolls of the Imperial Japanese Navy.

As the *Yorktown's* largest Stars and Stripes battle flag broke from the masthead, men on the flight deck began making their way aft to where man-ropes and cargo nets were being lowered over the starboard side. Eppler and I followed. Halfway aft along the island structure, we passed the open hatch to the flight deck head. Turning toward the hatch, Eppler growled, "To hell with it, I gotta go!"

Near the after end of the island I stopped, looked at the crowd gathering in the area, turned and made my way back toward the bow. The thought in mind was that if the ship did capsize, I wanted to be clear of the superstructure or any other entanglement including the mass of men gathered aft. Abreast of the forward starboard gun gallery, one deck below the flight deck, I spied a small group of sailors lowering two lines over the side. The lines were not man-ropes as I first thought. They were long gasoline hoses used to fuel planes on the flight deck. I joined them as the first man climbed over the life line and started down the hose. Others fell into line to follow the pioneer. I took off my shoes, dropped my gun belt and holstered forty-five to the deck, inflated my life vest, then fell into line to await my turn.

Water and Oil

Slipping into the oily water, I turned to swim away from the dangling gas hose, just in case one of those above lost his grip or in panic let go and fell. The eye-stinging vapors from the fuel oil spreading on the water were quite enough to contend with.

"What are we supposed to do now?" The question came from a teenage sailor wearing the white helmet of a plane handler, floating in a kapok life jacket beside me. Pointing to a camouflage-striped destroyer seventy-five yards away I answered, "head for that tin can, Mac!" Taking my own advice, I then struck out in that direction, my new-found water buddy splashing along beside me. He appeared to be a strong swimmer, but neither of us would set a record in a hundred-yard freestyle race wearing the bulky life jackets.

Within a few yards of the destroyer, my aviator's life jacket began to ride up on my body, its sharp edges where the vest wrapped around my chest cutting into the pit of my arm. The upper section of the jacket curved around the back of my neck. The bottom section wrapped around my chest, the two sides closing across my back were secured by a short strap on one side snapped to a ring on the opposite side. Rolling onto my back, I reached back, took hold of both the snap and ring, and undid the snap. Pushing the strap down and under the belt of my pants I had just closed the snap into the ring when the jacket surged up under my neck. Startled, I tugged the jacket down and rolled over.

"I thought you were in trouble. I was going to give you a tow," explained the young sailor. "I'm okay," I answered. I didn't say that, for a moment when I almost lost hold of the snap and ring, I wasn't so sure.

As we neared the destroyer's bow, manila lines with a large loop in the end of each one were being thrown to men in the water who then slipped the loops over their heads and under their arms to be hoisted aboard. One of the lines landed in the water just beyond our grasp. Before either of us could reach it, it was suddenly withdrawn. The ship started moving rapidly astern and from its 1MC we heard the command, "BATTLE STATIONS, BATTLE STATIONS. AIR ATTACK, AIR ATTACK!"

We were stunned. Motionless, we watched the destroyers and cruisers move out at high speed and begin circling around the drifting *Yorktown*. Rolling onto his back and looking up at the sky, the youngster beside me questioned, "good God, haven't they done enough already?"

Rescue

"Come on, Mac," I urged, and began swimming away from the drifting carrier that appeared to be the same distance behind us each time I glanced back. No air attack developed and it seemed an eternity before the cordon of

circling ships slowed their pace and the destroyers again approached. Grab-
bing the first line that splashed into the water near me, I slipped into the loop
and was hoisted to the forecastle of the destroyer *Balch*. One of the destroyermen shouted, "give us a hand, Buddy!" Joining a group on one of the lines I
pulled with the rest of them, hoisting men aboard. I had last seen my swimming partner climbing over the life line; he had also made it safely on deck.

It was not long before the chill of my wet clothing and the realization that
I was tiring brought the decision to clear the area and I headed aft. As I
stepped out onto the main deck just aft of the superstructure, I was met by
two sailors. One held a large coffee pot by its bail while the other one thrust
toward me a large, white, general-mess soup bowl filled with hot coffee.
"Drink this!" he ordered. Holding the bowl in both hands I raised it toward
my mouth. As it touched my lips, my hands began to shake uncontrollably. A
few drops of the hot brew entered my mouth as the rest spilled over my chin
and down the open neck of my shirt. *Damn, that feels good* flashed across my
mind. I can't remember the flavor of the coffee, but its warmth—unforgetta-
ble.

The area in the lee of the superstructure was warm. The steel deck heated
by the fire rooms below was another matter. It was hot on my stockinged feet,
forcing me to shuffle from place to place as I watched the *Balch's* crew bring
more refugees from the *Yorktown* aboard. Some came alongside aboard a life
raft or crowded into the *Balch's* motor whaleboat. The majority arrived at the
cargo nets hanging down the port side the same way as I did, swimming.

Some, fatigued or wounded, were towed in by other swimmers. Two of the
swimming rescuers were *Balch* crewmen. This duo, wearing only swimming
trunks and towing a light line, repeatedly swam out and retrieved many who
were unable to make it on their own. At one point I heard a voice from the
after deck, calling them to come in and rest; they waved back and continued
with their work. Later I would learn that the rescue efforts I watched was a
carefully thought out routine, based upon the *Balch's* experience with the *Lexington* in the Coral Sea.[10]

The wounded were quickly lifted aboard in a metal framed wire-mesh
stretcher that was lowered into the water, then the patient floated into it. One
of the wounded brought a bit of mirth to those watching. As he was being
floated into position over the metal basket, one of his legs twisted to the side at
an odd angle. "Be careful, that man has a broken leg," called a voice from the
bridge. A feeble grin showed on the man's pale face as he called back, "never
mind my leg, get my *ass* aboard!"

My watching ended when a corpsman led me forward to the wardroom,
where he swabbed the fuel oil from my eyelids and ears. Another crewman
then took my clothing to be dried in a boiler room while five others and I tried
to clean the remainder of the bunker oil from our faces, hair, and hands in a
nearby shower. Emerging from the shower, I donned a set of underwear
donated by the ship's captain, took the blanket offered me and returned to the
wardroom.

The first minutes of June 5, 1942, found me wrapped in a blanket, sitting with five similarly clad figures on a settee in the wardroom. Half awake, foggily, we watched a team of doctors and corpsmen working around the mess table as they cut, sewed and bandaged the wounded as they were rotated by.

At dawn's first light it was standing room only on the *Balch's* decks where refugees from the *Yorktown* waited to learn what the new day had in store. At daybreak the bulk of the survivors transferred by high-line, in "coal sacks" to the cruiser *Portland* without incident. Aboard the cruiser I sat down to a breakfast of bacon, eggs and toast; my first food in more than thirty hours. [11]

✳   ✳   ✳   ✳

Yorktown's Final Hours

As mentioned in Chapter 3, *Yorktown* photographer's mate Bill Roy was responsible for most of the well-known photos and film footage of the ship at the Battle of Midway. Here he describes not only his escape from the sinking carrier, but how he managed to take and preserve those historic pictures amid the chaos of battle and the trauma of abandoning ship:

> Without power, nothing could be done to correct the list. The switchboard had been destroyed. The ship was in total darkness. It was difficult to move around because of the heavy list to port. Captain Buckmaster and the DCO (damage control officer) both believed the ship would capsize in a few minutes. The captain gave orders to abandon ship.
>
> I went to the photo lab, starboard side, hangar deck. It was burned black and gutted. Since the fire was out, I left a still camera on the counter. I had the movie camera and filmed some of our sailors in the water. I took off my shoes and placed the camera near the rail and asked an officer passing by to hand it down to me. When I looked up, he was gone.
>
> I had taped up three cans of exposed film and stuffed them under my dungaree shirt and kapok life jacket. The hand lines were fifteen feet short of the ocean because of the list to port. A mess attendant was tangled up in the lines and hollered that he could not swim. I got him free. We both got to the armor belt and I gave him a gentle push and jumped about fifteen feet after him. I got him to a life raft. Life rafts were scarce and overloaded; about twenty-five sailors in them or holding on. Wounded were sliding under water, so we secured them.
>
> As each wave broke over my head, oil and gas vapors burned my eyes and nose, making it difficult to breathe. I was covered with bunker oil. Some sailors swallowed oil and water, then vomited trying to hang on. Wind and waves kept all of us against the rough side of the steel hull, which was tearing at our

skin. It was difficult to get away. We were all afraid the *Yorktown* would roll over, sink, and take us down. I gradually worked my way towards the stern. Captain Buckmaster had gone off the stern, and I heard him hollering that he could not hold on much longer. He was holding a young sailor. Some of the better swimmers went to his rescue. Before long, a motor whaleboat took Buckmaster in tow.

All of our destroyers were weaving back and forth about 300 yards out. They were on high alert and would quickly move out if an air or submarine threat developed. It was dark when I was finally pulled by a boat towards the destroyer *Hammann*.

I was dragged aboard, and laid on the steel deck totally exhausted. I looked for a place to go. All deck space was packed with survivors. I went below. The mess tables were being used to operate on the wounded. Some of them were covered with blankets, waiting and in shock. I finally went topside and found an open hatch. That night, totally exhausted, I slept on sacks of potatoes out of the cold and wind.

Hammann's crew had given most of their spare clothing to survivors of the carrier USS *Lexington* at Coral Sea the month before, but I did get a shirt and a pair of pants. Then we came alongside the cruiser *Astoria* to transfer the wounded. I saw a *Yorktown* photographer on *Astoria* and passed up the cans of film to him.

Captain Buckmaster was on the *Hammann* and sent word that he was organizing a salvage party. I volunteered. *Hammann* returned us to *Yorktown* early on the morning of June 6th.

The first order was to put out the fires in the forward rag locker. It was still burning near bomb and torpedo magazines and the aviation gas storage tanks. We next cut away the port five inch guns. I made photos. Then I was asked to help the medic identify and bury the dead left on the flight deck. Next, I helped lower new aircraft from the hangar deck overhead and push them overboard to get the weight off the port side. I asked Captain Buckmaster if I could have one of the torpedo planes. He said "you got it, Roy" as it went over the side to its 17,000-foot deep grave. I then went back to the bow to help remove the second five inch gun and make photos.

At 1:36 PM that afternoon, the 20 mm. gun started firing and I ran across to starboard just in time to see the bosun on the bow of *Hammann* using a fire axe to cut the bow lines. The destroyer's turbines were screaming as they were backing down. The ship's skipper, Commander Arnold True, was trying to break loose from *Yorktown*. Four torpedoes had been fired from the Japanese submarine *I-168*. *Hammann*, hit by one torpedo under the bridge, blew up alongside *Yorktown* and broke in two. Sailors were catapulted off the bow or blown overboard. *Yorktown* was hit by the next two torpedoes on her starboard side. She rocked up and rolled hard. Great explosive sheets of fire, oil, water, and metal blew up between the two ships. The fourth torpedo missed astern. I was knocked over into a bulkhead. Some *Yorktown* sailors were blown overboard. Others were thrown in every direction. I picked myself up and made three sequential photos of the *Hammann's* stern half drifting back with sailors clinging on. When the stern section sank, many of the ship's men were in the water. Then, as her eighteen depth charges reached their set depth, they exploded. The *Yorktown* rose up out of the water, shaking and rolling again. There was only foaming water showing in the last photo I made, where *Hammann's* stern had sunk.[12]

I went off the starboard side to board the *Vireo*, which had cut its towline on *Yorktown*. We picked up survivors, some of whom were wounded. We also picked up some of the dead. Captain Buckmaster performed sea burial services for two officers and one enlisted man.

We then transferred to another destroyer. Early the next day, June 7th, 5:30 AM, *Yorktown* seemed to be on an even keel. We still had hopes to salvage the ship and save her. The list was then noticed to be increasing rapidly to port, and, at 7.01 AM, *Yorktown* turned over to her port side and sank stern first.

I was on the bridge of the destroyer taking pictures with a K-20 aerial camera. It was the only camera that had film. Captain Buckmaster told the destroyer skipper, "take me through the debris where *Yorktown* sank." We cut through the flotsam. Buckmaster said "come about and go through again." We did. Buckmaster made the same request a third time, but the destroyer skipper declined, indicating that the time had come to head back to Pearl Harbor.[13]

CHAPTER 7

▼

OVER THE ENEMY FLEET

Those Wonderful Blue-tipped Bullets

Commander Rochefort, Lieutenant Fabian, and their respective ComInt teams in Pearl Harbor and Melbourne felt that they had done a credible job of divining virtually all of the enemy's op-order for Midway. Commander Layton, the CINCPAC intelligence officer, was convinced of it and had presented their analyses and predictions to Admiral Nimitz, who had accepted them as fact and planned his defenses accordingly. But were they *fact*? That would not be known for certain until Japanese surface vessels in quantity were sighted inbound toward Midway. Until that actually happened, all such ComInt predictions were only predictions, thus far unproven. To OP-20-G in Washington they were not only unproven, they were dangerously wrong.

The first inkling that Rochefort and Fabian had gotten it right came at 0843 Midway time on the morning of Wednesday, June 3rd, when a PBY patrol plane reported two small vessels headed for Midway, about 700 miles out. While that inspired a lot of interest on the atoll and in Task Force 16 and 17, two small vessels (Japanese minesweepers, as it turned out) were not what anyone was looking for. But the Americans only had to wait a few minutes, for at 0925 came the electrifying report from another PBY commanded by Ensign J. H. Reid: "MAIN BODY." Reid and his crew had spotted the Japanese transport group, carrying the troops slated to conduct the amphibious assault of the atoll.[1]

Ensign Robert A. Swan was Reid's navigator and also one of the plane's pilots. A retired USNR commander, he joined the Roundtable very shortly after Bill

Price got it going in 1997, and he gave us the following report of his momentous flight:

On June 3rd, 1942 I was flying with Jack Reid in PBY-5A No.04982, on a regular search mission out of Midway. Since we had the sector heading straight towards Wake Island, we anticipated getting attacked by a Mitsubishi type 96, since the enemy knew exactly how far out our patrols were going. We covered a 700-mile arc around the northwest, north, and northeast of Midway, and most days at least one of our planes would be attacked by the enemy at the point where we turned parallel to Midway and flew another one hundred-plus miles before returning to base.

When we first arrived at Midway and started our patrols, one of our crewmen became somewhat worried about our ability to find Midway on the return trip, even though we started our flight a couple of hours before daylight to give us a better chance of finding the island on the way home. (We flew about 1500 miles over water without any modern navigation aids, and with radio silence and blackout.) He put an extra 150 gallons of gas in our tank, which we continued to keep there as a safety measure. Fuel was very short on Midway and when the B-17s arrived, their four engines used so much of it that the Marine planes were not permitted to fly. We were given only enough fuel to complete our search mission, assuming no navigational problems.

In debriefing after our flight on June 2nd, I learned that we were scheduled to patrol the sector towards Wake island on the 3rd. That almost guaranteed that we would be attacked at the end of our outbound leg. Some B-17s arrived that day, and when I went to the mess dugout to get a beer I met some Army crew members. I mentioned the Mitsubishi attacks in our discussion, and the fact that we knew we were hitting them with our .50 caliber machine guns but we weren't knocking them down. That was when the B-17 crewmen mentioned the blue-tipped explosive .50 cal. shells. They assured us that if you hit one of the enemy planes with one of those explosive shells, it would blow them up. (Remember, we were young. We believed what they told us.) They gave me five of those fantastic (?) shells. The next day I gave three to our starboard gunner, Chief Radioman Musser, and two of them to our port gunner, Pat Fitspatrick. We all were very anxious to have the enemy attack us so we could destroy them!

On the 3rd, at our outbound turning point, we still hadn't been attacked. I was at the navigator's table and Chief Musser was behind me at the radio position. We discussed our disappointment and decided to go another fifteen minutes in hopes that we would be attacked! The command pilot, Jack Reid, agreed that it was okay since we had that extra fuel. We went another fifteen minutes—nothing. We decided on a second fifteen minute extension and were only a few minutes into it when the general quarters alarm sounded. I ran up between the two pilots, looking up to see the enemy, and they tapped me on the shoulder and pointed down—there were eleven enemy ships heading straight towards us and towards Midway.

We immediately broke radio silence with "main body." They received our message both at Midway and at Admiral Nimitz' headquarters at Pearl Harbor. They began asking us to amplify; more information was needed. Jack Reid dropped the plane down to nearly sea level and told me to head north for fifteen minutes then turn and go behind them. We tried this twice. The first time we ran into seven more ships and the second time we ran into another seventeen. We finally got behind them and we would climb up till we could see and identify them, send the info back, then drop down and go on to the next group of ships. They kept us there for over three hours.

Why the enemy didn't spot us, I'll never know. We had radar on our surface ships at that time but evidently the Japanese did not. At least, not on that group of ships.

Our radio finally told us to return to Midway. We were low on fuel but the base didn't know we had that extra 150 gallons. Reid "leaned out" the engines as much as possible and used every way he knew to extend our flight distance. The enemy was coming behind us so we didn't dare run out of fuel and land in front of them. Jack's and my memories differ. I am certain that we made it back and landed on the landing strip at Midway. Jack thinks that we lost one engine and landed in the bay at Midway. I know it was close but I think Jack was mixed up. We did have to land in the bay the next day during the battle.

I'm aware of two things since then that are quite interesting. In the 1950s, when Admiral Nimitz heard a report about my speech on this subject at the officers club at NAS Alameda, he told a Navy captain friend of mine that he wished he had heard the speech, saying that ours was the most important radio message he had ever received. The admiral said that it allowed him twenty hours to bring his carrier forces back closer to Midway and to prepare for an attack there, and not be concerned that the primary Japanese thrust was at Dutch Harbor, Alaska. As I recall, an enemy carrier group attacked several points in the Aleutians about June 3rd, causing some among our forces to doubt that Midway was to be the primary target. They thought our fake message indicating water problems on Midway could have caused the enemy to send their own fake message indicating Midway to be the target, while it was actually the Aleutians.

One other thing I heard was that the commander of the enemy naval landing force was court-martialed for being fifty miles ahead of his assigned location, causing him to be spotted by our patrol plane. Actually, he had been in his assigned position, but *we* were fifty miles ahead of where *we* should have been. I know they did not see us, and it wasn't until months later that the enemy learned that we had been where we found them. They then assumed that *they* were in an unplanned position, rather than us.

The foregoing report by Commander Swan is a prime illustration of the value of the dialogue conducted on the Roundtable. While virtually every book about the Battle of Midway mentions the discovery of the Japanese invasion force by a PBY, they generally don't reveal why it *really* happened as it did: Ensign Reid and his crew wanted to blow up a Japanese patrol bomber with some blue-tipped explosive bullets![2]

✳   ✳   ✳   ✳

A Ring of Coral

If you are well-versed in the details of the Battle of Midway, or if you've studied Appendix B at the end of this book, you know that its unlikely outcome was the result of several interwoven circumstances and events involving strikes from the three American carriers, *Yorktown, Enterprise,* and *Hornet.* The Roundtable's roster has been blessed with air group veterans from each of the three, and from them we have learned a great deal about the contributions (and in some cases, the failings) of their respective squadrons during the course of the three-day battle.

Two of those veterans, Tom Cheek and Clayton Fisher, have been especially eloquent and voluminous in providing both lengthy narratives as well as many brief anecdotes about their experiences during the battle and in connection with related events. Cheek's story, a large piece of which concluded the last chapter, continues here with his account of the fight over the Japanese carriers as the *Yorktown* air group pressed home its attack. As you'll see, he had a front-row seat—or more precisely, center stage—during the battle's most critical few moments:

> The naval and air action known as the Battle of Midway has been captioned with various titles. From an American viewpoint it has been called the greatest naval engagement in world history! However, the Japanese have chosen to view it as the battle that defeated Japan in World War II. Though they go mainly untitled and many untold, it seems fair to say that there are as many versions of the battle as there were men who fought there. Undoubtedly, each one recalls the action as he viewed it, from his own place in the arena and the phase of the action that was of his own immediate concern.
>
> The arena itself centered on a ring of surf-spumed coral, known as Midway Atoll. Relatively unknown to the world, the atoll is a mere pinpoint on a navigational chart, located eleven hundred miles northwest of Pearl Harbor. Midway is a small dot of sand and coral that the Japanese high command considered essential to their conquest and control of the Pacific. Formed on the summit of an extinct undersea volcano, the atoll's encircling reef, fifteen

miles in circumference, shelters a broad, shallow harbor with an off-center setting of two low sand and shell islands, appropriately named *Eastern* and *Sand*. At the time of the battle, both islets were equipped to operate large seaplanes. Land-based aircraft operated from Eastern's crisscrossed hard surfaced runways.

With the capture of Midway Atoll, the Imperial Japanese Navy anticipated achieving two objectives. The primary goal was the luring of the American aircraft carriers to their annihilation in open battle. And the second, using the captured atoll as a springboard, was the decimation of Pearl Harbor and the capture of the Hawaiian Islands, thus depriving the United States of its only Pacific base.

Forming Yorktown's Air Group

The Midway action has been hailed as an "incredible victory." I'll not argue with that. Nor do I believe that time or the historians will find fault with that assessment. For myself, the mere mention of the name *Midway* instantly calls up the memory of one very long, seemingly endless day. June 4, 1942, began at 0115 for Doyle C. (Tom) Barnes and myself, aboard the aircraft carrier *Yorktown* (CV-5). We were on temporary additional duty from Fighting Two on USS *Lexington* (CV-2), having been ordered to Fighting Three following a brief tour to waters off Tokyo with Fighting Six in the *Enterprise* (CV-6). The room that we shared in warrant officers country was port side, slightly forward of midship and one deck below the waterline. Although we had climbed into our bunks early the evening before, sleep was restless. The faint vibration of machinery through the hull, the swish and hissing surge of water past the skin of the ship did little to hurry time along. Asleep, yet not asleep, my mind drifted through the events of the past few days. The three short days following *Yorktown's* return to Pearl Harbor, May 27th, from the Coral Sea engagement in which she had been heavily damaged (and we lost the *Lexington*) had been busy ones. Pearl Harbor and its NAS Ford Island, as well as NAS Kaneohe on the windward shore of Oahu, in a hush-hush atmosphere, whirred with activity. Rumors! If what you heard failed to catch your interest, wait a moment, there were others in the mill.

While the *Yorktown* received emergency repairs at the navy yard, a new air group had been hastily assembled from pilots, planes, and squadrons available in the area. As one wag put it, "it was a collection of all available spare parts!" Said in jest, it was a statement very close to fact. Fighting Three was composed of twenty-four new F4F-4 Wildcat fighters and twenty-seven pilots. Only the CO, Lieutenant Commander J. S. "Jimmy" Thach and Ensign R. A. M. Dibb, fresh from flight training, were permanent VF-3 pilot personnel. The majority of the pilots, sixteen, were from *Yorktown's* own VF-42. Six others with original orders to VF-8 on the *Hornet* were classmates of Ensign Dibb.

The remaining three pilots to complete the roster were Lieutenant Commander Don Lovelace, Barnes, and myself.

Formerly Thach's executive officer, Don Lovelace had been detached from VF-3 with orders to reorganize and command Fighting Two. On being informed of the coming operation, Don had volunteered to return to his old assignment as VF-3's executive officer and rejoined the squadron on the afternoon of May 28. Composed of Fighting Three, Torpedo Three, Bombing Three, and Scouting Five, the makeshift air group had landed aboard *Yorktown* on the afternoon of May 30th. But not without incident. Lovelace was killed instantly when an F4F failed to catch an arresting wire, soared over the crash barrier, and smashed down on him as his aircraft was being parked.

With its air group aboard, *Yorktown* immediately departed the area on a northerly heading, its announced destination, "Point Luck." Hearing the announcement, crew members questioned one another, "where in hell is *Point Luck?*" Then added, "what next?"

A Powerful Enemy Force

What next—what all the secrecy had been concealing was revealed the following afternoon. All pilots and available ship's officers were assembled in the wardroom for a briefing. We had been told that a very large force of the Imperial Japanese Navy was on the move. Its objective, the capture of the circle of coral reef and two sand islands we called Midway Atoll. In the situation summary that followed that startling announcement, the briefing officers had little difficulty making themselves heard. The IJN force was not only large, it was heavily-gunned and fully capable of achieving its objective. The Japanese had committed over 200 vessels to this operation, and 127 of them were combat types: eleven battleships, twenty-two cruisers, sixty-five destroyers, twenty-one submarines, and eight aircraft carriers.

The principal Japanese commands for the operation were: (1) the Advance Force (submarines), (2) the Aleutian Force, (3) the Midway Invasion Force, (4) the First Carrier Striking Force, and (5) the Main Force (battleships). Of primary importance to us would be the First Carrier Striking Force, Vice Admiral Nagumo's task force that had carried out the attack on Pearl Harbor. A battle-hardened group, it was now composed of the fleet carriers: *Akagi* (Red Castle); *Kaga* (Increased Joy); *Soryu* (Blue-Gray Dragon); and *Hiryu* (Flying Dragon), supported by two battleships, two heavy cruisers, and eleven destroyers. Missing from their usual places in this force were the fleet carriers *Shokaku* (Soaring Glorious Crane), and the *Zuikaku* (Happy Crane); they remained in Japan nursing wounds received in the Coral Sea engagement.

To counter the First Carrier Striking Force we had only Task Force 16, the *Enterprise* and *Hornet* with Rear Admiral Spruance, and Task Force 17, with Rear Admiral Fletcher aboard the *Yorktown*, which was still nursing her wounds from the Coral Sea. Support for our three carriers would be fourteen heavy cruisers, one light antiaircraft cruiser, and fifteen destroyers, plus a scouting line of submarines.

It was a hushed, stunned, group that listened intently as the briefing team further revealed a detailed résumé of the Japanese attack plan: on June 1st the Aleutian Force would commence its approach to the Aleutian Islands with the objectives to (1) attack Dutch Harbor on June 3rd, and (2) begin the invasion and occupation of designated islands on June 5th. The Aleutian Force was in fact a red herring. Its main objective was diverting attention away from the flotillas converging on Midway. On June 3rd the Midway Invasion Force, escorted by light carrier *Zuiho*, was to commence its approach from southwest of Midway, timed to arrive in the area on the morning of June 5th. Also on June 3rd, the First Carrier Striking Force was to begin its approach from the northwest, timed to commence air strikes on the atoll at first light the morning of June 4th. Bombardment by surface ships was planned to begin and continue through the night of June 4th, with the landing of invasion troops on Midway to begin the morning of June 5th. The Main Force (Admiral Yamamoto), composed of battleships and light carrier *Hosho*, were to maintain station 300 miles northwest of the First Carrier Striking Force, in readiness for the moment of opportunity to engage any U.S. carriers that may appear.

While the Japanese scenario unfolded, Task Forces 16 and 17 would take station well to the north and east of Midway; circling in the shadows, warming the bench while waiting their turns at bat. If the strategists guessed right and all went as planned, they would be called on to step into the batter's box and deliver a flanking attack on the First Carrier Striking Force on the morning of the fourth of June

The Game Plan

In the days that followed the briefing, it had been like reading the book then going to see the movie. The Japanese had carried out their schedule with clockwork precision. Now the wait was almost over. When Tom Barnes's voice queried in the dark, "are you awake? Let's go get some coffee," I reached for my flight clothes, shoes and socks. We were sitting in the dimly lit wardroom sipping coffee with the ship's XO, Dixie Kiefer, when General Quarters sounded. After the pilots had gathered, the group commander laid out our plan of attack, then closed with an emphasis that we must first wait—wait for the discovery of the Japanese carriers, hopefully before their scouts found us.

The success of our game plan relied heavily upon the element of surprise. Arriving in the VF ready room just off the flight deck in the forward section of the island structure, we checked the flight roster grease-penciled on the plexiglass schedule board. Both Tom and I were each assigned to lead a four-plane division, but Tom's assignment was not to his liking. His division was listed as *standby*. "How did you work that?" he asked, pointing to my name as leader of the second division of the eight-plane strike escort. The fighter escort for

VT-3 would be, 1st division: Lt. Cdr. J. S. Thach, Ens. R. A. M. Dibb; Lt.(jg) B. T. Macomber, Ens. E. R. Bassett. 2nd division: MACH T. F. Cheek, Ens. Dan C. Sheedy, Lt.(jg) E. S. McCuskey, Ens. M. K. Bright.

As navigational data appeared on the teleprinter screen, we entered it on our aircraft plotting boards. First to be plotted was Point Option, that mythical point that traveled at a set speed on a predetermined course, and from which all maneuvering of the task force was reckoned. From Point Option we computed our courses, estimated flight times and fuel consumption to and from the expected position of the First Carrier Striking Force. The answers we came up with were anything but encouraging. From the standpoint of fuel, the anticipated position of the Japanese force was beyond the effective combat range of our Grumman F4F-4s. Someone else had reached the same conclusion, for shortly an order came down to scratch the VF escort. Torpedo Three would have to go it alone. Thach bolted from the ready room, heading up the ladder in the direction of the bridge. Returning half an hour later he erased the names of McCuskey and Bright from the schedule. The escort would go, he announced, less my second section. Six F4Fs would ride herd on VT-3's twelve TBDs. The two SBD dive bomber squadrons, VS-5 and VB-3, would go without fighter escort, depending instead on speed and altitude for protection.

Continuing his briefing, Thach stressed the need for complete radio silence, which would be broken only in a combat situation, and then first names, or nicknames, would be used as call signs. This was a practice already in use by the *Yorktown*. "Jimmy," he continued, would be his call sign and then noted a problem. Among us, there were two Toms, Barnes and myself. Thach found an immediate solution. Turning to me he said, "we will call you Sam!" I remained *Sam* to Thach through the ensuing years of our association.

Escorting the Torpedo Bombers

At dawn's first light, we listened as *Yorktown* launched its first combat air patrol of six F4Fs, followed by ten SBDs to search sectors in the expected direction of the enemy carriers. Then tension began to mount in the ready room as the first enemy contact reports appeared on the teleprinter screen. A PBY searching from Midway was the first to break the silence, reporting the sighting of a large formation of enemy aircraft on a course to Midway. Then Midway reported it was striking back with bombing and torpedo attacks upon the Japanese force. Next was the report that Midway was under attack by planes from the First Carrier Striking Force. Finally the news we waited for: a PBY had sighted and reported the position of the enemy carriers. There was a rush to plot this reported position of the IJN carriers and to revise our courses. It was our turn to step up to the plate.

Task Force 16, the *Hornet* and *Enterprise*, operating twenty-five miles south of the *Yorktown*, began launching their two strike groups at 0700. Each group was composed of two units of SBD dive bombers, one TBD torpedo squadron, and ten F4F-4 fighter escorts. Departure from the task force was delayed by each group until its fighter and dive bomber units had climbed to altitude and formed as an attack group with the group commander in the lead. In the case of the *Enterprise* group, that was at twenty thousand feet, which proved to be a time, and most importantly, a fuel consuming method of rendezvous. The torpedo squadrons, VT-8 and VT-6, the last to launch, proceeded independently on course to the target at lower altitudes.

Held in reserve, *Yorktown's* strike group waited. Then, first to launch from *Yorktown* at 0840 were the torpedo-laden TBDs, closely followed by the SBDs, each armed with either a five hundred or a thousand pound bomb. VT-3 immediately departed on course to target while the SBDs circled the task force climbing to altitude. To conserve fuel, takeoff for the fighters was delayed until 0905. The faster cruising speeds of the F4Fs and SBDs would allow them to overtake the lumbering TBDs before they reached the target area.

When the order came to man our aircraft, Thach gathered us in a huddle outside the ready room. His instructions were short and to the point. "Whatever happens, stick together! None of this *lone wolf* business! You will only get yourself killed and won't do the rest of us any good! Another thing: lean your mixture as much as you can. Save your fuel! Cheek, you and Sheedy stick close to the torpedoes, just astern and about a thousand feet above. Stop anyone trying to get to them. I will be three or four thousand feet above you and give you high cover. Lets go!"

Thach was the first to sight the TBD formation, and with a slight waggle of the ailerons he raised the nose of his fighter and began a gentle climb. Glancing down and ahead I caught sight of the torpedo planes and moved to take position on them. Torpedo Three was cruising in a compact two division, stepped-down formation. In each division there were two three-plane sections flying in the standard vee pattern. The first division flew in a left echelon while the second division tucked in close to the lead section in an echelon to the right. The pattern afforded the rear seat gunners a broad field of fire, a fact that would soon be very evident.

Due to the difference in our cruising speeds, to maintain station above and to the rear of the formation I began slow, lazy turns to the right and left of course. I had just started a slow drift back to the left of course when a geyser of water suddenly erupted from the sea ahead and to the left of the formation. Startled? Yes! Explanation? None would come to mind at the moment. Days later I would learn that the bombing squadron commander's bomb had inadvertently been released when he set the bomb's electrical arming switch. He immediately broke radio silence and warned the other pilots to arm their bombs manually, but not before two others lost their bombs in the same manner. There was no detonation as the unarmed missile struck the water. What I had witnessed was the splash of a thousand-pound pebble dropped into the sea.

Initial Strikes Against the Japanese Carriers

As we cruised toward the target, events of which we were totally unaware had been taking place. The strike group from the Japanese carriers had brushed aside Midway's defending fighters and bombed and strafed the atoll's installations, inflicting moderate damage and light casualties. In return, Midway aircraft had harried the First Carrier Striking Force with a series of unco-ordinated, single-group torpedo, glide, and high level bombing attacks. Though the torpedo and dive bombing crews suffered major losses in these attacks stretching out over a period of an hour and a half, in the end not one of the Japanese carriers had its paintwork scratched by an American bomb or torpedo.

The *Hornet* air group was having its problems. They had failed to find the Japanese carrier force, their ten escorting F4Fs were running short of fuel and would soon ditch after failing to make it back to their carrier. The SBDs would also soon be facing a fuel shortage and abort their mission. Some would divert to Midway while the remainder returned to Task Force 16, having never sighted their target. The *Enterprise* air group was faring little better. The SBDs led by the group commander had also failed to find the target at its anticipated position and were continuing to search. After climbing to twenty-thousand feet, the ten escorting fighters from *Enterprise's* VF-6 had mistakenly followed *Hornet's* VT-8 instead of their own VT-6 when they departed on their mission. Torpedo Eight chose to fly a more southerly course than did the rest of the *Hornet* air group, and flew directly to their target and their deaths. Arriving over the target, VF-6 reported it was also running low on fuel, aborted the mission and returned to *Enterprise*.

While fending off his persistent attackers, Admiral Nagumo had been advised that a second attack against Midway defenses was needed. In response, he had ordered his reserve aircraft, which had been armed with torpedoes and armor piercing bombs for a strike against naval forces, rearmed with land bombs for a second attack on Midway. Then, notified of the discovery of the U.S. task forces by one of his scout planes, he had countermanded his first order and directed all aircraft be rearmed for action against ships. As a result of the crews' haste to carry out the last order, unsecured ordnance, bombs, and torpedoes littered the carrier decks. Bomb stowage and magazines were left open, and planes that had returned from Midway were being refueled.

No Target Sleeve

We were approaching an area of tall cumulus clouds, rising from 1500 foot bases in towering, grayish-white columns across our course when the torpedo formation made an abrupt change of course to the right. I followed, penciling the time and new compass heading on the left sleeve of my flight jacket. Adrenaline began to flow—something was about to happen.

I also had a decision to make. The TBD formation was now on course between two of the large cumulus buildups that were joined at their base by a shelf of cloud. The shelf extended from the cloud base to at least five hundred feet above my altitude. Should I climb over the shelf or drop down to the formation's level and go under the cloud deck as it appeared they would do?

Moments later the question was of no consequence as black puffs of anti-aircraft fire blossomed below and ahead. Then an object I thought to be a belly tank whirled down in the path of the formation. Looking up, I saw my first enemy aircraft, a Zero fighter. Silhouetted against the cloud shelf, the Zero was in a shallow dive making a head-on run at the lead TBD. Puffs of white spouted from the Zero's engine cowling as, at extreme range, the pilot tripped off a short burst from his 7.7 mm guns. Without hesitating, the Zero rolled into a steep climbing left turn, then leveled off in a wide, sweeping flat turn to the right. I was momentarily spellbound watching the fighter's clean, seemingly effortless maneuvers. Within seconds it was in position to make a firing run on the last plane on the formation's right flank. Nosing down slightly the pilot continued his curving approach, five hundred feet above and slightly to my right, as though I had not yet been seen. I moved my engine controls into combat power range, and pushed the throttle to the forward stop. Easing back on the control stick until the F4F was hanging on the prop, I brought the gun sight pip to an almost full deflection lead on the Zero's nose. The index finger of my right hand squeezed down on the gun trigger set in the molded grip of the control stick. The six .50 caliber wing guns rumbled. I held the trigger down just long enough to see the red stream of tracers converge into the Zero's engine and start to drift back into the fuselage. The thought flashed through my mind, *right down the target sleeve's throat.*

But this was no target sleeve. The Zero's nose bucked up momentarily, dropped back, then the plane came diving down in my direction. At that moment my guns were firing and the tracers were curving up and into their target. I was literally hanging in air. The muzzle blast and recoil of the six fifties was all that was needed to push my overloaded, underpowered F4F over the edge into a control-sloppy stall. As I let my fighter's nose drop and started a recovery rolling to the left, the Zero swept past on my right, black smoke and flames spewing from the engine, a river of fire trailing back along its belly. Clearly visible, the pilot sat rigidly facing straight ahead. *He is dead* flashed across my mind. If alive he would have been watching me, looking for any movement of my control surfaces, anticipating my next move. Teruo Kawamata, PO3/c, Imperial Japanese Navy, would be listed as missing in action that night.

Rolling into level flight, the throttle still firewalled, I tried to bring my guns to bear on two Zeros diving in on the formation's left quarter. The Wildcat's straining engine could not build up maneuvering speed fast enough. With the pipper of the gun sight at a point well ahead of the pair, I snapped off a short burst. As the tracers crossed their diving path the Zeros abruptly zoomed skyward. Their climbing ability was stunning to watch, they were out of sight and mind in seconds as I rolled to the right, reversing course. With airspeed increasing, the Grumman began to respond to my mind's commands rather than my deliberate moves. Time ceased to be measured; hands and feet moved automatically evoking control responses, moving the plane as one with my body as I turned and twisted to face each new situation. I moved to intercept a lone Zero diving in on the last TBD on the right. Just short of coming into firing range, it too zoomed up and out of my sight. Reversing course to the left I scanned the sky for more attackers and saw none. Looking to the left, back across our course, I watched as a Zero trailing black smoke and flame crashed into the sea. A mile beyond an F4F made a last spinning turn as it too disappeared nose first into the ocean. Only rippling rings in the water marked the F4F's impact, while a puffball of black smoke hovered over the spot where the Zero had disappeared. Several other such puffs of black marked similar ruffled spots of water. *Grumman or Zero*, I wondered, turning my attention back to my own line of flight.

The TBD Gunners Score

The lack of Zero attackers had only been momentary. Diving in on the last section of TBDs on the left came a pair of Zeros. As before I was not in position to intercept and without hesitation snapped a burst of tracer in their direction. The results were the same as before, an exhibition of the climbing ability of this nimble fighter. The thought struck home, this was not one to tangle with in a dogfight, at least not with an overweight F4F-4.

Again reversing course to the right I was startled and alarmed to see that the TBDs had increased speed; the distance between us had doubled. A duo of Zeros were just pulling up from a run on the trailing plane on the right flank of the formation. At that moment a Zero dove in front of me aiming at the center rear of the group. I rolled after him, sliding into his tail, aiming for a no-deflection shot. All the while, so sure of my target, I was mentally painting a Rising Sun on my Grumman's fuselage. As my finger tensed to squeeze down on the trigger, the Zero seemed to shudder, then pitched forward into a near vertical dive into the sea as I pulled up in a climbing turn to the right. The TBD gunners had beaten me to the punch. But the inning was far from over.

I was snapped out of a momentary trance as a burst of tracers, shoulder high, swept past on the right side of the cockpit. Nosing down and twisting left, glancing back I could see no one. A burst of tracers brushed across my left wing. I snapped the fighter tightly to the right; again I could see nothing tailing me. Hesitating (a mistake), I allowed the F4F to level off. Immediately 7.7 tracers zipped past on both sides of the canopy and I heard or felt the thud of hits on the armor plate behind my seat. The 7.7s abruptly stopped, replaced by 20 mm. cannon tracers, seemingly the size of oranges, floating past in slow motion on both sides of the canopy. I violently kicked the F4F into a vertical turn to the left and found a Zero tucked in under my tail. The turn had caught him off balance, he was drifting rapidly to the right. I snapped the Grumman back to the right hoping to catch him in a scissors, facing my guns. As the Wildcat rolled past the horizontal a fiery stream of red tracers flashed over the canopy, seemingly just inches above my head. It was like a broad stream of fire, leaving a mental impression of heat. The Zero was not in sight as I completed the turn, and I immediately swung the fighter back in the direction of the torpedo squadron.

The last TBDs in the formation were just passing from view under the cloud shelf. To the right of the formation the plane that had last been under attack was now in a curving glide down to the right. A parachute blossomed behind the TBD and from the side a Zero knifed down toward it. I felt help-less—hogtied—there was nothing I could do to stop what I thought was going to happen. The TBD, then the chute hit the water.

Dangerously close to the water and without firing, the Zero pulled up to the right, climbing in my direction. I glimpsed other Zeros above and to my right. Shifting my gaze to the instrument panel and steadying the fighter on course, I flew into the cloud deck. Passage through the murky cloud was brief in time, but as the seconds ticked by questions raced through my mind. Where was Jimmy and his high cover? Where were the puffballs of AA coming from? Where was Dan Sheedy? I had not seen Dan since we came under fire! Was that Dan's F4F I saw go in?

Rapid Fire

All those questions remained without answers as I burst from the cloud cover into a clear narrow avenue between two towering cumulus columns. I fully expected to see the torpedo group ahead as I came into the open. They were not in sight, but others were. A thousand feet above my right shoulder flew four or more Zeros. Three hundred yards off my left wing, on course and at my level paced another Zero. I snapped to rigid attention as I realized the speck in the middle of my gun sight was a Zero coming straight at me. *Wait for him to close* was a momentary thought instantly overruled by a reaction that closed my finger down on the trigger. Tracers spewed out, pieces of metal from the Zero's engine and cowling flashed as I released the trigger, pulled up and rolled to the left. Still in the turn I began firing as the nose of the plane on my left appeared in the outer ring of my gun sight. Tracers raked through its engine and the length of the fuselage before I released the trigger and passed astern. Rolling into level flight, I flew straight for the billowing cloud that had been to the left as I broke into the open leaving the first cloud deck. With my attention riveted on my flight instruments, the dim gray light of the cloud closing around me was a welcome feeling. Once in the cloud I made a brief adjustment to flying on the gauges, then made a ninety degree turn to the right, reduced power and began a slow descent. There were two reasons for this action. First, the turn should shake off any Zero that had followed me into the cloud. The one I had last fired on evidently flew through the first cloud deck with me. Secondly, and hopefully, when I again broke into the open I would be in the vicinity of the torpedo squadron.

It was not to be. As I broke free of the cloud base, I searched to the right and ahead for my torpedo planes. There were no aircraft in sight. As two puffballs of AA blossomed in the direction I was searching, I looked closer—still nothing in sight. Then one, two, three more puffs of black popped up, each successively closer to me. Realizing I was the target, I glanced down to the left and found a large cruiser of a design I had never before seen. With its bow splitting the water in a foamy white wave ("a bone in its teeth") whatever its destination, the ship was wasting no time getting there. I pushed over and rolling right, dove for the ocean, leveling off at a hundred feet above the water. Swinging back to the left I found what the clouds had kept hidden from me. There before me was the target, the First Carrier Striking Force. Ahead and on a course to my left were three large carriers, all with bow waves and stern wakes that indicated a high rate of speed. These were later identified as *Kaga*, *Akagi*, and *Soryu*. The fact that there should have been a fourth carrier, *Hiryu*, failed to register in my memory. *Kaga* was in the lead with *Akagi* not more than three miles broadside to and directly ahead of me. *Soryu*, which I compared to *Enterprise* in size, was a mile beyond and to the right of *Akagi*, and appeared to be just starting a hard turn to starboard. Flashes of gunfire spotted the decks of nearby escorts, but I saw no shell burst or possible targets. It appeared I had the sky to myself.

The Flames of Hell

A brief thought flashed across my mind: should I make a strafing run on the nearest carrier? Then as I looked back to *Akagi*, hell literally broke loose. First the orange-colored flash of a bomb burst appeared on the flight deck midway between the island structure and the stern. Then in rapid succession followed a bomb burst midship, and the water founts of near misses plumed up near the stern. Almost in unison on my left *Kaga's* flight deck erupted with bomb bursts and flames. My gaze remained on *Akagi* as an explosion at the midship waterline seemed to open the bowels of the ship in a rolling, greenish-yellow ball of flame. A black cloud of smoke drew my attention to *Soryu*, still in a turn to starboard, she too was being heavily hit. Dense black smoke billowed from the entire length of her hull. All three ships had lost their foaming white bow waves and appeared to be losing way.

I circled slowly to the right, awe-struck, my mind trying desperately to grasp the full impact of what I had just witnessed and the scene still in motion. In reading the script, the briefing team had voiced this destructive happening as only a hoped-for possibility. The infernos I now watched in creation were not being viewed from a comfortable seat in a movie, but from atop a parachute pack in a Grumman fighter!

"Group rendezvous! Rendezvous!" The command piercing into my ears from the headphones in my helmet jerked me back to reality. I was also startled by the realization that except for an occasional sputter of static, the abrupt command was the first radio transmission I had heard the entire time we had been airborne. I reached for my microphone and began to call, first "Jimmy," then "Dan," finally "any station!" I desperately wanted the sight of a friendly set of wings. My headphones remained silent.

At briefing, the rally point after the attack had been given as twenty miles north of the target. Japanese ships were visible in that direction, and to get there it would take fuel that I did not have to spare. Thach's admonition popped to mind, *none of this lone wolf business!* It was time to get out of here. Pulling the plotting board out of its slot under the instrument panel, I checked the return heading to Point Option and *Yorktown*. Swinging the fighter's nose onto the desired compass heading I scanned the sky in all sectors for aircraft. There were none in sight, neither friend nor, thankfully, foe.

A last look in their direction found the three carriers now almost dead in the water. Each vessel's position was marked by a black cloud of smoke towering above that rolled and boiled in a manner indicating it rose from an area of intense heat. Climbing to the base of the low hanging clouds to protect myself from being jumped from above, I set the engine controls for maximum range. A visual sweep of the area for aircraft informed me that I was still on my own. A few minutes later my right arm suddenly went numb. The hand loosed its grip on the control stick, the limp limb dropped down and the forearm came to rest on my lap. In a momentary state of panic I gripped the stick with my left hand while my mind whirled, sorting the facts of this new situation. From the shoulder down the limb was without feeling and without pain. As time slowly ticked by feeling and motion began to return, and within ten minutes I again had full usage of the limb. Though still shocked and puzzled by what had happened, the concern of coping one-armed with what might lie ahead dropped from mind. Finding a U.S. ship, preferably a carrier, before I ran out of fuel again became my main concern.

Dan Sheedy

Cruising at fifteen hundred feet, just below the base of the scattered clouds, the droning beat of the engine lent a bit of reassurance. Still, time passed slowly and the horizon ahead remained free of any sign of friendly forces. My mind refused to remain idle. The blast of red tracer that had zinged over my head puzzled me. I wondered—did the Japanese have Zeros equipped with .50 caliber guns? The answer to that would come days later when Dan Sheedy and I met again in a hanger on Ford Island. Dan related that he had called on the radio hoping I would turn sharply right or left and give him a shot at the Zero on my tail. He'd fired as I rolled into my turn, thinking that I'd heard his warning. Though he missed the Zero (and me) it was enough to make the Zero pilot look for safer air space.

I would also learn that Dan had then come under attack from a diving Zero that sprayed his cockpit with 7.7s, wounding him in his right leg and shoulder. Stunned, he doggedly followed me through the first cloud, emerging just as the Zero I had fired on in the head-on pass exploded as it passed beneath me. Turning to the right to avoid the debris from the disintegrating plane, he was immediately jumped by the group from above. Taking hits in and around the cockpit, he dove away from his attackers, leveling the fighter off just above the ruffled sea. Only one of the attackers followed, and within seconds Dan faced this last opponent. From directly ahead, skimming the water, the Zero came at him in a head-on pass. Both pilots opened fire then rolled into opposite turns to avoid the other's approaching plane. The Zero pilot, eager to again bring the F4F under fire, pulled his plane into a vertical turn. As Dan watched, the silver-gray fighter dipped its wing tip into the top of a low swell. The Zero cartwheeled across the surface and disappeared in a shower of spray. Scanning the sky around, Dan found himself alone. The fighter's cockpit was a shambles of destroyed instruments, including the compass, and one wheel of the landing gear dangled from its wheel well. With no compass to guide him, Dan remembered that the sun had been at his back on the way out from the *Yorktown*. Hoping for the best, he swung the nose of his battered plane into the sun. His sun-line course led him to the *Hornet*, but not to a safe landing aboard. On landing, his tailhook engaged an arresting cable just as the damaged right landing gear collapsed. As the plane slid to the right in a jarring stop, the right wing crashed down on the deck and a burst of fire erupted from the .50 caliber wing guns. A two-second burst sprayed into the after superstructure of the ship, killing five and wounding twenty of *Hornet's* crew.

The fate of the man swinging from the parachute was another thought to wonder about. Fifty years would go by before I would learn that twenty-three year old Ensign Wesley F. Osmus had been picked up by the Japanese destroyer *Arashi*. Interrogated and forced to divulge information as to the composition of the U.S. forces, Osmus had been executed that night and his body thrown into the sea.

"Three CV Burning!"

As I flew on, the only sound was the drumming of the engine. My headphones remained silent, not even the occasional crackle of static that I had heard before. An attempt to tune in the *Yorktown's* YE homer brought only continued silence. With all senses on full alert, I continued visually sweeping the sea and sky ahead. Finally, just forward of my right wing tip, barely visible in the distance, a faint streak of white on the blue-gray water caught my eye. Looking closer I found it trailed behind a genuine made-in-the-USA destroyer, on a course parallel to mine, but speeding in the opposite direction. Without hesitation I turned toward the ship, throttled back and dropped down to five-hundred feet.

As I neared the destroyer, to the left and near the horizon I caught sight of other ships, one of them a carrier, reversing course to port. I held my course for the destroyer and two miles from its starboard beam, began a precisely banked and level turn to the left. Having very exactly completed the two required identification turns, I headed for the carrier, unchallenged by the destroyer. Approaching on the carrier's starboard quarter, I recognized it as the one I had hoped for, the *Yorktown*. From the signal bridge a light began blinking a blur of dots and dashes in my direction, at a speed far too fast for me to read. Circling the ship to the left I reached for my Aldis lamp and tried to send the message, "THREE CV BURNING." In the time it took to flash a few letters of the message, I was already passing from the view of one wing of the bridge, only to be greeted on the opposite side by the blinking code, "REPEAT, REPEAT." As I rounded to starboard of *Yorktown* for the second time, three F4Fs dove past me on the right. It was the skipper. One plane was missing from the division. I joined up in the missing plane's spot just as the leader's landing gear began extending.

Tripping the tail hook extension handle with my left elbow, I began cranking down my own landing gear. With the wheels down, I reached to lock the tail hook lever in the extended slot. The lever was still in the retracted position, the hook had descended by its own weight as expected. With considerable effort I forced the lever forward and into the locked down slot. I gave it little thought. As the pilot in the plane ahead looking back gave me the thumbs up signal meaning, "your gear down, hook extended," I returned the sign; his was also in the required position. I entered the approach pattern following in turn, flew up the groove, and as the landing signal officer swept a flag across his throat in the sign to cut my power, snapped the throttle back and dropped the Wildcat onto the deck. Immediately I sensed something had gone haywire. As the fighter slammed to the deck there was no tap of the tail hook or the surging forward of my body as an arresting cable snubbed the plane to a halt. Instead there was the sensation of uncontrolled motion that follows when one unexpectedly steps on a very slippery surface. No hook, nor a bouncing hook? Having a hook that bounced along the deck and over, instead of catching an arresting cable was not a new sensation. There had been a siege of them when we flew the Brewster F2A-3 Buffalos from *Lexington*. Thankfully, there was only one barrier crash as a result. In times past, I had witnessed more than a few barrier crashes, some with fatal results. Luckily my hooks had always caught a wire before, but this one failed to catch!

Hard Landing

In the mere seconds that followed, my mind raced as the plane rolled forward. Halfway up the deck my plan of action was clear. I reacted as the crash barrier loomed ahead. Jamming the control stick full forward, I followed it with my body. Bending forward, tucking myself into a ball, I tried to get my head as close to the cockpit deck as possible. A propeller blade grabbed one of the barrier's snaring cables, bringing the engine to a sudden stop. The F4F cartwheeled forward, crashing to the deck on its back. With the windshield crushed flat, the cockpit was held just above the deck by the turtleback and protective armor plate behind the seat. Hanging upside down by the seat belt, I was momentarily dazed and disoriented. The thought of fire flashed to mind. I reached to cut the ignition switch—with the wrong hand, and to the wrong side of the instrument panel. Voices and the sound of trampling feet turned my attention to the shaft of light on my left at deck level. All I could see of a face that was trying to peer into the cockpit was its nose. I yelled, "Get this SOB off of me!" The nose disappeared and I heard a voice sing out, "he's okay!" In response to the voice the tail of the plane began to rise. I tripped my seat belt and scrambled clear of the wrecked fighter. As I gained my feet and stood erect, my eyes settled on a barn-sized camera that was focused on me. Indignant rage seized me and as I started a haymaker in the photographer's direction, someone gripped my right arm held it in check. It was a flight surgeon. "Let's get down to the sick bay," he ordered. Unaware there was a trickle of blood down the right side of my face, I jerked my arm from his gripping hand, turned and started for the ready room.

Half way there I met Thach. "Are you okay?" He asked, and without waiting for an answer, continued, "What happened?"

"I got one Zero for sure," I said, but as I started to continue Thach broke in.

"No, no, what did you see…the ships," he demanded.

"There were three carriers," I replied. "I saw bomb hits on all of them and I think one torpedo hit on one. They were all burning like hell when I left." Thach turned and ran through the hatch into the island and up the ladder to the bridge. I followed him through the hatch and turned left into the crowded ready room where I found Dibb and Macomber. Bassett was missing, so was Sheedy. Questions came at us from all directions. I repeated what I had told Thach, adding that I had seen the one F4F go in, and that I had not seen Sheedy after I turned to meet the first Zero. I soon learned that the high cover I had counted on had been corralled by a swarm of Zeros and had to fight their way out.[3]

If you read any of the familiar works on the Battle of Midway, including the best of them such as *A Glorious Page In Our History* or *The First Team*, you'll find

Warrant Officer Tom Cheek credited with just one confirmed aerial kill and, in some accounts, one other damaged or unconfirmed. For the most part, he is honored for simply surviving the melee with swarming Zeros rather than ably fulfilling his assigned task of protecting the torpedo bombers. After all, VT-3 was nearly wiped out, like VT-8, with only two planes and three airmen making it back to the task force alive.

But a close examination of Cheek's narrative above shows that he contributed far more than that to the cause, probably directly saving the lives of those three VT-3 airmen plus certainly destroying two and most likely three Zeros that morning, not just one. The first of the three was that of PO3/c Teruo Kawamata, his confirmed kill that he flamed just as the Zero was about to attack the TBDs. Number two was the one Cheek fired on in a head-on pass, which Sheedy later reported had exploded. And number three—the probable—was the one he fired at in a left turn immediately thereafter, during which he watched his tracers rip into the Zero's engine cowling and fuselage before he lost site of it.

But beyond that, Cheek related four incidents above in which he shot down or chased enemy fighters away from VT-3: the first was Kawamata's, then he took long range shots at two, then one, then two more attackers, in each case causing the Zero(s) to break off their runs at the torpedomen. Would the two *Yorktown* TBDs that made it back to their task force that day have instead been shot down without Cheek creating havoc with at least seven and probably eight of their attackers? Under the circumstances described by those three surviving airmen, that seems more than a fair bet.

Cheek told the Roundtable that his official score of just one confirmed Zero is based on his initial report to squadron commander Thach upon landing on the *Yorktown*. At that time he wasn't aware that the Zero he'd fought in a head-on duel had exploded behind him. That wasn't known until he met up with Sheedy at Pearl Harbor several days later. And while the fate of the plane that he fired at and hit when he banked left (immediately after the head-on encounter) is uncertain, it's likely that, at the very least, that Japanese pilot was in no position to threaten the TBDs while suffering .50 caliber holes in his engine cowling and fuselage.

Thus, with a likely three Zeros shot out of the sky plus five others chased away from VT-3, it would seem reasonable to elevate Cheek to a level of importance in the Battle of Midway that's quite a bit loftier than history has afforded him so far.

*   *   *   *

Luck and Doctrine

There is one vital element of the battle that every author and every veteran agrees upon: *luck*. There was certainly no shortage of bravery, skill, and tenacity on either side at Midway, but the proverbial and mysterious gods of war were clearly granting a large measure of favor to the Americans during those bitter three days. There are many examples that can be cited, but perhaps the most striking of all is the appearance of three U.S. Navy dive bomber squadrons, purely by chance, over the Japanese carriers at the same moment. What makes that occurrence even more remarkable is that it only happened because VB-6 and VS-6 from the *Enterprise* benefited from two other chance happenings that had to occur as they did and when they did, else those two squadrons would have missed the fight altogether. First, submarine USS *Nautilus* attempted an attack upon the enemy carriers and was chased away by IJN destroyer *Arashi*; and second, the destroyer doggedly pursued *Nautilus* far to the southwest of *Arashi's* assigned screening position (see Appendix B). Because of that, the commander of the *Enterprise* air group (CEAG), Lt. Cdr. C. Wade McClusky—who had led his dive bombers on a very circuitous route around and behind the enemy's actual track—found *Arashi* in a location it would not have been without *Nautilus* inadvertently leading it there. He adjusted his course to conform to *Arashi's* heading as it sped back to the Japanese fleet, and found it just as Lt. Cdr. Maxwell Leslie showed up from a different direction with the *Yorktown's* VB-3. It was that simultaneous arrival of three dive bomber squadrons high over the target while the Japanese were fully absorbed with seemingly endless low-level torpedo attacks that unexpectedly gave the Americans their key to a smashing victory.

Clayton Fisher was flying with the *Hornet's* air group at that moment, involved in a separate drama that will be covered in depth in the next chapter. He gratefully acknowledged McClusky's crucial role at Midway with this message to the Roundtable in 2003:

> A lot of us BOM survivors owe our lives to Wade McClusky. If those two squadrons Wade was leading had not made contact on June 4th, who knows whether the *Hornet* and *Enterprise* might have been sunk instead of the four Japanese carriers.

I watched Admiral Nimitz decorate Wade with the Navy Cross on the flight deck of the *Enterprise* at Pearl Harbor shortly after the BOM. I have never forgotten that ceremony!

Fisher's comments above are consistent with the praises afforded McClusky in all of the familiar histories on the Battle of Midway. But unfortunately, adulation for the CEAG's performance on June 4th was not universal among his fellow pilots. In his defense, he was new to dive bombers; his previous experience had mostly been as a fighter pilot. That may explain why, according to VB-6 commander Dick Best, he violated doctrine by leading VS-6 down on the "near" carrier (*Kaga*) when the position of the two squadrons in formation dictated that it should have gone after the "far" carrier (*Akagi*). The mistake very nearly caused both squadrons to attack only one of the four carriers.[4]

Ensign Lewis A. Hopkins was a one of Best's pilots that day, flying in the SBD section led by Lt. Joe Penland. After Midway he was assigned to the *Hornet* where he fought in the Battle of the Santa Cruz Islands during the struggle for the Solomons. After the war he specialized in jet aircraft engineering and development assignments, retiring as a rear admiral in 1974. He offered the following response to Fisher's letter above, from his unique perspective as one who had flown with McClusky against the Japanese carriers on June 4th:

> As a pilot of Bombing Squadron 6, flying SBD side number 6-B-12, I was in the formation led by McClusky. Remember at that time I was an ensign relatively new to Bombing Six, but I had two areas of expertise. First, being technically inclined, I knew how to manage my engine settings so that I could get maximum flight duration. Second, I was good at navigating and could keep accurate track of my location. With that in mind I have the following to offer. When we launched from the *Enterprise* for the June 4th morning attack, the location of the IJN was a reconstructed one, based on a number of fragmentary reports. There was, however, one piece of hard information, namely that the Japanese planes that attacked Midway had approached on a bearing of 320 degrees.
>
> Taking note of that, when we reached the reconstructed location at which we had estimated the IJN would be, and finding they were not there, my opinion is that we logically should have taken up a course of 320 degrees from the island. We would have located the IJN considerably sooner.
>
> Secondly, after locating the IJN, and after Lt. Cdr. McClusky had assigned carriers to VS-6 and VB-6, he violated his own instructions and attacked the nearest carrier. Luckily my skipper, Dick Best, had the foresight to shift from his assigned target, thus perhaps saving the day.

Also, it was obvious that fuel was a major factor as McClusky led our formation well past the reconstructed enemy location. The fuel factor was aggravated by the inordinate time involved in the forming up via a "deferred departure" from the *Enterprise*.

Summing up, in my opinion McClusky erred in continuing for fifteen minutes past the IJN's estimated position instead of taking up a course of 320 degrees from Midway; and secondly, he violated his own instructions as to target assignments. Nevertheless, as is so often the case, luck plays a large part in the outcome, as evidenced by the simultaneous arrival of the *Yorktown's* planes from a totally different direction.

McClusky's alleged dive on the wrong target was an annoyance that Best never forgot or forgave. The issue is discussed further in Chapter 12.

✻ ✻ ✻ ✻

Wingman

Ironically, the Roundtable over the years has focused more on the USS *Hornet* air group and its veterans than those of the other two American carriers, *Enterprise* and *Yorktown*. The irony is in the fact that, with the singular exception of Torpedo Squadron 8, none of the *Hornet's* squadrons contributed anything to the sinking of the three Japanese carriers struck by McClusky and Leslie's dive bombers on the morning of June 4th, nor were they directly involved in the sinking of the fourth and last carrier that afternoon. But those very circumstances—particularly the fact that the *Hornet* fliers were no-shows during the most critical few minutes of the battle—have long been the catalysts for interest and controversy among all who have studied the Battle of Midway to any degree.

That interest has quite naturally been manifest on the Roundtable, and it has been ably reinforced by the many eloquent contributions of one of the *Hornet* air group's key veterans, Commander Clayton Fisher, for whom the BOM was but one of numerous instances in which he dodged the proverbial bullet. Fisher began his military career in 1937 by enlisting in the tank company of the Wisconsin National Guard, 32nd Division, which he fortuitously left to attend college in 1939. The 32nd Division was mobilized in 1941 and sent to the Philippines, where its tank company suffered horrendous casualties in the defense of Bataan and on the infamous Death March—only ten men survived as POWs. He became a naval aviation cadet in 1940, was commissioned as an ensign in 1941, and reported to Bombing Squadron 8 (VB-8) aboard the brand new *Hornet* in August of that year. Wind sheer nearly caused him to crash while landing his SBC4 dive bomber at an Army airfield in the Canal Zone in March of 1942, and on the very next day a tailhook failure on his aircraft almost sent him into the drink while landing aboard the ship as it exited the canal. After making five combat sorties during the BOM, he was shot down and very nearly killed in the Battle of the Santa Cruz Islands, and he later ditched in the Atlantic off the Florida coast when his F6F Hellcat's engine died on a training flight. As if that wasn't enough, he made a discretionary career move in 1951 that inadvertently sent him to still more combat, flying F4U Corsairs against well-defended North Korean targets such as the deadly bridges at Toko-Ri. He retired from the Navy in 1962 and commenced a somewhat safer career in real estate.[5]

The flight of the *Hornet* air group on the morning of June 4, 1942 had two broadly distinguishing elements, both well known and much-discussed in all histories of the battle: (a) the ship's torpedo squadron, VT-8, led by Lt. Cdr. John Waldron, arbitrarily broke away from the rest of Cdr. Stanhope Ring's air group while searching for the enemy carriers, with the result that VT-8 was the only *Hornet* squadron to find and attack the target. As a result it was completely wiped out by Japanese defenses without scoring a single hit. And (b), Ring then led his other three squadrons on a fruitless "flight to nowhere," which cost him his entire fighter escort lost in the sea when the ten F4Fs ran out of gas, adding two more pilots to the *Hornet's* KIA list for the day. Ring's two SBD squadrons then returned to the ship after contributing nothing to the fight against the enemy carriers. (Most of VB-8 first diverted to Midway after spotting its rising column of smoke that served as a convenient locating beacon. The *Hornet* planes returned to their carrier after refueling on the island.)

As disappointing as those failings were, they were the result of command decisions rather than any lack of courage, resolve, or skill on the part of the involved aircrews. Each of Ring's pilots faced some tough decisions involving his commander's orders, the limitations of his aircraft, and the inherent confusion resulting from poor communications during a highly convoluted combat scenario. Each did what he believed to be his best under those severely trying conditions.

Ensign Fisher had a key role that morning, as one of two SBD pilots assigned to fly as wingmen to the group commander. In 1979 he'd composed a detailed narrative of his experiences at Midway, which he provided to the Roundtable upon joining in 2000. He takes up the story here on the eve of the battle, June 3rd:

> June 4th was going to be the big day. The Japanese carrier task force was closing the distance so that their aircraft could reach and attack Midway

Island. After briefings in the various ready rooms early in the evening, most of the pilots retired to their staterooms. The entire ship was unusually quiet. There were no pilots moving around the dimly blue-lit passageways. It was a strange and eerie feeling. I felt that, as an individual pilot, my odds of survival the next morning were minimal even if we achieved our planned surprise attack on the Japanese carriers with all their experienced air groups. We had heard about the successes of the Zero fighters shooting down our aircraft during the Coral Sea battle. I have read postwar Japanese accounts that their pilots were partying, playing their record players—maybe *China Nights*—that evening. They evidently were very confident they were going to have an easy time attacking Midway.

I wrote letters to my wife and my mother and told them I was resigned to whatever fate had in store for me, and if we lost the battle and I was killed, I knew our country would eventually defeat the Japanese. Frankly, I was very worried and scared. Nobody wants to die. We had always had fatal aviation accidents. Younger pilots usually didn't worry too much—it was always going to happen to the other pilot.

This evening was totally different. Tomorrow I could be one of those "other pilots."

Early on the morning of June 4th, the *Hornet* was ordered to launch all of its available aircraft to search for and attack the Japanese carriers. Our attack group consisted of Fighting Squadron Eight (VF-8) flying Wildcat F4Fs, Bombing Squadron Eight (VB-8) and Scouting Squadron Eight (VS-8) flying Dauntless SBDs, and Torpedo Squadron Eight (VT-8) flying Devastator TBDs.

Ensign Ben Tappan of VS-8 and I had been "volunteered" that morning to fly as wingmen on Commander Stanhope Ring, the commander of the *Hornet* air group (CHAG). Ring intended to fly above the dive bombers to coordinate the air group's attack. I was just plain demoralized! Our three planes would be the first aircraft to be attacked by Japanese fighters. The experienced Zero fighter pilots would try to take out the flight leaders first. I wanted to be in my own squadron formation and have all those fast-firing twin .30 caliber rear guns from about sixteen dive bombers protecting our tails. Our squadron doctrine was to try to stay in formation as long as possible for mutual protection before breaking up to start our dives. The torpedo squadrons had to fan out and break up their formations to make their runs, which is one reason why they were all going to be such sitting ducks for the Zeros.

First to Launch

My assigned aircraft was in the front position of the SBDs in the flight deck stack. My plane had a heavy aerial camera mounted in its belly, and because of that additional weight my plane only had a 500-pound bomb hung on it. All the other dive bombers were loaded with 1000-pound bombs.[6]

Mine was the first dive bomber launched from the *Hornet*. I was excited and the adrenalin must have been flowing as I started rolling down the flight deck. I remember waving at the people on the bridge as I passed by.

After forming up, we started a slow climb to around 14,000 feet. We had to use a lot of engine power to climb because of those 1000-pound bombs. As we were climbing, I never could see VT-8, which should have been below us at about two thousand feet. We flew over some cloud layers that could have obscured their position.

We had to use our oxygen masks, which were older vintage than the masks the fighter pilots used. When we reached our altitude, I was collecting ice inside the mask from my breath. The mask was apparently not sealing out the outside air. I was having difficulty breathing and I had to periodically removed the mask to clear the ice. All pilots and crewmen were wearing summer flight suits and the air temperature became very cold up there.

As our formation was approaching the estimated position of the Japanese carriers, there was nothing in sight and we were close to the maximum range of the dive bombers. There was unlimited visibility, and I could see a large column of black smoke to the southwest of our position that I thought was coming from Midway Island.

The air group was operating under a radio silence doctrine until we would make contact with the enemy. The CHAG continued on our original southwest course and gave me hand signals to form a scouting line, pointing down at the VS-8 formation. A scouting line meant that all aircraft would break formation and get in a line abreast with large intervals between each aircraft. That also meant we were going to continue on our original course.

Alone

I dropped off my wing position and dove down to try to get close enough to pass the CHAG's order to the leader of VS-8, Lieutenant Commander Rodee. Just as I started to get into position near Rodee's aircraft, he started turning his formation in a 180-degree turn and assumed a course heading back to the *Hornet*.

I felt I could not abandon the CHAG, and tried to locate him. All I could see was empty sky. It was a very scary feeling being all alone up there. I turned back and tried to join up on VS-8. I could just barely see their formation, and not wanting to burn excess fuel to close the distance, I just dogged behind. I finally could see the *Hornet* and was able to join the formation while approaching the task force.

After landing, I walked into the ready room where I was met by Ensign Christofferson. He had not flown that morning and was very upset. He told me I was the only pilot that had returned from our squadron (VB-8), and that no fighter pilots or torpedo pilots from *Hornet's* attack group had returned. The fighter pilots had all ditched after running out of fuel, and some of them would later be rescued by PBYs. All the torpedo pilots had been shot down and Ensign Gay was the only survivor. VT-8 had a detachment flying six of the new Grumman TBF torpedo bombers from Midway Island. All were shot down except a plane piloted by Ensign Bert Ernest. He managed to return to Midway Island in his badly damaged plane. He had a small wound on his face; one of his gunners was killed and the other gunner was badly wounded.

Some of the VB-8 pilots landed at Midway Island. Two pilots had to ditch in the lagoon inside the atoll. One plane ditched at sea, and the pilot and gunner were rescued by a PBY. The CHAG and the remainder of the VB-8 pilots were able to reach the *Hornet* before running out of fuel.[7]

*   *   *   *

Pilots, Man Your Planes!

Captain Roy P. Gee, USN (Retired), was another VB-8 pilot who, like his friend Clay Fisher, ultimately became a frequent contributor to the Roundtable. Gee's path to naval aviation and the *Hornet* paralleled that of Fisher's: he began as an army ROTC cadet while in high school in the 1930s, got a private pilot's license while attending the University of Utah, then volunteered for naval aviation in 1940. Like Fisher, he reported to VB-8 in August 1941 and shared all of the squadron's experiences for the remaining brief life of the *Hornet*. He had stateside assignments for the rest of the war, then went on to fly AD Skyraiders in the Korean War, followed by a tour as XO of the USS *Essex* (CV-9). He commanded a U.S. Navy C-130 turboprop squadron during the Vietnam War, followed by assignments in Washington and with NATO. Retiring in 1972, he returned to college in order to earn a degree in history, some of which he had helped to make. Here are his recollections of VB-8's morning flight on June 4, 1942, the first day of the battle:

> We went to general quarters at 0630. All *Hornet* pilots and crewmen were at flight quarters in their ready rooms. A PBY flying from Midway had spotted the Japanese task force. The teletype in VB-8's ready room was steadily clicking away with navigational data that I diligently copied to my chart board, as did the other VB-8 pilots. The required information consisted of following elements: (1) enemy position, course, and speed, (2) own task force position, course, and speed, (3) wind speed on the surface and at various altitudes, (4) latitude and longitude of the operational area plus magnetic compass variation. Using these four elements, each pilot was responsible to prepare his own

navigational solution for flying a relative motion course to intercept and attack the enemy, and also the return course back to our carrier.

CHAG (Commander, *Hornet* Air Group: Stanhope C. Ring) had his own navigation solution, as did our VB-8 CO, Lt. Cdr. Ruff Johnson, VS-8 CO Lt. Cdr. Walt Rodee, and VT-8 CO Lt. Cdr. John Waldron. The VF-8 CO, Lt. Cdr. Samuel ("Pat") Mitchell, remarked that he would use the solution that was chosen. The squadron COs' solutions were different from CHAG's, but he overruled them and said that they would all fly his navigational solution. Lt. Cdr. Waldron strongly disagreed, and subsequently decided that he'd follow his own solution. He told his Torpedo 8 boys to follow him—he would lead them to the enemy.

Suddenly, "PILOTS MAN YOUR PLANES" was announced. We all wished each other good luck as we left the ready room for the climb to the flight deck and our SBDs. I met my R/G, Radioman First Class Canfield at our assigned aircraft and went over our mission and recognition charts with him. I don't know which particular aircraft (side number) we flew that day. My only record of that went down with the *Hornet* at the Battle of Santa Cruz.

After completing an inspection of the SBD and its bomb, Canfield and I climbed into the cockpits. As I sat there waiting for the signal to start engines, I got the same feeling of apprehension and butterflies in the stomach that I got before the start of competition in high school and collegiate athletics. The butterflies left after takeoff as I focused on navigating and flying formation. Our two squadrons (VB-8 and VS-8) rendezvoused in two close-knit, stepped-down formations on each side of CHAG's section, which consisted of CHAG and VS-8 wingman Ens. Ben Tappman and VB-8 wingman Ens. Clayton Fisher. CHAG's section was flying above and somewhat separated from VB-8/VS-8 and was escorted by ten VF-8 F4Fs. As we proceeded to climb, we soon lost visual contact with VT-8. We were maintaining absolute radio silence and were on oxygen, and our engines were on high blower. I eased my fuel mixture control back to a leaner blend in order to conserve fuel as we leveled out at 19,000 feet and proceeded on our assigned course.

Diverted to Midway

We continued flying on a westerly heading for some time and were getting close to our point of no return without seeing anything of the Japanese fleet. Our CO, Lt. Cdr. Johnson, decided to break away and fly towards Midway because some of our pilots didn't have enough fuel to return to the *Hornet*. So we left CHAG, VS-8, and VF-8 and headed toward Midway, but shortly after we turned, Lt. Tucker banked his three-plane section away and headed in an easterly direction. As the remaining VB-8 SBDs headed towards Midway, Ens. Guillory suffered engine failure and made a forced water landing. He and his R/G, ARM2/c Cottrell, were observed to safely leave the aircraft and get into a life raft. They were later rescued by a PBY.

As we approached Midway, the skipper signaled us to jettison our bombs. Afterwards, as we continued our approach to the Eastern Island airfield, we received sporadic AA fire that caused minor damage to some of the planes, but it quickly ceased after our SBDs were recognized as friendly. Shortly thereafter, Ens. T. J. Wood ran out of gas. He and his R/G, ARM3/c Martz, were safely rescued after ditching their aircraft. Ens. Forrester Auman ran out of fuel on his landing approach and safely ditched in the lagoon, where he and his R/G, ARM3/c McLean, were rescued by a PT boat. After the remaining 11 SBDs had landed, we taxied to an area where our aircraft were refueled and rearmed with 500 lb. bombs. Refueling from gasoline drums was necessary due to fuel trucks being damaged from the Japanese air attack. The runways had not been damaged, but certain buildings and the water system had been hit.

Midway Air Operations had notified *Hornet* of the arrival of VB-8. Lt. Cdr. Johnson was ordered to return to the ship and to attack any Japanese ships that we might find while en route. So we departed Midway and returned to the ship without incident. We were recovered aboard at about 1400 with our 500 lb. bombs intact. When I entered the VB-8 ready-room, I was shocked to learn that none of VT-8's fifteen TBDs nor VF-8's ten F4Fs had returned, and that all the crews had been declared MIA. I went to the wardroom to get something to eat and paused to look at the empty chairs that were normally filled by my friends from VF-8 and VT-8. It was a sorrowful site, but I could only dwell on it for a moment—the announcement came for all VB-8 pilots to report to the ready room immediately.

With all of VS-8 and most of VB-8 back aboard the *Hornet*, the ship was capable of mounting a second strike if needed, albeit without its torpedo squadron or much in the way of fighter escort. But the call to action came nonetheless, as the *Hiryu*—the last surviving Japanese carrier—was discovered by a scout from the *Yorktown*. The *Enterprise* sent off twenty-five SBDS from VB-6, VS-6, and VB-3 (which had taken refuge there when the *Yorktown* could no longer conduct air operations), followed somewhat later by sixteen planes from the *Hornet's* VS-8 and VB-8, the latter including Ensigns Fisher and Gee. Gee described the subsequent action as follows:

Upon entering the ready room, I was informed that we were launching on a mission to attack the Japanese carrier *Hiryu*. The attack group would consist of nine VS-8 SBDs carrying 1000 lb. bombs and seven from VB-8 carrying the 500 lb. bombs that we'd loaded on Midway. No VF escort would be available. The enemy ships were located approximately 162 miles out, bearing 290 degrees. I plotted my course for intercepting the enemy formation and returning to the *Hornet*. Lt.(jg) Bates, the VB-8 flight leader for this mission, briefed us on tactics for the strike. We were ready to go.

Since we'd seen no action that morning, I thought that this could be VB-8's first exposure to real combat. We were ordered to man our planes at about 1540. I met my gunner, Canfield, at our SBD for the second time that day, and we completed our same routine and boarded the aircraft. We went through the takeoff checklist after I started the engine, then we were ready to roll when our turn came. As I approached the take-off position, I was given the *stop* signal followed by the *hold brakes* signal, and was then handed over to the Takeoff Control Officer (TCO), who held a stick with a brightly colored flag in his right hand. When the deck ahead was clear, the TCO rotated the flag above his head, which was the signal for me to rev the engine to full take-off power while holding the brakes and keeping the tail down with the elevators in the full-up position. The TCO made eye contact with me, then suddenly bent forward on his knee, pointing the flag towards the bow. That was my signal to release the brakes and let 'er rip. It's an exhilarating way to take off in an airplane, and old-time carrier pilots can recount many interesting tales.

The Hiryu in Flames

We were safely airborne and proceeding to our rendezvous point. Our VB-8 SBDs, led by Lt.(jg) Bates, joined up with VS-8 and Lt. Stebbins, who was the strike leader. The *Enterprise* had also launched a much larger strike group about thirty minutes before ours.

By the time we arrived in the target area, the *Enterprise* group had already finished their strike. That had cleared the upper altitudes of Zeros, leaving our approach over the enemy force unopposed. The *Hiryu* was observed to be completely on fire, so Lt. Stebbins directed us toward other suitable targets. He took VS-8 toward one while signaling Lt.(jg) Bates that our squadron was to bomb a nearby cruiser. We maneuvered to make our attack out of the sun from 15,000 ft. There were puffs of AA fire all around us.

Just as we were approaching the dive point, we noticed several explosions on the ocean's surface, quite some distance from the target. Looking up, we saw a flight of B-17s high above us. They'd dropped their bomb loads right through our formation, missing us as well as the enemy ships!

We then tailed off into our dives. Lt.(jg) Bates had the lead plane (bomb 50 ft. off the starboard bow) followed by Ens. Nickerson (100 ft. astern). I was next (hit astern). The second section dove next with Ens. White first (miss), followed by Ens. Friesz (miss wide), followed by Ens. Barrett (hit on starboard quarter), followed lastly by Ens. Fisher (no release). During the dive, what looked like orange balls were popping up at me and continued coming from all directions during my high-speed retirement at sea level. Following the strike, all sixteen of *Hornet's* SBDs rendezvoused unscathed and returned to the ship, landing back aboard at dusk. VB-8 had at last lost its combat virginity.

Japanese records did not record a hit on any of the *Hiryu's* screening vessels on June 4th, although Ensign Gee's bomb was seen by both his R/G and his section leader to strike an enemy cruiser. Gee was awarded the Navy Cross for this action, but he generously tells anyone who listens that it "actually should go to my gunner, to my plane captain, and to all the hard-working ordnance and maintenance crews who really were flying with me when I made the attack. Without their expertise, no aviator can do his job."

✳   ✳   ✳   ✳

Riding the Bomb

Clay Fisher also related the attack upon *Hiryu's* screening ships for the Roundtable, during which the "no bomb release" episode was another dodge-the-bullet experience for him. He remembers the flight like this:

> In 2004, I had the opportunity to meet "Bud" Merrill, a *Yorktown* SBD pilot during an event at Chicago's Midway Airport. Bud told me he flew from the *Enterprise* on the June 4th afternoon attack against the *Hiryu*. Those *Enterprise* and *Yorktown* SBDs got at least four direct bomb hits. That proved fatal, and *Hiryu* was finally sunk by two torpedoes fired by Japanese destroyers.
>
> I've done some research about the price those dive bomber pilots paid to sink the *Hiryu*. We all have read about how the BOM was won in approximately ten minutes on the morning of June 4th, but it was the *Hiryu's* dive bombers and torpedo planes that caused the sinking of the *Yorktown*. In the afternoon the *Hiryu* was still operating and it had to be destroyed for closure of the battle.
>
> The *Hiryu* was protected by a high combat air patrol of some very experienced Zero fighter pilots who caught the *Enterprise* and *Yorktown* SBDs just as they were rolling into their dives. Ensign Weber was the first to be shot down (he'd scored a hit on the *Akagi* during the morning strike). Next were Ensign Butler and Lieutenant (j.g.) Wiseman. Merrill told me those two crashed into the sea almost simultaneously. The Zero pilots knew they had to take out the SBDs, and aggressively pressed home their attacks, firing mostly their 20 mm. cannons.
>
> Merrill said that his plane was hit by 20 mm. shells, his gunner was seriously wounded from shrapnel, and his controls became hard to move because

of damage to the cables. His plane and one other were judged unsalvageable upon their return to the *Enterprise*.

I have always known that the *Hornet* SBD pilots lucked out that afternoon by not having the Zeros to contend with. I didn't realized, until I talked to Merrill, just how deadly the Zeros were during that particular mission. Such was the aggressiveness of the Japanese defenders that if the SBDs had been intercepted slightly earlier, more of them would have been lost and the *Hiryu* might have survived that day.

Our launch from the *Hornet* was delayed by the recovery of VB-8's SBDs that had landed on Midway in the morning. The *Enterprise* and *Yorktown* SBDs had already hit the *Hiryu*, so our flight shifted to a cruiser, which I think was the *Tone*. I was "tail end Charlie," the last *Hornet* plane to dive. I still had the camera on my plane from the morning flight and was supposed to turn it on just before I started my dive. The camera would supposedly record the formation's bomb hits. The camera switch was mounted in a difficult position that required me to reach behind my head. Between trying to arm my bomb, adjusting my position to start my dive, seeing my first AA, and wondering when we would be hit by the Zeros, I just plain forgot to turn on the camera. The BOM had very few action pictures taken, and I have always felt that I missed an opportunity to record a little bit of history with that camera.

I observed Roy Gee's bomb hit amidships of the cruiser we were diving on and my camera should have recorded that hit! Also the camera would have shown a string of bombs exploding just off the port side that were dropped by a flight of B-17s. They almost dropped their bombs through our formation! The Japanese must have thought the SBDs and the B-17s were delivering a coordinated attack. Anyway, I knew a B-17 crew was going to think they hit the ship, rather than Roy.

My bomb failed to release. Unfortunately, I had collapsed my dive brakes a little prematurely in order to accelerate out of my dive, and I suddenly realized I was getting a really wild ride, pulling a lot of Gs. My airspeed indicator had pegged! Pulling out, I passed just astern of a destroyer I hadn't seen due to a low layer of clouds. The water just below and behind my plane was being splattered by shrapnel—the destroyer's gunners had misjudged their aim because of my terrific speed! My air speed indicator had stayed pegged until I was clear of the AA. I thought the needle was stuck, but I finally decelerated and could read my real speed, about 180 knots. I finally got back to a normal 140 knots. I never knew how fast that old bird was going!

*   *   *   *

An Elusive Target

Unsure whether the Japanese had still more carriers in their Midway fleet, Task Force 16 continued a maximum search effort on the following day, June 5th. While there were a number of false reports concerning potential targets, the only enemy ship attacked was the destroyer *Tanikaze*, late in the afternoon. Clay Fisher, on his third combat sortie of five at the Battle of Midway, had this report on the attack against the lone Japanese vessel:

> On the next day, *Hornet* and *Enterprise* dive bombers were launched to attack some reported cruisers and destroyers. We flew about 230 miles, almost to the limit of our range, and finally passed over a huge oil slick from the sinking of the *Hiryu*. We continued on course and finally found a lone Japanese destroyer, the *Tanikaze*. Due to its high speed and some super evasive action, none of the dive bombers could get a direct hit. As I was getting into position to dive, two AA shells exploded close enough to rock my plane. I made my dive and could see the muzzle flashes of the ship's guns firing at me. I missed close astern; I had misjudged the destroyer's speed. As I circled around behind its stern to pick up the return course for the *Hornet*, I watched other dive-bombers in their dives. One never pulled out, exploding on impact with the water. Lieutenant Sam Adams, a *Yorktown* pilot flying off the *Enterprise* was killed.
>
> We did not have enough fuel for trying to form up, so we returned to the carriers strung out in a long column. We were running out of daylight and knew we would have to make a night carrier landing. Some of us had only made one night carrier landing on our shakedown cruise.
>
> A few of our pilots became lost because they could not pick up the weak radio homing device ("YE") from the *Hornet*. We had been briefed that the coded signals from both carriers would be the same, but they were different. Some of the *Hornet* pilots could only hear the *Enterprise's* stronger homing signals and used the wrong courses to the task force. The *Hornet* turned on a powerful searchlight and pointed it to a vertical position to provide a homing beacon. A couple planes ran out of gas in their landing approaches and were rescued by a destroyer. Ensign Don Adams from Bombing Squadron Eight was preparing to ditch his plane while he still had engine power. His radioman spotted a light and Don was finally able see the *Hornet*. He got astern of the ship, made a straight in landing approach, and ran out of gas when his tail hook engaged the arresting gear wire!

In a significant footnote to this story, the saga of the *Tanikaze* has to be included near the top of the long list of highly remarkable events in the Battle of Midway. On the afternoon of June 5, 1942, the little ship was attacked by elements from no less than *six* squadrons from Task Force 16 (VB-8, VS-8, VB-6, VS-6, VS-5, and VB-3) plus two flights of Army B-17s, and in the process dodged what appears to have been *one hundred and thirty seven* bombs without a direct hit![8]

✳   ✳   ✳   ✳

Mogami and Mikuma

In yet another of the Battle of Midway's bizarre occurrences, the submarine USS *Tambor* surfaced in the midst of a Japanese formation early in the morning of June 5th, causing the IJN heavy cruiser *Mikuma* to collide with sister ship *Mogami* while taking evasive action. That left the latter with major damage to its bow, causing it to lose speed and leak a long trail of fuel oil. A PBY Catalina spotted the pair after dawn, drawing an initial attack by the depleted U.S. Marine strike group from Midway, then bombing runs by B-17s, all to little avail. The American carriers were sidetracked by the *Tanikaze* incident later that day, but joined the fight against the two cruisers on the following morning. Roy Gee takes up the story here, commencing with his return to the Task Force 16 the previous evening:

> By the time we approached the task force, darkness had enveloped the ships and it didn't seem that a deck landing would be possible. Suddenly their lights came on and we were ordered to land. I followed Lt. Vose into the landing pattern, and Canfield and I went over the carrier landing checklist: wheels down and locked, flaps down, tailhook extended. I picked up the LSO and his lighted wands as I turned into the groove. My approach speed was good, but I was a little high. The LSO gave the high-dip signal, meaning I was to drop the nose, come down about ten feet, and resume my approach attitude. The LSO then gave me the *Roger* signal, followed shortly by the *cut engine* signal, and I landed the aircraft, catching the third wire. This was my first night carrier landing in the SBD, and I felt very good.
>
> After my tailhook was cleared from the arresting wire and put in the up position, I revved the engine in order to quickly clear the landing area and move forward so that the barriers could be raised in time for the next plane to land. After the propeller stopped turning and the wheels were chocked, Canfield and I climbed down and proceeded to our ready rooms. As I went through the hatch and down the ladder, I felt uncomfortable with the sur-

rounding bulkheads and passageways. Somehow, they looked strangely unfamiliar. And for good reason: as I entered what I thought was VB-8's ready room, I discovered that I'd landed on our sister ship, the *Enterprise!* Of course, Lt. Vose had done the same thing.

They told me I'd be assigned to fly another search on the following morning, so I was billeted in a room and told to go to sleep. Three additional *Hornet* pilots (Ens. Doug Carter of VB-8, Ens. Jim Forbes of VS-8, and one other whose name I don't remember) had also landed aboard *Enterprise.*[9]

I awoke about 0500 on June 6th and remembered that I was on *Enterprise* and scheduled to fly a 200-mile search that morning. I hopped out of the bunk, washed myself a little, slipped into my flight suit, and hurried to the wardroom for breakfast where I encountered an atmosphere similar to the one in the *Hornet's* wardroom the previous morning: many missing pilots would never again sit in the empty chairs. I have never forgotten that feeling.

I finished breakfast and went quickly to the ready room to prepare for the mission. The search group was launched at 0700, and Canfield and I were flying a sector to the southwest at 1500 ft. I was on autopilot, making it easy to keep track of my relative position from the task force as the search proceeded. After about an hour I noticed several silhouettes on the horizon ahead. As the distance closed, I could see that they were four ships in formation on a southwesterly course. I dropped down to 800 ft. and tracked them for several minutes in order to record their position, course, and speed, and also to determine their ship class from my IJN silhouette cards. The two larger ships were cruisers with pagoda-type superstructures, and the other two were destroyers. (I later learned that the two larger ones were the Japanese heavy cruisers *Mogami* and *Mikuma.*)

Remaining at a safe distance out of AA range, I dictated a message for CTF 16 to Canfield. The message contained the enemy formation's composition, relative position, course, and speed. Canfield sent the message by radio but got no confirmation that it had been received. He was concerned that a problem with his radio transmitter might have prevented the task force from receiving the message. It was already 0835 and I decided to get out of there and back to task force ASAP. Arriving over the *Enterprise* at about 0930, I dropped them a message containing the data on the enemy cruiser formation that we'd located. I then returned to the *Hornet's* air pattern to await recovery. After she launched a strike group, I was recovered aboard at about 1015. I proceeded to the bridge in order to brief Captain Mitscher on the details of my sighting. After reporting to the VB-8 ready room, I was told that I wouldn't be flying any more that day.

*   *   *   *

Last Sortie for the TBD Devastator

Based on Gee's scouting report, the *Hornet* sent a strike against the two Japanese cruisers and their two accompanying destroyers. Both cruisers were hit but did not sink, prompting Rear Admiral Spruance in Task Force 16 to mount a more aggressive second strike from both carriers. He decided to send the fleet's last three TBD Devastators with the dive bombers, thinking that the two enemy cruisers could most likely be sunk by torpedoes.

ARM3/c Ronald W. Graetz was possibly the luckiest torpedo squadron radioman-gunner in the American task force at that time, for he was supposed to have been killed on the morning of June 4th, like all but a few of his fellow R/Gs who rode in TBDs that day. In 2005 he explained in the following letter to the Roundtable how he manage to dodge that cruel fate:

> ARM2/c W. D. Horton, ARM3/c D. L. Ritchey, and I were in the same class at Aviation Radioman school. We all reported aboard the *Enterprise* at the same time, however I was originally assigned to VB-6. A lot of the guys in that outfit were unhappy about the squadron and it rubbed off. When I volunteered for submarine duty, the VB-6 personnel officer didn't like my attitude and I got transferred to First Division (the deck force). After about two months, Horton went to Lt.(jg) Rombach, the communications officer of VT-6, and got him to request my transfer to VT-6. I flew with Rombach as his R/G until I was replaced in May 1942 so I could go to gunnery school at Kaneohe Bay. That is why I wasn't riding with Rombach as his gunner at Midway.

Lt.(jg) Rombach's assigned R/G on the June 4th flight of VT-6 was ARM2/c W. F. Glenn. Both died in the mass sacrifice of the three torpedo squadrons on that fateful day. By luck of the draw, Graetz was not assigned to fly that morning, having lost his billet as Rombach's gunner due to a fortuitous training assignment. But his number did come up when the decision was made to send all remaining TBDs against the *Mogami* and *Mikuma* two days later. Having seen only four of his squadron's fourteen Devastators return from their previous flight (with one of them deliberately jettisoned as a lost cause), Graetz could not have been overjoyed at the prospect of joining them on another mission. But it turned out to be a far more benign event than that experienced by his fellow gunners on June 4th. He remembers it this way:

When we prepared for that flight, Warrant Officer Mueller, one of the pilots, told me that they wanted that ship sunk (the *Mikuma*) at all costs because they thought a flag officer might be aboard it. However, we were to keep in mind that these three TBDs were the only three remaining torpedo planes in the entire Pacific Fleet, and they wanted all three back!

As we came over the horizon and saw the cruiser, the first SBDs were just beginning their dives. We never got close to the target, but every once in a while our three-plane formation would turn towards the cruiser and attract its anti-aircraft fire. We flew a big circle around it and watched the dive bombers pound the hell out of that ship. It looked like a huge bathtub, full of scrap iron and junk. An aerial photographer took a picture of it that was posted on the bulletin board for all to see. It was one of the most pleasant flights I ever had.[10]

$$* \qquad * \qquad * \qquad *$$

Empty Chairs

The *Hornet* launched its second strike against the two cruisers that afternoon, with Clay Fisher taking his bomb-laden SBD up for the fifth time at the Battle of Midway. Here is his report of the final combat mission in the three-day battle:

The *Hornet* and *Enterprise* launched about twenty dive bombers to try to finish off the cruiser and the two destroyers that had been bombed that morning. We found the cruiser dead in the water and a lot of men in the water. The destroyers near the cruiser were picking up survivors. The VS-8 flight just ahead of us hit the cruiser with two 1000-pound bombs and triggered a huge explosion. The debris must have reached over 1000 feet.

The destroyers started pulling away from the cruiser. The CO of VB-8 diverted us to bomb the destroyers. I selected a destroyer that was in a shallow turn and increasing its speed. The ship did not put up any AA, probably because of survivors from the cruiser exposed on the open deck. It was easy to line up for a dive bombing run. I dropped my bomb from about 1500 feet and my gunner told me we got a direct hit near the stern. The destroyer went dead in the water. Ruff Johnson, our squadron CO, confirmed the hit. I later found out the destroyer was the *Arashio*. Due to superb damage control efforts by its crew, the ship did not sink and was able to reach Wake Island. There was terrible suffering among the wounded survivors while en route to Wake.[11]

The Battle of Midway was finally over. I was emotionally drained and physically very tired. I had flown on all five of the attack missions launched from the *Hornet* and had logged seventeen combat hours. When I sat in the officers' wardroom, I looked at two completely empty tables. Each squadron had their own table and the VF-8 and VT-8 tables were empty. As I looked at those tables I could remember some of the pilots' conversations and jokes.

I visited VT-8's ready room. It was completely empty except for the pilots' uniforms hanging on the hooks, left there after they had changed into their flight suits. As shipmates of the deceased men, some of us we were assigned the job of inventorying their personal effects, then packing them to send to their next of kin. Another pilot and I inventoried Lieutenant Moore's and Ensign Bill Evans's personal effects. It was a very emotional and depressing experience.[12]

Late in 2005 Fisher received a copy of Jon Parshall's new book on the Japanese navy, *Shattered Sword: the Untold Story of the Battle of Midway*, which includes considerable detail on his bombing of the *Arashio*. He provided this appraisal of the book to the Roundtable, along with some fresh thoughts on the plight of the enemy destroyer:

I finished reading *Shattered Sword*. The descriptions of the demise of the four Japanese carriers and terrible suffering of the personnel sort got to me. The descriptions of the abandonment of all those Japanese sailors from the *Mikuma* brought back stark memories of that afternoon. I was just approaching the *Mikuma* and I witnessed the huge explosion which I thought were her magazines. As I circled around to get at the *Arashio* I saw a large group of men in the water to the port area of the *Mikuma*. I felt sorry for them and knew some of the bomb misses must have killed quite a few of them. The *Arashio* had been picking up some of those men and was moving slowly away from the *Mikuma* on a straight course. I wasn't high enough to make a dive bombing run so I pushed over in fairly steep glide bombing run. The *Arashio* was not firing at me; I guess they had too many survivors from the *Mikuma* exposed on the open main deck. I was lined up so good in my dive that I released at about 2000 feet. Ferguson, my gunner, told me I had a direct hit near the stern, and VB-8 skipper Ruff Johnson also witnessed the bomb hit. I think we all carried 1000-pound bombs that afternoon because of the short distance we flew.

According to the description in *Shattered Sword*, the bomb killed thirty-nine men.

I found the sympathy for his former enemy that Fisher exhibited in the foregoing anecdote to be typical of that expressed by many Battle of Midway veterans that I've known and interviewed over the years, particularly the aviators. In the years after the war, a lot of them met and became friends with many Japanese, often including former adversaries. Knowing them personally and long removed from the emotions of both youth and war, the bitter enemy into whose midst one could drop a thousand-pound bomb without remorse became a real human being that one could meet, know, and even befriend. That seemed to bring forth refreshing feelings of compassion in the former warriors that they'd have never imagined while locked in the midst of bitter combat.

CHAPTER 8

▼

THE FLIGHT TO NOWHERE

A Question of Leadership

In reviewing the sorties of the various American squadrons and air groups on the morning of June 4, 1942, one peculiarity is consistent in all of the familiar histories of the Battle of Midway: four separate flights of attackers from the atoll (Marine, Navy, and Army) had no difficulty finding the Japanese carriers. Torpedo squadrons from all three U.S. carriers found them. Dive bombers from the *Enterprise* and *Yorktown* found them. But oddly, the entire air group from the *Hornet* (less VT-8) not only failed by a large margin to find any Japanese ships, but they suffered as many aircraft lost as they might have expected from bitter combat against an enemy fleet. Where did the *Hornet* air group really go on the morning of June 4th, and why?

Arriving at the answer is far from easy. Even at this late date, universal agreement remains elusive despite extensive, lengthy analysis at many levels over many years. But there is one key factor upon which virtually all reviewers agree: the ill fate of the *Hornet* air group that morning was clearly born of leadership problems at the highest level aboard the ship. The deck spot, launch sequence, squadron formation assignments, and especially the chosen course to the enemy fleet were all decisions reached by the air group's commanding officer, Stanhope Ring, in concert with his longtime friend, Captain Marc Mitscher.

In the case of Commander Ring, there was ample reason in the very beginning for his pilots to have grave doubts about his quality as an aviator and navigator, and hence his ability to effectively lead an air group—*their* air group—in battle.

Clay Fisher cited the misgivings he felt upon his initial meeting with the CHAG before the war:

> I met him for the first time on the *Hornet's* quarterdeck in September 1941 when I was checking in with my orders. I was so green I didn't even know you were supposed to salute the flag and ask the duty officer for permission to come aboard the ship! This was my first time on a carrier, and believe me, it looked huge.
>
> Ring gave me a tour of the hangar and flight deck. I noticed an SBC4, with "CHAG" painted on the side, tied down on the hangar deck. At the time I didn't know this was the group commander's aircraft. The biplane's landing gear was damaged, its "flying wires" supporting the wings were broken, and the wings were drooping. I never heard an explanation, but I assumed that CHAG had wanted to make the first carrier landing on the *Hornet*. It must have been a lulu! You had to work at making a bad landing in the SBC4!

Several members of the Roundtable are descendents or other relatives of Midway veterans who were either killed during the battle or who passed on in later years. Among them is Troy Guillory, Jr., the son of VB-8 pilot Troy Guillory, who had been a squadron-mate to Clay Fisher and Roy Gee. In 2004, Troy (Jr.) forwarded to the Roundtable another anecdote concerning Commander Ring's piloting skills:

> While reading the transcript of an interview that author Bowen Weisheit had with my father in 1983, I came upon an interesting bit of trivia. After the *Hornet* was commissioned in 1941, it was evidently quite an honor to make the first landing on a carrier. The first landing (and first crash) aboard the ship was made by Stanhope C. Ring with Ensign Guillory in the back seat. This was done in Ensign Guillory's SBC4. The plan was that Ring was going to make the landing, get out of the plane, and send Ensign Guillory on his way. "High and fast" was Father's description of the approach. They caught a "late" wire, hit the barrier, and chopped it down.

The hard landing described by Ensign Guillory could certainly have caused the type of damage described by Fisher, giving cause to wonder if the two anecdotes resulted from the same occurrence. But there is reason to believe that they were two separate events: Fisher reported aboard the *Hornet* in September 1941, two months *before* it was commissioned. And Ensign Gillory's SBC4 would not have had "CHAG" painted on its fuselage, as was the case with the aircraft seen by Fisher. But any carrier pilot, including the best of them, can expect a less-than-perfect landing at some point in his career. If denting a couple of biplanes during training flights was all there was to cast doubt on Ring as an avia-tor, one could argue that the case had not been proven.

But there was more. In the last chapter, Roy Gee commented that Com-mander Ring "had his own navigation solution" for the *Hornet's* launch on June 4th, a solution that Gee described as greatly contrasting with the track computed by VB-8's pilots. And of course, Ring's chosen track had led the entire air group to a costly failure. Gee also related an earlier incident in which Ring became lost while leading a training flight in the Gulf of Mexico. A fellow VB-8 pilot, K. B. White, had described it in a letter to Bill Vickrey, which Gee shared with the Roundtable in 2003. Here's an excerpt from White's letter:

> In 1982 my wife Auriel and I visited Hawaii, and I've just begun reading one of the books we purchased at Pearl, *Miracle at Midway* by Gordon W. Prange. Reference is made to Ring's performance, raising some questions about his ability…I had my doubts, too. In fact, on our first group rendezvous in the Gulf of Mexico prior to leaving for the West Coast, group commander Ring had to be escorted back to the *Hornet* by Gus Widhelm, all in good weather. He scared me. To his credit, he looked like a naval officer; tall, hand-some, and erect. He wore his uniform well.

Gee gave us another recollection about Ring as a dive bomber pilot in this 2004 message to the Roundtable. He is quoting from a personal letter he'd sent to Bill Vickrey in 1988:

> I think Cdr. Ring paid little attention to details. A case in point: I flew with him on a mission on 5 June to attack a Japanese cruiser, and he failed to release his bomb during his dive bombing run. When he landed back aboard with his bomb, he said he pressed the button on the throttle handle, but the bomb wouldn't release. The button on the throttle handle was used to trigger the pilot's microphone while flying formation so that he could maintain proper position without taking his hand off the throttle. The bomb release was forward of the throttle handle. A separate emergency release was available for the center rack. This handle pulled a direct wire attachment to the bomb release mechanism of the center rack in case the normal bomb release was inoperable. Cdr. Ring could have easily dropped his bomb by using the emer-gency release, but he didn't even know it existed, let alone the handle's loca-tion.
>
> In any case, I lost all my respect for CHAG. He left us after the Battle of Midway, receiving the Navy Cross and quick promotions to captain and rear admiral.

In his letter to Vickrey, K. B. White suggested that Stanhope Ring had the appearance and bearing of a competent and respectable naval officer. Indeed, nothing here is intended to reflect upon him as anything less than that. His apparent shortcomings were confined to just one narrowly defined area, his intrinsic ability as an aviator. Unfortunately, that one area was his most important at the Battle of Midway.

Clay Fisher commented further on Ring's qualities as a naval officer in this 2005 letter to the Roundtable:

> My opinion about Stanhope Ring as a naval officer and a Naval Academy graduate: I considered him a product of the peacetime Navy who had to make adjustments to the wartime Navy. I thought he represented a lot of line officers who elected to become naval aviators not out of a strong desire to fly, but to enhance their careers.
>
> Most of us naval aviators entered flight training through the AVCAD program because we wanted to fly, and some wanted to escape the expected draft into the army. All naval aviators could be plotted on a "bell curve" and most of us would have been considered average to above average because of the fairly rigorous elimination of weaker student pilots.
>
> Most of the senior naval aviators in the *Hornet* air group were above average, experienced pilots and had demonstrated their leadership qualities to us junior pilots. Ring was an exception. He was a decent officer in general terms, but he did not exhibit the qualities of a skilled pilot and navigator.

Thus it was a generally decent officer but, in the opinion of his subordinates, an unskilled pilot and navigator who led the *Hornet* air group into battle on the morning of June 4, 1942. With scant enemy contact reports and poor or non-existent communications, navigation was everything to have any chance for success.

*   *   *   *

A Question of Direction

Nearly all of the familiar histories of the Battle of Midway tell a consistent version of the *Hornet* air group's flight on the morning of June 4th: in essence, Commander Ring is said to have led his squadrons toward the southwest upon launch, generally on a track similar to that taken by the *Enterprise* air group, which was a bearing of approximately 240 degrees true from the task force (see Figure 1). That course, 240 true, was purportedly predicted by Ring, with

Mitscher's support, to result in an intercept of the enemy carriers if they maintained the course and speed that had been reported by Howard Ady (see Chapter 1). Ring then launched on 240 degrees true but missed contacting the Japanese fleet because of an unpredicted turn they made toward the northeast. Lieutenant Commander Waldron, leading VT-8, supposedly knew the Japanese would turn and broke away from Ring toward the north where he and his squadron indeed found the enemy and eternal glory. Ring, it is said, then turned toward the south, thinking that he'd possibly arrived at the intercept point after the Japanese carriers had passed. With dwindling fuel, he then brought his planes back to the *Hornet* without sighting any enemy ships, but not before losing his entire fighter escort in the ocean due to empty tanks, plus three of VB-8's SBDs that vainly tried to make it to Midway.

It's no wonder that the familiar histories of the battle all relate the foregoing story because they're all mostly based on the same source, Captain Mitscher's official after-action report of the USS *Hornet* at Midway. Oddly, neither Ring as air group commander nor any of his squadrons submitted their own reports as required by naval regulations. Indeed, such after-action reports from the other air groups and squadrons engaged at Midway exist in abundance, including those from the *Enterprise*, the *Yorktown*, and from the atoll itself. But nothing survives from the *Hornet* save the singular report by its commanding officer, which until recent years has been taken at face value by all.

In spite of lacking support from other official sources, there are at least a few factors that tend to suggest that Mitscher's version of Ring's flight was accurate. George Gay, the sole survivor among the *Hornet's* VT-8 pilots, stated in his book that his squadron's course "was a constant 240 degrees." Additionally, he says that Waldron told him before launching that Ring "is going to take the whole bunch *down there*. [Emphasis added.] I'm going more to the north…"[1] *Down there* would be consistent with a course of 240 degrees true. Also, Clay Fisher told us in the previous chapter that…

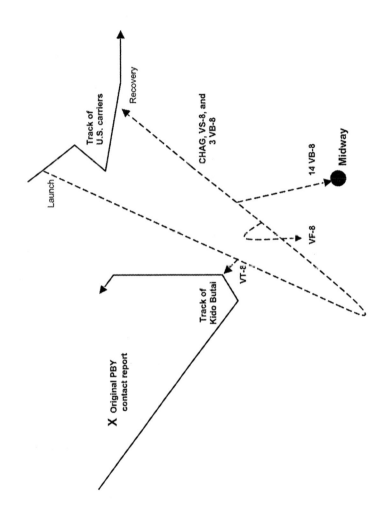

FIGURE 1. *Hornet* air group tracks according to the ship's official after-action report. This chart and Figures 2 and 3 are greatly simplified for clarity and are not to scale.

...the air group was operating under a radio silence doctrine until we would make contact with the enemy. The CHAG continued on our original *southwest* course [emphasis added] and gave me hand signals to form a scouting line...

So despite the strange paucity of after-action reports from Ring and his squadrons, there was never any particular reason to doubt Mitscher's tale of his air group's flight on June 4th. It was universally believed that the CHAG had dutifully following a logical southwesterly course to the enemy's expected location, just like the *Enterprise* and *Yorktown* squadrons, but had failed to sight the target because he simply made an unlucky choice in turning south at the end of his search, instead of north like VT-8. With supporting recollections like those of Gay and Fisher, the matter had remained completely devoid of controversy.

New Evidence

But that all changed one day nearly forty years after the battle. Two of the *Hornet's* VF-8 pilots were killed trying to ditch when their Wildcat fighters ran out of fuel. One of them, Ensign C. Markland Kelly, Jr., had been a college friend of a Marine Corps aerial navigation instructor named Bowen P. Weisheit. While examining a minor artifact from the Battle of Midway in 1981, Weisheit was puzzled. The object, from a PBY crew that had rescued four of Kelly's squadron mates, had inscribed upon it the latitude and longitude of the pickup point where the four survivors were found. Weisheit's problem was that the location recorded by the PBY's commander seemed to be very far removed from the spot where the *Hornet's* official after-action report says all the pilots had ditched—much *too* far. He consulted a chart of the area and was surprised to see that his friend Kelly had gone into the water *over a hundred a fifty miles* from of the position indicated by Mitscher.[2]

That caused Weisheit to wonder a great deal about his friend's death. Why didn't Kelly survive the ditching, and above all, why does on-scene evidence—the PBY artifact—show that he died at a location that is drastically different from that shown in the U.S. Navy's official record? Resolved to seek out the answers and equipped with the navigation skills to thoroughly analyze anything found, Weisheit then embarked on a crusade to learn every possible detail about the actual tracks flown by the *Hornet's* squadrons on the morning of June 4th at Midway.

It didn't take long for his quest to bring a positive result. Through extensive interviews with *Hornet* ship and air group veterans, Weisheit was stunned to learn that upon launch, Commander Ring had led his fifty-nine planes on a course of 265 degrees true. That was nearly *due west* of the ship, not southwest (course 240 degrees) toward the presumed location of the Japanese fleet, as had been universally accepted for over forty years. That meant that each of the *Hornet's* squadrons, including Kelly's VF-8 and the heroic torpedomen of VT-8 had flown a track that was substantially at odds with that portrayed in the official record and all of the familiar references (see Figure 2).

Testimonials

Among Weisheit's several veteran interviews, two were critical to establishing that Ring had flown a westerly course of 265 degrees upon launch. The first was with the ship's air operations officer during the battle, John G. Foster, who told Weisheit that the air group had flown nearly due west from the ship (due west would be 270 degrees true). The second was with Rear Admiral Walter F. Rodee, U.S. Navy (Retired), who had flown with VS-8 as its CO that morning. Weisheit published his notes from that interview in his book, *The Last Flight of Ensign C. Markland Kelly, Junior, USNR.* The following is the key excerpt:

Weisheit: "…do you think that Waldron did not take the course that was given to you, or did you not take the course?"

Rodee: "We took the given course…we took the bearing and course they gave us."

Weisheit: "You don't remember what it was?"

Rodee: "It was about…"

Weisheit: "Two-four-zero?"

Rodee: "No, it was about two-six-five."

Weisheit: "Two-six-five?"

Rodee: "Yeah, two-six-zero to two-six-five. It was almost due west."[3]

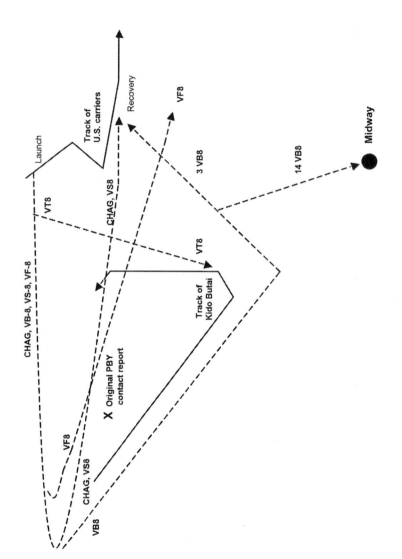

FIGURE 2. *Hornet* air group tracks as discovered by Major Bowen Weisheit.

It's noteworthy that Weisheit gave Rodee every chance to tell him that the air group had flown the time-honored 240 degree course, but the admiral knew better and wouldn't be swayed.

The appearance of the *C. Markland Kelly* book resulted in one of the Roundtable's lengthiest and most detailed deliberations. Weisheit findings, if accurate, would turn a major portion of the history of the Battle of Midway completely on its head. But were his discoveries factual? Did Ring actually take off from the *Hornet* in a direction that afforded no chance for finding the enemy carriers?

One of the Roundtable's veteran members provided very solid testimony that supported Weisheit's findings. Richard T. Woodson, a retired Navy chief petty officer, had been a radioman-gunner aboard one of the VS-8 SBDs on the morning flight, and he had observed VT-8 immediately after launch. He told us a little about it in March, 2004:

> About a half hour or so after we had all joined up in a wide scouting line, I observed VT-8 heading about 40 degrees to our port. I have no real idea of the true heading and I mentioned to Don Kirkpatrick, my pilot, about the new heading that Waldron had taken. Maybe this will help.

The direction that Waldron and VT-8 turned—left or right—when they broke away from the rest of the air group is the key to the entire debate. Note in Figure 1 that the traditional view had been that VT-8 broke to the *right* from Ring, heading toward the northwest in order to engage the enemy fleet. But in Figure 2 we see that in order to find the Japanese carriers, he had to break to the *left* if the air group had flown west from the *Hornet* rather than southwest. A turn to the left is exactly what Chief Woodson saw that morning, as well as several other air group veterans interviewed by Weisheit. *None* of the witnesses to VT-8's flight supported a break to the right when Waldron led them away from the air group, and there is no way he could have found the enemy fleet by breaking left from a southwesterly course of 240 degrees.

Midway's Beacon of Smoke

What, then, do we make of Clay Fisher's strongly-held view that Ring's course was more or less the same as that flown by the *Enterprise* air group? Did the CHAG head west instead of southwest because of deficient skills as a navigator? Here is what Fisher told the Roundtable about it in 2002:

I think the discussions about faulty navigation is just plain bunk! All the VS-8 and VB-8 pilots were pretty good navigators. We flew a lot of 200-mile search missions and never lost a pilot to poor navigation. Prior to the early morning flight of June 4th, we all read the last known position reports of the Japanese carrier task force off the information screen at the front of the ready room. A periodic flow of information came across that screen from the ship's navigator. All the ready rooms got the same information. We all plotted in the course to the Japanese carriers' location on our plotting boards.

Our three carriers were not so far apart that the obvious courses to the target for each squadron should have varied by more than a few degrees. After you got on course you just adjusted your directional gyro to your compass heading and occasionally readjusted the gyro. All Cdr. Ring had to do was fly the compass heading that had been determined. He did not use our ready rooms, so we had no way of knowing what course he plotted or intended to fly.

I sure don't think our course was 265 degrees. If we had flown 265 degrees, I don't see how the VB-8 SBDs would have made it to Midway.

Fisher, then, couldn't buy into a nearly due west heading of 265 degrees upon launch from the ship. He explained why in this 2004 letter to the Roundtable, having just completed a review of Weisheit's book:

> I have always maintained that I saw a large column of black smoke from Midway at about 0945 to 1000, or about 75 minutes after departing the *Hornet* around 0830. We had unlimited visibility and were flying above 14,000 feet, probably cruising at 145 knots while flying at least 170 miles. In *Miracle at Midway* by Gordon Prange, Lt. Cdr. McClusky, leading the *Enterprise* SBDs, reports "some of the pilots on the formation's far left could see smoke rolling up from the stricken base."[4] None of the Japanese carriers had been attacked at that time.

Fisher subsequently explained in a telephone interview that it was that black column of smoke from Midway that convinced him the *Hornet* air group could not have flown a track such as that postulated by Weisheit. Had he been that far removed from the atoll, he doesn't believe he would have noticed any smoke, since it had only been seen by pilots on the left, or Midway side of McClusky's formation. So the traditional view retains at least one significant adherent, despite compelling testimony to the contrary by the likes of Foster, Rodee, and Woodson.[5]

Then there is George Gay's account in his own book, *Sole Survivor*. If the *Hornet* air group's outbound course of 265 degrees true is to be accepted, why does Gay say that his squadron flew a constant 240 degrees? Weisheit has an answer for that, too. In Figure 2, note that Ring and his squadrons briefly flew together on a westbound course from the ship, then after about a half hour in the air, Waldron broke to the left on a new heading that then comprised the majority of his flight. Weisheit believes *that* is the segment of VT-8's sortie that Gay remembers, and he backs it up with detailed technical analysis of a clue in *Sole Survivor*. Gay said that, en route to the enemy fleet, the moon was centered over his engine cowling.[6] Weisheit calculated the true bearing of the moon on June 4, 1942 from the point north of Midway where Waldron turned his squadron to port, and established it as 234 degrees.[7] While that's not *exactly* 240 degrees, it's worth noting that Gay wrote his book in 1979, thirty-seven years after the battle, and the only references that he had to jog his memory at that late date were those familiar accounts based on Captain Mitscher's official report, all claiming a course of 240 degrees for the air group. It's no wonder that "two-four-zero" would thereby readily come to mind while Gay was trying to remember a compass reading plus a magnetic correction to a true bearing from thirty-seven years in the past.[8]

✳   ✳   ✳   ✳

Rationalizing a Westbound Course

So Commander Ring apparently led his squadrons on a very curious track, due west of the ship on a course that actually crossed the enemy carriers' path at a point *behind* their position reported by Howard Ady nearly four hours before the *Hornet* fliers got there. By that time, at an average speed of about twenty-five knots, Vice Admiral Nagumo and his four carriers would have been nearly a hundred miles away on their advance toward Midway. Thus, Ring's chosen course had no chance whatsoever of making contact with the Japanese strike force, leaving us to forever wonder what in the world he could have been thinking.

Noted naval aviation author John Lundstrom offered the Roundtable two plausible theories to explain Ring's mysterious course. The first, originally appearing in his 1984 book *The First Team*, is a suggestion that Ring might have been mindful of Howard Ady's original contact report of only *two* Japanese carriers. Knowing that the enemy was bringing at least four and as many as six of them to Midway, perhaps he was seeking those that were following the two in the lead that Ady had seen.[9] While that brings a measure of sanity to what otherwise seems an unfathomable decision, it's still a stretch to believe that elements of the

Japanese strike force would be trailing their leaders by four hours and a hundred miles. Their fleet carriers had done nothing like that at Coral Sea or Pearl Harbor, and the IJN was notorious for conforming to past practice. Hence it seems unlikely that they would do it at Midway.

Also, that theory runs up against George Gay's quotations from Waldron, although they are not supported by any documentary evidence and are dependent upon the quality of Gay's memory when he wrote his book. For example, Lundstrom told the author that when Gay quoted Waldron as saying Ring was going to take the whole air group "down there," that could have been an inadvertent but convenient distortion on Gay's part. Waldron may have said that the group commander was going "*out* there" if he'd learned that Ring was intending to head west. A check of Samuel Elliot Morison's history of the Pacific war or Walter Lord's *Incredible Victory* while composing his book could certainly have led Gay to think that Waldron must have said "*down* there," which he then duly recorded.

But Lundstrom subsequently developed an alternate theory that does not require any quibbling with Gay's account, although it does have its own significant stumbling block. Here is his idea, from a 2004 message to the Roundtable:

> My take on why Ring went west instead southwest is that he became disoriented. He had very little recent flying experience and was rusty at best. During the *Hornet's* shakedown cruise, he got the air group lost on a training flight and someone else had to guide them back to the ship.
>
> I believe the original intention on June 4th was for the group to go southwest like the *Enterprise* group. McClusky went on about 226 degrees to get between Midway and any possible Japanese advance and Lindsey [VT-6] who flew on 240 degrees alone. Waldron reacted to Ring moving west first by arguing and then breaking off to the left on his own to head southwest. Ring just kept going west out to 225 miles, long after the fighters broke off.
>
> Bowen Weisheit discovered this in the early 1980s when he researched the loss of his friend Mark Kelly. Bowen thinks Ring deliberately went west, but I don't think so.

This suggestion fits nicely with Clay Fisher's recollection that Ring's announced course was not especially different from that plotted by VB-8's pilots in their ready room prior to launch, namely, toward the southwest at approximately 240 degrees true. He had stated as much to the Roundtable shortly before Lundstrom's new theory appeared:

> I flew wing on the *Hornet's* air group commander. There were no navigational problems. We all had plotted in the enemy's estimated position and knew what course heading we would be flying. If CHAG had decided to fly a different course than what we plotted in our ready rooms, I would have been aware of the new course.[10]

The above scenario fits another Waldron quote from Gay, who said that he remembered his squadron commander's last words to him before takeoff: "Follow me! Don't think I'm lost, because I think those two [Japanese] forces will swing together north of where the group is headed. By the time they [the rest of the *Hornet* air group] locate the Japs, we should be there. I hope we aren't late."[11] *North of where the group is heading*—if that quote from Waldron is authentic, then he seems to have been telling Gay that "the group" was supposed to head more to the south, the traditional 240 degree course once again.

But as tidy as all that seems, Lundstrom's later theory has a large problem. In his interview with Weisheit, Admiral Rodee was definite that the *given* course was 265 degrees. It wasn't simply a navigational error on Ring's part. Rodee repeated it during a separate exchange with researcher James Sawruk, who had aided Lundstrom in the development of *The First Team*. Rodee indicated to Sawruk that he still knew some four decades after the battle that 265 degrees was the chosen course because he'd written it in his flight log, which he still had.[12] And of course, one can only accept Gay's quotation from Waldron as verbatim if nothing is allowed for errors of memory over a thirty-seven year span.

In any event, whether Ring's preferred course was consistent with what his pilots plotted or significantly different, the preponderance of testimony and evidence indicates that he did take a westerly course of approximately 265 degrees true from the *Hornet*, either by intent or through error. The result was a flight for each of his squadrons that grossly contrasts in nearly every important detail with the official and familiar account.

*   *   *   *

A Compass Error That Wasn't

In his book, Bowen Weisheit offered the opinion, backed up by apparently extensive documentation, that a fault in the *Hornet's* gyrocompass caused inaccurate signals to be transmitted by the ship's "YE" radio homing device. The YE system worked in concert with the special "ZB" radio receiver in each aircraft: a brief transmission containing a letter of the alphabet was sent in Morse code from a rotating directional antenna on the ship, with a different letter indicating that the antenna was, at that instant, pointing at a specific bearing relative to true north. A pilot hearing any particular letter on his ZB receiver could match it to a predetermined list, thus giving him the bearing from his aircraft's current position to the carrier. For example, if the letter "A" indicated the antenna was pointed toward 090 degrees true—due east—and that's the letter the pilot clearly heard in his headphones, then he knew he only had to fly the reciprocal of that bearing—270 degrees, or due west—in order to get back home.

The key to the system's reliability was synchronizing the rotating antenna to the ship's gyrocompass, which in turn had to be precisely calibrated. A gyrocompass error could cause the YE transmitter to send a letter code in the wrong direction, giving any pilot who relied on it a false bearing back to the carrier. Weisheit believed that he'd found evidence indicating that such an error existed in the *Hornet's* gyrocompass on June 4th, contributing to the loss of VF-8's fighters. Presumably, they failed to find TF 16 at least in part because they were following an erroneous YE bearing.

But the Roundtable's *Hornet* veterans did not support that notion. Clay Fisher was especially adamant that any fault with the ship's YE system would have been painfully noticed well before the battle:

> Weisheit states in his book on page 47 that "upon the *Hornet's* return from her shake-down cruise, the ship's navigation officer mentioned in his report that there had not been enough time to swing the magnetic compass. In the *Hornet's* report of the June 4th operation, the flight launch, flight recovery, and the flight attack course were reported as 20-30 degrees too high."[13]
>
> This seems strange to me because if the *Hornet's* compass was that far off, I probably would not be writing these comments. I flew ten 200-mile single plane searches off the *Hornet* prior to the BOM. After the BOM I flew another twenty-nine 200-mile searches. On a couple searches a very faint ZB signal enabled me to find the *Hornet*.
>
> The YE/ZB homing device was so simple and easy to use, I really don't understand why the VF-8 pilots had so much trouble. All they had to do was fly the magnetic compass course determined by the lettered sector. The sector letter radio signal would have become stronger as the distance was closed to the *Hornet*. I have come to the conclusion that the VF-8 pilots had the correct ZB letter sector and were actually very close to the *Hornet*. As an SBD pilot, if I identified a sector letter I knew, I definitely was not lost! I can only assume the VF-8 pilots just didn't trust their ZBs.

Fisher's point that he (and by extension, scores of other *Hornet* pilots flying hundreds of individual sorties) unfailingly got back to the ship each time through the proper use of the YE/ZB system is a strong indicator that nothing was wrong with it on June 4, 1942. Richard Woodson had offered the Roundtable a similar comment in 2003:

> The YE transmitter sent its signal on frequency of 43 mc/s, which was received on the ZB receiver from an approximately twelve-inch antenna on the underside of the SBDs, and converted through the RU receiver to something we could interpret. The coding used by *Hornet* was apparently accurate since I received a signal on the late afternoon [June 5th] intercept of an IJN destroyer and it got us back. That would seem to indicate the YE/ZB was good enough to get us home and not 30 degrees off as someone mentioned recently. I flew four flights with Don Kirkpatrick during the BOM and we never got lost. We used the YE/ZB several times during our long range search flights.

So while Weisheit seems to have clearly established that the air group flew a lengthy westerly track from the *Hornet* rather than the shorter southwest course claimed in the official record, that alone seems to have been the primary problem for VF-8 and his friend Ensign Kelly, rather than anything related to the ship's homing system. Any problems with the YE/ZB would appear to reside aboard the squadron's F4Fs—most likely incorrect use or interpretation on the part of the pilots—rather than in the ship's equipment. The multitude of safe landings by Fisher, Woodson, and their many fellow airmen allow no other conclusion.

*   *   *   *

Naval Careers at Stake

In the sorrowful saga of the *Hornet* air group's opening sortie at the Battle of Midway, one enigma remains: if multiple respected witnesses both in the planes and aboard the ship knew that Ring had departed on a westerly course of 265 degrees true rather than the plotted 240, why in the world does the ship's after-action report say that nothing like that occurred? The inference by some is that Captain Mitscher, then a new selectee for rear admiral, viewed Ring's debacle on the morning of June 4th as reflecting poorly on his own judgment and performance, since he had been a primary participant with the CHAG during the pre-launch planning. The ship's after-action report, then, was simply a cover-up for both Mitscher as well as his friend Ring. The mysterious absence of *required* after-action reports from Ring himself as well as all of his subordinate squadrons lends strong credence to that view. Professor Alvin Kernan provided the Round-table with an in-depth analysis of the situation in the following letter from May 2004. In it he articulates a set of strongly held beliefs that have been frequently heard from veteran and historian alike:

> Mitscher, the commanding officer of the *Hornet*, thought for a time that his career was over, so badly had his air group performed. Commander Stanhope Ring, the actual leader of the air group, might well have seen himself commanding a dry dock somewhere out in the boondocks. After all, how can one explain such a big-time mistake that had thrown away almost one-third of the American strike force in what came to be known as "the flight to nowhere?"
>
> The answer is that lifetime naval careers were at stake, and a cover-up began almost immediately after the battle. After-action reports were explicitly required, on the standard Navy form dedicated to the purpose: "(a) to be filled out by the unit commander immediately upon landing after each action or operation in contact with the enemy, and (b) do not 'gun deck' the report. If data cannot be estimated with reasonable accuracy, enter a dash in space for which no data is available."[14]
>
> But there were no reports for Ring's *Hornet* air group, nor for Scouting 8, Bombing 8, or Fighting 8. So Marc Mitscher's after-action report for the entire ship, the *Hornet*, became the official document describing what had happened during the Battle of Midway. His brief report says correctly that the position of the enemy at the time of launch was "155 miles distant, bearing 239 degrees T from this task force." It lets readers think, however, that the unspecified "prescribed bearing" that Ring took corresponded to a direct line to the enemy's assumed course. The report goes on to say that the *Hornet* planes flew *south* of the Japanese carriers, for the enemy had "reversed his course and started his retirement."
>
> The report says that a message was received about the Japanese change in course, but *Hornet* "did not break radio silence to report this to the planes." Unaware of the enemy change in course, Mitscher's report goes on, Ring had flown south of the target and made the mistake of searching still farther to the south when he crossed the point where he expected to encounter Nagumo. Had Ring "turned north, contact would probably have been made," Mitscher concludes.
>
> The effect of the report was to transform Ring's failure into an understandable mistake for which no apologies need be made. "The strike flew south of the Japanese, (but) the torpedo planes flew a different course to the enemy." A map attached to Mitscher's report appears to substantiate that Ring flew south of the Japanese on a course of about 240 degrees, that he turned towards Midway in a search, and then returned to the ship. Why the fighters would have taken the course indicated on this map when they were low on gas is left as anyone's guess.[15]

Mitscher's commander, Rear Admiral Raymond Spruance, did not approve of the way the *Hornet* had conducted the battle or written its action report. At the beginning of his own report to CINCPAC, he casts doubt on Mitscher's accuracy with unusual frankness: "Where discrepancies exist between *Enterprise* and *Hornet* reports, the *Enterprise* report should be taken as the more accurate." But the Mitscher report and map were not questioned, at least openly, and in time came to stand as the official representations of the flight of the *Hornet* air group on the morning of June 4th.

Did Mitscher personally invent the story told by his report and its map? Not likely. He and Ring had served together at the Bureau of Aeronautics in the 1930s, and he was known for his loyalty to his officers. After the BOM, he continued to support his old friend Ring, not only recommending him for his Navy Cross but choosing him as his chief of staff in patrol wings he commanded after Midway. But his Midway report was surely put together by his officers, and there had to have been a lot of collusion, or, more likely, quiet agreements among a network of academy graduates who saw their careers as the paramount consideration. But Mitscher signed the report, and he was responsible for all that was in it. Whether he ordered the cover-up or not, he had to have known what was going on.

In 1947, a Naval War College strategic and tactical analysis of the Battle of Midway called attention to the *Hornet* air group's failure to sight the enemy fleet and turn *north* (so they accepted Mitscher's report). The report blamed Mitscher only to the extent that "the commanding officer should ensure that flight leaders are properly briefed." But by then Mitscher had been canonized as *The Magnificent Mitscher* for his performance as the commander of fast carrier forces later in the war.

*   *   *   *

The Traditional View Persists

Should Bowen Weisheit's findings be taken seriously among the professional cadres of the U.S. Navy? It would seem that that has happened in large measure. Rear Adm. C. A. "Mark" Hill, Jr., a World War II submarine veteran who ultimately served as an Assistant Chief of Naval Operations, wrote a review of Weisheit's *Kelly* book for *Wings of Gold* magazine, the journal of the Association of Naval Aviation. The review was published a few months after the appearance of the book's first edition in 1993, and in it Hill introduced Weisheit's revelations in these terms:

Once tactical decisions in major battles are documented as part of an offi-cial history and become a matter of folklore, it is not only difficult to change the record but often equally difficult for professionals to accept that change.

With that lead-in, Hill went on to outline Stanhope Ring's course as has been reported down through the decades, then contrasted it with a summary of Weisheit's discovery, focusing particularly on the testimony of respected naval aviators like Admiral Rodee. He summarized his review with these comments:

Indeed, it is the outcome of [Weisheit's] research that makes this short book such a vital supplement to what we have known or believed about per-haps the most significant sea fight of this century…In the words of English philosopher Josh Billings, "it's not that we don't know the truth; it's that we know it so poorly." But to avoid falling prey to the corollary dictum that "his-tory is a fable agreed upon," every Naval Aviator, every Naval Officer who served in WWII and every student of Naval History should have Bowen Weisheit's little book in his library.[16]

Hill's article in *Wings of Gold* soon came to the attention of former Chairman of the Joint Chiefs of Staff, Admiral Thomas H. Moorer, himself a World War II Navy pilot, who was deeply impressed. The admiral invited Weisheit for a per-sonal interview to discuss the book, and the visit stretched to two hours. He reported that during the interview Moorer took one look at the book and told him, "oh, the Navy hadn't gotten [a] thing right!" The admiral then set about to ensure that all USN libraries got a copy, with the first order going to the U.S. Naval War College.[17]

Even so, the traditional view of the *Hornet* air group's errant flight at Midway persists in professional writings about the battle. A significant example is found in Capt. Bruce R. Linder's 1999 article in the U.S. Naval Institute's *Proceedings* on the subject of a personal letter written by Ring in 1946, then filed away and not discovered until more than fifty years later. The letter is a detailed summary of Ring's recollections of his command decisions and the resulting developments for his air group at the BOM, and as one would expect, it parrots the *Hornet's* official after-action report with regard to the course he flew on the morning of June 4th. While Captain Linder's analysis of the letter is otherwise thorough and articulate, he passively accepts Ring's explanation of his course without challenge, despite the fact that Weisheit's countering argument had then been known and highly respected in much of the naval air community for at least six years.[18]

Thus, it seems that the matter will never be resolved with finality as long as Walter Lord and Gordon Prange's best-sellers continue to be the general public's main window to the Battle of Midway and as long as Bowen Weisheit's *Kelly* book simply gathers dust on forgotten library shelves.

CHAPTER 9

▼

MIDWAY WAS BECKONING

A True Hero of Midway

While the principal focus on the Battle of Midway has always been on the atoll and the three U.S. carriers and their air groups, there were thousands more American sailors and airmen serving on the many cruisers and destroyers screening Task Force 16 and 17, as well as aboard numerous submarines and other supporting vessels. Combat action around those ships was often no less arduous than that experienced by the defenders of the atoll, the embattled crew of the *York-town*, or the gallant airmen who braved Zeros and flak over the enemy fleet. Destroyermen suffered occasional casualties and damage to their ships by the torrent of AA fire from the task force that eventually had to fall to the surface, sometimes hitting an unintended target. Submarines—most notably the *Nautilus*—courted violent death in vain attempts to attack the enemy carriers with unreliable torpedoes while dodging Japanese depth charges. Crewmen from the destroyers and cruisers sometimes went beyond the call of duty in rescuing badly wounded survivors from the *Yorktown* when it was abandoned on June 4th, and from both the *Yorktown* and the *Hammann* when those ships were torpedoed two days later.

The heroism of Seaman First Class Art Lewis particularly comes to mind. Lewis, an athletic eighteen year-old, dove into the ocean without a life jacket from the USS *Balch*, dragging buoyed lines behind him that he hauled out as far as four hundred yards from the ship, thereby saving several men who otherwise would have drowned. Tom Cheek was a witness to the daring rescues performed by Lewis and a shipmate, as mentioned in Chapter 6. The seaman's courage is underscored by the fact that he knew as he dove in that his ship might have to get underway at any moment if another air attack developed or if a Japanese submarine should be detected. In that case, Lewis would have been left behind in the water and could not have been expected to survive. Such were the tales of many of the victors of Midway that, for the most part, have never before been told.[1]

✳   ✳   ✳   ✳

Loss of USS Hammann

The Battle of Midway included both triumphs and tragedies, both legendary and unheralded, in the air, on the atoll, and aboard the ships. The sacrifice of the torpedo squadrons is paramount among the tragedies due to the bitter loss of nearly all of their airmen and planes in desperate attacks against well-defended targets. Somewhat less renown but equally tragic in terms of lives lost was the torpedoing of the destroyer USS *Hammann* on June 6th, as it was tied up alongside the *Yorktown* to provide electrical power for a gradually succeeding salvage effort aboard the carrier. Japanese submarine *I-168* hit the *Yorktown* with two of four torpedoes fired at her and a third caught the *Hammann* amidships, tearing the small vessel in half and sinking it in a matter of minutes.

Aboard the *Hammann* that day was Fireman First Class Elmer Jones, who joined the Battle of Midway Roundtable in 2001, bringing with him a gripping saga of survival. Bill Price forwarded it to the members in serial fashion over a two-week period, and it was subsequently compiled into a single document for the Roundtable's web site. Here is Jones' story:

> I did not enjoy boot camp. Although I did not particularly hate it, I certainly did not like getting up at 0400 to take down my hammock and go to the basement to scrub it. We had to do this once a week. After I got aboard ship, I recognized how important cleanliness was. When you have that many men in close proximity, it's a primary concern to all. If memory serves me right, we had twelve weeks training, and then transferred to the outgoing unit. They put a list of the ships available on the bulletin board and lined us up alphabetically and told us to pick what ship we wanted. There were four of us who had become good friends and wanted to stay together. Three wanted to go on a big ship, but I wanted a destroyer. So I said if there is a big ship left when we get up there, I'll take it with you, but if there isn't you'll all pick the *Hammann*. I won.
>
> In May 1940 we were sent to the Norfolk Navy Yard to meet our ship. We had to take a ferry across the bay and after we got off and were waiting for the

bus, I told Marshall Jones, "let's get off this floating dock." He looked at me kind of funny and explained that we were standing on a concrete pier. It felt to me like I was just floating up and down, and by the time we got to the base I was so seasick I could not eat supper. I thought, *my god, I signed up for six years of this?*

When we got aboard ship, my first watch was lookout on the bridge, and I stood there with the sea air striking me in the face and thinking *this is not too bad after all.* And then I suddenly vomited! I turned my face seaward and it went all over a ship's boat directly below. I bet the seaman who had that boat as a cleaning station would have killed me if he had known who did it. After that I had very little seasickness.

The Black Gang

Our first foreign port was Guantanamo, Cuba. In peacetime the Navy rigged awnings over the deck when docked or anchored in the tropics. The bos'n's mate wanted to teach us recruits who was boss and he was giving us all a bad time. I looked back aft and there was a bunch of men flaked out under the awnings we had put up. I asked one of the older men, "who are those guys laying down back there?" He told me that they were the *black gang,* or the below-decks engineers. They did not do topside work in the tropics except in an emergency. That night I met an old chief machinist's mate on deck and asked him how to get into the black gang. He told me I was talking to the right man. He wanted four recruits to transfer in, so I got my three buddies and we all went to the engine and fire rooms. (Understand, I am not lazy. I just didn't like to rig awnings!)

The North Atlantic

The north Atlantic was the most horrendous physical duty of my six years in the Navy. Also, it was the only time I even considered missing the ship intentionally. When they told us we had to make another trip to Iceland, most of us would have given anything not to have gone. Anything you did on topside, you risked your life. You could not eat or sleep in a normal manner. You had to strap yourself in your bunk. On the mess deck, they sometimes just strapped large pans of boiled potatoes, beef, and bread on the tables and we would walk by to grab some bread and meat for a sandwich, plus a cold potato to go. You then looked for someplace to brace yourself while you ate.

In the engine room on the centerline of the ship is an instrument that records the ship's roll. Once we went over to sixty-nine degrees. When we got back to the Boston Navy Yard, they noticed the sixty-nine degree reading and said that it was impossible. If you did that, you'd never get back up. We did.

The men in the fire room said we dipped water in the stack. It was certainly not a pleasure cruise.

Few people knew that we were engaged in a sea war with German submarines back then. Under the "rules" at that time, we could take convoys over to England, but as long as we did not go within a set distance from shore, the German subs would not fire at U.S. Navy ships. But when we got to Iceland, I believe it was the USS *Kearny* I saw there with a hole in her side from a torpedo.

Into the Pacific

Everyone was rather apprehensive about entering the war zone in the Pacific. It was certainly a new experience for all of us. It was like on-the-job training, except that if you didn't do your job right you might all die. I really thought we would go right out, hunt down the enemy and slug it out. I had no conception of how much jockeying for a favorable position they had to do, and how important that would be for the pilots who had to find the enemy and then wonder if they had enough gas to make it back. It seemed like we sailed around day after day doing nothing but drills and staying alert. We set a record for 117 continuous days underway.

We would take oil from a tanker at sea and sometimes we'd even get mail. I was glad when we would go alongside a British supply ship, because they would usually give us honey. The cooks would then make biscuits; a real treat. But when they gave us a bunch of mutton I could have shot them! There was even a story going around that General MacArthur had a sheep ranch in Australia and we were required to use so much mutton. When the cooks made mutton stew, I'd usually grab some Spam and bread and take it to the engine room.

The Coral Sea

My battle station was on the lower deck on pump watch. I saw nothing that went on topside. It's hard to be a coward on a ship. A destroyer is only 327 feet long so you can't run anywhere; you just stay on your station and sweat a lot more than usual. You soon developed an attitude that the only thing you can do is your particular job and you hope everyone else does his. If any man fails to do his task, it can cost the ship and many lives.

After the battle was over I went down and went to bed. The *Lexington* had been badly damaged, but they made some repairs and I believe were making fifteen knots. I had just gotten to sleep when someone woke me up and asked me if I wanted to see the *Lexington* go down. I thought he was kidding, but went topside and there it was, a mass of flames. They were abandoning ship and we had a boat in the water to pick up survivors. If I remember right, we lost that boat and its crew. The destroyer *Morris* was in close to the carrier, and when planes started exploding they backed out so fast it tore a section of the bridge off. The *Hammann* then moved in close and continued to pick up survivors.

After the battle we were all low on oil and the Japs had sunk our tanker, so we had to lay in port at the Tonga Islands to wait for another tanker. After we had refueled and headed for Pearl, we knew the *Yorktown* had been badly damaged so we figured we would all get a nice long rest. However, we thought it odd that they brought some engineers out to meet the *Yorktown* while it was still underway for Pearl. Midway was beckoning.

Agony at Midway

We were reluctant about going out to the Midway area. We knew something big was about to happen but they didn't tell us what it was until after we got underway. It was still like on-the-job training for us. The Japs had done some of this before, but we had not. It seemed to me that one of the most tragic mistakes was not really testing our torpedoes. I remember we would put a dummy warhead on them, and then we'd retrieve them with a boat after they were fired. We never really gave them a true test. I believe at the time they said they cost $12,500. That would have been a pittance compared to the value of a real test.

At my battle station below decks, the only thing that made you aware of the battle was the frenzy of speed. If their bombs missed the carrier and we had a near miss, you might feel the jar. We were elated when we heard the results of the battle. I was on the 1JV phones, which was the communication circuit between the bridge and the engine room, and what little I could hear during the battle was rather discouraging. But it was hard to believe the final reports.

When they passed the word on *Yorktown* to abandon ship, we pulled in close to pick up the survivors. I understand that the carrier's skipper, Captain Buckmaster caught a lot of criticism for abandoning ship too soon. Monday morning quarterbacking is awfully easy, but with the number of lives involved and the condition of the ship, I thought he made the right decision. After all, less than a month before we saw what developed with the *Lexington*, which according to what I'd seen was abandoned in better shape than the *Yorktown*.

Commander True, *Hammann*'s skipper, gathered some of the *Yorktown*'s men that we'd picked up to go back aboard the carrier to see if they could save it. *Hammann* tied up to the injured ship so we could furnish electric power and fire hoses to fight the fires that were still burning. When the *Hammann* was torpedoed, that's why we sank so fast: with all those cables and hoses passing through open hatches and doors, we had no watertight integrity whatever. I have read that we sank anywhere from ninety seconds to four minutes. I have always said it was U.S. Navy peacetime regulations that sank the *Hammann*.

The Navy had a regulation that if you were dead in the water for so long and it was not practical to jack the main engines by hand, then you must close the main bulkhead steam stop and engage the mechanical jacking gear. Now this was fine in peacetime so that you didn't warp the main turbines, but it should have been ignored at Midway.

All morning I had manned the foam generator to fight fire on the *Yorktown*. We had a twin cartridge unit in order to switch back and fourth to replace one cartridge while the other was being expended. The crew on the 0800-1200 morning watch was there and I remember the chief of the watch was just pacing back and forth with an agitated look on his face, frequently glancing at the still open steam stop. I then saw something hard to believe. Enlisted men were never to touch a commissioned officer and vice-versa, but the engineer, Mr. Ray, walked around in front of the chief, took him by the shoulders, looked him right in the eye and said "Chief, settle down. There is nothing to worry about. If anything should happen, there's a tug that can pull us out of here at a moment's notice." I do not believe Mr. Ray saw me there or he would have called the chief to one side first. The chief did not want to close that bulkhead steam stop. I thought Mr. Ray was correct. I felt just as safe as if I was standing out in the middle of a Kansas wheat field. Within six hours Mr. Ray was dead. The next time I saw the chief he was sitting in a bar called "The Lodge" at the corner of Turk and Larkin street in San Francisco and he was wearing a warrant officer's uniform.

Torpedo Strike

I still say if *Hammann* had been on that picket line, we would have picked up that submarine. Our sonarmen were really good. I have not heard to this day a satisfactory explanation why it was not detected. We never knew the sub was there until they saw the wake of the torpedoes. I have read that the Jap commander said he got inside the picket line, was too close and had to go out and come in again. I will have to give him a "G" for guts. It should never have happened.

I had the 1600 to 2000 watch and had been on pump watch on the lower deck about ten minutes when I heard the 20 mm. guns firing and thought, *my god, is it an air raid?* I thought sure there were no more enemy carriers in the area. The bridge rang up "emergency astern" on the engine order telegraph, but of course there was no steam. At that moment a torpedo hit and things flew everywhere. It was instant darkness, the generators were probably thrown out of alignment and stopped immediately. I am sure there was a second torpedo hit, or one that went off underneath *Hammann* and that's probably what broke the keel. I don't remember hearing abandon ship; it was obvious that we'd have to. They always said wear your life jacket at all times, but few if any did. I always hung mine on the hand rail and said I would grab it as I went up the ladder. Didn't happen. When I got topside it suddenly occurred to me I had no life jacket. I saw a great big black lump on the deck and it dawned on me that it was the life jackets that the *Yorktown* survivors had left there. They were completely covered with old black oil from our ruptured fuel oil tanks. I rammed my hand into the mess as far as I could and pulled one out. Saints be praised, it was a good one.

I started aft and went from port to starboard at midship, and this put me directly under our nest of torpedo tubes. Now, I knew next to nothing about them but there was a cable that ran from the torpedo back to the tube. I asked a torpedoman what that was for, and he told me that when a torpedo is fired, the cable pulls a metal strip out of the torpedo, which arms it. All the cables had been pulled. The torpedo motors were running wide open and made a hell of a noise, and I thought if they had magnetic warheads they could go off any time.

I ran for the stern and it was already rising out of the water. I saw a torpedoman who was checking the safety settings on the depth charges. I jumped. I will never be able to describe the feeling at that time. If you jump into the ocean, the ship could suck you down or if it blew up it would probably kill you, but if you ride the ship down you knew damn well you were dead. It did not take long to decide. Four of us jumped at the same time. The ship had started sliding bow first and we all yelled for the torpedoman to jump, but it was too late. At about that instant there was a terrific explosion. Great walls of water and fuel oil rolled over us and about the time you caught your breath and wiped the oil out of your eyes another wave would hit you. I nearly drowned. I remember saying to myself, *Mildred, your little brother will never be twenty-two.* Mildred was my older sister. My birthday was June 7th, and someone was trying to kill me on the 6th.

Rescue

One of the men near me in the water said that I had blood running out of my nose, ears, and mouth. I told him, "so what, you have too." I finally got ahold of a raft and hung on until the USS *Benham* picked us up. The *Benham* had rigged cargo nets over the side for us to climb aboard. Now, a rope cargo net is not the easiest thing to climb when you're in good condition, which I obviously wasn't. I made it almost to the top and just gave out. Another *Hammann* fireman, Carl Hunstein, pulled me aboard and laid me down by the fire room hatch, then sat down on the other side. The next day I asked someone where Carl was, and they told me he was dead. I said that I knew better, because he'd saved me from falling back into the ocean while trying to get aboard. Apparently, he immediately thereafter just sat down and died of his injuries.

I was placed on a stretcher, and noticed that the *Benham's* crew dumping dead bodies over the side. When they were ready to send one over, they would blow a whistle and everyone was supposed to come to attention. My stretcher bearers set me down right in line with the dead bodies. I let them know I was still alive!

The *Benham* went up to flank speed upon departing for Pearl Harbor, and when you do that on a destroyer the crews' quarters really shake. They thought the main thing was to get us to the hospital, but finally a doctor asked the *Benham's* captain to slow down because the vibration was killing the men. The doctors had no experience with the kinds of injuries we had sustained, so they opened up one of the dead men in order to see what they were dealing with. They said their intestines looked like they had been shot with buckshot and were full of holes. One of the injured men gave his keys to another sailor and told him if they didn't do something for him soon, he was going to jump over the side. The next morning at roll call, he wasn't there.

A Destroyer By Choice

When we got to Pearl, Admiral Nimitz was there to greet us. They sent me up to a mobile hospital called the Red Hill, and I was there about two weeks. Then, it was back to Naval Station Treasure Island (in San Francisco Bay) for reassignment. There was a new destroyer ready to go into commission, and they said all who wanted to stay together could go aboard. Our new ship was the USS *Gansevoort*, DD-608.[2]

✳   ✳   ✳   ✳

Cruiser Scout

In Chapter 3 we read of Ralph Wilhelm's experiences at the Battle of Coral Sea, as recorded in the detailed journal that he kept while serving as a SOC pilot on USS *Portland* until August 1942. The journal is equally loquacious on the details of the Battle of Midway, from his perspective aboard one of Task Force 17's heavy cruisers. Wilhelm's writings also provide a uniquely human element to the story that you don't find in the history books. He takes up his narrative here on the morning before the battle, June 3rd:

Wednesday, 3 June, 5th Day at Sea. Byron had the dawn patrol. Al and I had the mid-day, and Mike the evening patrol. This morning about 0900 we received word that Dutch harbor, Alaska had been bombed at 0600 by the Japs. A second report came in later that they had received a second attack at 1030.[3] It also said that there were four bombers and fifteen fighters, which doesn't sound right. I hope the army bombed their carrier or whatever they had.

At the time of the attack we were about 350 miles north of Midway, steaming north. Shortly after, we turned south and are now heading for a point 200 miles north of Midway, at which we should arrive at 0600 tomorrow morning. Two orders of the day for tomorrow have been printed this evening. The first said that the Japs were expected to attempt the taking of Midway today, tonight, or tomorrow. About a half hour after it was printed, the executive officer came down and personally helped gather them all up. Evidently, the captain didn't like the paragraph mentioning Midway because they were reprinted with those few lines deleted. The commander told Bob that possibly if they did get in a fight, we would be told to shift for ourselves and attempt to fly to Pearl, 1200 miles away, by refueling at French Frigate Shoals along the way. To be on the safe side, we each made a chart of the islands between Pearl and Midway. I also have my spare laundry bag ready for taking with four canteens of water, five emergency rations, and a flashlight. Scuttlebutt has it that the Japs have four carriers and a large occupation force out here somewhere.

I bought a Bulova watch today to replace the one I lost in Pearl when I dove in the water. I also got a new wallet, a Shavemaster electric razor, and two bottles of perfume. I wrote Kay an anniversary letter and will send some perfume the next time mail leaves. [4]

Thursday, 4 June, 6th Day at Sea. At about 0900, the fighters on patrol sighted a submarine. They machine gunned it and a DD depth charged it; they think it was sunk. At 1000 we heard that two CVs and two BBs were sighted 180 miles off Midway Island and about 240 miles from us. The island had been bombed at this time, evidently from these carriers. The Army reported another force of CAs, DDs, and ten transports to the south of Midway, evidently waiting until it had been bombed by the carriers before they attempted to land troops. The Army has been bombing the Jap forces since last night and this morning claimed to have already damaged a carrier, set a battleship on fire, and sank a transport. [5]

We recovered our two planes at 1130. The remaining flights were called off, so I didn't fly today. We were on an alert all day so had only sandwiches for lunch. At about 1400 the 17 SBDs returned to the *Yorktown* and reported that they had sunk an enemy carrier. At 1415, as our SBDs were circling the carrier to land, it all started. At first I saw the CV challenging some bogeys. Then about five miles out on the beam of the formation I could see many dog-fights going on between our fighters and the Jap planes. I saw seven planes shot down in flames before the ships were bombed. Three pilots bailed out. Then all hell broke loose again and the Jap dive bombers made their attack. Only about eight got through after our fighters finished with them but that was drastic for the *Yorktown*. It looked like one bomb went right down her stack. A few near misses fell around one of the DDs. It seemed to last about ten minutes and then there were hardly any planes in sight.

The *Yorktown* was smoking badly and looked just about like the *Lexington* looked a month ago before she sank. Task Force 16 sent over the *Vincennes*, *Pensacola*, and two DDs to help us. We continued to run in circles around the carrier while they tried to put out the fire. Two SBDs made crash landings in the water when they ran out of gas and were picked up by a couple of the ships. About 1600 the carrier was able to put out the fire and she looked all right again except she could only make 20 knots and had to steer with her engines because a near miss on her stern probably damaged her rudder. We made all preparations to take her in tow but we didn't have to.

About 1630 we received a message from the *Yorktown* to "prepare to repel air attack." The CV launched about seven fighters and then the Jap torpedo planes came in sight. There were about seven that came straight in and seemed to fly in formation. They flew for the carrier and dropped their fish. We put up a tremendous barrage, even firing the eight-inch turrets, but most of them got through. The fighters jumped on them afterwards and I don't think many got away.

The *Yorktown* abandoned ship shortly after the attack and the survivors were picked up by the DDs. One of the destroyers was going to come alongside and transfer survivors to us, but just as soon as one line was thrown over, they were told to cast it off. About 1900 when everyone was taken off the *Yorktown*, we all turned east and left her sitting there alone, looking as though she would roll over any minute. An hour later the *Enterprise* and a few other ships came in sight. She sent us a message that the *Hornet* was thirty miles east of her and that both of their air groups were out after the fourth enemy carrier. That news sounded good because we then knew that the Japs were receiving more damage than they had given us.

The destroyers transferred some of their injured to us this evening, after dark, for medical treatment. This is a big battle and should last for many days yet. Today should go down in history.

Friday, 5 June, 7th Day at Sea. The boss and I had the dawn inner air patrol from 0600 until 1100. At about 0830 the DDs took turns coming alongside and transferred 1550 survivors from the *Yorktown* to us. We also fueled them. The *Astoria* has the admiral and his staff aboard and this afternoon they departed with four DDs to go back and try to help salvaging the *Yorktown*.[6] There are quite a few officers aboard that I know very well. Lt. Mead is also here. McCarthy and a couple more *Enterprise* pilots are also here because they couldn't find their own carrier so came back to the *Yorktown*. Mac was the fellow I saw make the forced landing in the SBD. He hit the dashboard so hard he had his head bandaged up.

The *Yorktown* pilots confirm the report that my class made Lt.(jg), so now I have to get the dispatch aboard so I can start getting paid.

There are sure a lot of people on here. Two fellows are sleeping on the deck in my room. They say that only two of the twelve TBDs sent out ever returned.

We started steaming towards Oahu at twenty-five knots this evening because we are to meet the submarine tender *Fulton* tomorrow and transfer the survivors to her for transportation to Pearl. That means we won't go in. Task Force 16 is still engaging the enemy.

Saturday, 6 June, 8th Day at Sea. At 1300 we met a tug which was on its way to help tow in the *Yorktown*. About 1400 the *Fulton* came alongside and we commenced transferring the survivors. They rigged three "trolley cars" and sent them over two in the basket.

I typed out a memo to the communications officer of the *Fulton* and asked him to please send over a copy of the dispatch concerning my promotion. This he did, so now all I have to do is get the captain to swear me in. He has been pretty busy tonight so will get him tomorrow.

The stretcher cases were hoisted over to the *Fulton* by cranes. About 2000, when we had only ten more men to transfer on stretchers, the DDs got a sound contact and we cut the lines to the *Fulton* and the ships scattered. After dark we transferred the remaining men in a motor launch.

We are to rendezvous with the *Astoria* and the *Platte* in the morning so we can fuel. The scuttlebutt is that we are to join the *Saratoga* when she gets here in a couple of days. The *Yorktown* is supposed to have received a couple of fish from a submarine, which righted her a little bit.

I wrote to Kay and had McCarthy mail it for me.

Sunday, 7 June, 9th Day at Sea. Well, today I made lieutenant (j.g.) and my pay and allowances jump up from $264.25 to $371.01 per month.

Al and I were to have the dawn patrol but as it turned out, I was the only one to fly. About 0600, just at sunrise, quite a number of people sighted a yellow flare a couple miles behind us. The *Morris* was sent back and also I was catapulted to try to locate its source. I searched for an hour and a half but couldn't see a thing. I was hoping I might see a lost pilot in a life raft but I believe it must have been a submarine because the emergency recognition for subs this morning was a yellow flare. When I returned we had joined the other ships and the tanker was alongside us. Two *Astoria* planes were up for the inner air patrol so I was recovered.

I took the oath of acceptance for lieutenant (j.g.) from the captain at about 1630. Then, this evening, I bought two boxes of cigars and passed them out in the wardroom and warrant officers' mess for dinner, and to the men in the division.

We are supposed to meet the *Saratoga* in the morning. We got the news today that Dutch Harbor had been attacked again yesterday and that the *Hammann* was sunk by a submarine yesterday.[7] The good news of the day was 4 CVs sunk, 1 damaged, 1 BB sunk, 2 badly damaged (one of which was probably sunk), 1 CA sunk in 15 seconds by two 1600 lb. bombs from an Army bomber, 4 badly damaged, and many transports and destroyers sunk or damaged.[8] There are many enemy subs in this area, so we might go somewhere else; where to, I don't know. We are on course 130 degrees, which is toward Pearl.[9]

CHAPTER 10

▼

FINDING KIDO BUTAI

The Fog of War

Nothing is more prominent in the lore of the Battle of Midway than the gripping saga of Torpedo Squadron 8, the first element of the U.S. task forces to arrive over the Japanese carriers. VT-8's story has all of the drama that a Hollywood screenwriter could ever want: its charismatic leader, John Waldron (who even resembled John Wayne to a remarkable degree), the squadron's reportedly grueling training regimen, Waldron's emotional disagreement with his commander over tactics before the battle, and the squadron's desperate, gallant fight in the face of impossible odds, bringing forth comparisons to the Alamo, the Charge of the Light Brigade, and Custer at the Little Big Horn. It's only natural, then, that review and analysis of Waldron and his squadron would also be frequent and detailed on the Roundtable, as you have found in other chapters.

One of the interesting elements of the VT-8 story is the fact that, as George Gay described it, Waldron purportedly led his planes "just as straight to the Jap fleet as if he'd had a string tied to them."[1] On the other hand, none of the other squadrons from the American task forces had nearly the same degree of success in finding the target. Some believe that Maxwell Leslie's VB-3 from the *Yorktown* also scored a bull's eye in finding and attacking the *Soryu*, but that was not exactly true, as will be shown.

The apparent contrast between Waldron's (and to some degree, Leslie's) ability to find the target vs. the problems faced by the *Enterprise* squadrons and the rest of the *Hornet* air group prompted this inquiry from Bill Price in 2004:

Among all the questions about Midway that remain unanswered are two concerning the leaders who took their men into action—how they found *Kido Butai* [the Japanese carrier force] after they had launched. The Midway-based planes attacked the carriers on the original course reported by Howard Ady. But *Kido Butai* then changed course and headed northeast for recovery of their Midway strike aircraft, and I don't believe there was any sighting and reporting of that new course.

It is well documented how the *Enterprise* dive bombers finally located *Kido Butai*. Using Howard Ady's contact report, Lt. Cdr. McClusky plotted an intercept point for his air group, but no carriers were in sight when he arrived there. He continued south and, finding nothing, turned on a dogleg to the right. With gas gauges moving toward half of a tank, he then turned back to the north. Smoke was soon spotted on the horizon: the destroyer *Arashi* heading back to Nagumo's task force. McClusky followed and soon spotted the carriers, north of their original course. As the *Enterprise* SBDs prepared to make their dive, Lt. Cdr. Leslie's SBDs arrived from the *Yorktown*. The two air groups struck the Japanese carriers almost simultaneously.

Leslie's squadron had left the *Yorktown* an hour after the *Enterprise* planes had launched, yet they came together on the Japanese carriers at the same time. The mystery is how the *Yorktown* squadrons located the Japanese carriers on this different course. It is known how the *Enterprise* planes arrived there, but nothing reveals what led the *Yorktown* planes to the target. The answer was not any sort of guidance by radio, as both fleets observed radio silence.

So the question remains, how did the *Yorktown* air group set a course to *Kido Butai's* new location? The answer will be a significant contribution to understanding the "incredible victory."

The second question centers around Torpedo Squadron 8. It also struck the Japanese carriers on their new course, one that was a considerable departure from that reported by Ady. VT-8 was the first carrier-based group to find Nagumo's carriers. How did its skipper, Lt. Cdr. Waldron know where the carriers would be? Waldron had broken away from the *Hornet* air group on its flight to nowhere, and as well as can be determined, he almost flew directly to his target after it had departed from its known original course.

Does anybody have any documentary evidence to answer these two key questions? If so, you will make a substantial contribution to the history of the battle.

The first response to Price's two-phased question came from ComInt veteran Mac Showers, although it couldn't quite be categorized as "documentary evidence." The admiral was thinking more along the lines of the *Miracle at Midway* in this case:

Regarding Bill Price's questions, you simply have to remember and rely on the fact that, through the fog of war, God was at Midway. Over sixty years later, documentary evidence probably cannot be produced. But with "God as my co-pilot," you've also got to remember that He is still a very good navigator...just for what it's worth.

*   *   *   *

Sighting Reports

While no one was prepared to argue Admiral Showers' point, most were still looking for a tangible reason for Waldron and Leslie's perceived foreknowledge of where Nagumo was headed at the critical moment. USS *Enterprise* vet Alvin Kernan offered what some considered the obvious answer:

> On the *Yorktown* side [TF-17], one simply has to assume that by the time their strike was launched an hour or so after the TF-16 strike, word had seeped through that Nagumo had turned north and his new course could be plotted. On the whole, the *Yorktown* air group performed so much better in the battle than the *Enterprise* group and especially the *Hornet* group that one can reasonably assume the Yorktowners were much more alert about course changes.

Professor Kernan was alluding to the frequently-heard assumption that the *Yorktown* squadrons and perhaps some of the others benefited from followup PBY contact reports or other enemy position reports radioed to them after launching. Unfortunately, that theory had been disposed of long ago through the interviews conducted by Gordon Prange. *Miracle at Midway* reported that neither Spruance in TF-16 nor Fletcher in TF-17 received any contact reports subsequent to Ady's original one, despite multiple overflights and attacks upon *Kido Butai* by Midway-based squadrons.[2] The lack of followup reports while en route to the enemy fleet was also confirmed to the Roundtable by Tom Cheek in this message from 2004:

> Regarding the suggestion that we got some sort of enemy posit [position] reports after we launched: there weren't any.

So at the outset, we can dismiss external help of any sort as the reason Waldron and Leslie's squadrons seemed to have little or no difficulty finding their targets. But then, Australian historian James Bowen came forward with a suggestion that was closer to the mark, at least in the case of Leslie:

> I gave some thought to the manner in which Lt. Cdr. Leslie's *Yorktown* Air Group appeared to fly almost in a direct line to Nagumo's carriers. I wondered whether that was a case of good luck or good judgment. After reading Prange's *Miracle at Midway*, I became persuaded that it was a case of good judgment, namely, superior operational staff work on *Yorktown*, possibly aided by the fact that *Yorktown's* air group was launched much later than the air groups on *Enterprise* and *Hornet*. Perhaps the closing of the distance between the American and Japanese carriers facilitated finding *Kido Butai* by the *Yorktown* Air Group.

Bowen's considerations of good judgment ("superior operational staff work") coupled with good luck were indeed appropriate to the *Yorktown* air group. Good judgment was evident in their decision, born of experience, to launch their SBDs and TBDs ahead of the fighters, allowing the air group to effect a "running rendezvous" en route to the target. The faster fighters, leaving the carrier last, easily caught up to the other squadrons without wasting precious fuel orbiting the task force while their lumbering charges launched and formed up. (That's exactly how TF-16 did it, which proved fatal for the *Hornet's* VF-8.) Good luck was also a factor, as the Yorktowners' late launch (about an hour after TF-16) fortunately brought less cloud cover than experienced by the *Enterprise* and *Hornet* squadrons, further facilitating their running rendezvous. The result was that Leslie's VB-3 and Thach's VF-3 were able to observe and follow Massey's VT-3 as the latter led the air group along its base course toward the southwest.

*   *   *   *

Splashes

The goal of American carrier air groups at that stage of the war was a coordinated, simultaneous attack by the squadrons of each ship, and the Yorktowners very nearly pulled it off through superior planning and some good luck. But that still didn't get them directly to the target. One more important scene needed to be played out before that act was completed, and its star was ARM3/c Lloyd Childers, the R/G in Warrant Officer Harry Corl's TBD in Torpedo Squadron 3.

Childers was scanning the sea below him in all directions, out to the horizon, looking for the cause of some mysterious splashes he'd seen on the ocean's surface. The splashes had been the result of a few bombs from VB-3, flying nearly overhead, accidentally being released due to faulty arming switches (also mentioned in Chapter 7 by Tom Cheek). Mystified by the strange splashes, Childers continued turning about in his cockpit as the squadron droned on, wondering what in the world could have caused them. Thus, while earnestly searching the sea on the starboard side of his aircraft, he noticed a wisp of smoke on horizon— the enemy fleet! He called Corl's attention to the smoke, Corl rocked his wings to signal the squadron commander, and Lt. Cdr. Massey responded by turning VT-3 toward the smoke.[3] Lt. Cdr. Leslie, tracking VT-3 from above, saw the turn and led his dive bombers around on a following course. VT-3 then proceeded toward its brutal destiny at the hands of the Japanese CAP, allowing Leslie and VB-3 to pounce upon the undefended *Soryu.*

So it was superior staff planning, some luck with the cloud cover, and the sharp eye of ARM3/c Childers that had enabled VB-3 to find *Kido Butai* after Nagumo had turned away from the Yorktowners' intersecting track.

$$*\qquad*\qquad*\qquad*$$

Nagumo's Turn

Next, VB-8 pilot Roy Gee took us back to the question concerning Waldron: did the VT-8 skipper have some sort of sixth sense that told him Nagumo was going to turn? Did that enable him to find the elusive target that Cdr. Ring and the rest of the air group completely missed? Gee got us headed toward the answer with the following contribution:

> Lt. Cdr. Waldron objected to CHAG's course as the wrong one to intercept the Japanese carriers, but Ring ordered the squadron COs to fly his course. After our launch and rendezvous, he led us west on course 265 degrees true. VS-8 pilot Ben Tappan then heard an altercation on the radio between Ring and Waldron concerning the course to the enemy fleet. The *Hornet's* air operations officer also heard it, noting the time as 0815. At that moment several VS-8 and VF-8 airmen observed VT-8 break away from the air group, heading to port. By turning to the southwest, the exasperated VT-8 skipper led his squadron on a course he knew would intercept the Japanese carriers.

Whether Waldron knew that Nagumo would turn northeast had not yet been established, but there's one thing that he definitely did know at that point: as suggested by Roy Gee above, he had to know that the Japanese carriers reported by Howard Ady couldn't possibly be in the direction the air group was then heading, for that course was going to take them *behind* the point where Ady's PBY had originally spotted the enemy over two hours previously. Those carriers had to be much more toward the southwest (where the *Enterprise* air group had gone), and Waldron knew that's where he had to go, too, with or without support from Ring and the other *Hornet* squadrons.

We know from Bowen Weisheit's research that Waldron then turned VT-8 to the southwest on a course that would put the moon dead center in George Gay's windscreen, a course that also led directly to the point *Kido Butai* would have crossed the air group's track had they flown southwest from the *Hornet* in the first place. That takes us to the issue of Nagumo's turn: how did that affect the fortunes of VT-8? A look at Figure 3 gives the answer: Waldron, like Leslie, actually did *not* fly "straight to the Japanese carriers," as alleged by George Gay and as has been parroted by various writers over the years. That is evident from the Nagumo Report, which states that VT-8 was first spotted at a distance of thirty-five kilometers and at a relative bearing of fifty-two degrees to *Chikuma* while that ship was on a course of 070 degrees true, or toward the northeast.[4] Those facts place VT-8 about twenty-one miles *southeast* of the Japanese when first spotted. That being the case, Waldron must have flown toward his own calculated point of intercept (CPI) after breaking away from the rest of the *Hornet* air group. He missed *Kido Butai* by something in excess of twenty-one miles to the southeast, then turned to starboard in order to engage after someone in his squadron spotted the Japanese ships off to the right, more or less like Childers was to do for VT-3 some forty minutes later.

Thus, it is rather unlikely that Waldron's course upon breaking away from Ring was predicated on any sense that *Kido Butai* was going to deviate from its known track. Even if it were true, the fleet's turn actually availed Waldron nothing, which will be explored further in Chapter 12. What's far more likely is that he simply employed his superior navigation skills to plot a new base course to the original CPI that he'd computed back on the *Hornet* from Ady's original contact reports (see Figure 3). His new course was accurate enough to get him close to the target, just a little to the east; close enough to engage the enemy and ultimately decide the outcome of the battle.

*   *   *   *

A Critical Sequence

Returning to Leslie, we need to remember an important chain of events. From *A Glorious Page In Our History*, we know that Japanese DDs laid down signaling smoke during the VT-8 attack, and it was that smoke that VT-6 spotted, on the horizon far to starboard, while they were flying toward the *Enterprise* air group's CPI.[5] Without that smoke generated due to Waldron's attack, VT-6 very possibly would have missed the fight altogether, flying straight to their air group's CPI and finding nothing.

The attack by VT-6 led to the generation of still more smoke by the Japanese screening ships, which very likely helped Lt. Cdr. Leslie in VB3 find his target. As the *Yorktown* air group proceeded on its base course (as it happened, well to the east of *Kido Butai's* track after Nagumo had made his turn), VT-3 was in the lead, with VB-3 following overhead. Childers in VT-3 saw smoke on the horizon as explained above, leading eventually to the destruction of *Soryu*.

Without that smoke generated from the VT-8 and VT-6 attacks, VT-3 (and therefore VB-3), would very likely have flown on to the TF-17 CPI, finding nothing, leaving *Soryu* to survive the morning if not the entire battle, with untold consequences for its outcome (see Figure 3).

In trying to analyze this multi-faceted issue, a few Roundtable members commented on the time of launch of the various squadrons, suggesting that there was a wide variance between the launch of VT-8 and VT-6 and a much wider one between those two and VT-3. There were also suggestions that VT-3 must have gotten to the target much quicker that the other two. What one needs to remember, though, is that TF-16 (*Enterprise* and *Hornet*) used a "deferred departure" launch as opposed to the *Yorktown's* "running rendezvous," meaning that the TF-16 TBDs got off the deck *last*, while those on the *Yorktown* got off much earlier, ahead of their escorting fighters. The result of that procedural difference is that the torpedo squadrons actually launched closer together on the clock than is generally believed. The specific VT launch times were:

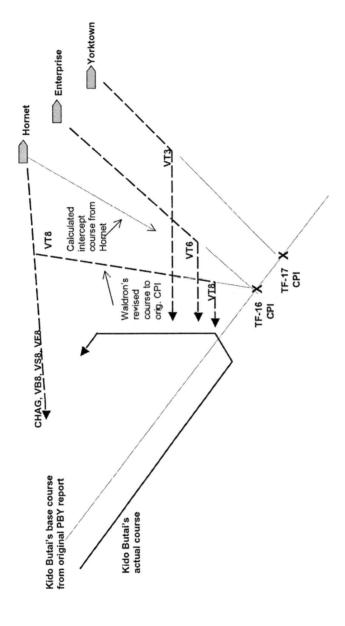

FIGURE 3. This chart demonstrates that all three torpedo squadrons deviated sharply to the right from their base courses upon sighting the Japanese carriers. Note also that Lt.Cdr. Waldron, after breaking away from Cdr. Ring's westbound course, may have simply computed a new base course to TF-16's original calculated point of intercept (CPI).

VT-8: 0755
VT-6: 0806
VT-3: 0840[6]

Thus, it is evident that VT-6 lagged VT-8's launch only by a few minutes, and VT-3 was only a little more than a half hour behind.

Now let's look at the flight times for each of the VT squadrons. VT-8 was first spotted by the Japanese one minute after they made their turn to the northeast, at 0918. It took seven minutes for Waldron's planes to reach the point of attack, which is recorded as 0925. VT-6 is first sighted at 0938, and is fully engaged by 0945. VT-3 is sighted at 1002 and is over the cruiser screen at 1014 and attacking at 1015 (all times from the Nagumo Report). Comparing that data to the above launch times for each squadron, we have the following elapsed times from launch to attack:

VT-8: 01:30
VT-6: 01:29
VT-3: 01:35

Thus, the flights of all torpedo squadrons were of a consistent duration, with minor differences attributable to the forming maneuvers of each air group plus variances in the distance that each traveled to the target. There might also have been some slight differences in speed of approach.

The conclusion from all that is that there is nothing remarkable about the launch times, flight distance, flight duration, or attack times of the three torpedo squadrons (and by extension, VB-3). Considering the position of their respective carriers and their respective times of launch, they all got to the target on their chosen course in about the amount of time that one would expect.

In summary, then, and to answer Bill Price's original question, *no one* "flew straight to the Japanese carriers." Waldron apparently picked a sensible new course based on his original CPI and Ady's contact report, and turned toward that CPI when it was evident that the *Hornet* air group was headed the wrong way. He came close to a bulls-eye thanks to Nagumo turning the fleet almost directly toward him. VT-6, not encumbered with a base course that was doomed to failure upon launch, was dutifully tracking toward the *Enterprise* air group's CPI when smoke from the fight with VT-8 caused them to change course to starboard. The *Yorktown* air group did exactly the same thing a short while later for the same reason and under the same circumstances.

The result of this remarkable sequence, initiated by Waldron, was three enemy carriers out of action within the hour. Without Waldron's initiative and the subsequent chain of events that he started, it's unlikely that the *Yorktown* air group would have found *Kido Butai*, hence VB-3 would not have attacked *Soryu*. Without those repetitive VT attacks, all of the Japanese fighters would not have been drawn down to the wavetops when McClusky arrived on scene, thereby giving the CAP a decent chance for spoiling the SBD attack upon *Akagi* and *Kaga*.

Upon closing this discussion on the Roundtable early in 2005, I had to admit that a few elements of the subject were assuredly open to further investigation or even debate. But that is simply intrinsic to the Battle of Midway, for all of its unknowns will never be inarguably resolved. The most that anyone can do, now or in the future, is to analyze the documented record, interview the veterans who were there at the time, then draw reasonable conclusions.

The final comment came from Admiral Showers, who had started it off by attributing Waldron and Leslie's success to the "fog of war" or perhaps divine providence. He ended it in a similar vein:

> Most all of you engaged in this discourse know far more about aerial navigation than me, and I have to believe that your solution is as close to correct as we'll get. But that takes me back to my original view, which is in agreement with Chaplain Linzey's thesis: "God was at Midway."

CHAPTER 11

▼

THE MOST AND THE BEST

One Above All Others

As stated previously, the principal advantage of reviewing an important chapter in U.S. history on the Battle of Midway Roundtable is the fact that a large number of the men who actually made that history are current participants. That being the case, I endeavored over the years to exploit that advantage to the extent possible, mindful of the inevitable time all too soon when each of those men will be an honored memory, having given all that there is to be gained.

To that end, I proactively sought their opinions on various aspects of the battle by means of formal surveys on four occasions over a period of two years. The first one appeared in October 2003, which I introduced as follows:

> If you had to name *one* participant who was *the most important* combatant in the entire battle, who would it be? That is, what one person (in any service, anywhere, on either side) would you say played the single most important role in deciding the outcome of the battle?
>
> In this discussion we'll not only include the warriors on Midway and on the ships and planes, but those who contributed direct support elsewhere, i.e. the signal intelligence groups, the Aleutians diversion, the commanders at Pearl and Washington, etc. Which one of all those was *the* most important? You can only name one.
>
> Here are a few choices that come to mind:
>
> - Wade McClusky, whose squadrons crippled two Japanese carriers in five minutes.

- Dick Best, whose on-the-fly tactical decision resulted in the destruction of *Akagi*.

- Admiral Nimitz, whose grand strategy of ambush worked to near perfection.

- Admiral Yamamoto, whose flawed strategy of deception led to the turning point of the war.

- Lt. Cdr. William Brockman, whose USS *Nautilus* started a chain of events that led to McClusky finding Nagumo's carriers.

- Lt. Cdr. John Waldron of VT-8, who started a chain of events that ultimately drew all Japanese fighters down to low altitude, leaving McClusky and Leslie mostly unopposed.

- Admiral Nagumo, who left his attack aircraft on board far too long.

- Admiral Fletcher, whose on-scene strike plans were a masterful combination of vision and luck.

- Cdr. Joseph Rochefort, who virtually sat in on Yamamoto's staff meetings.

- The shipyard master at Pearl, who got *Yorktown* into the battle when it should have been impossible.

- Howard Ady, who made the crucial first discovery of the Japanese carriers.

- Bill Tremblay, representing the codebreakers without whom the Japanese plan for Midway would never have been discovered.

There are probably a few others you can add to the above list. Anyway, name your single most important player in the battle and let us know.

After the survey votes were tallied, first place turned out to be a tie between Admiral Nimitz and HYPO's Commander Joseph Rochefort. The responses were quite interesting, for there was an unexpected statistical difference between those from our BOM veterans vs. those from other members. While our non-veteran members cast their votes across a broad spectrum of numerous choices, the BOM vets were more solidly lined up behind the two winners, casting over half of their votes for Rochefort and Nimitz. Insight into their thinking was provided by several of the vets who offered detailed explanations for their reasoning. Here are some examples:

Mac Showers: I'll cast my lot with Commander Joseph J. Rochefort. My own opinion stems from his loyalty and dedication to providing Admiral Nimitz with all the best intelligence available, whether it came from Melbourne, Washington, or HYPO. Also, he was my boss and one of my career mentors, and the proudest part of my naval service was to have been associated with him.

But my second and more important reason comes from the late Captain Ned Beach, who stated in one of his books, "Midway has also been called a battle won by intelligence, for there was no way Nimitz's meager forces could have met the Japanese fleet without the advantage of foreknowledge of Yamamoto's plan…He was defeated by one man, whose special genius enabled him to give Admiral Nimitz the invaluable background that made all the difference between fighting blindly and fighting with full awareness of the enemy's plans. To Commander Joe Rochefort must forever go the acclaim for having made more difference, at a more important time, than any other naval officer in history."[1]

Phil Jacobsen: I could be considered to have a conflict of interest, but as a tie-breaker, my vote goes to Joseph J. Rochefort. Without the information he and his contemporaries provided, our carriers would probably have still been in the South Pacific. Midway would not have been built up to withstand the first Japanese onslaught. It would have been too little too late to try to reinforce Midway and return the carriers to that locale. While the Japanese landing may not have been easy, I believe that Midway would have been lost to the overwhelming Japanese force, for the interim at least.

Chaplain Stan Linzey: Consistent with the title of my book [*God Was at Midway*], I would have to cast my vote for God! For I do, indeed, believe He directed the course of action at Midway as the book indicates. On the other hand, if we are speaking humanly, then I vote for Commander Rochefort.

Bernie Cotton: In attempting to define the most important participant, I would say that the Battle of Midway would not have occurred had it not been for Joe Rochefort. He undoubtedly is number one.

Clay Fisher: I think there are two categories of "combatant," *support* and *operational* personnel. I have selected Admiral Nimitz as the most important support combatant. I selected Dick Best as the most important operational combatant. In my mind Dick Best represented all those SBD pilots who got direct hits on three Japanese carriers on the morning of June 4th. Those direct hits turned the tide of the battle in about ten minutes.

Bill Roy: Admiral Nimitz, for leadership, vision, inspiration, and courage!

Newton Delchamps: Admiral Nimitz, for if we had lost, he'd surely had gotten the blame!

Elmer Jones: From my point of view it was probably Elmer Jones! But that aside, it would be hard to point out one person or group to give the most credit, from Nimitz, Rochefort, and right on down the line to those brave pilots who had very little combat experience. But I'm glad that we had Nimitz on our side!

Roy Gee: Admiral Yamamoto has my vote as the most important combatant in the entire BOM. Without his plan to engage and destroy what remained of the U.S. Pacific fleet by capturing Midway, there might not have been a BOM. By spreading out his huge armada across the central Pacific, he weakened his overwhelming superiority. His overconfident forces screwed up, and gave our boys the opportunity to find them and kick their butts!

We've got to be thankful that Yamamoto never concentrated his forces and completely surrounded Midway atoll with battleships, cruisers, destroyers, and carriers, in which case he could have really crushed us in spite of our excellent intelligence.

Bryan Crisman: In 1998 I began a written rendition of this battle for my grandson, entitled "Intervention Won the Battle of Midway." The more I thought about it and recounted the events, the more that I'm convinced that God intervened to bring victory in this and many other battles, and the ultimate victory over both the Germans and the Japanese. Therefore, my nominee is *God.* I know that this is not the answer that you are seeking, but it is my true belief since the United States was too ill prepared to engage the Japanese with any expectation of success without His participation.

Otis Kight: The most important person in the Battle of Midway? As the world well understands, the Navy's ladder of success is upholstered in *dungaree.* I nominate any of the several thousand [enlisted sailors] that fought, right after the three hundred plus that died, as the most important. Without the Dungarees, nothing would have gotten done.

Tom Cheek: My vote would go to Jimmy Thach. Without his insisting on fighter cover for VT-3, the enemy CAP would not have been drawn down and the SBDs would have found themselves in a melee that would have scattered them from Hell to Breakfast. Thach's division was at mid-altitude and in the clear when the CAP sighted him and attacked. From that point the Japanese spotted VT-3, more easy meat.

As I recall, John Lundstrom gives the number of Zeros as thirty plus. Together it makes an interesting pyramid of facts.

Tom Cheek's comment above provided the Roundtable a bonus, for in all of our previous analyses as to whether the torpedo squadrons should get credit for drawing the Japanese CAP down and way from the dive bombers, the role of the VF-3 escort in that particular regard had never previously come to light, nor is it evident in the popular histories of the battle.

Finally, Rear Adm. Lew Hopkins' response provided a fitting epilogue to this survey:

> I often am asked to give a speech on the BOM, and in order to make it interesting I entitle it "Ensigns at Midway." I point out that as of 1020 on the morning of June 4th, the IJN had not been scratched. But at 1026 three IJN carriers were headed for the briny deep. How did that happen? Because some twenty-nine U.S. Navy ensigns and others "carried the mail"; in this instance, the bombs that did the actual damage. There could not have been a victory without their SBDs.
>
> Of course, there were many others along the way whose actions were critical in the victory. Here are my comments about them and my final analysis as to which was the most important.
>
> Commander Rochefort: if he had not persisted in following up on what his codebreaking was telling him, he never could have convinced Adm. Nimitz that an opportunity existed to ambush the IJN.
>
> Admiral Nimitz: if he had not had faith in Cdr. Rochefort's code analysis, he would not have ordered the *Enterprise* and the *Hornet* to return and rearm for Midway. Just think what courage and risk-taking was involved there. Had he not made the decision to deploy the carriers, the Japanese would have taken Midway, and then what?
>
> Rear Adm. Spruance: he was in place because of Cdr. Rochefort's analysis and Adm. Nimitz's decision. Yet, he also took some risks. He was willing to roll the dice, so to speak, and commit his entire air groups on the morning of June 4th.
>
> Lt. Cdr. McClusky (I was in his group): what a decision he made! Without question, he was willing to sacrifice his entire flight of thirty-two SBDs to get a chance to attack the IJN. I was one of them, and I knew that what he was doing was putting me and all the others in jeopardy. When he made his decision [to search beyond his calculated point of intercept] I resigned myself to not returning to the *Enterprise* because of fuel exhaustion (I was one of the few to make it back with a "teaspoon" of fuel left). But because of McClusky's decision, the *Kaga* and the *Akagi* were sunk.
>
> Lt. Dick Best: what a spur of the moment decision he made. In the excitement of a pending attack on the massive IJN fleet, he diverted his dive to the *Akagi*, which otherwise would have survived and could have been very instrumental in subsequent attacks upon the American carriers.

The three torpedo squadrons: their tenacity in attacking the IJN with their attendant losses drew the Zeros down, leaving the SBDs to make their dives free from harassment.

The Midway atoll defenders: their ferocious defense made Nagumo decide on a second attack, resulting in a rearming debacle that precluded the assembly of a strike force against the American carriers.

The Almighty: there is absolutely no argument that luck played its role, or was it really *luck*? Without the presence of a Japanese destroyer's wake, McClusky might have wandered over the ocean until all of our planes ran out of fuel. Without torpedo planes finding the IJN before the SBDs arrived, who knows how effective the SBDs could have been [in the face of Japanese fighters at their altitude]?

A case can probably be made for still others, but I make my final choice on the one whose action was absolutely the key to the victory; whose action, had it *not* been taken would surely have made victory impossible. That person is Commander Rochefort, because he was the first link in the chain of events. Without his primary achievement, the IJN would have arrived at Midway with minimal opposition and the atoll would have been theirs.

✳   ✳   ✳   ✳

On Midway Atoll

Initiating a discussion of the Battle of Midway usually brings forth images of Torpedo Squadron 8 gallantly charging into a maelstrom of Japanese fighters, followed closely behind by scenes of McClusky, Best, and Leslie's dive bombers turning three enemy carriers into floating infernos. The discussion may then turn to the brilliance of Admiral Nimitz, the tactical acumen of Admirals Fletcher and Spruance, and perhaps to the endless controversy concerning the flight of the *Hornet* air group as the battle was joined. Admiral Nagumo's infamous torpedoes-to-bombs-to-torpedoes vacillation inevitably comes up, and the folly of Admiral Yamamoto's strategy is nearly always included. But what very often gets missed in the discussion is the heart of the battle itself: Midway. The exciting drama of the air-sea attacks and their crucial impact on the outcome of the battle invariably overshadows what transpired on the atoll itself.

Of course, the cause for that is that the war on Midway was essentially over after one mostly ineffective Japanese air attack. By 0900 on the first day of the battle, the atoll had been relegated to the background as the fight raged for the next two and a half days on and over distant waters. That fact was evident on the Roundtable from the beginning, as matters concerning the defenses on Midway were rarely discussed. Mindful of that, I would occasionally stimulate the participation of our atoll veterans by offering an inquiry specific to their experience, or by guiding a discussion in a manner that included them. Our roster had always been blessed with the presence of several retired and former Midway Marines as well Navy vets from the island's small craft, PBY squadrons, and VT-8 detachment, and I wanted to ensure that their contributions to the dialogue were not overlooked.

In that spirit, then, I crafted a followup survey to the previous one, in which no combatants on the atoll got significant notice. This time I was looking exclusively for the "most" or the "best" from Midway itself:

> That "most important participant" survey we recently completed was so informative and educational that I thought we'd try another. This one is for everyone who fought the battle on or from Midway itself: the Marines, the PBY squadrons, the VT-8 TBF detachment, the PT and other USN crews, and the AAF squadrons.
>
> Same rules as before: name *one* individual who was present on the island, or flew from the island during the battle that you think is the most important, significant, or memorable of all. Of course, this is another one of those situations where each of us would be tempted to answer "everyone who was there." That's understandable, but for purposes of this survey, stretch your imagination and name a single person who you'd put at the top of the list without any reservations. And note that someone could have been exceptionally *memorable* during the battle without having been particularly *important* to its outcome. He could have had very little impact on BOM itself, but might still have performed acts of courage or inspiration that warrant special attention.
>
> Who, then, was the most memorable in your recollection who served on or from the atoll?

The bulk of the responses acknowledged the incredible courage and brutal sacrifice of the Marine pilots and gunners of VMF-221 and VMSB-241, each of whom was either flying a very obsolete Brewster F2A fighter or SB2U Vindicator dive bomber, or a more modern F4F or SBD in which they'd had virtually no training or flight time. VMF-221 skipper Maj. Floyd Parks and VMSB-241's Maj. Lofton Henderson were most frequently named, followed closely behind by Marine Captain and SB2U pilot Richard Fleming, who was awarded the battle's only Congressional Medal of Honor. Those sentiments were best expressed by Midway Marines Walt Grist and Bill Lucius, who had these comments:

Walt Grist: I would like to bring up two Marines who had a very important part in the battle of Midway but are seldom ever mentioned. They are Major Lofton Henderson and Major Floyd (Red) Parks.

Major Parks was the commanding officer of VMF-221 and led his squadron against the incoming strike on Midway on the morning of June 4,1942. He may have been the first casualty of the battle. He was shot down almost immediately as the attack started. But VMF-221 disrupted the Japanese strike force so badly that their mission was not completed and a second strike was called for. It was during turmoil on the Japanese carriers in preparing for an unplanned second attack that an American carrier was discovered, forcing the Japanese to change their bomb loads again. The courageous pilots of VMF-221 led by Major Parks started it all.

Major Lofton Henderson was commanding officer of VMSB-241, and led the spearhead strike from Midway on the Japanese task force without fighter support. Even though that first strike was not as effective as later ones, it was the first and it started the dispersion of the enemy fleet. Their maneuvering [in the face of attacks from the atoll] was what slowed the recovery and rearming of their Midway strike force, a principal cause for confusion on the part of the Japanese commanders.

Those two men may not have been the most important combatants in the battle but they deserve consideration as major participants.

Bill Lucius: There are a number of individuals who should be considered: Red Parks who led the initial assault but died in doing it, or Dick Fleming who dove to his death on a Japanese ship and earned a Medal of Honor, or Eastern Island commander Major William Benson, who also lost his life when his dugout received a direct hit, or Bill Staph, a Marine gunner and rough and tumble guy who personally knocked the lugs off the 500-pound bombs with a sledge hammer and a hacksaw so they could be used on the B-17s. I could go on and on, but everyone there in one way or another was a hero.

*   *   *   *

Midway's Signature Scene

Having established our veterans' opinions on the most important personnel involved in the battle, my next thought was to try to get their feelings as to the most memorable and significant incident, event, or circumstance that they either experienced or became aware of during the battle. That survey began like this:

Thanks to you BOM veterans, historians, authors, and other experts on the Roundtable, we've all leaned a great deal about the battle in recent months and years. So now that we have that depth of knowledge, what one scene of the entire battle do you find most memorable? That is, pick one specific event that you either personally witnessed as a participant, that you saw in a photograph, or that you can visualize from reading history: the one event or scene that you might consider the most memorable of all about the Battle of Midway.

Like the last survey, you'll have many prime choices from which to choose, and picking the best one over all others may be a challenge. But give it your best attempt. If you had to select but one such event or scene that most typifies the BOM to you, what would it be? Make your own choice, but to get you started, here are some possibilities:

- That famous photo of SBDs over the smoking *Mikuma* and *Mogami*.

- The flag being raised over Midway immediately after the air raid.

- TBDs gamely pushing on in the face of slashing attacks by Zeros.

- Howard Ady spotting two Japanese carriers.

- Bill Tremblay, somewhat wide-eyed, finding "attack" and "AF" in an intercept.

- Marines in doughboy helmets, at the start of the John Ford film.

- Lloyd Childers firing his .45 at a Zero.

- *Hammann* tied up alongside the listing *Yorktown*.

- Ground and hangar deck crews waiting for returning planes that never returned.

I'm sure that you can imagine any number of additional choices. Now, which one immediately comes to mind when you think about the Battle of Midway?

This survey was a very rewarding exercise, for the responses from our BOM vets were particularly interesting and generally revealing of strong, personally poignant emotions. The clear winner was the *Enterprise* and *Yorktown* SBDs diving upon three Japanese carriers, which is perhaps easy to understand from the perspective of a young sailor or Marine facing what he'd been told was an overwhelming enemy force bent on killing him. The stunning success of the dive bombers removed that threat, giving perhaps thousands of young Americans a lease on further life that they didn't expect to have. Admiral Showers put it rather succinctly on behalf of all BOM veterans:

My immediate and most vivid event is the dive bombers attacking the *Akagi*, *Kaga*, and *Soryu*. Any way you slice it, that was the guts of the battle, and nothing else ranks as high!

Several other vets made similar comments about the dive bombers, but they frequently added their visions of events they'd personally experienced and in some cases had burned into a bitter memory. Elmer Jones had perhaps the bitterest of them all:

> For me it was the USS *Hammann*. I will never forget watching the stern half sink out of sight, followed by the tremendous explosions of the depth charges.

Ron Graetz had his own piercing memory, one that meant he'd barely escaped death in a VT-6 Devastator at Midway because a shipmate had gone out in his place:

> I guess I am alive today because I was not scheduled to fly on the morning of June 4, 1942! The most memorable scene from that date for me was standing on the catwalk on the starboard side aft and watching 6-T-9, my usual aircraft, rolling forward for takeoff. Aboard that plane was Ens. Rombach, with whom I had flown for most of the time I was in Torpedo Squadron 6, and radioman-gunner Wilburn Glenn, one of my closest friends. Glenn was facing aft, and was alternately signaling two thumbs up, then clasping his fists over his head, like a winning boxer. He continued doing that until the plane left the forward deck of the *Enterprise*. That plane was one of the ten out of the fourteen we sent out that did not return! We lost two great people that day in 6-T-9, and other scenes and memories of the BOM take a "back seat" to that for me.

Another TBD veteran, Lloyd Childers, could easily have cited any number of tense scenes that he'd experienced in his desperate personal duel with the Japanese CAP, but oddly enough, the one he remembered best had little to do with shooting at or getting shot at by Zeros:

> As R/G in 3-T-3 (VT-3), I was facing aft, fending off Zeros during the initial run-in and did not see much of what was ahead. When the AA got heavy, the Zeros departed and I turned around to view our targets: three huge Japanese carriers at about a half mile, churning the water at thirty knots or more, turning hard to make it difficult for our torpedo-lugging TBDs. That unforgettable scene was beautiful and awesome, but terrifying!

Otis Kight had a rather unique principal memory, of a scene recounted in Chapter 6 by Bill Surgi. Kight had also observed Taisuke Maruyama's Kate as it crossed the bow of the USS *Yorktown* after making its torpedo run, its wounded gunner, Giichi Hamada, limited to hand gestures at the Americans as his plane crossed the carrier's flight deck:

> One vision comes to mind very often, aboard the *Yorktown* during the torpedo attack. That rear gunner in the Japanese plane that crossed our bow—he was shaking his fist at us! At the time I considered it a supreme gesture on his part, but after sixty-two years of meditating, I consider that he should have been spraying 7.7 mm. bullets at me instead. That's what I did during future missions in a TBF. I used the fifties!

This survey had nicely accomplished its purpose of drawing out our BOM veterans' sharpest memories of the battle, but perhaps the most profound response came from one of our stalwart non-veteran members. Ted Kraver, an Arizona software engineer who was introduced to the Roundtable by Clay Fisher, capped the survey for us with this haunting vision of the battle not as it was in 1942, but as it is today and will be forevermore:

> My visualization of the Battle of Midway is five carriers, a cruiser, a destroyer, and over a hundred aircraft resting on the bottom of the Pacific 12,000 feet down: a littered battlefield, undisturbed by time or man.

*   *   *   *

Portraying Midway

The final survey was perhaps the most important, for it related to the Battle of Midway's entire body of recorded history. I asked all of the members, but particularly our veterans of the battle to give me their well-considered opinion and critique of the principal books, movies, and other media productions relative to the BOM. It occurred to me that the men who had made the history would be best able to judge attempts by others to record and portray their stories.

Their responses were highly interesting for their unexpected nature: instead of railing against what many see as the flagrant inaccuracies in most of the books and all of the movies, the veterans tended to favor those works that told their story in the most thorough and perhaps even entertaining style, despite an occasional factual flub. It turns out that such points of detail, much of which the casual reader would label as unimportant or esoteric, are more of a concern to authors and historians than to the warriors of Midway themselves. That was evident in their top choice for a book about the battle, Gordon Prange's *Miracle at Midway*. As you will find in the next chapter, Prange's book ranks rather low for accuracy on the list of BOM references, frequently getting the minor particulars wrong, or worse, appearing to abet some of the battle's more persistent myths. But even with such failings exposed on the Roundtable, the veterans still tended to prefer *Miracle at Midway* and to a slightly lesser extent, Walter Lord's venerable *Incredible Victory*, both of which told the story in a masterful narrative style as opposed to the cold, factual accounting found in some of the respected scholarly works.

The veterans were a little more critical of the movie and television renditions of the battle, as evidenced by these opinions from PBY pilot Robert Swan, Midway Marine John Gardner, and *Enterprise* bomb loader Alvin Kernan:

> *Robert Swan:* About the use of voice radio on the PBYs in the 1976 *Midway* movie: that "Strawberry Five" call sign was made up. Besides, we were too far from Midway for voice radio. Maybe they can do it nowadays, but back then our radiomen had to use Morse code.

> *John Gardner: Incredible Victory* and *Miracle at Midway* are a draw. Both are excellent. The History Channel sixty minute production [*Command Decision*] of a year or so ago was very, very poor!

> *Alvin Kernan:* I thought both movies [*A Wing and a Prayer* and *Midway*] were poor. The wrong ships and wrong planes troubled me, as did the tacky love stories. There was no sense of the real tension in battle.

Gardner's comment on the History Channel production was consistent with the responses from all other members, veteran and non-veteran alike. Kernan's appraisal of the two BOM movies was also typical. But Admiral Hopkins had a more favorable view, at least of the 1976 *Midway* movie, imparting a salient value to it and other video productions about the battle not considered by many of the vets:

> My nominee for the best book is *Incredible Victory* by Walter Lord. As for the movies, I liked *Midway* best. The core information in the film is sound. Its real value lies in constantly re-running it and others like it on the cable TV

channels, which serves to keep this important historical event before the public.

But in the main, our combat veterans had surprisingly little to say about the Battle of Midway in the media. I had assumed at the outset that they would solidly support the more accurate histories such as those by Cressman and Lundstrom, and that they would have much to say about the battle's portrayal on the screen. I was wrong on both counts, and in retrospect, it shouldn't be surprising. Having lived the history himself, it's perhaps understandable that a Midway veteran wouldn't be particularly moved by a version of it written by someone who was never there.

CHAPTER 12

▼

FACTS AND FABLES

An Expanding Body of Knowledge

Knowledge about the Battle of Midway has expanded almost continuously since the final shot was fired on June 6, 1942, and the commanding officers (or in some cases, the senior surviving officers) of the various U.S. squadrons and air groups began writing their official after-action reports. Unfortunately, from the historian's perspective, those reports were almost universally flawed in one or more important regards, and in Chapter 8 we found that they could seriously and perhaps even deliberately mislead the reader with regard to important facts about the battle. Yet they were all that existed in the record of events at Midway until 1947 when the Japanese after-action report became available.[1] That added a great deal of new insight on what had actually happened five years previously, and the publication of Volume IV of Samuel Elliott Morisons's *History of United States Naval Operations in World War II* two years later helped further to bring about a modestly good, if less than perfect understanding of the battle among the general public.

Of course, Morison's work was largely based on interviews and after-action reports from both sides, and in some instances the Japanese accounts were as flawed as anything that had been penned in English. The situation changed little throughout the 1950s and early 1960s. A few minor works on the BOM appeared during those years but for the most part, they all simply repeated the known and flawed existing account, or in some cases they managed to further cloud the historical record on their own. Walter Lord's *Incredible Victory*, published in 1967, was the first general market book that exhibited a diligent attempt to present the full, true story of Midway based on exhaustive research. It became a best seller as a result, despite perpetuating some of the misinformation (most notably, the subject of Chapter 8) that was still believed to be true at that time. In 1982, Gordon Prange's *Miracle at Midway* brought a further enhanced view of the battle with still more research and veteran interviews, and it became the number one best seller of all Midway references. But, while giving a refreshing new look at many aspects of the battle, it also hung on to some of its time-honored myths and it suffered from historical or technical errors not found in the other works, as described in Appendix D.

Finally, in 1984, the first detailed account of the Battle of Midway to avoid the usual myths while covering the subject thoroughly and accurately was John Lundstrom's *The First Team*, even though Midway only comprises the last third of the book and its focus is mainly on just the fighter squadrons. It was revised in 1990 and remains a top choice for a Midway reference among many serious authors and historians. The same can be said for a somewhat lesser-known work, *A Glorious Page In Our History*, by lead author Robert Cressman and a corps of supporting coauthors and researchers. The book was first published in 1990 and is into its fourth reprint at this writing. Unlike *The First Team*, the entire volume is totally centered on the BOM, and it exhibits a level of thoroughness and accuracy that rivals that achieved by Lundstrom but with its own unique style and content.

As for the Japanese side of the battle, *Midway: the Battle That Doomed Japan* by Mitsuo Fuchida and Mastake Okumiya had long reigned as the principal reference, having first been produced for domestic consumption in Japan in the early 1950s. The appearance of the English language version in 1955 provided what came to be accepted as a veritable bible on the Imperial Japanese Navy at Midway for decades after. But a new major work on the subject, *Shattered Sword: the Untold Story of the Battle of Midway*, co-authored by Jon Parshall, has convincingly demonstrated that the Fuchida book was as egregious as any of them in promulgating some of the most common myths about battle.[2]

It can therefore be seen that the body of knowledge about the BOM has progressed on a rather rocky but continuous basis from 1942 to the present day, and even the appearance of Parshall's revealing new book will not by any means be the end of it. The Battle of Midway Roundtable has analyzed and debated numerous "unanswerables" during its nine years of intense discourse, and until such time as answers are found to all of them (which is not considered at all likely), the learning will continue.

What follows, then, are several of the issues fielded on the Roundtable from time to time that are among the common myths, imponderables, or popular paradigms about the Battle of Midway. As you will see, most are judged as fables, but some are factual or in need of further discovery before a final conclusion can be drawn. I have labeled each accordingly, based on the preponderance of opinion from the Roundtable's veterans and experts.

✳   ✳   ✳   ✳

1. The Midway Water Ruse

Contention: the "Midway is short of water" ruse was a ploy by the codebreakers at HYPO to find out if "AF" was the Japanese geographic code for Midway. Consensus: *fable*

This matter was covered in some detail in Chapter 4 and it is one of the most common mistakes made by those attempting to tell the story of the BOM, whether in print or on the screen. It may have originated from a pervasive misunderstanding of Walter Lord's account of the water ruse episode in *Incredible Victory*. Here is the key passage:

> Washington remained skeptical. For one thing, they still hadn't pinned down exactly what the Japanese meant by "AF." Rochefort was always sure it was Midway but he needed proof.[3]

Lord is actually stating the matter correctly here, but his choice of words has apparently been widely misinterpreted. In saying that "he [Rochefort] needed proof" and "they" hadn't pinned down the meaning of "AF," the casual reader can easily take that to mean that Rochefort himself as well as the entire ComInt organization was the "they" who needed the proof and hadn't yet pinned "AF" down. The fact that Lord said it was *Washington* who was skeptical while Rochefort was *always sure* is easily missed in the broader context. In reality, Rochefort's need for proof was solely in order to sway the doubters at OP-20-G, not to bring assurance to HYPO because it wasn't needed there.

The misunderstanding got a big boost with the theatrical release of the blockbuster movie *Midway* only nine years after the appearance of Lord's best seller. Actor Hal Holbrook, playing Rochefort in the 1976 film, indicates to Nimitz (Henry Fonda) that he suspects "AF" means Midway and wants to try the water ruse in order to prove it, apparently to Nimitz and everyone else. Roundtable members believe that it got a further boost eight years later with the publication of Gordon Prange's *Miracle at Midway*, which states that Rochefort merely had a "strong hunch" that "AF" was Midway.[4] Thus, with the impetus of the battle's two top selling books and its iconic motion picture, the misunderstanding has become widespread.

ComInt veteran Phil Jacobsen clarified the matter rather bluntly for the Roundtable with this message in 2003:

> One of the most grievous errors is saying that HYPO only *thought* that "AF" might be Midway and implying that they were not sure. They were *absolutely* sure it was Midway back as far as April 1942 when Station C (Corregidor) identified "AF" as Midway in one of their first JN-25B decrypts. The only reason the "water shortage" message was thought up was to keep OP-20-G and War Plans chief Rear Admiral Richmond Kelly Turner ("Terrible Turner") off their backs with suggestions that other places were the target of the operation, such as Hawaii, the west coast, Fiji, Australia, Alaska, etc.
>
> The credit for the cryptologic success with the Battle of Midway belongs to Cdr. Rochefort and his Station HYPO gang with Melbourne not far behind. OP-20-G in Washington was not only a day late and a dollar short, but they almost messed up the intelligence side completely with their suggestions of other targets and their determination that "AF" was not Midway. And in the end, they claimed the lion's share of the credit!

*   *   *   *

2. Nimitz on Midway

Contention: Admiral Nimitz flew to Midway on May 2, 1942, in order to inform the garrison of the upcoming invasion and to find out what they needed to repel it.

Consensus: *fable*

This one apparently got started in 1949 through the misinterpretation of a passage in Volume IV of Morison's history. He describes the admiral's visit to the atoll accurately enough, but he is vague on the date, which is the key to the misunderstanding. As it's stated by Morison, one gathers that Nimitz went to Midway expressly to warn Navy Commander Cyril Simard and Marine Lt. Colonel Harold Shannon that the Japanese were headed their way, asking if they could withstand the forthcoming assault if he provided them with their requested rein-forcements.[5] But in reality, May 2nd was too early for that to be the case. There was little reason for the Americans to believe that anything actually might be brewing in the direction of the central Pacific area at that time. Positive identifi-cation of Midway as the target of a specific enemy operation did not happen before May 14th, as related in Chapter 4.[6]

Interestingly, Walter Lord actually got it right once again, stating that Nimitz mentioned no explicit threat to Simard and Shannon during his visit.[7] But Prange, as the author of the all-time top selling reference on the BOM, gets most of the credit for the misunderstanding by showcasing an April 29th dispatch from Nimitz to Admiral King that said that Midway could withstand a moderate attack but not a major one, and that he (Nimitz) intended to visit Simard and Shannon on May 2nd in order to develop stronger defenses for the island. Prange then goes on to say that while on Midway, Nimitz "did not take the two officers into his confidence," thereby creating the perception to many readers that CINC-PAC was aware of a specific Japanese threat at that time.[8]

Thus, the highly improbable notion that the Japanese plan for Midway was known to the Americans as early as a week prior to the Battle of the Coral Sea became passively accepted by many historians and writers at various levels. When the matter came up on the Roundtable in mid-2005, John Lundstrom set us all straight:

> I must take issue with the assertion that the reason behind Adm. Nimitz' trip to Midway on May 2, 1942 was that he knew that Midway was about to be attacked. The idea that Nimitz knew as early as May 2nd or even earlier that the Japanese were going to invade Midway is one of the most persistent myths of the battle. In fact, it was not until around May 8th, as the Battle of the Coral Sea wound down, that Cdr. Rochefort and Lt. Cdr. Layton became suspicious that the Japanese were not reinforcing their South Pacific offensive but might instead head to the east toward Midway or Hawaii. This is clearly demonstrated in the original radio intelligence documents, notably in a lengthy message Rochefort sent Washington on May 1st entitled "HYPO's Evaluation of the Picture in the Pacific" and in Layton's "CINCPAC Enemy Activities File" (which Nimitz called the "scorecard").
>
> In mid to late April, Nimitz, reacting to radio intelligence regarding major Japanese threats to the southwest and south Pacific island bases, conceived a plan to commit all four of his carriers for an extended period to those imper-iled areas to stop what he thought would be widespread Japanese attacks against the Port Moresby-Noumea-Fiji-Samoa line. Nimitz presented his plan to Adm. King on April 25-26th during their conference at San Francisco. King eventually approved, but was wary of committing so much strength away

from the central Pacific. He asked Nimitz on April 26th whether Midway would be secure against a "major attempt." Nimitz replied that Midway would need help from the Pacific Fleet to weather attacks by two or more carriers and promised to look into the matter of Midway's defense. That was the genesis of Nimitz's inspection trip, not any belief that there was a direct, immediate threat to Midway. Nimitz also went to Midway to raise morale and decorate those involved in shooting down a Japanese flying boat on March 10, 1942.

It was King, not Nimitz, who was concerned the Japanese might take advantage of the situation and move against the central Pacific while all the U.S. carriers were down south. On May 2nd, King admonished Nimitz and MacArthur not to get too wrapped up in the southwest Pacific. Acceptance of Nimitz's strategy "must not be construed as eliminating the possibility that enemy may attack Hawaii-Midway line or launch attacks against our line of communications via Gilbert-Ellice-Samoa line." The great irony is that after May 8th when Nimitz became aware of the impending threat to Midway-Hawaii, he couldn't get King to accept it!

✴   ✴   ✴   ✴

3. The Flight to Nowhere

Contention: Commander Ring led the *Hornet* air group on a mysterious westbound course from the task force on the morning of June 4th, instead of southwest toward the enemy carriers as indicated in the ship's official after-action report.

Consensus: *unresolved*

This matter was covered thoroughly in Chapter 8, so it only needs a brief mention here. The evidence compiled by Bowen Weisheit plus the testimony of multiple *Hornet* aviators who saw VT-8 turn to the left (thus affirming the westbound track postulated by Weisheit) would seem to firmly categorize this contention as factual. But two nagging and rather compelling contradictions remain: George Gay's quotes from Waldron himself, and Clay Fisher's sighting of the smoke column from Midway.

Gay's testimony is the easiest to argue with, for a number of respected historians have long contended that certain key elements of his book are contrived, giving reason to doubt almost anything in it. That seems quite true with regard to some his statements that can be checked against the historical record, such as how many Japanese carriers were afloat and burning during the night of June 4th and whether he could have seen three of them sink. But less arguable are Gay's purported recollections of Waldron's statements concerning Commander Ring taking the air group "down there," and the Japanese turning "north of where the group is heading." That's two separate quotes from Waldron that obviate Weisheit's theory if taken literally. Since any quotes from Waldron are absent in the independent historical record, Gay obviously was not just parroting known facts in reporting such quotes, giving reason to wonder why he would have made them up any differently than what Waldron had actually said. If that's what the VT-8 commander had really said, then a planned westbound course seems impossible to reconcile.

But Clayton Fisher's view of the smoke column from Midway's burning fuel tanks is even more troubling to the Weisheit theory than Gay's quotes from Waldron. Fisher has repeated it to me a number of times, both in writing and in face-to-face discussions, and his sincerity and clarity are quite convincing in every case. Stated simply, if the *Hornet* air group had flown west from the ship instead of southwest, the smoke column's position relative to the heading of Fisher's aircraft would have to have been very different than what he says he saw. Here is his most articulate explanation, from a 2005 message to the Roundtable:

> I first observed the huge vertical column of black smoke off my port wing at approximately ten to eleven o'clock. The shape of the column did not change at any time. We had unlimited visibility to the south. I thought I could see a line at the base of the column that might have been a coral reef but I decided that was an illusion. I remember the last time I looked at the smoke column, it was about nine o'clock off my port wing.

Since the *Hornet* was just a little east of due north from Midway when the air group launched, initially seeing Midway's smoke column at a relative position of ten or eleven o'clock (or slightly left of dead ahead) could not have been possible if the formation been flying toward the west (see Figures 1 and 2). Furthermore, the smoke gradually moved more toward Fisher's left wing ("nine o'clock") as he proceeded, which is precisely what would have occurred if he'd been flying the southwesterly course. On the other hand, if he'd instead gone west from the task force, the smoke would have been seen at almost nine o'clock at the outset, and would have proceeded back toward the eight and seven o'clock positions (toward his aircraft's tail on the left side) as he flew on—if he'd been able to see the smoke at all from that great distance.

In the end, we are left with two very compelling arguments, both quite believable, that unfortunately are mutually exclusive: if one is true, the other is false, but how can anyone convincingly demonstrate that *either* is false? It would seem that we have no choice but to add this matter to the list of Midway's incongruities that will never be resolved beyond the level of personal opinion.

*   *   *   *

4. The Sacrifice of the Torpedo Squadrons

Contention: the sacrifice of the three torpedo squadrons on the first day of the battle was a key to the U.S. victory, by drawing the Japanese fighters down and away from the *Enterprise* and *Yorktown* dive bombers.

Consensus: *fact* (but with a notable dissenting view)

This matter was one of the most discussed and debated issues in the history of the Roundtable. It stems from the general public's fascination with the gallant charge of Torpedo Squadron 8, which left all fifteen of its TBD Devastators sinking around *Kido Butai*. It also left its sole survivor, George Gay, to write a book that became the one and only eyewitness account (on the American side, at least) of what had happened to Waldron and his men.[9] With added public exposure from a John Ford-produced short film that honored VT-8's aviators as fallen heroes, the squadron's lore became an essential fixture in all accounts of the BOM. The sacrifices of VT-6 from the *Enterprise* and VT-3 from the *Yorktown* were actually no less brutal or heroic, but it is inevitably Waldron and VT-8 that first pop into focus whenever the subject arises.

The heart of the contention is whether VT-8's sacrifice, coupled with those of VT-6 and VT-3, was responsible for bringing *Kido Butai*'s CAP down to the wavetops, leaving the upper altitudes undefended at the critical moment when McClusky and Leslie's three dive bomber squadrons appeared overhead. Zeros at high altitude had caused enormous grief for the SBDs in the Coral Sea, but their absence at Midway was a salient factor in the subsequent destruction of three Japanese carriers in the space of less than ten minutes. Was that directly attributable to multiple low-level torpedo attacks in the hour before the dive bombers appeared, or should the SBD squadrons' stunning success be credited to factors largely unrelated to their comrades in the TBDs?

Bringing Down the CAP

George Gay had started things off during an oral interview in 1943, during which he made this statement:

In our particular case I think [the Japanese fighters] would have been at [high] altitude after the dive bombers, which I think also was one thing Torpedo 8 and the other torpedo squadrons should be credited for, I mean, given credit for doing. They sucked those fighters down…it turned out to be beautiful bombing, because the fighters were not [at their altitude]. I don't say that there weren't any fighters up there to get after them; there weren't nearly as many as there would have been if they hadn't come down to get us. So I think that is one thing that helped save the day as far as the battle was concerned.[10]

Since none of the VT squadrons' torpedoes had hit anything, it was natural for writers to seek meaning in the terrible slaughter of the TBD crews, and Gay had conveniently provided it: without the vulnerable torpedo bombers luring the entire Japanese CAP to themselves like a pack of hungry wolves on the scent of blood, they would have trumped the SBDs like they did at Coral Sea, enabling one, two, or even three of *Kido Butai's* carriers to survive the morning. That would have rewritten the Battle of Midway in a manner that could only have been very bad for the American side, hence the torpedomen were bona fide heroes of the battle.

That's a very nice notion, but it has been challenged from time to time by some of the demanding experts on the Roundtable. An in-depth debate on the matter got started in early 2005 and continued for the next two months, with some asserting that the TBDs accomplished nothing in the battle, or at the most simply inconvenienced the Japanese carriers in trying to get their bombers spotted on deck. Others held that without the VT squadrons doing exactly what they did and when they did it, the Battle of Midway would have been known as more of an "incredible calamity" for the U.S. side than a victory.

Smokescreens

The matter arose during a discussion about, of all things, *smoke*. The Nagumo Report includes several log entries describing smoke generated by the task force's screening ships during the American air attacks. "Smoke" and "screening ship" has led over the years to the assumption that *Kido Butai's* cruisers and destroyers were liberally laying smokescreens in the vicinity of the carriers in order to hide them from attacking planes. In researching the subject, I found a couple of references that intimate such screening smoke was a vital factor in guiding both VT-6 and VT-3 to the target, which they otherwise would have missed.[11] Support for that belief came from Naval History Center archivist Bernard Cavalcante, who told the Roundtable the following:

I read through the entire Naval War College Analysis of the Battle of Midway. I found the following references to smoke on page 93: "The *Yorktown* dive bombers were guided to the Mobile Force by the smokescreens laid by the Japanese in order to confuse the *Hornet* torpedo planes. On this occasion the smokescreen had become a greater danger than an aid."

Cavalcante's comment elicited the following rebuttal from SB2C Helldiver pilot George Walsh:

> Smokescreens laid by destroyers were heavy white gases formulated to lay close to the surface of the sea to protect the ships against imminent surface attacks. From the air this smoke would blend into the cumulus clouds prevailing on June 4th. This smoke did not rise into the atmosphere to signal the location of the targets.
>
> The smokescreen would not have stayed with the Japanese ships as they traveled northeast at high speed. The smoke would have drifted off, carried by the wind to the northwest. This would put the dissipating wind on the port side of the Japanese fleet, opposite the direction of the approach by VT-6, VT-3, and the dive bombers. The low hanging smoke could have been blown miles beyond the fleet in the time that had elapsed between the attacks, and would probably have been largely dissipated by the wind anyway.
>
> It is more likely that the smoke that drew the attention of the torpedo squadrons would have been the normal smokestack emissions of such a fleet. These smoke signals would be directly over the ships at all times and would rise into the atmosphere. This suggests that screening smoke generated during the attack by Waldron at 0930 had nothing to do with the later action.

Whether deliberately generated smoke helped the torpedo squadrons (specifically VT-6 and VT-3) find *Kido Butai* is central to the issue of whether they significantly contributed to the American victory. The chain of events is presumed to have gone like this:

1. Waldron defies his commander and takes VT-8 directly to the Japanese carriers.

2. Their screening vessels generate smoke in order to signal the location of attacking aircraft to the defending CAP fighters and AA gun crews. (Key point: without Waldron's initiative, no such smoke would have been generated at this moment.)

3. VT-6 is proceeding on its programmed track, well east of *Kido Butai*, when they notice the above smoke on the horizon to starboard, much of which had been laid intentionally due to VT-8's attack. VT-6 alters

course toward the smoke and engages. Without it, they'd have missed the fight altogether, and the Japanese CAP would have had no reason to abandon the upper altitudes.

4. Similarly, the *Yorktown* air group is following their plotted track east of the action, when one of their airmen spots smoke on the horizon to starboard, which again presumably includes screening or signaling smoke put up because of VT-6. To underscore the key point, *that* smoke would not have existed without Waldron's initiative. (See Figure 3.)

5. VT-3 alters course to engage, the *Yorktown's* dive bomber squadron (VB-3) follows them around, and because of that the SBDs are able to attack and mortally wound the carrier *Soryu*. Again, without the deliberately-generated smoke from the fight with VT-6, the Yorktowners very likely would not have found the enemy fleet that morning, meaning that those CAP Zeros still would have had no reason to descend from their usual patrolling altitude.

Generated smoke, then (by this reckoning), was crucial to getting VT-6 and VT-3 into the fight, which was ultimately necessary for VB-3 to dive upon and neutralize *Soryu*. They succeeded in doing so because the sequential VT attacks attracted the Japanese CAP down to the deck and kept them there, thus giving both the *Yorktown* and *Enterprise's* SBDs a free ride.

But if we are to credit VT-8 with causing the enemy to produce smoke that served as a beacon for VT-6 (and ditto VT-6 for VT-3), what do we do about George Walsh's rejoinder that it could not have happened that way since screening smoke is always white and hugs the surface?

That sent me to the VT-3 veteran who had actually first seen the smoke, retired Marine Lt. Colonel Lloyd Childers, who had been flying as a Navy R/G that morning with pilot Harry Corl. He joined the Roundtable 2002, bringing aboard his invaluable firsthand knowledge of the flight (and plight) of the TBD squadrons on the morning of June 4th at Midway.

I telephoned Childers one afternoon, hoping he would tell me that the smoke he'd spotted was white. I started out by asking him to explain the circumstances at the time

"It was actually sort of accidental," he said. "We had been flying at about two thousand feet when all of a sudden I saw splashes on the surface below us. I thought we were under attack, so I started twisting about, looking in every direction for whoever was shooting at us. While turning my head to starboard, I noticed the smoke on the horizon and told Corl. He rocked our wings to attract Massey's attention [the squadron commander], who then turned us all toward the smoke."

"Splashes on the surface?" I asked. "In the middle of nowhere?"

"It was those bombs from VB-3," Childers replied. "The *Yorktown* SBDs had those faulty arming switches. They starting arming their bombs and a few of them accidentally released, almost through our formation."

"Ah, right," I said. That particular anecdote had been dramatized rather effectively in the 1976 *Midway* movie. "Now, tell me, about the smoke you saw on the horizon—was it white?"

"No, it was just a wisp of dark smoke."

"Dark?" (There went a good theory!)

"Yeah, it had to be darker than the horizon or else I wouldn't have been able to see it."[12]

Confirmation from Fuchida

At that point, then, the smoke that had beaconed VT-3 (and probably VT-6) into the fight did not seem to have been purposefully generated screening smoke. Walsh said such smoke was white, and Childers had been drawn by a wisp of dark smoke, which is what ordinary stack smoke would look like. I just let the matter drop until a few days later when, quite coincidentally, I happened upon this passage in the standard Japanese reference on the battle, Fuchida's *Midway, the Battle That Doomed Japan*: "A destroyer in the van section of our ring formation suddenly hoisted a flag signal, 'enemy planes in sight!' Emitting a cloud of black smoke to underline the warning, she opened fire with her antiaircraft guns."[13]

Black smoke—well, okay, now! It would seem that IJN destroyers at Midway weren't necessarily emitting white smoke after all. That took me back to square one with regard to what Childers and his counterpart in VT-6 had seen, namely that it very well could have been smoke produced as a result of Waldron's attack after all. That notion was reinforced by a message from Bernie Cotton that arrived a few days later:

> During my early days in the Navy I was assigned to a four piper, USS *Manley* (DD-74), and when we were ordered to make smoke, believe me, it was black and never white. Later on (the 1950s) the newer DDs had smoke canisters on the fantail and they did make white smoke.

The concept of white screening or signaling smoke (in 1942, at least) took a further hit when I found a photo from the Battle of Leyte Gulf (1944) showing destroyers assiduously laying very dark smokescreens.[14] Another photo in the same reference did show a DD laying a light gray smokescreen, but it now seemed clear that the smoke seen by VT-6 and VT-3 in 1942 very well could have been defensively generated by *Kido Butai's* screening ships.

The Opposing View

That being the case, it then seems reasonable, if not proven, that a large measure of credit indeed should be given to John Waldron's initiative in starting the aforementioned chain of events, without which VB-3 arguably would not have found the *Soryu* that morning. Given that, we next needs to decide if one, two, or all three of the VT squadrons were *directly* responsible for the SBD squadrons getting a pass from the Japanese fighters as they approached their tipover points. One naturally has to respect the opinion of IJN authority Jon Parshall on such matters, and he gave it to the Roundtable in February 2005 via the following message, which argues against VT-8 getting any credit for drawing down the CAP:

> I think the whole matter of VT-8's sacrifice has been misinterpreted. Bear in mind that a Zero can climb from sea level to 15,000 feet in about five minutes flat. So this whole business of the VT attacks pulling the Zeros down to the deck is only marginal to the whole air defense equation. VT-8's attack being a full hour before the dive-bomber attack meant that the Zeros had all the time they needed to re-assert CAP stacking, had they not subsequently been occupied with VT-6 and then VT-3. Likewise, in my opinion the problem was less one of proper stacking (although that hurt) than it was of the CAP having no central direction, and having been yanked laterally all over the place during the preceding hour. They could handle single-vector, single-altitude threats okay. It was a multi-directional, multi-altitude attack that killed them. Frankly, if you did an analysis of the fighters that were present during VT-8's destruction, I bet you'd find that they had all been landed prior to the 1020 attack anyway. That doesn't argue very strongly for some notion that VT-8's attack introduced some sort of permanent impairment on the Japanese. So, frankly, much as I admire the sentiment of trying to find meaning in VT-8s bravery, the cold facts don't really bear that out, because strictly in terms of its effect on the conduct of American attacks, their sacrifice introduced no difficulties on the Japanese CAP that couldn't have been undone in a matter of minutes, let alone an hour.
>
> Where it *did* have meaning is in its delay of Nagumo's counterpunch. If Nagumo was going to strike at the Americans before the hammer fell at 1020,

he had to start spotting his decks at about 0930 at the latest. But he was busy with other stuff, the first being VT-8's fifteen minute immolation. Had Nagumo begun spotting his decks at 0920, and had nobody shown up until VT-6 at 0940, he might have been about fifteen minutes shy of being ready to go. At that point, with only *Kaga* being chased down by VT-6, Nagumo might have been able to launch at 1000 with *Akagi* and CarDiv 2 [*Soryu* and *Hiryu*]. Or he might have even waited for *Kaga* to be ready, then launched at 1010. Bear in mind that it only took the Japanese about seven minutes to launch 121 carrier aircraft during the morning strike on Midway. So, my overall stance is that VT-8's sacrifice didn't affect *Kido Butai's* defensive equation at all, but it affected its *offensive* operations a great deal. I think we need to be content with that.

While everyone respected Parshall's analysis above, few agreed with its premise. The principal criticism was articulated by VB-8 pilot Roy Gee, who had this observation:

> We know for a fact that swarms of Zeros attacked the torpedo planes and shot most of them down. As one torpedo attack was finishing, another was starting with no let up, then the SBDs commenced their attacks just as VT-3 was departing. The VT-6 and VT-3 attacks did clear the upper altitudes of Zeros, dooming *Kido Butai's* air defense envelope to collapse to its lower level. It was the gallant and brave attacks by VT-8, VT-6, and VT-3 that caused that collapse, thereby allowing our dive bombers to bomb at will and easily destroy three IJN carriers. Their attacks led to the immediate destruction of *Kaga, Akagi,* and *Soryu*, and assured victory at Midway for the U.S. forces.

In discussing the matter with Gee by phone, he further clarified his point this way: "You have to remember that the Japanese were subjected to no less than *five* separate torpedo attacks [B-26s and TBFs from Midway, then the three VT squadrons] over a period of only two hours or so, and the last three all came within the final hour. Despite their intense training and combat experience, the repeated attacks down low got those Zero pilots accustomed to the need for fighting at low altitude. By the time VT-6 and VT-3 showed up, they had to *expect it*. They weren't disappointed. VT-3 paid a terrible price for being the final bait, but they got it done. The Zeros were down low with them, not up there with McClusky and Leslie's SBDs."

"What about the fact that the Zeros had an incredible ability to climb?" I asked. Couldn't they have gotten to the SBDs' altitude any time they wanted?" I was trying to advocate Parshall's point on that issue.

"Sure they could," Gee replied. "But the fact is, they *didn't* at Midway. What they *could* have done had no bearing on what they *did*. They stayed down there with the TBDs. The rest is history."

A Cumulative Result

Screenwriter Paul Corio then followed up with this passionate argument in favor of the VT squadrons:

> I find it absurd to say that the VT squadrons' contribution to the victory at Midway is somehow contradicted. How can we ignore the fact that VT-8's heroic charge caused a major disruption in the enemy carriers' launch proceedings, forced them to undertake evasive maneuvers, and occupied their CAP down on the deck? This was but the first of three successive blows dealt by the relentless courage and unwavering resolve of the TBD crews, who in three waves just minutes apart disrupted and delayed the launch of a massive strike force that would have likely blown our carriers out of the water.
>
> Because of the critical timing of the disruptions successively wrought by VT-8, VT-6 and VT-3 over a thirty to forty-minute span, when the SBDs arrived over the fleet (as the Zeros were dealing with the last of VT-3) the decks of the Japanese carriers were packed with fully armed and fueled planes, most all of which would have been long gone if the TBD crews hadn't charged in as they did when they did. Let's not forget that the skies high above the fleet were also totally devoid of Zeros, thanks again to the cumulative effect of the sacrificial charges of *all three squadrons.*
>
> The attacks by the VT squadrons were indispensable to the victory. Their sacrifice set up the timing of the "Miracle at Midway" by perfectly setting the table and then opening the door for the SBDs, giving them wide open shots at perfect targets.

The traditional view supported by Corio and most others, as well as Parshall's opposing opinion are both very well-reasoned. Yet, in the final analysis, we are left with the inescapable fact that when the SBDs struck, *none* of the many Japanese fighters then in the air met them at their altitude, in stark contrast to what happened in the Coral Sea. That unlikely circumstance had to have occurred for a reason, and the only one in sight is the repetitive low level attacks by Midway and task force torpedo planes.

*   *   *   *

5. Nagumo's Turn

Contention: Waldron was able to lead VT-8 straight to the Japanese fleet because he knew they would turn north rather than continue steaming toward Midway.

Consensus: *fable*

As explained in Chapter 10, Waldron's purported foreknowledge of the enemy's course is one of the most commonly recurring themes among the lore of VT-8, but it is easily dispelled by a close examination of the Nagumo Report. In its usual incarnation, the story asserts that Waldron had a prescient sense that the Midway-bound Japanese carrier force would have to turn to the northeast at some point in order to recover their strike from the atoll, or that they would do it as soon as their scouts found American ships in that direction. As it happened, *Kido Butai* did exactly that and Waldron found his target more or less as he'd predicted.

While it's quite true that Waldron led his squadron on a near-beeline to the enemy fleet, the fable arises from the belief that he did so *because* Nagumo turned his ships to the northeast as predicted, rather than *in spite of it*. That was initially brought to my attention by Tom Cheek in the following message from 2003:

> I've sometimes wondered why Waldron got so much credit for finding the Jap carriers because he supposedly knew they would turn. Looks to me like all he did was fly to the point where the *Hornet* group commander had intended to go in the first place. The fleet turn didn't amount to anything as far as VT-8 was concerned.

I didn't particularly recognize the importance of Cheek's observation until more than a year later when the subject of Commander Ring and the *Hornet* air group at Midway became a major topic on the Roundtable. I wondered what Cheek (who, regrettably, had passed away by that time) had meant by saying *Kido Butai*'s turn "didn't amount to anything" with regard to Waldron's presumed adroitness. A simple glance at the Japanese timeline provided the answer: VT-8 would have encountered their target where they did *regardless* of the turn. Here are the key ship's log entries from the Nagumo Report:

"0917: Course 70 degrees. Number 3 battle speed." [This is the turn to the northeast.]

"0918: Maximum battle speed. Noted enemy plane sighting signals from all ships."

"0918: *Chikuma* sites 16 [sic]enemy planes bearing 52 degrees to starboard, elevation 2 degrees, distance 35 kilometers."[15]

The obvious problem with the contention that Waldron only found the enemy carriers because he knew they would turn to the northeast (approximately course 70 degrees, in fact) is the lack of a time lag between the turn and his arrival on scene. *Kido Butai* executed its turn at 0917, and VT-8 was spotted by the screen not more than one minute later. If the carriers were then steaming at a reasonable twenty-five knots, that's less than a half mile of distance after the turn. The conclusion is therefore inescapable that VT-8 would have easily found its target whether Nagumo turned or continued on his original course toward Midway. Call it luck, foresight, excellent navigation, or all three, Waldron had led his planes exactly where he'd intended: to the spot where *Kido Butai* would be when he crossed their known original path at his predicted time of intercept. With only a half mile of ocean separating the carriers from the location of their turn and the location where VT-8 was first seen on their run-in, the turn itself was of no consequence to what followed.

*   *   *   *

6. *What George Gay Saw*

Contention: George Gay was adrift in the midst of the Japanese carriers, watching three of them as they were attacked by American dive bombers and then as they sank.

Consensus: *part fact, part fable*

This controversy got its start while the battle was still raging. After he was rescued by a PBY on the afternoon of June 5th, Gay was immediately debriefed on Midway. Rear Adm. Showers told the Roundtable about the importance of that debrief in this message from 2004:

During the battle, I was in the ComInt shop [Combat Intelligence Unit, Pearl Harbor] getting the Japanese messages, and we knew from intercepts that the first three carriers had sunk. But this information was TOP SECRET

ULTRA. The next day, George Gay was rescued and debriefed. In the SECRET debrief report, he said that he had seen the three carriers attacked, burn fiercely, and sink. That report enabled us (and Admiral Nimitz) to accept what we knew from ComInt at a lower classification, and the admiral was able to issue his after-action report about the carriers sunk.

On the next day, John Lundstrom followed that with the actual CINCPAC message from June 5th that outlined Gay's debrief. The message is time-stamped 0625 on June 6th, which was 1825 (6:25 PM) on June 5th, Midway time:

MESSAGE 060625 JUNE 1942 CINCPAC TO CTF-16, INFO CTF-17: ENS GAY TORPRON 8 RESCUED AND NOW ON MIDWAY X HE MADE DROP AND SCORED HIT BUT WAS SHOT DOWN ON DEPARTURE BY 0 FIGHTERS CLOSE TO CARRIER X WHILE HIDING UNDER CUSHION AND NOT INFLATING LIFE RAFT UNTIL DARK HE SAW FOLLOWING X QUOTE X CARRIER SLIGHTLY SMALLER THAN TWO GIANTS BURNING AND A SHIP THOUGHT TO BE A BATTLESHIP ON FIRE X THEN SAW SEVERAL HITS DIVE BOMBERS FROM HIS GROUP AND BOTH BIGGEST SIZE CARRIERS STARTED BURNING FIERCELY X CRUISER TRIED TO RESCUE PERSONNEL FROM CARRIER NEAREST HIM LATER BEGAN FIRING TO SINK IT X IDENTIFIES THIS SHIP AS KAGA OR AKAGI X CARRIER HE HIT WITH TORPEDO AND LATER BY DIVE BOMBERS NEARLY DEAD IN WATER ALL AFTERNOON X DESTROYER LATER CAME ALONGSIDE NEAREST CARRIER AND TOOK OFF PERSONNEL X NEAR MORNING HE HEARD A NUMBER OF TREMENDOUS EXPLOSIONS X ALL 3 CARRIERS WERE SEEN BURNING FIERCELY X JAP PLANES CIRCLED OVERHEAD A LONG TIME X UNQUOTE NOW THAT ENEMY IS WITHOUT AIR CONSIDER IT FAVORABLE OPPORTUNITY ATTACK BY LIGHT FORCES.

Breaking the above message down to its essentials, it says that (a) Gay saw a "smaller" carrier (probably *Soryu*) and a battleship burning, (b) he saw two larger carriers (had to be *Akagi* and *Kaga*) attacked by SBDs and start to burn, and (c) he saw a cruiser trying to sink one of the large carriers. Then (d) he heard explosions on the morning of June 5th, and finally, (e) he saw all three carriers burning, although exactly when he saw them burning and from what distance isn't stated. Except for the cruiser firing at one carrier, the message mentions nothing in connection with any of them sinking.

Midway Timeline

It is instructive at this point to outline what really happened. Here is the actual sequence of events for all four Japanese carriers:

> June 4th:
> 0936: VT-8 under attack by Japanese CAP
> 0942: All VT-8 planes shot down (Gay presumed in the water at this point)
> 1022: McClusky's SBDs dive upon *Kaga*
> 1023: Best's SBDs dive upon *Akagi*
> 1028: *Soryu* hit by bombs from Leslie's SBDs
> 1705: *Hiryu* bombed by *Enterprise* and *Yorktown* SBDs
> 1915: *Soryu* sunk by torpedoes from Japanese DD, location 30-42.5N, 178-37.5W
> 1925: *Kaga* sunk by torpedoes from Japanese DD, location 30-23.3N, 179-17.2W
>
> June 5th:
> 0510: Japanese DD fires one torpedo at *Hiryu* in scuttling attempt
> 0520: *Akagi* sunk by torpedoes from four Japanese DDs, location 30-30N, 178-40W
> 0915: *Hiryu* finally sinks from bomb damage and torpedo, location 31-27.5N, 179-23.5E
> 1250: Gay rescued by PBY[16]

Looking back at the CINCPAC message, then, the only thing wrong with it is the mention of a burning battleship (none were hit during the BOM), the cruiser firing at a carrier (nothing like that in Japanese records), and the fact that the hits seen on *Soryu*, then *Akagi* and *Kaga* were out of sequence; all minor points. If Gay had left it at that, there would have been no controversy.

But he didn't. In his 1943 interview, Gay stated once again that he had been adrift in the midst of *Kido Butai*, watching all three Japanese carriers burn. Two of them burned all night, he said.[17] Then, years later, he stated in his book that he saw the SBDs bomb all three carriers, after which all three and their escorts "steamed right over me." He then says that two of the carriers were scuttled in the night, and that another went down at dawn on June 5th.[18] The "two" would have to be *Kaga* and *Soryu*, going down in the early evening of the fourth, followed by *Akagi* on the following morning. Note the discrepancy there with his 1943 interview in which he'd stated that he watched *two* carriers burn all night. That wasn't possible since two of them were gone shortly after dark, leaving only *Akagi* anywhere near him (*Hiryu* was still afloat but more than sixty miles away).

A Limited View

The controversy got launched right there because of the relative distances between the three carriers at the locations where they sank. The latitude-longitude coordinates logged by the Japanese (above) provide the following separation among the three:

> *Kaga* sank 39 nautical miles southwest of *Soryu*.
> *Kaga* sank 33 NM west-southwest of *Akagi*.
> *Akagi* sank 13 NM south of *Soryu*.

Since Gay indicates he was in his raft while watching the three ships sink, his field of vision had to be limited to that possible at three to four feet above sea level, which is not more than just a few miles under ideal conditions. That raises a fundamental problem in his claim of watching *Kaga* and *Soryu* sink, since they did so just after sundown and Gay didn't get up into his raft until after dark. Seeing two ships sink that are thirty-nine nautical miles apart while one's head is barely above water is just a bit beyond the pale. If you can put that aside, even if he was perfectly positioned at the midpoint of the above three locations, his minimum distance to the farthest of the three would have been more than fifteen miles. If, as is more likely, he was rather close to *Akagi* (whose sinking he describes in some detail as opposed to the other two) then his separation from *Soryu* and especially *Kaga* would have been even greater. (See Figure 4.)

Thus it is reasonable to question whether Gay could possibly have seen all three carriers sink, and the detail-focused members of the Roundtable did exactly that with a certain vigor. That occurred a number of times through the years, but it is best illustrated by the following exchange initiated by Jon Parshall early in 2004. He believed that *Kido Butai* had moved far north of where Gay ditched before being attacked by the SBDs, thus making it nearly impossible for the pilot to have seen much of anything:

> From everything I've read, Gay's accounts are simply not to be trusted, or must be used with utmost caution. Much of what he says he saw while in the water is not supported by known facts, so it seems to me that whatever he says must be independently confirmed. Unfortunately, that's really hard to do, given the lack of survivors within the squadron. Gay's remarks may well have been constructed with a knowledge of contemporary accounts of the battle and designed to corroborate them.

In response, Gay's banner was taken up by screenwriter Paul Corio, then in the midst completing and marketing his script centered on the torpedo squadrons at Midway. He strongly countered Parshall's opinion with the following:

> The charge that a great veteran like Gay fabricated his story is a serious allegation. The doubts seem to arise from the purely speculative assertion that the Japanese fleet *may* have moved beyond his field of view by the time the SBDs attacked. Only Gay himself really knew the positions of the carriers relative to him from the time he was shot down until the SBDs' attack, and I believe the facts as we know them greatly favor him being in position to witness the carriers' destruction.
>
> VT-8's TBDs were initially spotted by screening ships at around 0920. Gay, as the last plane in line, likely didn't reach his drop point for at least ten more minutes, or at around 0930. He states that after dropping his fish he flew beyond the destroyer screen (several more minutes gone, several miles put between him and the carriers) before being shot down, around 0940. Then after several more minutes spent escaping his plane and attempting to rescue his gunner, he dodged strafing Zeros until they stopped shooting, which occurred because the fleet was overtaking his position in the water, likely around 0945. At that moment the fleet is bearing down on his position and VT-6 is about to attack. The carriers again start evasive maneuvers. Instead of passing beyond Gay's position, they circle and turn relatively near him until the end of VT-6's attack. Since the time of VT-6's final forays virtually coincide with the spotting of VT-3 at 1010, the maneuvering and turning of the carriers continued unabated until the SBDs hit at 1020.
>
> Also, the details about what Gay saw both in his book and in his 1943 interview are very compelling in their vivacity. It's hard to conceive that his explicit details and vivid visuals were entirely the products of an imagination. Also, Gay's willingness to recount his story to Admiral Nimitz shortly after his rescue is further evidence that he was telling the truth. He would have been taking a huge risk by giving concocted information to Nimitz himself if it had turned out to be contradictory to the dive bombers' after-action reports and debriefings.

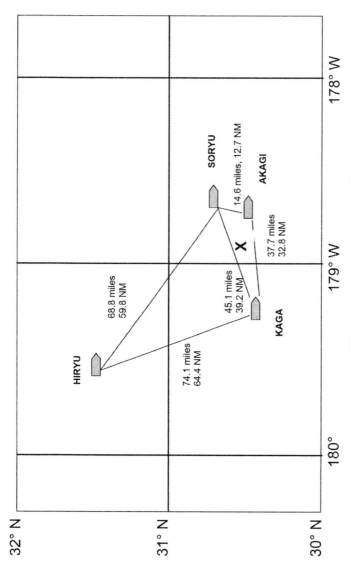

FIGURE 4. This chart shows the location at which each Japanese carrier sank, as recorded in the Nagumo Report. The optimum position in which George Gay could have been floating while watching (as he says) *Akagai, Kaga,* and *Soryu* sink would have been at point "X," placing him within about 15 miles of *Akagi.* But he would have been up to 20 or more miles from the other two, casting strong doubt that he could have seen, at the most, more than one of them actually sink.

Both of the above positions contain important points. Parshall hit upon the suspicion held by many that Gay's 1979 book was written as much to conform to then-known history as it was to reflect his own recollections. On the other hand, Corio rightly observes that, given the fact that Gay flew some distance beyond *Kido Butai* before ditching, it's at least possible that the fleet could have steamed somewhere near his vicinity and more or less stayed there while dodging continuous attacks by VT-6, VT-3, and finally the dive bombers. There are several minor elements to Gay's story that appear blatantly wrong, such as seeing SBDs drop one bomb then pull up and dive on another target.[19] But as for the primary assertions in his book—that he witnessed the dive bombers' attack, saw all three carriers on fire, and saw all three of them sink— only the latter one can be considered as inarguably false, given the times of their sinkings and especially their distance from each other and from Gay, regardless where he was at the time. (It's noteworthy that that claim was absent in his Midway debrief and in the 1943 interview.)

In the sum, then, the accounts by George Gay at Midway must be labeled as part fact and most assuredly, part fable.

✻   ✻   ✻   ✻

7. Bombing Doctrine and McClusky's Target

Contention: Lt. Cdr. C. Wade McClusky, leading *Enterprise* SBD squadrons VB-6 and VS-6, nearly caused a very serious mishap by diving on the wrong enemy carrier. VB-6 skipper Lt. Richard Best then saved the day by quickly ad-libbing his attack plan, resulting in the destruction of *Akagi*.

Consensus: *fact* (but with some unresolved questions)

While the saga of VT-8 is generally considered the archetypical tragedy of the Battle of Midway, the attack by the *Enterprise* and *Yorktown* dive bombers less than an hour later has to be its signature triumph. The sudden and unexpected fatal crippling of three enemy fleet carriers by the SBDs in the space of about five minutes inalterably decided the winner of the battle just as it had barely begun.

Below and Behind

But it very nearly didn't turn out that way because of an odd mixup between McClusky and Best that remained relatively unknown for a quarter century after the battle. In 1967 Walter Lord first brought the snafu into general view by noting that McClusky had radioed Best to attack *Akagi* with VB-6 while he and

VS-6 would dive on *Kaga*. Lord says that at that time VB-6 was "below and behind" the group commander and VS-6. However, Best didn't receive McClusky's radio message, and believing that *Enterprise* bombing doctrine proscribed his squadron to attack the nearest target (*Kaga*), he lined up his planes to do precisely that. At that instant McClusky and VS-6 "streaked down from above" in front of Best toward *Kaga*. Best abruptly aborted his dive and managed to redirect two of his squadron's pilots to join him in diverting to the farther target, *Akagi*. Through skill and a good dose of sheer luck, those three bombs scored one solid hit and two damaging near misses on Nagumo's flagship, enough to take it out of the battle and the war. McClusky, VS-6, and the balance of VB-6 went on to dispatch Kaga.[20]

Below and Ahead

That became an issue on the Roundtable in 2005 when I noticed an interesting discrepancy between the above account in *Incredible Victory* and the same tale as related in *Miracle at Midway*. Gordon Prange and his coauthors stated that Best and VB-6 were below and *ahead* of McClusky and VS-6, not behind them as reported by Lord. Best himself also stated it that way in a personal interview posted on the Internet.[21] Since the "Best-below-and-ahead" version thus seemed more prevalent, I got to wondering how McClusky and VS-6 could have dived in front of Best from above if Best was ahead of them. Then, another look at Best's Internet interview confused the issue further. Here's the relevant passage, to which I've added emphasis to certain key words:

> I started dropping down to 15,000 feet…this put me well below and *ahead* of the AGC [McClusky] so that when we sighted the Japanese carriers I was 5,000 feet under him. He assigned targets by radio, which I didn't receive. When abreast of the nearest carrier, I called him to say that I was attacking according to doctrine (i.e., leading aircraft take the *far* target and trailing planes take the *nearer* targets) and thus share the surprise. I turned toward the nearest carrier [*Kaga*]…and when nearly over the target with my division in column, I started to open my dive flaps, when right in front of me and from above, the AGC and Scouting Six came pouring in. Furious at the foul-up, I tried to cause my squadron to rejoin, but without success, I took my first section of three planes toward the next carrier [*Akagi*].

If the above quote is accurate, it appears that Best contradicted himself. First he states that he was *ahead* of McClusky, then he explains the doctrine itself (*leading* squadron hits *far* target, etc.), then he says he started to push over on the *near* target, even though he was in the lead. Then he faults McClusky for also diving on the near target, even though that would be correct according to the doctrine as he explained it.

It seemed as if the third sentence in Best's quote above should read "this put me well below and *behind* McClusky…" It all makes sense with that change, including the fact that Best saw McClusky and VS-6 diving in front of him. It also conforms to Walter Lord's account of the incident. Believing I'd found the logical answer to the riddle, I telephoned the Roundtable's expert on VB-6, Rear Admiral Lewis Hopkins, who had flown in the second division of Best's squadron during that attack. After explaining why I was calling, I asked the key question:

"Admiral, just before your air group dove upon the two Japanese carriers, what was the position of your squadron relative to McClusky and VS-6?"

"We were below and in front of them," he replied.

"In *front* of McClusky?" I asked. There went another fine theory.

"Sure. We had to descend because one of the guys had an oxygen failure. When you head down, you gain speed. So we wound up ahead of the rest of them."

Another Doctrine

That left me more puzzled that before, since Hopkins had supported the view of both his squadron commander and the authors of *Miracle at Midway*, even though the opposite version as set forth by Walter Lord was the only one of the two that made sense. As if that wasn't enough, the issue was severely muddled further by the following message from Bill Vickrey:

Jim Murray was a chief ARM and flew in Best's rear seat as his R/G on June 4, 1942. I spent a good bit of time with Best and Murray at a couple of *Enterprise* reunions, and Jim and I had a great deal of correspondence over the years. In fact, he was writing a letter to me when he died, and a nurse sent the unfinished letter on to me. Jim wrote an unpublished memoir and graciously gave me a copy. Here is an excerpt from that memoir:

"Shortly after sighting the Japanese carrier force, the commanding officer (Lt. Best) of Bombing Squadron Six (VB-6) deployed his squadron into its three division attack formation and proceeded to attack the nearest Jap carrier (IJN *Kaga*). This was in accordance with Air Group Six attack doctrine. This doctrine specified that the dive bomber squadron carrying the heaviest bomb load will be the low squadron in the step-down formation and its target will be the closest to the air group formation (fuel use compensation). The other dive bomber squadron with the lesser bomb load will attack the next available target. [Murray is alluding to an ordnance load in which VS-6 launches from the

Enterprise first with 500-pound bombs, then VB-6 follows behind with 1000-pounders, taking advantage of additional takeoff room on the flight deck.]

"This did not happen at Midway. At the moment the first division of Bombing Six reached the roll-over point, the air group commander's section, followed by Scouting Squadron Six came diving down from above, narrowly missing 6-B-1 [Best and Murray's aircraft], forcing it and the rest of the division to 'bail-out' to avoid a mid-air collision. 6-B-1, 6-B-2, and 6-B-3 proceeded toward the next carrier in line, the IJN *Akagi*. 6-B-5 (Roberts) and 6-B-6 (Halsey) did not follow the first [division] but went their own way. The second and third division leaders ignored their commanding officer's radio command to follow him and instead followed VS-6 and attacked the *Kaga*.

"The group commander, in leading and participating in the attack on the *Kaga,* not only usurped Bombing Squadron Six's target and broke up their formation, but put himself into a position where he could not direct the overall attack. As a result, the group commander's three planes, Scouting Six's fifteen planes, and ten planes of Bombing Six all attacked the IJN *Kaga*. Three Bombing Six aircraft did attack the [*Akagi*]."

Thus, into the already confusing mix of doctrinal definitions and recollections from Lord, Prange, Best, and Hopkins we added the brand new and unrelated definition of the USS *Enterprise's* bombing doctrine as supplied by Commander Murray, Best's former R/G: "the squadron carrying the heaviest bomb load attacks the near target, and that with the lighter load goes after the far target." I found it truly remarkable that two veterans who went into battle *in the same aircraft* could hold two such differing views as to what their air group's dive bombing doctrine really was.

Radio Protocols

But there was still more. I noted another problem with Best's account: he said he'd radioed McClusky that he was "attacking according to doctrine." I don't mean to denigrate Richard Best at all here, for in the final analysis he was a major hero of the battle whose quick thinking in the midst of a foul-up sank an enemy carrier that otherwise would have survived. Still, "I'm attacking according to doctrine" seemed to me an odd choice for a radio transmission at that time and under those circumstances. Radio communications were tenuous throughout the Battle of Midway, and anything that remotely could be subject to misinterpretation should have been avoided. Was that the proper time to expect anyone in the air group to correctly interpret what "doctrine" was and react accordingly? Surely a more sensible transmission at that point would have been "I'm attacking the near carrier," or "I'm attacking the carrier on the left," thereby removing all ambiguity.

Remember that in the BOM era, pilots typically used brief, clear radio calls, employing their own first names as call signs and limiting themselves to very simple phrases like, "Jim, come on down!"[22] In that scenario, "I'm attacking according to doctrine" appears much too formal for the circumstances, and I had to wonder if that's what Best had really transmitted then, or if that's what he preferred to say years later when he related the tale to an interviewer while remembering his anger toward McClusky. Of course, it's largely academic since apparently no one heard either Best or McClusky's radio transmissions at that time. But it does add further confusion to the issue and especially to Best's account of it.

In summary, (a) we have Richard Best's definition of the *Enterprise* air group's bombing doctrine and his contradictory statement concerning exactly who was in violation of that doctrine, (b) we have Walter Lord affirming the same definition for the doctrine but with VB-6 in an opposite position in the formation from that stated by Best, (c) we have Cdr. Murray's completely different definition of the bombing doctrine, and finally (d) there is reason to question what Best said he tried to tell McClusky by radio just before starting his dive.

But in the end we are left with three inescapable facts: Best and McClusky did start to dive on the same target, the more experienced Best then modified his attack literally on the fly and thus helped in large measure to win the entire battle, and finally, scores of authors and academic professionals have reviewed this matter for nearly a half century and have not found fault with it. That being the case, the contention that Best saved the day by overcoming an inadvertent error perpetrated by McClusky must be admitted as factual, despite some nagging confusion factors.

*   *   *   *

8. *"All Battle Flags Flying"*

Contention: After a prolonged death struggle, the USS *Yorktown* finally sank with dignity like a proud lady, going down "with all battle flags flying."

Consensus: *fable*

The issue here is rather minor, although it has been inflated out of proportion by one crusading veteran. It arises from Captain Buckmaster's official after-action report in which he said:

> About 0530 on the morning of June 7 the list of the *Yorktown* was noticed to be rapidly increasing to port and, at 0701, *Yorktown* turned over on her port side and sank in about 3000 fathoms of water with all battle flags flying.[23]

"All battle flags flying" was actually just a touch of poetic license on the part of the battle-worn captain, for the presence of *any* such flags on U.S. warships in 1942 was doubtful, as explained by Otis Kight with this revelation:

> From *Naval Customs, Traditions and Usage*, published by the U.S. Naval Institute, 1939: a two-line paragraph on page 866 says, "2815. The use of battle flags at the fore and main has been discontinued. During battle the ensign shall be hoisted at the gaff only."
>
> Somewhere there is an inkling that the "battle flag" was a much larger one, used only in battle so the enemy could see it much easier. Economy also ruled that a less expensive flag (smaller) would be beat to shreds just as fast as one that cost twice as much!

Indeed, an examination of the several on-scene photographs taken of the *Yorktown* during the battle by ship's photographer Bill Roy and perhaps others shows only a single national ensign flying from the carrier's foretruck as the crew abandoned on the afternoon of June 4th. Nonetheless, the notion of the beloved ship somehow going down gracefully and gloriously with streaming banners has become an accepted notion in the lore of the BOM.

Samuel Eliot Morison, writing only a few years after the battle, described the *Yorktown's* sinking rather accurately, noting that the ship simply "rolled over and sank...with her loose gear making a horrible death rattle."[24] That was supported on the Roundtable by eyewitness accounts from our veterans who watched it happen at the time. Ship's photographer Bill Roy was particularly passionate in response to fictionalized images of *Yorktown* sinking in some vainglorious style. He told us his view in this message from 2003:

> On the early morning of June 7, 1942, *Yorktown* was dead in the water and appeared to be on an even keel. She started to roll to port, then went down stern first, going faster and faster, with rumbles and roiling water, as compartments filled and burst from the water pressure. There was no wake, no forward movement.

> It is my hope that historical research done by those who talk about *York-town* and artists who paint her take the time to research the facts from the more than adequate records, reports, photos, and surveys to correctly reflect the truth about this fine ship, and not slander her reputation about what her last hours were like.

Roy's comment was mainly in response to an Internet site sponsored by another BOM veteran who abhors the thought of the *Yorktown* giving up its life in any way other than valiantly charging into the waves with banners streaming. In recent years that veteran (not a Roundtable member) has mounted an aggressive, quixotic campaign to get the Navy to change the record of the *Yorktown's* demise to conform to his romantic view. He had been a crewman on a Task Force 17 destroyer, and has gone to great lengths to convince all who will listen that every account of the *Yorktown's* sinking by capsizing and noisily going down stern-first (including official U.S. Navy photographs showing exactly that) are a nefarious conspiracy designed by undefined parties to sully the proud name of a great ship. He even went so far as to take the stage during the official 2005 Battle of Midway commemoration in Washington to trumpet his bizarre theories, to the consternation of the admiral commanding the local naval district.[25]

While the foregoing is a rather rare case of someone deliberately embellishing the account of *Yorktown's* final minutes, others have unknowingly helped to promote the myth. Walter Lord gave it a subtle boost with the following in *Incredible Victory:* "There were the usual noises, but to most of the men she went quietly and with enormous dignity—'like the great lady she was,' as one of them put it."[26] *Enormous dignity* was hardly they case, though, as the giant vessel first rolled over on its topside, then ingloriously slid backwards into depths amid the clatter of collapsing bulkheads and loose equipment. Captain Buckmaster's "all battle flags flying" artfulness was subsequently repeated, often in quotes but occasionally without, in a great many writings about the BOM, to the point that the image has become more or less accepted as fact.[27]

In reality, though, it is clear from the various extant photographs that only one national ensign was hoisted on *Yorktown* from the moment it was abandoned until it sank. That one flag might have been the largest available on the ship, such as its holiday ensign, but "battle flags" per se simply weren't there. It's also clear, from accounts by *Yorktown* veterans on scene at the time, that the great ship's demise proceeded in a decidedly ungraceful manner. Those who continue to believe otherwise are simply hanging on to a very nice fable.

*   *   *   *

9. Conspiracy Theory

Contention: President Roosevelt had foreknowledge of Japan's intention to attack the U.S. fleet in Pearl Harbor, but let it happen in order to force America into the war.

Consensus: *fable*

I explained at the beginning of Chapter 3 that certain key historical events both before and after the Battle of Midway have provided relevant and important subject matter for the Roundtable. The most obvious example is the Pearl Harbor attack, the seminal act in the naval war that was to bloody the Pacific in the following months, to Midway and beyond.

As it happened, Pearl Harbor was the source of the most prolonged and harangued discourse in the Roundtable's history, commencing in 2001 with the temporary participation of Mr. Robert Stinnett, the author of a very popular best seller, *Day of Deceit: FDR and the Truth About Pearl Harbor*, and continuing sporadically for the next two years. The thesis of Stinnett's book is that the President, through JN-25 intercepts that made their way to the Oval Office in 1941, was fully aware that the IJN intended to assault Pearl Harbor, but saw that as a means to break the public's isolationist views, making it possible to jump into the war and thus save England and Europe from the Nazis. Therefore, in Stinnett's view, Roosevelt conspired to not only refrain from action in the face of the Japanese threat but also to deliberately deny the on-scene commanders in Hawaii any knowledge of what they were about to endure.

Rebuttal

Don McDonald, a retired cryptologist with the National Security Agency, was quick to descend upon Mr. Stinnett and his theories, offering the Roundtable a lengthy critique of *Day of Deceit* in May 2001. Here are some excerpts from the critique, written after Stinnett had given a presentation to a meeting of cryptologists at which McDonald was present:

> Our February speaker, Robert B. Stinnett, discussed his book *Day of Deceit*. His theory is that FDR was willing to accept Pearl Harbor casualties

because they would be a price justified by shaking our country out of its isolationist leanings and embracing the war he wanted.

Stinnett's theory differs significantly from the many other "FDR Knew" conjectures published in the past because it involves a new source for the intelligence FDR allegedly received about the impending Pearl Harbor attack. The new theory holds that we got such intelligence from high level Japanese naval message traffic that the U.S. Navy was reading at the time. Supposedly, the President arranged to have Admiral Kimmel, Commander of the Pacific Fleet, kept in ignorance of the attack. To keep the conspiracy a secret, the theory requires that FDR and the Navy, plus the Secretaries of State, Navy, and War Department, and everyone else who had read this critical intelligence took part in the subsequent fifty-nine year cover-up, which Stinnett says his research finally exposed.

As hard as he tries, Stinnett can't find proof that [intelligence pointing to a Japanese attack on Pearl Harbor] ever existed. He assumes that it must have come from our exploiting *high-level* Japanese naval traffic. In his book he makes much of the fact that when he did his research, many records concerning our efforts to exploit this traffic were classified and not available to him. He contends that rebuff was part of the Navy's cover-up. But within the last two years many key records have finally become available in the National Archives. Historian Stephen Budiansky points out in his review of Stinnett's book (U.S. Naval Institute *Proceedings*, December 1999) that those old records show unmistakably that prior to Pearl Harbor, the high-level Japanese cryptographic systems involved *had not* been broken to the point where any useful intelligence was derived from them or *could have been* derived from them.

On pages 292-293 of his book, Stinnett reproduces two messages which would have been "smoking guns" except for the awkward fact that they weren't read until 1942!

[Stinnett] is clearly wrong about JN-25, and as a result, FDR's name doesn't belong in the book's title. Nor do I think the word "truth" belongs there, because his book is useless as history. He ruins all of his admirable research by recklessly twisting every scrap of his evidence to support his theory. He ignores or glosses over powerful, conflicting evidence; he ignores simpler explanations involving human incompetence; he indulges in 20/20 hindsight; and he pads his book with a lot of peripheral or irrelevant evidence. Cryptologic historian David Kahn wrote what many consider the definitive history of the subject in his *The Codebreakers*. He reviewed *Day of Deceit* in the *New York Review of Books*, November 2, 2000. There he sums up Stinnett's work succinctly in these words: "…he misreads the record, misunderstands intelligence, mishandles facts, and misdirects readers."

An Early Warning?

As the discussion proceeded on the Roundtable, John Gardner's report of a message read to him and his fellow Marines on Midway on December 5, 1941, warning of the "Japanese fleet maneuvering in your area" was offered as evidence that CINCPAC knew something was coming toward the Hawaii/Midway area at that time (see Chapter 5). But that contention was easily put to rest with the following explanation that I was able to offer the Roundtable myself, based on a modest background in naval communications plus a reluctance to draw conclusions from shallow inferences:

> The problem with this story is that we don't have the message in hand for review, and it has apparently been lost to history—not found in any message archives from CINCPAC. Consequently, we don't know who the addressee(s) on the message were, and exactly what "your area" meant without drawing baseless assumptions. Was Lieutenant Cannon reading a message addressed specifically to Midway, or did the Marines' communications center copy a general message intended for much broader dissemination? We don't know, for example, that the message wasn't actually intended for the western Pacific area (meaning the Philippines), of which Midway is perhaps the eastern fringe. Elements of the Japanese fleet "maneuvering" near the Philippines on December 5th would have been entirely plausible.
>
> Alternately, did "Japanese fleet maneuvering in your area" refer to the two destroyers that approached and shelled Midway two days later? That's another possibility that can't be discounted in this instance.
>
> In any case, my inclination is to stick with the facts, which are very limited here. We don't know anything about this message except what John Gardner reported, which is only the text. We don't know when the message was originated; only its apparent date of receipt on Midway. We don't know to whom it was intended; only that a radioman on Midway copied it. And most especially, we don't know what "area" CINCPAC was referring to in the message. With all those unknowns, this will never be more than just another intriguing anecdote, incapable of impacting much of anything one way or the other.

The Challenge of JN-25 in 1941

But the heart of the debate was Station HYPO's alleged ability to copy JN-25 before December 7th, and thus funnel Japanese plans up the chain of command to the President himself. That notion was mercilessly thrashed by the Roundtable's ComInt veterans, who knew from first-hand experience what Station HYPO could and couldn't do in 1941 with regard to Japanese navy intercepts:

next to nothing, to be exact. Admiral Showers explained it like this, no doubt with drawn sword:

> The "revisionists" of history are those who develop a preconceived notion and then seek and usually find anecdotal evidence to validate their notion. The Stinnett book is a prime example of that procedure. It is also dead wrong, full of what appear to be intentional misinterpretations that he twisted to support his theories.
>
> Breaking the Japanese code (JN-25) was not a sudden, one-time accomplishment. It was worked on for months by a great many persons (USN, British, Australians, Dutch) with some slowly developing success. The major task was to discover and understand the nature and the structure of the system being used: code groups, code group meanings, additives, keys to additive tables, etc. This initial step had been pretty well accomplished prior to December 1941, but the further key to *reading* messages was recovery of code group meanings. There were over 50,000 of them in the JN-25 "dictionary" and each had to be recovered, *one by painful one*!
>
> Prior to December 7, 1941 the effort against JN-25 was steady but not an all-out job. HYPO, for example, wasn't even working on it. We were laboring (unsuccessfully) against the Japanese flag officers' code. Also, prior to the war, the Japanese were transmitting a relatively light volume of JN-25 traffic. Cryptologists require a high volume of traffic in order to acquire "depth" in any system. That had not become possible until after the war began and the Japanese greatly increased their transmissions in JN-25.
>
> As U.S. mobilization took effect, there were major increases in cryptologic and linguistic effort by the Naval Security Group to recover JN-25 code group meanings. After about three months of concentrated effort we had recovered enough of them to enable us to commence making sense out of Japanese message texts. Through research, very hard work, and with some lucky breaks, we slowly were able to create intelligence out of even partial message texts. That was when we were able to detect the operation leading to the Battle of Coral Sea, immediately followed by even better understanding of the traffic setting up the operation for Midway.
>
> Believe Phil Jacobson. Believe Dwayne Whitlock. Believe me. We were all participants at the time, in one way or another. There was no prior reading of JN-25 before the war! There was no prior knowledge of the Japanese plan to attack Pearl Harbor! I can state with absolute confidence that, as much as he wanted the U.S. to become involved in the war, FDR had no "secret" information that has been covered up to this date. Anyone who believes that has simply been brainwashed by the revisionists who from time to time have floated theories without the backing of inarguable evidence or incontrovertible proof.
>
> This is the true story as clearly as I can state it. I urge all to lay aside these suspicions and dreams and accept the facts of history as experienced by those

of us who lived it. To continue to promote revisionist fiction is a gross disservice to future generations who will not have the benefit of getting the truth from those of us who were there.

Phil Jacobsen then pointed out the fundamental weakness of Stinnett's theory, the one that sends it and all FDR conspiracy fantasies to the dust bin: for the President to have known in advance about the Japanese attack, he couldn't possibly have acquired the knowledge by himself. His top commanders had to know it, too, and that's where the theory collapses:

> It wasn't just the top U.S. commanders who had to have foreknowledge of the Japanese plan to attack Pearl Harbor—the entire ComInt chain of command down to my own shipmates at Station Cast in Corregidor, Station H at Heeia/Pearl Harbor and Station N, Washington D.C. must have also been in on it. Are we to believe that our own U.S. Navy intelligence associates, enlisted as well as officer, were part of a massive conspiracy that caused the lives of some 2,500 of our shipmates? All of them to a man deny such nonsense!

Jacobsen's point echoed the same sentiment that Don McDonald had stated at the outset, and it seemed to effectively end the debate at that time. Clearly, a secret so damning that was, of necessity, held by so many people at the multiple ComInt levels between the cryptologists in the field and the President in Washington would have been leaked at some point in the six decades between then and now. Yet that has never happened—not one White House typist, not one Navy Department messenger, not one OP-20-G cryptologist, not one IBM keypunch operator at HYPO—*no one* in sixty years has ever come forward with the smoking gun that validates any FDR conspiracy theory relative to Pearl Harbor or anything else. Without a smoking gun, such theories are little more then marginally interesting mind games.

Stephen Budiansky, cited above by McDonald, was a participating member of the Roundtable during a few of its earlier years. On a television documentary produced in 2004, he joined a panel of experts who were tasked with convincing viewers why Stinnett's book had to be branded a fable. While the panel provided an abundance of testimony on why that is so, Budiansky eloquently boiled it all down to one concise statement: "Stinnett obviously believes his own theories," he said. "He's just simply wrong!"

*   *   *   *

How a Myth Is Born

This detailed examination of some of Midway's fables was an interesting exercise, for in the process it became clear how easily one of them can arise. All that is necessary is for a respected source, preferably a major one like Morison or Lord, to either make a minor misstatement on a point of fact, or worse, to actually state the matter correctly, but in a way that is easily misinterpreted (as in the "Midway is short of water" ruse). In either case, by the time the tale has been repeated and enhanced by succeeding generations of historians and academics, a minor misstatement can become embedded history.

An example of how that happens came to my attention while working on Chapter 10. In contrasting the June 4th launch sequence between the carriers of Task Forces 16 and 17, I noted that the *Yorktown* sent off its TBD torpedo bombers *ahead* of its SBD dive bombers and F4F fighters, or at least that's what Walter Lord reported in *Incredible Victory* in 1967. The same thing was echoed in succession by Prange, Lundstrom, and Cressman between 1982 and 1990.[28] Then, in reading Jon Parshall's *Shattered Sword*, I came upon the following description of *Yorktown's* launch: "The SBDs went first, followed by the TBDs, the latter heading off immediately to the southwest..."[29] That piqued my interest, since I knew Parshall to be very meticulous in his research, yet his launch sequence conflicted with every previous account of the same event.

Of course, the big advantage on the Roundtable in researching a point in history is that you can often get the straight story by asking the guys who actually made the history. I sent the following message to VT-3 veteran Lloyd Childers:

> Lloyd, when you launched from the *Yorktown* at the Battle of Midway, which squadron launched first: VT-3 or VB-3? I've always understood that the torpedo planes launched first, but one source says that Lt. Cdr. Leslie and VB-3 launched *ahead* of VT-3. What is your recollection as to who launched first?

Childers' reply was another myth-buster:

> Russ, my memory is that VT-3 launched last because there was some doubt that most of our TBDs could get airborne with a torpedo. In fact, T-3 [Childers' aircraft] just barely made it. We dropped quickly off the flight deck

to a few feet above the water. I recall hearing that the skipper's T-1 had new engine that had about 100 more horsepower.

Of course, that not only made eminently good sense—the heavy TBDs needed maximum deck space in order to get going—but spotting twelve of them in front of two other squadrons would have assured the leading aircraft a very short flight off the ship's bow! That important fact should have been evident at the outset to Walter Lord and all who came after him, but they'd all missed it. Curious, I followed up with a question to John Lundstrom, asking how he thought the obvious error could have crept into nearly all accepted accounts of the battle, including his own. His nothing-held-back response not only explained exactly how he and others had gotten it wrong, but why Parshall and his coauthor Tony Tully had gotten it right:

> It's because we were stupid and weren't thinking. We all made the mistake of putting VT-3 first because that's the way the *Yorktown* report reads. It's wrong; VB-3 went off first, then VT-3. I realized the error years ago when doing research on an upcoming book, and advised Parshall and Tully.

That's the sort of thing that has helped to sustain a high interest in a continuing dialogue with our Battle of Midway veterans on the Roundtable. At this late date more than six decades after the smoke cleared, there are still some things to be learned.

CHAPTER 13

▼

WHAT IF

Analysis Through Alternative History

The title of this chapter is also the title of an interesting anthology compiled by Robert Cowley on the subject of alternative history. The book speculates on what would have transpired if certain key events that significantly affected the history of the world had turned out differently. For example, the premature death of Alexander the Great (entirely possible for the young, aggressive warrior) would have replaced Greek influence with Persian in the Mediterranean region, obviating the advent of Greek philosophies (i.e., democratic principles) in the Roman Empire and subsequently in modern Europe. Indeed, there may have *never been* a Roman Empire nor one of its principal consequences, Christianity.

Not surprisingly, the Battle of Midway is included in the book because of its stunning impact on World War II in the Pacific. The author of the BOM chapter, history professor Theodore. E. Cook, Jr., has the IJN winning at Midway because an astute Japanese radioman on occupied Wake Island decides that the "water ruse" message sent from Midway without encryption must be a fake, designed to ferret out the meaning of certain Japanese radio codes, which of course it was (see Chapter 4). The Japanese communications officer on Wake forwards his suspicions about the message to Tokyo, which then causes their intelligence analysts to assume the Americans are reading their codes. Thusly knowing that the enemy had probably intercepted his Midway battle plan and that their carriers would most likely meet him there, Yamamoto shifts his focus from the atoll to the enemy fleet. Nagumo, thusly armed with foreknowledge and thorough preparation for a carrier battle instead of a land attack, is able to overwhelm

Fletcher's forces instead of vice-versa, leading to the capture of Midway and ulti-mately Pearl Harbor. The U.S. eventually wins in the Pacific, but only through a lengthy, gargantuan effort that vastly eclipses what really happened.[1]

The Roundtable has always been fertile ground for such musings on alterna-tive history because so many vitally important aspects of the BOM could easily have turned out differently. However, Professor Cook's scenario really isn't among the best of them, as communications intelligence was never a strong suit of the Japanese throughout the war. Moreover, the garrison on Wake, a remote outpost not staffed with upper level officers having authority to deviate from established procedure, most likely would have promptly reported the Midway water plant intelligence exactly as they did under any circumstances. Failure to do so would contradict prior orders from Tokyo, and such flexibility did not exist in the notoriously rigid Japanese psyche.

But the BOM did have an abundance of situations that certainly could have—in some cases, *should* have—plausibly gone the other way. Unfortunately, analysis of such alternatives on the Roundtable was never overly popular with our Mid-way veterans. Admiral Showers offered this somewhat typical sentiment early in 2003:

> You know how I feel about revisionists. They cause me to use my delete key more than anything else. As to "what ifs," I know someone who is writing a book about World War II in the Pacific based entirely on "what ifs." I'll be happy to provide his name and address to anyone who wishes to waste time helping that pointless cause.

However, other Roundtable participants found a great deal of value in consid-eration of several what-might-have-been situations arising before and during the BOM. While the dialogue could turn rather intense if someone was promoting fantasized revisionism on the level of an FDR-Pearl Harbor conspiracy, there were other occasions in which simply acknowledging what didn't happen because of the American victory at Midway was deemed useful and positive. The impor-tant thing in such discussions was to separate revisionism from alternative his-tory.

The Perils of Revisionism

Revisionist history is the more aggressive of the two. The revisionist advocates a significant re-defining of an important historical event, with a view toward asserting that it actually happened in a manner or for a reason that is at odds with commonly accepted understandings. As such, revisionism is bound to fail unless its proponent brings forth new, verifiable facts that inarguably change the record. By that measure, Robert Stinnett's *Day of Deceit*, a prime example of revisionist history, is a failure because its fundamental thesis has proven to be far from inarguable.

But rather than uncovering new evidence that changes the historical record, a revisionist can also be successful by simply gathering together divergent pieces of archival evidence not previously considered in concert that, when taken together, compel a conclusion that differs from popular history. Jon Parshall accomplished as much in *Shattered Sword* with regard to the myth of Japanese flight decks at Midway being crowded with bomb and torpedo-laden Kates and Vals when the *Enterprise* and *Yorktown* dive bombers struck. Until Parshall and his coauthor Anthony Tully had meticulously compared the launch and recovery times of the Japanese CAP with the times of the various U.S. torpedo bomber attacks, no one had ever bothered to consider that the flight decks of the IJN carriers had to remain clear prior to the arrival of McClusky and Leslie's SBDs. The Japanese were frantically launching and recovering succeeding waves of fighters in the face of the maddening one-after-the-other assaults by American squadrons, and therefore had no chance to ready their bombers for a launch. The mayhem caused by U.S. bombs exploding amidst armed aircraft, charged fueling hoses, and scattered ordnance did occur, but it happened on the carriers' hangar decks, not the flight decks. The enemy aircraft seen on deck by various American eyewitnesses were largely Zero fighters, not an armed strike force. Thus a popular vision of the battle, considered axiomatic by most historians and artists, was essentially expunged through revisionist history.[2]

On the other hand, alternative history doesn't try to change anything. Instead, a major historical event is analyzed with certain key facts hypothetically altered—something that happened one way is postulated to have happened in a different manner that is reasonably believable. The supposed results of the altered facts are then reviewed in depth as to their effects upon subsequent history. The value of that exercise is an increase in the understanding of an historical event as it happened, as opposed to what almost happened or was likely to have eventually happened. As long as that was the goal of a Roundtable discussion, the veterans went along with it to a point, but any digressing into unsupportable revisionism tended to raise their hackles.

Viable Alternatives at Midway

With those unwritten rules more or less established, the Roundtable entered into frequent discussion and occasional debate on the outcome at Midway under various alternate scenarios. The BOM certainly had an abundance of circumstances that invite such considerations, like the remarkable degree to which the American cryptologists could read Japanese battle plans. Any moderation of HYPO's codebreaking achievements, entirely plausible, could have critically clouded CINCPAC's view of Japanese intentions. VT-8 skipper Waldron could have gritted his teeth and obeyed his immediate superior (eminently sensible!), staying with Stanhope Ring on his mysterious flight to nowhere. IJN destroyer *Arashi* could have maintained better screening discipline and broken off its lengthy chase of *Nautilus*, thus denying McClusky his guide to *Kido Butai*. Richard Best could certainly have completed the dive on *Kaga* that he started, leaving *Akagi* unscratched for perhaps the rest of the battle. The Japanese CAP could have met McClusky and Leslie's SBDs at their own altitude like they did in the Coral Sea, a given if Waldron sticks with Ring. VB-3's arming switches could have been wired correctly, meaning no splashing bombs to surprise Lloyd Childers in VT-3 and cause his diligent search for their source. These and several more twists of fate, none of which involve a serious breech of the extant conditions, could easily have changed the battle's outcome for the worse, profoundly altering the rest of the war in the Pacific and beyond.

But in the case of the Battle of Midway, there is an interesting problem in speculating about alternative outcomes. Nigel Moore, a Roundtable member in England, got to the heart of the matter with this passing comment attached to his application for joining the group in 2005:

> If what happened at Midway had been used as the plot of a novel, it would have been condemned as a totally unrealistic portrayal of events, something completely beyond anything that might possibly happen.

Therein lies the problem: the fact that the U.S. won at all at Midway was remarkable enough, but the total destruction of the Japanese carrier force was so astonishing that nothing conceivable in the realm of viable alternative history could have brought about a better result. Every postulation that didn't drift off into the sphere of the highly unlikely (and some that did, as with Professor Cook's free-thinking Japanese officer on Wake Island) ultimately brought a worse result for the American side than what actually occurred.

The result of such ruminations was a general consensus that the American victory at Midway, while clearly the result of a triumph of cryptology followed by a lot of dogged determination and courage, was admittedly aided in very large measure by successive strokes of downright luck, virtually all of which were good for the Americans and bad for the enemy. Chaplain Stanford Linzey, of course, held that "God was at Midway," and that was perhaps as good an explanation as any.

$$* \qquad * \qquad * \qquad *$$

Turning Point

The Battle of Midway has long been renowned as the fabled "Turning Point" of World War II in the Pacific. That notion became deeply etched in American naval history by Walter Lord's famous "no right to win" quote in *Incredible Victory*, which includes the assertion that the battle changed the course of the war. The book's jacket also trumpets a Winston Churchill quote that proclaimed, "at one stroke, the dominant position of Japan in the Pacific was reversed." Thus, the role of the BOM as the turning point in the war became an entrenched reality in the traditions of the battle, an accepted truth untouched by doubt or debate.

Until the advent of the Battle of Midway Roundtable, that is. At the risk of skirting the edges of revisionism, some of the group's members challenged the perception that the BOM had really affected the Pacific war all that much! Jon Parshall offered the opinion that, if one takes into account the results of the battle on Japanese naval air power and their fleet structure, you really need to look beyond Midway for a true turning point in the war:

> The battle is still commonly viewed as the "turning point" of the Pacific war, even though the notion of having a "turning point" in the larger context of a war whose outcome was pretty much pre-ordained is kind of oxymoronic. You can make a very strong case that if "Midway" didn't happen precisely when and where it did, it was almost inevitably going to happen sometime and somewhere else. Even if we'd lost at Midway, we weren't going to lose the war. It just would have taken longer.
>
> Additionally, the Japanese themselves did not seem to consider Midway as a turning point. They typically point to the fights in the Solomons, or even the defeat at Philippine Sea and the fall of Guam and Saipan in 1944 as being the battles where losing meant that they had lost it all. My vote is that the Solomons, by their grim attritional nature, were more damaging to the overall balance of the IJN than Midway. Among other things, battles like Eastern Solomons and the Santa Cruz Islands were clearly more responsible for wreck-

ing the core of the their carrier aviators as well as their force composition, much more so than Midway. Midway represented the point where the IJN lost its offensive force projection capability, but the Solomons represented the point where they utterly ceased to be effective.

As an inspired advocate of historical accuracy from the Japanese perspective, Parshall occasionally found himself rather lonely on the minority side of a subjective discourse. His resistance to the pervasive "turning point" tenet in Midway's lore would seem to have been an open invitation for more of the same, but it didn't turn out that way. Other members lined up with Parshall on this one, including ComInt veteran Phil Jacobsen, who had served on Guadalcanal in the Solomons as that campaign raged:

> My vote goes with Jon Parshall. The Japanese did not feel Midway was *the* turning point of the war. They called Guadalcanal the "fork in the road." Had we lost Guadalcanal, the war in New Guinea and elsewhere would have been much different and Australia would have been threatened again. One reason for MacArthur's early success in New Guinea, besides the excellent fighting spirit of Australian troops, was the fact that the Guadalcanal campaign siphoned off huge amounts of personnel, ships, and aircraft that were planned for New Guinea.
>
> Advocating Guadalcanal as the actual turning point in the Pacific does not degrade the great achievements scored at Midway. The BOM did stop Japan's unopposed free running of large carrier task forces, but I would suggest that a more serious review of the Guadalcanal campaign (land, sea and air) be made before deciding what was *the* turning point in the Pacific war.

Those are both well-reasoned arguments, but the majority were not swayed from the traditional view. Some pointed out that, without the unlikely victory at Midway, there *would not have been a Solomons campaign*, at least not in 1942. American forces would have been preoccupied in the central Pacific, possibly defending Pearl Harbor itself, leaving Japanese aspirations for choking off the American-Australian pipeline solidly within the realm of reality. That would portend a grave threat to MacArthur's meager forces then regrouping in Australia, plus the end of U.S. submarine bases in western Australia that supported the Navy's crippling campaign against Japan's merchant marine.

Midway's Impact Beyond the Pacific

That eventuality gave rise to the belief that the growing Japanese threat would have adversely affected prosecution of the war in Europe, since vital assets destined for the fight against Hitler would of necessity have been diverted to the Pacific. That notion gained a prominent advocate in the person of former U.S. Secretary of Defense Dr. James Schlesinger, who eloquently argued in the press that the "incredible victory" was essential to a timely invasion of the European continent in 1944. Admiral Showers came down on the side Dr. Schlesinger's ideas, as well as the traditional view of Midway as the turning point in the Pacific, with the following report to the Roundtable in March 2003:

> To try to refute BOM as the turning point in the Pacific war is to engage in something akin to the currently fanciful art of *what if.* What *could* have happened did not happen!
>
> Almost a year ago, the *Wall Street Journal* published a commentary by Dr. James Schlesinger in which he put forth the argument that victory at Midway was a primary enabler for the U.S. to carry out the Normandy landing in June 1944 and thus pave the way for the end of the war in Europe. To my knowledge, that thesis had not been expressed prior to the *Journal* article.
>
> In June 2002, just after the appearance of the article, I was in England for the annual Midway observances by U.S. military personnel stationed in Europe. Schlesinger's theory relating the BOM to the war in Europe was an exciting and immediate hit among the USN forces there. It became the centerpiece for every BOM observance ceremony that I had the privilege to attend during that period.
>
> In my view, the Schlesinger thesis has also created a stream of re-thinking about the significance of the Midway victory that has crept into several interpretations by our veterans and advocates alike. On June 5, 2003, the Washington area Midway commemoration dinner at the Army-Navy Country Club will feature Dr. Schlesinger as the keynote speaker. There is no doubt in my mind that his selection for that role and, indeed, the theme of his remarks that night will reflect his thoughts as expressed in the *Journal* a year before. His view is a fascinating new slant on the significance of Midway and adds credibility to the importance of our success there.

*   *   *   *

Hawaii Under the Rising Sun

After the attack on Pearl Harbor in December 1941, there was a persistent fear that the Japanese were about to, or would eventually return for a full-scale invasion of Hawaii. The fear increased dramatically as the assault upon Midway approached. Bryan Crisman, who had been the disbursing officer on the USS

Yorktown, gave the Roundtable a little insight on invasion apprehensions with this message in 2003:

> The U.S. Navy evidently took the Japanese invasion threat of Hawaii seriously, since demolition charges were being set in the dry dock and other places in the naval shipyard when *Yorktown* pulled out for Midway. They were set to start the destruction in Pearl Harbor if Midway fell.
>
> We weren't told much as junior officers on the ship, but we were told enough to realize that this battle had more serious consequences than the one at Coral Sea for the future of the United States in the Pacific Theater of the war. We were told that we must win or else!

It would seem that such fears were well founded. The Japanese indeed had a plan for invading and occupying Oahu in late 1942 after a successful Midway campaign. Shortly after the above "turning point" debate had run its course on the Roundtable, Bill Vickrey initiated what was to become another of the group's most expansive *what if* examinations. He started things rolling with this message in May 2003:

> Perhaps some of you have read *Hawaii Under the Rising Sun* by Dr. John J. Stephan, published by the University of Hawaii Press in 1984. A part of his prelude reads, "Many historians of World War II assume that this topic did not exist. In fact, the conquest and occupation of Hawaii constituted an important part of the Japanese Empire's war strategy. Seizure of the entire archipelago was a major objective in the Combined Fleet's long-term plans from the day after Pearl Harbor until the Battle of Midway."
>
> Dr. Stephan has an M.A. from Harvard in East Asian studies and a PhD. in Japanese history from the University of London's School of Oriental and African studies. He is fluent in Japanese and has lectured at Waseda University, Tokyo University, and the National Defense College in Tokyo. He lived in Japan for three years. I say this just to let you know that he is not another wild-eyed revisionist.

I found the notion of a serious Japanese plan for an invasion of Hawaii somewhat startling, never previously considered. Of course, their debacle at Midway obviated any such ambitions, but it was surprising to learn that they even *had* plans of that magnitude. Was it really true, or was this another case of imaginative speculation promoted by an alternative history zealot with an agenda? Phil Jacobsen had the answer:

I just ran across the Appendix to [Japanese] Combined Fleet Secret Order Number One dated 1 November 1941 in OP-20-G's World War II files. Section 14 is quoted in part as "...seizure of Midway is scheduled for early 1942. The occupation of Hawaii is set as about October 1942."

Of course, it didn't take long for Jon Parshall to summarize what many of us knew or suspected: pulling off a successful invasion of Hawaii would have been a tall order for the Japanese under any circumstances, with or without the possession of Midway:

[Dr. Stephan] makes it sound as if there was some sort of well thought out, long-term plan for taking Hawaii. That might have figured in the IJN's calculations, particularly at a staff level, but it wasn't like Prime Minister Tojo had his sights set on Oahu from day one. Far from it!

In terms of strategy, Japan's eyes were bigger than its stomach. Professor Stephan provides a lot of evidence that the Japanese were interested in Hawaii, but he has little information regarding concrete plans for operations, most likely because there really wasn't much. A mark of the seriousness of any military's intentions, of course, is the presence or absence of planning to achieve an objective.

Interestingly, one of the more concrete tidbits in Stephan's book concerns a study of a proposed Hawaiian operation undertaken by an IJN staff officer (Capt. Kami) in January 1942. Kami stated that Hawaii could be captured but supplying it would pose great difficulties because of a shortage of shipping. He estimated that Japan would have to feed nearly half a million Americans in addition to its own garrison. Most of the food would have to be carried across 4,000 miles of submarine-infested ocean. He also noted that 2,900,000 tons of supplies had been shipped to Hawaii from American ports in 1941, which worked out to about twenty-five ships monthly. Under Japanese occupation, given the swollen population, the figure would be higher: 3,000,000 tons annually, brought in by thirty ships a month. An additional thirty ships per month would be required to transport military equipment. Kami concluded that Japan's merchant marine, already stretched to the limit in carrying vital resources from Southeast Asia to the home islands, could not fulfill the task.[3]

Before anyone jumps to the conclusion that the Japanese would simply have let the islanders starve, bear in mind that one of the ostensible reasons for "liberating" Hawaii was the fact that its largest ethnic group was Japanese. The invaders couldn't very well let them starve, any more than they could their own people. Bottom line: there's no way they could have carried it off.

But just because a Japanese invasion of Hawaii didn't seem logistically feasible to a group of Western analysts long after the war, does that mean they wouldn't have tried it anyway? Admiral Showers made a case for a "damn the logistics" attitude on the part of the victory-disease infected Japanese if they had succeeded at Midway:

> The lack of Japanese resources notwithstanding, had the Midway operation been successful (not only in occupying Midway but also in destroying the remaining U.S. carriers), then the IJN would still have had carrier and air superiority throughout the Pacific, and further operations on their part would not only have been a capability but a likelihood.
>
> As the Roundtable knows, I dislike engaging in "what if" analysis, but in my discussions of the BOM, I always emphasize that Japanese success at Midway would almost certainly have led ultimately to their attempts to invade Oahu.

This dialogue continued for eight months on the Roundtable, through January 2004, with more input from members than on any subject since the "FDR conspiracy" debate two years previously. In the end, it seemed fair to say that, to the surprise of many, the Japanese did have at least conceptual plans for a full-scale invasion and occupation of Hawaii after a successful Midway operation, although assaulting and holding Hawaii would most likely have proven more than they could have managed. They simply didn't have the manpower for a large-scale, multi-front war (remember their vast commitment in China), and they didn't have the transport capacity for supplying what would have to be a very large Hawaiian garrison as well as the civilian populace. It would have been their "Bridge Too Far," ultimately leading to the deprivation that their occupying forces experienced on Wake Island, but on a much larger scale.

*   *   *   *

Midway and the Cold War

Among all of the "what if" scenarios, plausible and preposterous alike that have been analyzed on the Roundtable over the years, one clearly stands above all the rest and produces the most extensive postulations on resulting developments in world history: the outright defeat of U.S. forces at Midway for whatever reason and the resulting occupation of the atoll by the Japanese. Extensive analysis and debate from all quarters has left a consensus that in that event, (a) the U.S. would eventually win the war in the Pacific, but much later than September 1945 and at a much greater cost, including far more death and destruction among the Japanese. And, (b) as suggested by Dr. Schlesinger, America's "Europe First" policy in waging the Second World War would have been downgraded or even obviated altogether because great quantities of troops, armaments, supplies, and industrial output dedicated to the European campaign would had to have been diverted to the Pacific Theater. That latter circumstance brought the postulation of two divergent eventualities in Europe. In the first, a Normandy invasion in June 1944 becomes impossible, giving the Nazis enough slack in western Europe that they are able to hold against the Soviets in the east, thus surviving in Germany far longer than they did, with whatever horrors that might bring. Or, alternately, the lack of Allied armies in Normandy in 1944 could have meant a lack of Allied armies on the west bank of the Elbe River when the Red Army reached it in 1945. In that event, the steamrolling Russians would simply have kept going, perhaps putting all of the European continent under their thumb as the Cold War commenced.

All of which leaves one with the conclusion that nothing good could have come of a Japanese victory at Midway; not for the Americans of course, but also not for Europe for the next several years or maybe decades, and not even for the Japanese themselves.

CHAPTER 14

▼

ON THE LIGHTER SIDE

War is a terrible experience for those compelled to endure it, but it is inevitable that isolated incidents of humor and irony will emerge when it is carried on over great expanses of territory and time. Our Midway veterans on the Roundtable have entertained us over the years with some of their tales of serious or somber matters that turned out to be rather heartwarming, amusing, or occasionally even downright funny. Here are a few.

*　　　*　　　*　　　*

Having Fun In Biplanes

Clayton Fisher had more than his share of near-death experiences throughout his military career, from his chance avoidance of the Bataan Death March in 1942 (explained in Chapter 7) to dodging vicious AA fire over the infamous Bridges at Toko-Ri in North Korea ten years later. However, several of those experiences did not involve enemy fire, and a few of them were rather amusing—after he walked away from the aircraft, that is. He told us three such tales in 2001:

> *How not to exit an N3N trainer.* I'm sort of reluctant to tell all you people how dumb I was about my fifth hour of flight instruction in the old bird [the N3N, a two-place, open-cockpit biplane]. We had just reached about 1,500

feet and my instructor cut the throttle to simulate an engine failure. The previous day I hadn't gotten the nose over hard enough to maintain airspeed above stalling, so this time I really jammed the stick forward—and damn near got tossed out of the cockpit! The only thing that saved me was the death grip I had on the joystick. I hadn't fastened my safety belt!

I was wearing a parachute but the plane was probably too low for me to have time to open it. My instructor never knew that he nearly lost his student!

Showing off for the Army Air Force. In 1942, just before the *Hornet's* transit of the Panama Canal en route to the Pacific Fleet, I flew a patrol on March 5th, two patrols on March 7th, and my last patrol on March 10th. On March 11th, VB-8 flew off the *Hornet* and landed at the Army Air Force's Albrook Field in the Canal Zone while the ship made the passage through the canal. We Navy types didn't know that the Army pilots made straight-in landing approaches over a big hill very near the runway, so on our final approach we did a standard carrier-type breakup to land, making tight turns as we approached the end of the runway. When I was at about 150 feet, on the last of the final approach, I hit a down draft off that big hill. My left wing flipped down and it felt like I was going into a spin, at only 150 feet! But my wheels hit the runway just as the wings came level. It must have looked a lot better than it was!

Who needs a tail hook? The sequel to that experience happened when the squadron flew back aboard the *Hornet* in the Pacific on March 12th. The ocean was dead calm, which meant our deck landing speed when we hit the deck would be a little faster than normal. The SBC4s had armor plate and self-sealing fuel tanks installed before we deployed from Norfolk, and these modifications added a lot of weight. When I started on my final approach, I was remembering my experience at Albrook field and just couldn't get my airspeed down to about eighty knots. Nevertheless, the LSO gave me the "cut" at eighty-five knots, and then the fun started. I felt the tail hook engage, and then there was a huge crunch! I thought my landing gear had collapsed, except that the plane was still rolling, although laterally toward the left edge of the flight deck! I thought I was going to go over the side! I kicked full right rudder and jammed on full throttle, and the plane finally stopped with its tail hanging over the catwalk!

I was looking straight at the bridge and the island, and everyone I could see was laughing. *What was so funny?* Then I looked down the flight deck, about a hundred and fifty feet, and there was my tail hook and tail wheel, all tangled up in the arresting wire!

All SBC4s were then inspected, and every one of them had loose rivets in the tail hook assembles. They were all grounded, and none were ever flown again.

*   *   *   *

The Enemy On the Beach

In Chapter 5 we read Edward Fox's story of his introduction to the Marine Corps, his posting to the 6th Defense Battalion, and his preparations for the dreaded Japanese bombardment and invasion during the Battle of Midway. His narrative included an additional anecdote that I've saved until now:

> Near the end of May 1942, we were pretty sure the Imperial Japanese Navy had us in their sights for an invasion. During one of my night patrol assignments, I was doing my usual strolls during a hell of a storm; thick cloud cover, strong winds, heavy rain, and a high, roaring surf. As I trudged along trying to keep my weapon dry under my poncho, I noticed a dark shape in the surf, approaching the beach and directly to my front. All I could see was that it was black, man-sized, and crawling slowly toward my position. My adrenaline kicked in as I got into a prone position, brought my BAR up, and sighted in on the crawling object—*the enemy has arrived and here we go!* I let go three rounds, striking the target, and waited. There was no movement on the beach anywhere. Then the sirens sounded off and the entire island went into Condition Red. I did not move. I could hear my buddies calling my name, but I didn't know how many more of the enemy were in the surf. For several minutes I laid still and quiet. I finally observed my friends approaching in strength, so I called out that I had shot something in the surf.
>
> Sunrise revealed that I had shot a seal! I'd hit it with two rounds, so my first sergeant made me pay one dollar to the slush fund for missing with my third shot! But I did get a pat on the back from my CO, and one of the other officers gave me a case of beer. But still, I got razzed for quite some time for shooting an enemy seal!

*   *   *   *

How the Battle of Midway Got Its Name

The government forbade the keeping of private journals or diaries by military personnel during most of World War II in order to prevent potentially useful intelligence from falling into enemy hands; highly likely due to the occasional surrender of troops or when an aircraft is lost in hostile territory. However, that policy was not enacted until late in 1942, and the diaries legally kept during the first several months of the war have often been valuable resources for interesting tales of wartime experiences, serious and otherwise. SOC pilot Ralph Wilhelm kept such a journal, which helped him a great deal in compiling his Midway reminisces that you read in Chapters 3 and 9.

He had entered an especially prescient note in his journal at the end of the first day of action at Midway, June 4th. Bill Vickrey brought it to the attention of the Roundtable in 2002 with the observation that it may have been one of more profound comments recorded by anyone while actually engaged in the battle. Wilhelm had written the following:

> *Thursday, 4 June, 6th Day at Sea*. This has been a day that will live long in my mind. Just as the last battle we were in had a name, this also should have a name such as the Battle of Midway, or something like that.

While "The Battle of Midway" is an obvious title that doesn't require much thought, Wilhelm very likely may have been the first person in the world to document it as such.

✱   ✱   ✱   ✱

The Purloined Pie

One of the more admired sailors aboard the USS *Yorktown* was Baker 2/c Raymond "Jerry" Eichorn, who became a welcome participant on the Roundtable in 2001. The *Yorktown's* bake shop was very popular with the crew for its outstanding fresh biscuits and pies. While discussing Eichorn's addition to our roster, VF-42 veteran Bill Surgi even told me that in addition to being delicious, those hot biscuits served as very effective hand warmers while standing topside watches during the ship's frigid North Atlantic run in October-November 1941!

Eichorn had developed a reputation as something of a champion pie maker in the ship's galley, which was said by many of the crew to produce first-rate pies. Chaplain Stan Linzey, the former ship's band musician who gave us his survival story in Chapter 6, had an interesting tale about the *Yorktown's* pies in 2002:

> The pastries and pies in the *Yorktown* bakeshop were the finest in the U.S. Navy. We in the ship's band had a deal with the bakers. They would give us pies and the band would play the tunes they wanted to hear at the noon concert on the hangar deck. A real good deal for the band! It was a clandestine arrangement, but a good one! Then one of the bandsmen (no names men-

tioned) stole a pie one night and the bakers got irate! However, the good arrangement continued.

That prompted me to respond to the Roundtable, tongue in cheek, with the following: "Chaplain Linzey, could that pie thief have been an impetuous young clarinet player, so smitten with remorse that he decided to devote the rest of his life to the clergy?" Linzey came back with...

> Ha! This is great! You have a fine sense of humor, but no, that is not the reason I devoted the rest of my life to the clergy. I never took the pies, but I confess I ate my share. I have never had a pang of conscience about the deal. Maybe I should have!

*   *   *   *

How To Get Along In the Navy

The Roundtable has a second veteran of the *Yorktown* bake shop on its roster, former VF-42 deckhand and latter-day humorist Otis Kight. He was working temporary duty in the galley just before the Battle of the Coral Sea, which left him with the following memory:

> I put in three weeks in the bakery, the three weeks before Coral Sea. The night before, we were up to 0200 putting frosting on cupcakes, enough for the entire crew. They were then put in racks in order to cool for several hours. The next compartment forward was hit by a very large bomb the following day, and the impact on the bulkhead put a layer of cupcakes six inches thick on our next bulkhead aft! For the first time I was struck with a feeling of absolute fury, both for the damage control party that was wiped out in the adjacent compartment as well as the cupcakes wasted!
>
> But the contacts I had in the bake shop paid off very handsomely later, as we in Aircraft Handling Crew Ten were given a full pan of hot cinnamon buns right after the first launch, almost every day. Believe me, it was the next best thing to kissing girls we could experience! (This was at a time when the usual breakfast was boiled rice and powered milk.)
>
> I was shifted over to the laundry, which only worked from 2200 to 0200 because we had no air conditioning back then and four hours in the laundry was all one could stand. I got an additional thirty dollars a month for laundry duty. I worked there only a week, got a check for thirty dollars anyway, and a short time later got another check for $2.50 to even things out. I still have that

check. I was transferred to parachute school right after I got it and had to ship all personal stuff home. The $2.50 check got stuck in there somehow. I may have to cash it if I ever get hard up.

Through all of it, I learned a most vital rule: be particularly nice to cooks, bakers, hospital corpsmen, yeomen, pay clerks, dental techs, the leading chief, and your section leader. Life in the Navy can either be beautiful or it can get you no liberty, a screwed up pay record, a burred hypodermic needle, mashed potatoes all over your dessert, or ten mid watches in a row!

*   *   *   *

How I Made the USS Hornet's First Torpedo Run

In Chapter 6, Bernard Cotton told us how he was mourning the apparent loss of his brother "FX" Cotton in a VT-8 torpedo bomber on June 4th, only to stumble upon him at the end of the day, casually reading a comic book in the squadron armory. FX, an Aviation Ordnanceman rating, was his plane's bombardier when the squadron flew bombing missions as opposed to torpedo runs. Since VT-8 was launched from the *Hornet* with torpedoes, he did not fly that day, a technicality that had escaped his brother while watching the air group's departure from his general quarters station. However, FX was responsible for VT-8's very first "torpedo run," as he explains below, although he didn't exactly cherish the notoriety at the time.

I was not qualified as a gunner although at times I did fly as a gunner. All of our squadron's planes at Midway left with their regular crew. My big job was crawling into the cockpit upside down and sticking my head out the bottom to direct the loading of torpedoes. They were extremely difficult to get centered so that a one-inch projection on top of the torpedo would slide into a one half-inch hole in the bottom of the plane.

One day, the orders came to load 500 lb. bombs, so we had to unload the torpedoes. My job was to disconnect each torpedo's motor starting lanyard. The first one was sticking, so I used a little excess pressure on it, at which time I heard what sounded like the ship blowing tubes, combined with the firing of the 1.1-inch cannons. I stuck my head out of the cockpit and saw all hands clearing the flight deck on the double! I then noticed that the blowing noise was coming from under my plane—I had started the torpedo motor! We carried an emergency wrench in the cockpit and I used it to get the motor turned off.

So, I had the distinction of making the first "torpedo run" on the USS *Hornet.*

*　　　*　　　*　　　*

Showing the Flag

Bernie Cotton had another amusing tale from the *Hornet* for us, which he passed along to the Roundtable in January of 2001:

> On the lighter side, one of my early escapades occurred during the pre-commissioning detail for the *Hornet*. The ship was in the Portsmouth Navy Yard having various fixes put in. This was in the October 1941 time period. Also in the yard were a few British ships. I believe one was the HMS *Indefatigable*, and there was also a cruiser being repaired from bomb damage inflicted by the Germans. Thus there were a lot of Brit sailors on liberty in the town. It was not uncommon for them to look down on us, as America was not in the war at that time. A favorite statement from them was, "hey, Yank, when are you going to get that other stripe in your flag?" The gullible Yank would answer, "what stripe?" And the response would be "the *yellow* stripe!"
>
> So, while ashore one day, three of us encountered a rather noisy Brit. We invited him to the Thirtieth Division Club, which allowed hard liquor in individual lockers. The club did not sell any hard stuff but maintained your personal bottle in lockers and only sold the mixers. Anyhow, we went in. The guy was already three sheets to the wind, so we poured him all he wanted for a few hours and then invited him out to the local tattoo parlor where we continued to feed him from our bottle. He happily sat in the chair while the artist proceeded, at our insistence, to inscribe a five by seven-inch American flag on his chest. We paid the artist and left, speculating as to whether our guest would ever again take a shower in the Royal Navy!

*　　　*　　　*　　　*

Cribbage With the Admiral

John Kellejian was an electrician's mate who served aboard the USS *Enterprise* throughout the war, having a hand in twenty of the twenty-two battle stars earned by the ship. One of his favorite memories is that of Admiral Halsey. Kellejian's battle station on the *Enterprise* during the first year of the war was on the flag bridge, which put him in direct contact with the admiral. "Bull" Halsey was noted for a ferocious temper, but Kellejian remembers that he could be quite personable with the enlisted men whose work placed them in his midst.

One day during a general quarters drill, things were fairly quiet on the flag bridge while the rest of the ship carried out a number of emergency action exercises. Halsey was a cribbage player, and he turned to Kellejian to ask if he knew how to play. The sailor had never heard of cribbage, so Halsey said, "don't worry about it, son, I'll teach you." With that the admiral whipped out his cribbage board and commenced to teach Kellejian the game. After he got the hang of it, Halsey told him that he was ready for the big time—they were now going to play for a nickel a round!

Kellejian was a little intimidated, to say the least, but he went along. As you might expect, he "lost his ass," as he described it to me, to the highly experienced admiral. Sailors rarely had any money aboard ship in those days, so he never paid up for his losses. Halsey seemed to generously ignore the debt.

Life went on. The war ended, as did Kellejian's enlistment not long after. He commenced his civilian career as a San Francisco police officer and gradually relegated his wartime experiences to fond but distant memories. Then one day, long after the war, he received a strange piece of mail. It was a summons, sent on behalf of the sister of William F. Halsey, the executor for the admiral's estate. Kellejian knew that Halsey had recently passed away, but he didn't understand the document. He telephoned the admiral's sister for an explanation.

"You're John Kellejian, who served with my brother on the USS *Enterprise?*" she asked.

"Well, yeah, sort of," Kellejian replied. "What's this all about?"

"You owe the admiral's estate two dollars and eighty cents," she said. Kellejian did a classic double-take, then realized that the hard-nosed but sometimes affable admiral apparently hadn't forgiven his 1942 cribbage debt after all. He'd carried it on his personal books all that time, as an amusing little anecdote, and his sister graciously passed the news on to Kellejian in the same spirit. Kellejian kept the "summons" as an interesting memento of the admiral. And no, he didn't really have to pay back the two-eighty.[1]

✳   ✳   ✳   ✳

Get Yamamoto!

The Roundtable's roster includes another veteran member who'd had an amusing personal experience with the great and occasionally infamous Halsey. Kenneth A. Boulier was a shipmate of William Tremblay in the communications intelligence unit at Corregidor and later Melbourne, Australia. He continued his

ComInt career after the war, retiring from the National Security Agency in 1958. Because of the key role possibly played by Tremblay at Melbourne (see Chapter 4), I was very interested in anything Boulier might be able to tell me about his fellow codebreaker Tremblay or anything at all concerning the intercept of Admiral Yamamoto's battle plan for Midway.

As a Yeoman First Class in 1942, Boulier did have the same decryption duties as Tremblay but on a different watch. Consequently, as he explained it to me in a lengthy interview, he never heard much of anything about Tremblay's alleged find because such details were kept very close to the vest; not even shared between watch sections. He never knew about the "AF—attack" message until after the war. But he did have an interesting anecdote from his Melbourne days that he enjoyed telling.

It seems Admiral Halsey was visiting the ComInt offices at Melbourne in 1943, at about the time plans were being developed for U.S. Army Air Force fighters to shoot down Admiral Yamamoto's aircraft as the Japanese Combined Fleet commander toured his southwest Pacific bases. In another codebreaking coup by the wizards at Pearl Harbor and Melbourne, the complete travel itinerary for Yamamoto's tour, including dates, locations, and especially times, had fallen into U.S. hands. Boulier's watch section was working on enhancing their decrypted draft of the intercepted message when Halsey appeared for his visit. The admiral stopped by Yeoman Boulier's desk and asked, "what are you working on, son?" Boulier explained the Yamamoto decodes and what the Army intended to do with the information.

That apparently caught Halsey by surprise, for in the next instant he turned to the entire watch section and bellowed, "GODDAMIT, YOU PEOPLE KNOCK OFF THIS YAMAMOTO BUSINESS! I'M GONNA GET THAT SONOFA-BITCH MYSELF!"

*   *   *   *

Past Enemies, Future Friends

There were several commemorations of the fiftieth anniversary of the Battle of Midway in 1992. Interestingly, one of them was in Japan, at a gathering of survivors from the carrier *Hiryu* and its air group. The *Hiryu* was one of the four carriers brought to Midway in 1942 by the Japanese, all of which were permanently out of the war by the afternoon of June 4th (*Hiryu* sank on the morning of the 5th).

Bill Surgi, as one of the more active participants in VF-42 and *Yorktown* reunions, decided to attend the *Hiryu* gathering and was welcomed by the Japanese veterans. There he met a torpedo plane pilot, Taisuke Maruyama, and the two commenced an enduring friendship. It seems that Surgi had seen Maruyama before: on the afternoon of June 4th, 1942, when the "Kate" torpedo plane in which Maruyama was riding as an observer crossed the *Yorktown's* bow after making a torpedo run against the ship. He was wielding a camera at the time, and Surgi caught a good look at him as the aircraft flew by.

Maruyama subsequently made a number of trips to the U.S. for various commemorative functions, including a 1998 symposium on the Battle of Midway held at the National Museum of Naval Aviation in Pensacola, Florida. There he met Roundtable member William Reece, who provided this impression:

> I did meet Mr. Maruyama in 1998 at the BOM symposium at the NMNA in Pensacola. He was there along with Dick Best, Lloyd Childers, Bill Leonard, Bert Earnest, and another Japanese vet, Takeshi Maeda (and I'm sure others whom I cannot remember right now). Mr. Maruyama spoke very clearly about the *Yorktown* attack and the intense antiaircraft fire from the U.S. screen as they bore in on her. He was very animated when he spoke, relating the attack as it developed. He'd urged his pilot to go lower to avoid the antiaircraft fire and said he was sure that they would all die. Their torpedo scored a hit on the *Yorktown*, near where Bill Surgi was stationed, that he described very excitedly. He spoke of the impact with a big "wooshhhhh!" and an upward motion with his hands. He told his pilot to get out of there, but the pilot replied that he could not turn without hitting the water with his wingtip, and that was when he flew across *Yorktown's* bow and into Surgi's view. He mentioned "your computer" and how it directed the antiaircraft fire. He was speaking of the USN's fire control directors on the ships screening the *Yorktown*. He was very colorful in his description.

Maruyama's "Kate" was one of the few surviving aircraft in the force sent to attack the *Yorktown*. They made it back to the *Hiryu*, only to suffer a strong counterattack by *Yorktown* and *Enterprise* bombers that ultimately sank the ship. The dramatic flight of the Japanese plane across *Yorktown's* bow amid a hail of antiaircraft fire became the subject of a painting that appeared in *Return to Midway*, by Robert D. Ballard, chronicling a National Geographic expedition that found and photographed the sunken *Yorktown* in 1998. As is often the case, the painting was graphically interesting but historically wrong, as Bill Surgi was quick to point out:

The painting on pages 100-101 by John Hamilton entitled "Attack on the Yorktown, June 4, 1942" in *Return to Midway* is a nice painting that does not reflect the actual scene. The painting shows four aircraft on our flight deck and the Kate going past the stern—not so. John Hamilton did a nice job of what someone *thought* had happened, or his references were misunderstood. I saw the Kate cross the bow, not the stern, and I could see the pilot hunkered down in front. The fellow in the second seat was holding a camera to take a picture of our ship. The third man, in the rear seat, was not using his gun. He held up his hand [in some apparent gesture] and I thought of stories I had read about chivalry. I thought he was saluting us.

The crew of that Kate was pilot Haruki Nakao, observer Taisuke Maruyama, and radioman-gunner Giichi Hamada, who was not using his gun as he was hit in the hand and foot and his gun disabled.

I attended the *Hiryu* reunion in Japan in '98 and met Maruyama, a pilot who was flying as an observer on the mission, and also Hamada, who explained to me that his arm waving was an expression of joy at still being alive and on his way home.

Oliver North, the host of the Fox News Channel's *War Stories* series, ran an episode on the Battle of Midway in 2002, which has been frequently repeated. Both Surgi and Maruyama were among several veterans and historians providing extensive on-screen narration for the program.

*   *   *   *

Why the U.S. Won the War

In addition to Bill Surgi, other members on the Roundtable have related instances where Japanese and American veterans of the Pacific war engaged in friendly meetings for the purpose of commemorating or researching wartime events. In 2001, author John Lundstrom told the group about such an encounter during which a Japanese veteran had a rather eloquent observation about one particular advantage possessed by the American side:

I recall an exchange with Sadamu Komachi during the 1992 commemoration of the Battle of the Coral Sea held in Pensacola. Mr. Komachi was an enlisted fighter pilot on board *Shokaku* from Pearl Harbor through the Battle of the Santa Cruz Islands, and an ace. He and I were on a panel, and I asked him whom among his squadron commanders he liked the most. He replied that he didn't like any of his officers. Later, we talked more about this in private. He said that officers, even the most junior and inexperienced, had to lead flights and missions. The lieutenants (junior grade) fresh out of flight training usually received top enlisted pilots as wingmen and at least some learned to treat them with respect. If not, Mr. Komachi told me, in the next battle the leader would go one way but the wingman another!

I told Mr. Komachi about our NAPs [enlisted pilots] and that during one combat mission by VF-6 in the Guadalcanal campaign, an experienced first class petty officer had as his wingman a green full lieutenant who happened to be the squadron XO. He just shook his head in total amazement and said that he now knew why the U.S. had won the war.

*   *   *   *

Miracle at Midway

In another event at which U.S. and Japanese veterans were present, Clay Fisher happened to meet a crewman from the IJN destroyer *Tanikaze*, upon which Fisher had tried his best to plant a bomb on the second day of the battle (see Chapter 7). The little ship had managed to dodge what actually turned out to be over a hundred bombs from several American squadrons, emerging mostly unscathed and living to fight for many months more.[2] Fisher remembers his pleasant and somewhat poignant encounter with the former enemy sailor this way:

> The *Tanikaze* had over a hundred bombs dropped on her, including some from B-17s, and had not been hit. I told the other pilots in our ready room that I thought someone on the ship was watching our individual dives and had directed those quick changes of direction as we approaching our bomb release points. There *was* a crewman on the destroyer's bridge who did exactly that, and I got the opportunity to meet him in Coronado, California nearly fifty years later.
>
> I have his written account of what happened on that that terrible day for his ship and its crew. As a signalman, his battle station was on the bridge. When the air attacks commenced, he volunteered to be a lookout and positioned himself on his back with his body partially protruding through a bridge window hatch. He could see and track each dive bomber in its dive, and passed his recommended course changes through a sound powered telephone to the commanding officer who had directly taken over the helm. His actions saved his ship and its crew. The signalman's name was Masashi Shibata. He survived the war and became a very successful businessman in Japan.
>
> Mr. Shibata, his wife, and the other two *Hornet* pilots, Commander Don Adams and Captain Roy Gee and myself along with our wives, met the Shibatas for dinner at the Hotel Del Coronado in 1991. Mr. Shibata gave each one

of us a small scale model of the *Tanikaze*. I gave him a miniature pair of naval aviator's gold wings. During the course of the dinner I proposed a toast to Mr. Shibata and the courageous crew of the *Tanikaze*. I said we had won the war but the *Tanikaze* had won the battle on that day. He thanked me with tears running down his face.

*   *   *   *

Hi, Honey, I'm Home!

During the Second World War, naval aviation training was almost as dangerous as naval aviation combat. If a pilot survived basic flight school and was marked for carrier duty, he then had to undergo the rigors of FCLP (field carrier landing practice), then CarQuals (carrier qualifications), and his first landing and launch at sea, followed by any specialty training pertinent to his type of aircraft. As the war progressed, most also had to learn to cope with the hazards of night missions. A great many student pilots and even some of their instructors were killed in mishaps connected with such inherently hazardous training.

In late 1943, Clay Fisher was a flight instructor flying F6F Hellcat fighters at Naval Air Station Melbourne, Florida, on the Atlantic coast near Orlando. Melbourne contributed its share to the tally of training flight fatalities during the war: sixty-three pilots were killed in mishaps during the base's three and a half years of operation.[3] Many young Melbourne wives became widows upon receiving the dreaded news about their missing pilot husbands while anxiously awaiting word in the company of fellow wives who had gathered in the home to provide moral support. One night in December, Anne Fisher was faced with the terrible likelihood that husband Clay had finally failed to dodge one of his many bullets, although she wasn't aware of it at the time. Clay told the story to the Roundtable in 2002, and it's a rather somber tale until you get to the ending, which when visualized is probably as hilarious as anything a Hollywood scriptwriter could dream up:

> I ditched twice, the first time at the Battle of the Santa Cruz Islands in an SBD and the second time in a Hellcat, over the Atlantic about twenty miles east of Melbourne, Florida. It was December 1943, and I was on my third training flight that afternoon, herding student pilots. My engine quit on the eighth of a series of overhead gunnery runs. I had been chewing out a student on the radio for getting out of position, and then I got out of position! So I

added maximum power to recover my engine and get back into position in order to avoid some serious personal embarrassment.

Then I think the engine just got tired and quit! I landed in the water and was rescued just before dark by a crash boat from the naval base at Fort Pierce, Florida. After inflating my rubber raft, I heard an ominous hissing sound: the emergency valve that you used by mouth to help keep a raft inflated had developed a slow leak. The valve had not been properly tightened when the raft was packed. I had trouble trying to tighten the valve with wet gloves, but finally got it closed. The raft was now very limp. My butt was low in the water and my feet hanging over the edge of the raft! I was soaked and getting cold.

I then had to avoid a large group of sea turtles that surfaced near the raft. After that, my next problem was that I was floating in the gunnery lanes, and wartime training did not stop just because one pilot was down. I watched the tow plane and the type of gunnery runs being made, checking the fighters in order to determine if I was in any danger. The tow planes fortunately passed over very quickly, so I was only exposed to "friendly fire" for a short time.

Fritz Falkner, an instructor who had been an *Enterprise* fighter pilot at the Battle of the Santa Cruz Islands, circled me as darkness was approaching and started firing his guns into the water nearby to point out my position to the crash boat, which then picked me up. I had an empty stomach, not having had anything to eat since that morning, and the boat crew gave me a pint of whiskey because I was cold. Thus I became thoroughly soused and got a little rowdy by the time the crash boat docked!

Now I need to explain that I was on temporary duty at that time from Vero Beach, which the station wagon sent down from Melbourne to pick me up had to pass on its way back to the base. I told the driver to just let me off at Vero Beach, which he did—my wife, who had recently delivered our first daughter was staying in a Vero Beach hotel. That night, the other Navy wives living in the hotel knew I had crashed at sea but were not yet aware that I'd been rescued. Some of them were with her in the room when I opened the door and walked in on everyone, soaking wet, drunk, and dragging a parachute pack!

When Fisher originally told me that story, I had a very colorful vision of the comical scene that must have ensued: his wife Anne, not aware that he'd crashed, flies into a rage at his ridiculous state. The other wives present are relieved to see him in one piece and frantically try to calm Anne down while explaining what had almost happened and why they really had been there in the first place. But alas, it wasn't to be. Mrs. Fisher told me during a meeting in 2005 that she'd simply been delighted to see him, wet flight suit or not. Apparently, conditions were such in those days that a fighter pilot who returns home each night under *any* circumstances was a welcome sight to his family.

*   *   *   *

Fahr! Fahr!

As one might expect by now, this chapter could only end with yet another funnier-than-fiction tale from Otis Kight. We find him on the *Yorktown*, just as it is departing Pearl Harbor en route to Midway. Admiral Nimitz had been aboard for a morale-building visit with the officers and crew, and it was now time to head for war. Kight told the Roundtable about it in this message from 2001:

Upon pulling into Pearl after Coral Sea, with our larders empty except for spaghetti, dried milk, and powdered eggs, we did a humongous amount of resupplying. Naturally, there was a lot of packaging to be disposed of, and the shipboard incinerator was never lit while in port. So, we toted all this paper, cardboard, thin wood, and other flammables down to the incinerator, which was inside a little compartment of its own. The firebox was crammed full after a while, so the packaging was just piled around it in the compartment.

We were just about abreast of the submarine nets going out to sea when the incinerator was lit off. After a few minutes we heard on the flight deck and everywhere else the 1MC speaker system could reach, an announcement in a slightly anxious and very Southern tone that shouted, "FAHR, FAHR! THEY'S A FAHR IN THE INCINERATOR!"

On the flight deck, my shipmates and I looked at each other with the unspoken opinion that that seemed quite a good place for a fire! We waited for the joker on the 1MC to add that there was also one in each of the boilers!

Instead, about thirty seconds later we heard the very frantic Dixie drawl announce, "FAHR, FAHR! THEY'S A FAHR IN THE INCINERATOR! NO SHIT, THEY'S A FAHR DOWN THAR! THIS AIN'T NO DRILL!"

Of course, what had happened was foreseeable: after the firebox was lit off and burned down some, the Caretaker of Trash opened the firebox door and a bunch of burning material fell out onto the piles around it. The paint was completely burned off the inside of the compartment, and big sheets of five-coats-of-paint-never-chipped came tumbling down on the deck.

But it was worth it to lighten the somewhat anxious mood we had while leaving port for Midway. When CINCPAC comes aboard and gives you his personal attention, the gut starts getting tight. The only thing more serious was a *fahr* in the incinerator!

CHAPTER 15

▼

THE IMPOSTERS

A Hero of Just About Everything

Prior to 2004 I'd never given any thought to the possibility that someone claiming to be a veteran of the Battle of Midway could have been anything less. My impression of each of the veterans I came to know, whether in person or via the Internet, was that he was a true gentleman with a personal story of the battle that had actually happened as he related it. I knew, of course, that a vet might occasionally color his tale with an inconsequential embellishment, but it never occurred to me that I'd ever find one of them to be an outright falsehood.

But I did, and sadly, more than once. The first occurrence was in November of 2004. Roundtable member Harold Towne, the grandson of VT-8 pilot George M. Campbell, referred me to an Internet site honoring one Tyler J. Venneman, said to be a heroic veteran of the Battle of the Coral Sea as well as Midway. The web page was on a site belonging to an army artillery regiment's memorial association. Mr. Venneman, it said, began his military career in the Navy, then switched to the Army where he performed more heroics as an artilleryman in Korea and Vietnam. The web site even included a photo apparently showing Mr. Venneman, bedecked with row upon row of medals and ribbons on his blazer, posing for a photo with President George W. Bush and Secretary of State Colin Powell.[1]

But my initial review of the web page caused an instant case of raised eyebrows, for Mr. Venneman was said to have been an aerial gunner with VT-3 at Coral Sea and Midway. VT-3, of course, was a USS *Saratoga* squadron, and neither the squadron nor the ship were present at Coral Sea. But it was the Midway claim that really stopped me. Venneman had supposedly been wounded in action while flying as the radioman-gunner for VT-3 pilot Wilhelm Esders during the dramatic and costly torpedo attacks on the first day of the battle. That was blatantly untrue. Esder's gunner that day was ARM2/c Robert B. Brazier, who died of wounds received while defending his TBD from swarms of attacking Zeros. In fact, only one of VT-3's radioman-gunners was still alive at the end of the day, and that was our own Roundtable member Lloyd Childers.

I did some fast checking to see if perhaps Venneman had actually flown with VT-6 at Midway instead of VT-3. Five VT-6 gunners had survived the battle, but in view of the misstatement concerning VT-3 being at Coral Sea, I had a hunch that I would find no Vennemans on the VT-6 flight roster. Not only was my hunch correct, but his name did not appear on *any* flight roster, in *any* squadron from the three American carriers at Midway.

Two other claims of exemplary naval service by Mr. Venneman were found on the same web site. One asserted that he had served aboard the destroyer USS *Hobson* during the invasion of the Philippines in late 1944, and the other said that he had then joined an Underwater Demolition Team (UDT or "frogman") unit with which he participated in landing operations at Okinawa in 1945.

Suspicious because of the flawed Coral Sea and Midway statements, I undertook an investigation of these last two, with results as expected. The first, USS *Hobson*, was quite easy to research, thanks to the Naval Historical Center's Internet site. It turned out that the destroyer had served in the Atlantic fleet, a veteran of the Normandy and Southern France invasions, but she never made it to the Philippines nor anywhere else in the Pacific. The UDT matter took a little more work, but not much. There is no organization in the U.S. Navy that is more protective of its traditions and reputation than the SEALs, who started life as the UDTs of World War II. My inquiry about Mr. Venneman to the director of the Naval Special Warfare Archives brought the expected negative result: "We do not have Tyler J. Venneman in our database…his name does not appear in the list of UDT men trained at Fort Pierce or Maui, nor does it appear on the roster of any UDT unit."

It should be said at this point that I held absolutely no animosity for Mr. Venneman. Indeed, I had never met or talked with the man, and so far I'd proved nothing other than the fact that an artillery association web site had posted some incorrect statements concerning his naval service. I had *not* discovered anything that totally excluded Venneman as a Battle of Midway veteran. He still could have been there, but in some capacity not yet revealed. With that frame of mind,

I searched him out on the Internet and found both his home address and an e-mail ID. I sent him the following message:

November 8, 2004

Dear Mr. Venneman:

I found your name on the [artillery association] web site, and noted that you are listed as a Navy veteran who was wounded in action during the Battle of Midway.

We are the Battle of Midway Roundtable, an international organization devoted to preserving an awareness of that great battle, and especially to honoring the men who fought and won it. We would be pleased to include your experience during the battle among our published veterans stories, and to include you on our roster of honored Midway veterans.

Could you, or someone on your behalf please contact me with basic information about your service during the battle? Info on your assigned ship/squadron/aircraft, rate or rank at the time, action during the battle, and the circumstances that caused your wound would be appreciated. Also, if you were aboard one the ships or aircraft that were lost at sea, details of your rescue and survival would be of high interest.

We invite you to review our web site (URL below), and look forward to adding you to our distinguished roster of Battle of Midway veterans.

Sincerely,

—R. W. Russell, editor

Battle of Midway Roundtable

http://www.midway42.org

I also included my home telephone number and address. No response was received.

I wanted to be very thorough here, for I was rapidly putting myself into a situation where I'd be publicly exposing an apparently bogus veteran. I called one of our members who is a wonderful resource for anyone researching U.S. Naval history: Bernard "Cal" Cavalcante was a mainstay at the U.S. Naval Historical Center in Washington for many years. If Venneman had flown strike missions at Coral Sea and Midway, he most likely would have been awarded the Distinguished Flying Cross, since virtually all Navy and Marine Corps radioman-gunners who flew at Midway got either the DFC or an Air Medal. In addition, he would have earned a Purple Heart for his wound while purportedly flying with VT-3. If Venneman had received any of those awards as well as a host of others that would be attendant with naval air combat in the Pacific, Cavalcante would have a record of it. He didn't. There was no record whatsoever of any U.S. Navy medals or awards presented to a Tyler J. Venneman.

I ended this matter in a brief series of entries in *The Roundtable Forum*, posting my e-mail exchanges with the artillery association webmaster and the Naval Special Warfare Archives director, plus my unanswered inquiry to Mr. Venneman himself. The response from our members was totally positive, with this message from attorney Dan Hamilton being typical:

> Thanks for your work on the "Bogus" BOM vet issue. It simply dilutes the honor due to those who served to allow unearned claims to pass without having the record corrected. I hope there is a misunderstanding somewhere and that this instance is not one of those sad *wannabe* cases. However, if it is, it's good to know that someone is out there checking. Good work!

I was glad to be done with this affair for I felt no joy in it. As Mr. Hamilton observed, it was simply something that had to be pursued to a conclusion for the sake of our real Midway veterans. I happily moved on with my usual weekly task of collecting e-mail input from our members in order to produce *The Roundtable Forum*. I was finished with the bogus vet investigation business.

*   *   *   *

Shooting Up the Soryu, and Other Fables

That lasted all of two weeks. In early December I was contacted by George Walsh, Jr., the son of one of our members and the city editor for *The Daily Gazette* in Schenectady, New York. Mr. Walsh was seeking verification concerning a Mr. Ed Holden, who had been a featured speaker during a big event at a local aviation museum. Mr. Holden had regaled the crowd with tales of his bravery at the Battle of Midway, in which he described flying as a radioman-gunner in an SBD Dauntless, creating havoc on the Japanese carrier *Soryu* by machine-gunning the flight deck and setting parked aircraft on fire. Holden also made exciting claims of further action in World War II as well as nearly all subsequent conflicts, major and minor, recounting a list of heroics that made Tyler Venneman's résumé seem a little tame.

Mr. Walsh knew from his father, a dive bomber pilot during the war, that real Battle of Midway veterans generally comported themselves in a much more reserved manner than exhibited by Mr. Holden. With suspicions aroused, he asked his dad for guidance and was eventually referred to me. Fresh from my experience with Mr. Venneman, I very quickly disposed of the claim about attacking the *Soryu* by providing Mr. Walsh a list of the pilots and gunners who had flown against that ship. Naturally, Mr. Holden's name was not on the list. I then called my friend Cal Cavalcante once again for another search of possible DFC or Air Medal awards in the Naval Historical Center's archives, and of course, there were none to be found.

Mr. Holden also claimed to have flown a TBF at Iwo Jima in 1945 as a squadron mate to future president Ens. George H. W. Bush. Mr. Walsh dispensed with that fable on his own, though, by noting in President Bush's biography that he'd been shot down in 1944 and was back home training new pilots when Holden allegedly arrived over Iwo Jima three months later. Walsh then arranged a meeting with Holden and confronted him with what the historical record had to say about each of his lofty claims. The old guy gave in, admitting that his entire spiel had been a fabrication. He said that he thought he'd been doing a good thing by somehow contributing to the younger generation's appreciation for what our veterans had accomplished in the Second World War. He agreed to tear up his notes (he had given many such speeches over the years) and avoid any further fantasizing of his war record, which he said consisted only of patrol flights off the east and west coasts.

Walsh wrote up the story for his paper, which published it on December 10, 2004. You'll find the article in its entirety in Appendix E.[2]

*   *   *   *

Exposing One of Our Own

The good news with regard to Mr. Venneman and Mr. Holden was that neither was a member of the BOMRT, one of our very own whom we'd been honoring for months or perhaps years. But even that small consolation was absent in the third and most troubling case.

Randolph Wyler is one of the nicest old guys that you'd ever care to know.[3] He joined the Roundtable shortly after I took it over from Bill Price in 2002, and I subsequently met him in person at the annual Battle of Midway anniversary dinner in San Francisco. We immediately hit it off during that first meeting, for he impressed me as an affable and friendly fellow, full of good cheer for anyone who'd bother to talk with him. He displayed a number of miniature medals on his formal jacket that night, and he told me they had been awarded for his service as a radioman-gunner in an SBD at both Coral Sea and Midway. He said that he'd flown behind Lt. Cdr. Robert Dixon, skipper of VS-2 (USS *Lexington*) at Coral Sea, and again with Dixon in VS-5 (USS *Yorktown*) at the BOM. This sounded a lot like Mr. Venneman's tale, but that episode did not occur until much later. I had no reason to doubt Wyler at that early stage.

Nothing came of it for more than a year, and Wyler continued as an honored veteran member of our Roundtable. I met up with him again at various functions in the San Francisco Bay area, including the 2004 BOM anniversary dinner where he was awarded a special certificate for his Midway service by the guest of honor, Marine Corps Major General Jon Gallinetti. Then, in July of 2004, I placed an article in *The Roundtable Forum* that made mention of him flying with Lt. Cdr. Dixon at the Battle of Midway. That elicited a quick response from Bill Vickrey:

> I'm sure someone else has picked this up, but Wyler did not fly with Bob Dixon at the BOM as Dixon was not there. He is famous for his message "scratch one flat top!" at the Battle of the Coral Sea. I have no record of Wyler flying at Midway.

Whoa! What's this? Dixon was not at Midway? I had learned by this time that any data about the BOM provided by Vickrey was to be relied upon. But what did it mean? Was Wyler confused about which pilot he'd flown with during the battle? That seemed unusual, since he'd also stated that his aircraft had scored one of only two bomb hits on the Japanese carrier *Akagi*, a crucial, historic accomplishment about which you'd think every detail would forever remain crystal clear. It must be just some sort of misunderstanding, I thought, so I replied to a recent message from Wyler with a request for a telephone interview:

Randy:

I received your message, and it was nice to hear from you. Would you please give me your phone number? I'd like to call you to ask some questions about your time aboard the *Lexington*, etc.

Thanks,

—RR

No response was received, and that was a bit odd since up to that point he and I had maintained rather consistent contact by both e-mail and occasional in-person encounters.

But I let it go. The importance of the situation wasn't so apparent to me at that time, and I had many other things to occupy my attention in those first months of the Roundtable's new format. However, that changed rather quickly when I was suddenly confronted in December of 2004 with the reality and seriousness of bogus veteran assertions, thanks to Mr. Venneman.

With that fresh experience behind me, I immediately began to look into the published Coral Sea and Midway claims for Wyler, and there were a great many. One document was on the USS *Yorktown* (CV-5) association's web site, another was found on a web page detailing the presentation made to Wyler at the San Francisco BOM commemoration in 2000, and still more were found in a veterans' biographies pamphlet produced in 2003 by the organizing committee for the San Francisco anniversary events. Included in those three sources were the following statements about Wyler:

1.   Flew as gunner with pilot Robert Dixon at the Battle of Coral Sea
2.   Flew as gunner with pilot Robert Dixon at the Battle of Midway
3.   Was in the second SBD that bombed the *Akagi* at Midway
4.   Flew as a gunner from USS *Yorktown* at the Battle of Midway
5.   Flew from USS *Hornet* at the Battle of the Santa Cruz Islands
6.   Worked on F4U Corsair fighters for Major Gregory Boyington and his famous "Black Sheep Squadron" (VMF-214) at NAS Barbers Point, Hawaii, prior to Boyington deploying to the South Pacific with the squadron.

None of that gelled with the facts uncovered through some simple research. Lt. Cdr. Robert Dixon's radioman-gunner at Coral Sea was ARM1/c Ferdinand J. Sugar, not Wyler. The Dixon-at-Midway issue had already been settled. The three SBDs that struck *Akagi* were from the *Enterprise,* not the *Yorktown*, and their crews were well known. Wyler's name does not show up on the flight rosters for either the *Yorktown* at Midway nor the *Hornet* at the Santa Cruz Islands battle. Finally, Major Boyington joined VMF-214 at Espiritu Santo in the South Pacific. The squadron was never at Barbers Point during its brief Boyington era, nor was Boyington. To top it off, Cal Cavalcante once again could find no record of a DFC, Air Medal, or anything else awarded to a veteran named Randolph Wyler.[4]

There were other, less tangible reasons for doubting Wyler's story. One thing I noticed by looking at flight rosters of the various strike missions was that squadron commanders seemed to assign their most senior and experienced ARM rating as their own R/G. That's why Lt. Cdr. Dixon had ARM1/c Sugar as his rear-seater during their flights at Coral Sea, and not someone who wasn't primarily trained in aerial communications and gunnery. An AMM or other rating did occasionally fly as the R/G in an SBD or other bomber, but generally not with the flight leader during a combat sortie.

Another reason was one that George Walsh had mentioned to me while researching his newspaper article on Mr. Holden: real Midway veterans generally did not trumpet their combat achievements with the level of bravado that seemed to accompany Wyler's accounts. It came to be apparent that, the more sensational the claim, the more likelihood for self-aggrandizing fantasy.

For all of those reasons, then, the conclusion was inescapable that my friend Randy Wyler was not a veteran of the BOM, or if he was, it was not under conditions that had thus far been revealed in public. I kept that latter thought in the back of my mind as I sought to make contact with him to resolve the discrepancies. Was he actually a BOM vet who had simply maintained aircraft on board the *Yorktown*? Had he intentionally fabricated an aerial gunnery fable over the years, or was he the victim of some trickery of an aging mind, actually believing accomplishments for himself that others had achieved?

Regrettably, it seems those questions will never be answered. At this writing, Wyler's family tells me he is in ill health and no longer able to cognitively discuss his wartime experiences. He now resides in an elder care facility, no doubt still content with his recollections of desperate aerial combat in the Pacific long ago. I reluctantly purged his name from our Midway veteran roster and archives.

*   *   *   *

A Matter of Honor

Investigating flawed claims of heroism at the Battle of Midway is not a task that I relished or sought, but once confronted with those issues, I felt compelled to persevere in each case in order to uphold the honor of our true BOM vets. Our motto on the Roundtable is "to promote awareness and understanding of the great battle and to honor the men who fought it and won it." There is little that dishonors those gallant warriors more than an impostor claiming to be their equal. Anyone making such bogus claims in public should be publicly exposed, and by the same token, any false claims due to misguided embellishments or innocent misunderstandings also need to be investigated and corrected with the same tenacity. That not only upholds the honor of our known veterans, but it also brings the possibility of finding the truth about someone who actually may have been present at the battle, but whose real experiences were not previously known or properly portrayed.

CHAPTER 16

▼

SAY HELLO TO THE GUYS

Falling Dominoes

Whenever I am asked to speak of the Battle of Midway to an audience, I always include what I call the "domino analogy" of the battle. That is, the improbable American victory at Midway can be viewed metaphorically like a serial string of dominoes, each standing on its end so that tipping over the first one causes all of the rest to fall over in turn. However, if any one domino within the row is removed before starting the sequence, the intended result will not occur: the last domino will not fall. If we line up such a string of dominoes and consider each one as representing a single critical factor necessary for the Americans to win the Battle of Midway, we can then call the last one "victory." If it eventually winds up on its side after tipping over the first domino, the U.S. wins. But if it remains upright, the victory belongs to the Japanese: a critical element necessary for the Americans to win was missing, hence the succeeding dominoes do not fall.

The domino analogy surfaced on the Roundtable in 2002, during Bill Price's stewardship, and it was debated at some length. In the end I was left with the conviction that nine specific factors *had* to occur *in the proper sequence* to bring victory to the American side in the manner that it happened, or perhaps in any manner. Other factors were suggested and argued during the discussion and some may indeed be valid, but these nine struck me as the few that absolutely had to be in place to deny the Japanese a triumph at Midway, including perhaps two or three sunken U.S. carriers:

1. American codebreakers *had* to be able to read JN-25 to the remarkable degree that they did.

2. The Japanese carriers *Shokaku* and *Zuikaku had* to sustain enough damage at Coral Sea to keep them home when the Midway fleet sailed (Yamamoto's original intent was to include all six of *Kido Butai's* carriers).

3. The shipyard crew at Pearl Harbor *had* to achieve their own incredible victory by getting the mauled *Yorktown* ready for sea in less than three days.

4. John Waldron *had* to brazenly disobey his commander's order (an astounding thing to do during wartime while engaged in combat!), breaking away from Stanhope Ring's errant course in order to find the Japanese fleet.

5. VT-6 *had* to spot *Kido Butai's* smoke resulting from its fight with Waldron.

6. Similarly, Lloyd Childers in VT-3, with VB-3 following, *had* to spot *Kido Butai's* smoke resulting from its fight with VT-6, thus providing the key for VB-3 to find the *Soryu*.

7. The Japanese CAP *had* to be lured to the wavetops because of successive assaults by five separate groups of torpedo planes, thus leaving the upper altitudes undefended when the dive bombers arrived.

8. IJNS *Arashi had* to chase USS *Nautilus* far from the Japanese fleet, providing a critically needed guide for Lt. Cdr. McClusky and his *Enterprise* SBDs.

9. Finally, McClusky's two squadrons *had* to arrive over *Kido Butai* at practically the same instant as Lt. Cdr. Leslie's SBDs from the *Yorktown*.

If *any* of the above nine circumstances had not occurred as they did and when they did, then the likelihood is very high that instead of three Japanese carriers destroyed on the morning of June fourth, it would have been two carriers, or perhaps one carrier, or maybe even none. And regardless how the Battle of Midway would have proceeded in any of those scenarios, the end result could only have been worse for the American side—probably *much* worse, very possibly to the point of losing the battle entirely and surrendering the atoll to the invaders.

Nine dominoes falling, each unfailingly after the preceding one, else all is lost. That is the characterization of the BOM that best explains, for this writer at least, why it endures to this day as the most chronicled, analyzed, and debated engagement of the Pacific war and why it continues to merit the exclusive focus of hundreds of Roundtable members around the world over sixty years after the fact.

＊　　　＊　　　＊　　　＊

Why We Had to Win

Regardless how the dominoes fell, the U.S. simply *had* to win at Midway. Lloyd Childers remembered how it was explained to his squadron prior to the battle. He told the Roundtable about it in 2003:

> Sometime late in May 1942, all of our flight crews were assembled in the ready room at NAS Kaneohe Bay to receive an intelligence briefing by a CINCPAC officer. He told us in his summary that "if only three TBDs out of your fifteen-plane squadron survive the run-in to deliver torpedoes, you will have accomplished your mission."
>
> I was stunned! I realized that I could have refused to fly anymore, but I'm not a coward. (In fact, our chief radioman did ask to be transferred to a non-flying job and Leo Perry took his place.)
>
> Then, on the morning of the battle and an hour or two before the *Yorktown* planes were launched, Captain Buckmaster came up on the 1MC. His last sentence was, "If we don't stop this enemy fleet today, there is nothing between here and San Francisco to keep them from going all the way." That really got my attention!

＊　　　＊　　　＊　　　＊

The Eloquence of Ensign Evans

Apprehension about the coming battle, as experienced by Childers, was widespread among the American aircrews, particularly those of the torpedo squadrons. Each of the pilots and gunners were fully aware of the palpable vulnerabilities of their aging TBDs. The Devastators had performed rather well in the Coral Sea, but there the enemy CAP was heavily involved with the dive bombers, who suffered substantial losses. There were few misconceptions on how the torpedo planes would fair next time in the event of a concerted fighter defense.

One of the TBD pilots was especially eloquent in recording his feelings. Roundtable member Tom Evans, the younger brother of VT-8's Ensign William R. Evans, shared with the group a few of his brother's letters mailed home before riding to his death with Waldron. In one of them, Ensign Evans offered this somewhat whimsical gesture, written on the back of a copy of the USS *Hornet's* plan of the day for May 23, 1942:

> Respectfully dedicated to those of the confused generation who, being born during a world war, were taught that Peace was the touchstone to man's happiness; and fought another war to make it so.

The pilot was quite a bit more pensive, though, in a letter in which his deep fears about the coming battle were apparent. His expressive, poignant prose in the following passage could serve as a fitting epitaph to all of the gallant American aviators who gave their last full measure at Midway:

> Many of my friends are now dead. To a man, each died with a nonchalance that each would have denied as courage. They simply called it lack of fear. If anything great or good is born of this war, it should not be valued in the colonies we may win nor in the pages historians will attempt to write, but rather in the youth of our country, who never trained for war; rather almost never believed in war, but who have, from some hidden source, brought forth a gallantry which is homespun, it is so real.
>
> When you hear others saying harsh things about American youth, do all in your power to help others keep faith with those few who gave so much. Tell them that out here, between a spaceless sea and sky, American youth has found itself and given itself so that, at home, the spark may catch. There is much I cannot say, which should be said before it is too late. It is my fear that national inertia will cancel the gains won at such a price. My luck can't last much longer, but the flame goes on and on.

Never Truly Gone

Ensign Evans' profound words tug at the heartstrings when considered in light of what he was to experience only a few days after writing them, and serve as a reminder that when we delve at length into the Battle of Midway, we are of necessity talking about many fine men who had to die before their time. And the sad reality of unexpected death even extends across the decades to the Roundtable itself, wherein we occasionally are forced to bear the news that one of our honored veteran members has suddenly departed on his last sortie.

That's an inexorable certainty in an organization centered on men in their eighties and nineties, something to which we cannot assign too much importance and must stoically accept as a fact of life. Indeed, throughout this book it has been my practice to avoid any differentiation between the reminisces of BOM veterans who are with us at this writing and those who have passed on, some even after learning with great anticipation that this book was in the works. On the Roundtable we hold to the belief that no Midway veteran will ever be truly gone until he is forgotten, and our intent is that each whose acquaintance we have made will live in honored memory as long as there is one of us left who cares.

Bill Tremblay, the Melbourne codebreaker whom we met in Chapter 4, was brought into the Roundtable by his friend and fellow Missourian, Midway Marine Ed Fox. One day early in 2003, Fox paid a visit to Tremblay at his rural home. The two visited for a while, talking about communications intelligence, the Battle of Midway, and the activities of the Roundtable. By that time Tremblay was no longer actively participating with the group, so in parting he told Fox to "say hello to the guys," meaning his friends and fellow veterans on the Roundtable. He passed away less than twenty-four hours later. They very nearly were his last words.

Tremblay's touching comment struck me as supremely eloquent in its simplicity. When the last veteran of the Battle of Midway has ascended to eternity, will we then finally be saying goodbye to them all? Will memory of those gallant warriors fade as their desperate struggle and sacrifice recedes deeper into the annals of history? Sadly, that is usually the case, even with conflicts that were more crucial to the U.S. cause than Midway. When was the last time you gave any thought to those battle-worn Revolutionary soldiers who in 1777 achieved their own incredible victory against a superior British force at Saratoga, without which there very likely would never have been a United States? If you are now raising your eyebrows and thinking *I didn't know that*, you have a lot of company, and that's my point.

But in the case of our Battle of Midway veterans, memory of their triumph and sacrifice should not fade from the American conscience. As long as the name "Midway" continues to adorn a magnificent aircraft carrier museum in San Diego harbor, as long as the U.S. Navy continues to mandate a formal annual commemoration of the battle throughout all of its commands, and as long as Walter Lord's "Incredible Victory" quote remains engraved at the Pacific Theater entrance to the World War II memorial in Washington, D.C., Americans will forever be invited and encouraged to "say hello to the guys" of Midway. They heard their nation's call during the dark, grim days of 1942, and I prefer to believe they will also hear its grateful gratitude for as long as it is acknowledged.

Chapter Notes

CHAPTER 1: ON LINE WITH THE GREATEST GENERATION

1. Lord, p. 95; Morison, p. 103 (footnote).

2. Price told the author that the Geddes dioramas were said to be huge, perhaps twenty feet to the side. There seems to be no record as to their ultimate disposition, but considering their great size, Price believes it likely that they were dismantled and discarded after being photographed. The problem may have been one of suitable storage space. A series of 14 black-and-white photos of the Midway dioramas can be found on the Naval Historical Center's Internet site in the "Photographic Section." Search photo numbers 80-G-701843 through 80-G-701902. Several of them are also included in Cressman.

3. Cressman, pp. 101-104. Best and his two wingmen succeeded in destroying the Japanese carrier *Akagi* while McClusky and the rest of the two squadrons were doing the same for the *Kaga*. Morison, Lord, and Prange report that the mixup between Best and McClusky was due to missed radio calls, but Best insisted that McClusky failed to follow doctrine in diving upon *Kaga*. See IMMF.

CHAPTER 2: CHANGES OF COMMAND

1. Adapted from Greaves, "Nimitz Arrives at Pearl Harbor." This anecdote by Captain DeLorenzo as well as all other writings by BOMRT members in this book (other than direct quotes from published works) have been edited for clarity by the author.

CHAPTER 3: HIT 'EM WHERE THEY AIN'T

1. See Appendix A for a complete listing of the Roundtable's Midway veterans.

2. This passage is the 8 May 1942 log entry in Wilhelm's personal diary, a copy of which he provided to the author in 2005. Other excerpts appear in Chapters 9 and 14.

CHAPTER 4: THE CODEBREAKERS

1. The term "HYPO" for Rochefort's operation at Pearl Harbor was probably not contemporaneous during the BOM era. It more correctly referred to the nearby intercept station at Heeia (Station "H"). In particular, Rear Adm. Showers has been emphatic in stating that the only name in use at that time was "Combat Intelligence Unit," which the personnel working there often shortened to "CIU." However, John Lundstrom found one instance where Rochefort apparently did call his command "HYPO," in a COMB net message dated 1 May 1942 (e-mail, Lundstrom to the Roundtable, 3 July 2003). The author's conclusion is that "HYPO" was a simple expedient used on a limited basis in written communications, and that it didn't become generally synonymous for the CIU until much later. A similar circumstance is found with regard to the common name for the counterpart station in Australia (see note 3 below).

2. See Layton, chapter 30.

3. The ComInt organization in Australia actually consisted of a receiver/intercept site at Moorabbin, the Australian navy's transmitter site at Belconnen, and the decoding section in Melbourne. The entire operation was variously known as "Station BAKER," "Belconnen," "Melbourne," and beginning in 1943, "FRUMEL" (Fleet Radio Unit Melbourne). "Melbourne" and "Belconnen" appear to have been the most commonly used terms in the BOM era. "Belconnen" was a misnomer for the overall command, but it was often used in lieu of "Melbourne" to avoid confusion with other military activities in that city.

4. Most sources refer to this circuit as COPEK, which was actually the name of the specific COMB net channel used exclusively for communication related to decrypted Japanese messages and intelligence derived therefrom (e-mail, Phil Jacobsen to the author, 4 August 2005).

5. Excerpted from Hannagan and Jacobsen.

6. See Sinclair.

7. See Parker (p. 43) and Jacobsen. Layton also comments on the March discovery of "AF," (pp. 376-377) although he isn't clear whether it was the result of work at Corregidor (communicated to HYPO via the COMB net) or if the discovery came from independent intercepts and analysis in Hawaii.

8. Layton, pp. 411-412.

9. Holmes, p. 89. Holmes does not identify which location initially copied and broke the message, although he does say that it was "intercepted in its entirety and immediately identified for what it was."

10. Whitlock (p. 14) strongly suggests that Melbourne deserves far more credit for discovering the Japanese Midway plan than indicated by Layton. He describes large quantities of analyses and partial intercepts (possibly including Tremblay's, although he doesn't go into that much detail) "sent to Com 14 (HYPO) from Belconnen, yet this fact is all but obscured in the credits cited by [Layton]…"

11. The exact text of the Japanese message was found by John Lundstrom while researching CINCPAC archives in Washington. He forwarded it to the Roundtable in April 2004.

12. Kernan, *Crossing the Line*, p. 47

13. http://community-3.webtv.net/loisdan/center5MEMORIES/

14. After this letter appeared in an issue of *The Roundtable Forum*, John Lundstrom pointed out that Nimitz, during his May 2nd visit to Midway, did not tell the atoll's commanders about the forthcoming Japanese attack because he hadn't learned of it that soon. He only discussed possibilities with them, recognizing Midway as an important bastion that the Japanese might covet, like Wake Island. See also Cressman, p. 31.

CHAPTER 5: DEFENDING THE ATOLL

1. This warning was construed by a few as evidence that the U.S. had foreknowledge of the Pearl Harbor attack. Why that was not the case is explained in Chapter 12.

2. Edward Fox's story is adapted from Bowen, "They Served Their Country at the Battle of Midway."

3. The four cruisers comprised Cruiser Division 7, which was accompanied by two destroyers, the *Asashio* and *Arashio*. However, the two DDs would not have participated in the bombardment, as they were left behind by the cruisers in the dash toward Midway on June 4th, apparently as a fuel-saving measure. (E-mail, Jon Parshall to the author, 22 August 2005.)

CHAPTER 6: ABOARD THE CARRIERS

1. Cressman, p. 44; Lundstrom, pp. 309-313.

2. E-mail message, Rich Leonard to the author, 14 April 2005. Until his death in August of that year, Admiral Leonard resided with son Rich, who facilitated his active participation with the BOMRT.

3. Adapted from Bowen, "The Fighting Yorktown (CV-5): Coral Sea and Other Reflections"

4. Kernan, *The Unknown Battle of Midway*, pp. 56-57

5. Kernan, *Crossing the Line*, pp. 51-52

6. Lundstrom, pp. 363, 387-388

7. Linzey, pp. 94, 135-136

8. Linzey's battle station on the "third deck" was two decks below the hangar deck.

9. Linzey, pp. 65-66, 68-70, 95-99

10. One of the heroic rescue swimmers was USS *Balch* seaman Art Lewis, who is discussed further in Chapter 9.

11. This report by Cheek is an excerpt from an unpublished document entitled "A Ring of Coral," which he provided to several individuals and organizations

over the years before his death in 2004. The narrative appearing here is adapted from the copy he originally sent to Bill Price.

12. This remarkable photo sequence can be seen in Cressman, p. 160.

13. Adapted from Bowen, "They Served Their Country at the Battle of Midway"

CHAPTER 7: OVER THE ENEMY FLEET

1. Cressman, pp. 52-54

2. Prange includes an abridged version of Swan's "blue tipped bullets" story on p.161.

3. This narrative is a further excerpt from Cheek's "A Ring of Coral." See Note 11 of Chapter 5 above.

4. See Chapter 1 and IMMF.

5. Over the years Clay Fisher has related many highly interesting naval aviation anecdotes to the Roundtable that are beyond the scope of this book, including several tales of his combat flights in Korea. Among the most notable are his strikes against the bridges at Toko-Ri, made famous by the James Michener book and subsequent Hollywood movie. As is often the case, the movie was spectacular with its daring jet fighter attacks against the bridges, but Fisher says that was ficti-tious. The bridges were primarily taken out by AD Skyraiders, not jets, while Fisher's Corsair squadron suppressed the AA batteries.

6. Lundstrom (p. 334) and Cressman (p. 86) state that the CHAG and his two wingmen were spotted on deck *behind* VS-8 and ahead of VB-8. But Fisher is adamant that his was the first SBD off the deck that morning, immediately after the fighters. As for the SBDs' bomb load, Fisher's memory here may be question-able as both Lundstrom and Cressman (op. cit.) indicate that VS-8 was fitted with 500-lb. bombs due to its shorter takeoff run. Only VB-8, toward the rear of the pack, had enough deck space to get off with the thousand-pounders. The offi-cial USS *Hornet* after-action report states that all of the dive bombers ("VSB") were loaded with 500-lb. bombs, but that seems hardly likely.

7. Adapted from Bowen, "The Battle of Midway, 4-6 June 1942: Commander Clayton Fisher's Story"

8. 58 bombs from the SBDs, 56 from the first B-17 flight, and another 23 from the second. The ship suffered damage to one gun turret due to a near miss. In addition to the loss of Lt. Adams and his R/G, one and possibly two B-17s failed to return as the result of this action. See Lord, pp. 268-270, Cressman pp. 149-151.

9. Cressman (p. 151) states that three VB-8 pilots and two from VS-8 landed on *Enterprise* that night.

10. Adapted from Greaves, "Last Mission of the TBD Devastator"

11. See Lord p. 272 and Prange, p. 342. Fisher's bomb hit the number 3 turret on the *Arashio*, killing many of *Mikuma's* survivors and blowing others into the sea. The ship temporarily lost steering, but was able to proceed on manual control..

12. Fisher, pp. 9-10

CHAPTER 8: THE FLIGHT TO NOWHERE

1. Gay, *Sole Survivor*, pp. 113-115

2. Enclosure (F) to Captain Mitscher's after-action report is a chart showing the purported movements of all *Hornet* squadrons during the battle. The loss of VF-8 on June 4th is indicated at a point roughly 120 miles northwest of Midway on an approximate bearing of 320 degrees true. The pickup point of Kelly's fellow pilots, as recorded by the PBY crew that rescued them, was about 210 miles northeast of Midway, on a bearing of 41 degrees true. Allowing for the known drift of the survivors' rafts, it is evident that Kelly and his comrades went into the water between 150 and 200 miles east-northeast of the area shown in the official record.

3. Weisheit, pp. 53 & 88

4. Prange, p. 259

5. While rather unlikely, it's not totally impossible that Fisher could have seen the towering column of smoke from Midway if he'd flown the course determined by Weisheit. In Chapter 6, Roy Gee reported VB-8's cruising altitude as 19,000 feet, and Fisher stated that the CHAG section was to fly above the squadrons; assume at least 20,000 feet in this case. Fisher told the author that conditions were "CAVU" when he saw the smoke (Ceiling And Visibility Unlimited). At 20,000 feet, the distance to the horizon over the ocean computes to 161 miles under CAVU conditions. Weisheit's track for the air group runs roughly 250 miles from Midway at the point where Fisher says he began to see the smoke. While that's well beyond the calculated distance to the horizon for Fisher at that moment, the smoke would have risen very high above the surface, making it visible at a far greater distance.

6. Gay, *Sole Survivor*, p. 115

7. Weisheit, p. 14 & Appendix H

8. Readers have found other faults in *Sole Survivor* that give reason to generally doubt Gay's accuracy. Roundtable members have pointed out a number of them over the years, such as his claim of attacking the carrier *Kaga* (it was the *Soryu*). His principle claim of having literally watched the death of three Japanese carriers while floating in their midst is challenged in Chapter 12.

9. Lundstrom, p. 333

10. In one of the many incongruities of the Battle of Midway, Fisher's friend and VB-8 squadron-mate Roy Gee had the opposite recollection. He told the author that when the squadron's pilots in their ready room learned of Ring's determined course, they were amazed at how different it was with what each of them had plotted. That would seem to support Lundstrom's first theory, while Fisher's version supported the second one.

11. Gay, *Sole Survivor*, p. 301

12. E-mail message, Sawruk to the author, 27 June 2005.

13. Weisheit is evidently referring to Appendix K in his book, rather than a ver-batim statement in the *Hornet's* after-action report, since no such statement

appears there. Appendix K is Weisheit's analysis of apparent differences between certain actual bearings and those recorded in the ship's log, i.e. "initial launch situation…wind from 130 T…*Hornet* log = 158 T…difference [is] 28 high."

14. Instructions printed at the top of a stock sixteen-section form entitled "U.S. Aircraft—Action With the Enemy." Examples are seen in the BOM after-action reports from the *Enterprise* air group.

15. Here Kernan has hit upon a further mystery in Mitscher's official report. Appendix F shows VF-8 flying *away* from Midway for a considerable distance at a time when they were supposedly much closer to the atoll than Fisher had been when he clearly saw its towering column of black smoke. The smoke would have been an obvious beacon to safety for the fighter pilots, had they actually been where Mitscher placed them in his report. With fuel tanks nearly dry, it's difficult to imagine why VF-8 would put a safe runway at their backs.

16. See Hill, "Ready Room Reading"

17. See Maryland State Bar Association

18. See Linder, "Lost Letter of Midway"

CHAPTER 9: MIDWAY WAS BECKONING

1. See Cressman, p. 135. Lewis was awarded the Bronze Star with Combat 'V' for his valor at Midway. He was not a member of the Roundtable due to being severely handicapped in his final years, but he was well known to many of its members. Despite his physical limitations, he was a regular attendee at the annual BOM commemoration in San Francisco where the author first met him in 2003. His personal story of gallantry was published in *The Roundtable Forum* after his passing in 2005.

2. Jones and the *Ganesvort* were in the thick of subsequent combat, participating in the assaults on Tarawa, the Marshall Islands, and the Philippines. The ship took a solid hit from a Kamikaze in December 1944, killing 34 of the crew. *Ganesvort* eventually returned to San Diego for repairs, which were completed after the war's end.

3. Wilhelm kept Hawaiian time in his journal, two hours ahead of Midway local time. The latter is used in most Battle of Midway references.

4. It would seem that the *Portland* had a well-stocked ship's store. June 3rd was the first anniversary for Wilhelm and his first wife, Kay, who passed away in 1988.

5. Japanese records confirmed that throughout the Battle of Midway, no hits were scored by any U.S. Army aircraft. With the single exception of a torpedo launched by a PBY at an oiler on the night of June 3rd, all damage to Japanese ships at Midway came from USN dive bombers. A U.S. Marine SB2U Vindicator from the atoll may have crash-dived on the *Mikuma* on June 5th, although that report is contradicted by some. See Cressman pp. 57 & 144, Prange p. 325 and Prange's endnote 20 on p. 425.

6. Task Force 17 commander Rear Admiral Frank Fletcher had transferred to the cruiser *Astoria* when the *Yorktown* became untenable as the flagship.

7. Wilhelm's journal on this page also includes a marginal entry concerning the sinking of the *Yorktown* on the morning of June 7th, but it's not legible in the copy provided to the author.

8. The "CA" (heavy cruiser) was actually the American submarine USS *Grayling*, which had to crash-dive in order to avoid the army bombs (see Prange, p. 341). Wilhelm's contemporary tally of enemy losses was typical of what was believed at the time. Both sides claimed far more attrition against the enemy than what occurred. The correct total for Japanese losses, as shown in most BOM references, was 4 CV and 1 CA sunk. Prange also describes damage to one DD on June 6th; see note 11 under Chapter 7 above. Additionally, one cruiser may have been damaged by a 500 lb. bomb from Roy Gee, as he related in Chapter 7.

9. This abridged excerpt from Wilhelm's journal is but one small portion of a very large volume that covers an eighteen-month period beginning in February 1941. His final entry reads "In August 1942, CINCPAC directed all naval personnel to stop maintaining a log of events for fear that some would end up in the hands of the enemy!"

CHAPTER 10: FINDING *KIDO BUTAI*

1. Gay, *Oral History; Battle of Midway*. Whether this particular statement by Gay was literally true is discussed in Chapter 12.

2. Prange, pp. 242 and 267

3. Childers related this account to the author during a telephone interview in July 2005.

4. ONI, p. 17

5. Cressman, p. 92. See also USS Enterprise CV-6 Association, "Battle of Midway, 1942," p. 3.

6. VT-8's launch time is recorded by Prange on p. 242; VT-6's by Morison on p. 120, and VT-3 by Cressman on p. 89.

CHAPTER 11: THE MOST AND THE BEST

1. Beach, pp. 449-450

CHAPTER 12: FACTS AND FABLES

1. Published as "The Japanese Story of the Battle of Midway" (OPNAV P32-1002), the 68-page document was sold by the U.S. Government Printing Office for thirty cents.

2. Parshall & Tully, pp. 436-442

3. Lord, p. 23

4. Prange, pp. 45-46

5. Morison, p. 85

6. Parshall & Tully (p. 92) date the initial American awareness of a Japanese operation in the central Pacific on May 9th, although nothing specific to Midway was identified that early.

7. Lord, p. 20

8. Prange, pp. 29 & 38

9. Whenever the term "sole survivor" is applied to George Gay, whether from the title of his book or otherwise, readers should recall that Gay was only the sole survivor of the VT-8 aviators who were flying from the *Hornet* that day. There were two other detachments of the squadron at that time, one on the atoll and another left back in Hawaii. Although the Midway detachment of six TBF Avengers was also nearly wiped out on June 4th, pilot Albert Earnest and radioman Harry Ferrier were actually the first two of VT-8's three survivors of the battle.

10. Gay, *Oral History; Battle of Midway.* This interview was conducted by the Navy on 12 October 1943 (Lundstrom, e-mail to author, 8 November 2005)

11. See Chapter 10, Note 5 above. While there has been misunderstanding in some quarters as to the purpose of the smoke generated by the Japanese screening ships, the point here is that it served as a beacon to guide VT-6 to *Kido Butai.*

12. There is a slight confusion factor in this anecdote from Lt. Col. Childers. He told the author that the bomb splashes occurred shortly before he spotted the Japanese smoke on the horizon, after the air group had been in the air about an hour or so. However, the official VB-3 after action report indicates the mishap occurred shortly after departing TF-17. (See Bombing Squadron Three, p. 2.) The author's assumption is that Childers saw the splashes earlier in the flight than he remembers and simply continued looking for a possible source from that moment on until he saw the smoke.

13. Fuchida & Okumiya, p. 143

14. Hornfischer, photos following pp. 148 and 341

15. ONI, p. 17. The times shown here are Midway local time on June 4th. The actual Japanese log used Tokyo time, 0617-0618 on June 5th in this case.

16. This outline was compiled from log entries in ONI pp. 19-20, 29, 34, 52-54; from Parshall & Tully pp. 336, 338-339, 353, 359; and from Cressman p. 148.

17. Gay, *Oral History; Battle of Midway*

18. Gay, *Sole Survivor*, pp. 125-126, 131

19. Ibid, p. 126

20. Lord, pp. 163-165. Nothing of this near-calamitous snafu appeared in the official after-action reports by Lt. Gallaher of VS-6, nor Capt. Murray of the *Enterprise*. The VB-6 report, authored by Lt. J. R. Penland on behalf of Best, mentions it briefly: see USS *Enterprise* CV-6 Association, "Bombing Squadron 6 Action Report, 4-6 June 1942."

21. See Prange p. 261 and IMMF.

22. "Jim, come on down," was the prearranged signal to be sent by Lt. Cdr. Eugene Lindsey in VT-6 to his fighter escort led by Lt. James Gray in VF-6, in the event the torpedo planes were attacked by Zeros. When that occurred, Lindsey was indeed heard by others calling for "Jim" to "come on down." See Lundstrom, p. 343.

23. See Naval Historical Center, "Battle of Midway: 4-7 June 1942, Online Action Reports: Commanding Officer, USS *Yorktown*, of 18 June 1942"

24. Morison, p. 156

25. E-mail to author from GSCM Richard B. James, command master chief, Naval Support Activity, Washington, 7 June 2005

26. Lord, p. 280

27. See Ballard p. 141, Cressman p. 167, and Linzey p. 103. On the other hand, Lundstrom (p. 426) got it right, saying that the ship sank with its "battle flag [singular] flying."

28. Lord p. 155, Prange p. 254, Lundstrom p. 340, and Cressman p. 89

29. Parshall and Tully, p. 189

CHAPTER 13: WHAT IF

1. Cowley, pp. 311-339

2. Parshall & Tully, pp. 229-231, 441

3. Stephan, p. 99

CHAPTER 14: ON THE LIGHTER SIDE

1. While this tale has not previously appeared in print on the Roundtable or elsewhere, it is well known among several of the group's members, as Kellejian has related it many times during various gatherings of BOM veterans. He told it to the author during the annual Battle of Midway observance in San Francisco in 2003.

2. *Tanikaze* was sunk by a U.S. submarine near the Philippine Islands on June 9, 1944, almost two years to the day after its miraculous escape at the Battle of Midway.

3. See Barnett.

CHAPTER 15: THE IMPOSTERS

1. Although the individual in question is very real, he is represented here by a fictitious name because the matter of his false claims has yet to be settled with finality. Any connection between the fictitious name and an actual person is an unintended coincidence that the author diligently sought to avoid.

2. Ed Holden is his actual name in this case, since he ultimately admitted his mendacity in public.

3. Another fictitious name. See Note 1.

4. Dixon's radioman-gunner at Coral Sea was confirmed directly to the author by Mark Horan, co-author with Cressman. Bill Vickrey's revelation concerning Dixon not flying at Midway is easily verified via an examination of flight rosters during the battle: see Cressman, pp. 90-105 and Hawkinson, Appendix 9. The identity of the *Akagi's* attackers is found in Cressman, pp. 102 & 104. The *Yorktown* air group's radioman-gunners are listed by name on Hawkinson, Appendix

9. Copies of the *Hornet's* air group roster at the Battle of Santa Cruz Islands were forwarded directly to the author by both Clayton Fisher and Roy Gee. The Boyington era of VMF-214 was Sept. 1943-Jan. 1944; see Sherrod, pp. 195 & 461.

References

BOOKS:

Ballard, Robert D., *Return to Midway*, Washington, DC: The National Geographic Society, 1999

Beach, Capt. Edward L., USN-Ret, *The United States Navy—200 Years*, New York: Henry Holt, 1986

Cowley, Robert and Stephen E. Ambrose (editors), *What If*, New York: G.P. Putnam & Sons, 1999

Cressman, Robert J., et al, *A Glorious Page In Our History*, Missoula, Montana: Pictorial Histories Publishing Company, 1990

Fuchida, Mitsuo and Masatake Okumiya, *Midway; the Battle That Doomed Japan*, New York: Ballantine Books, 1958

Gay, George H., *Sole Survivor* (Revised Edition), Midway Publishers, 1986

Holmes, W. J., *Double-Edged Secrets: U.S. Naval Intelligence Operations in the Pacific During World War II*, Annapolis, Maryland: Naval Institute Press, 1979

Hornfischer, James D., *The Last Stand of the Tin Can Sailors* (Bantam Paperback Edition), New York: Bantam Dell, 2005

Kernan, Alvin B., *Crossing the Line; a Bluejacket's World War II Odyssey*, Annapolis, Maryland: Bluejacket Books, 1997 (first edition)

_____, *The Unknown Battle of Midway: the Destruction of the American Torpedo Squadrons*, New Haven, CT: Yale University Press, 2005

Layton, Rear Admiral Edwin T. with Captain Roger Pineau USNR-Ret. and John Costello, *And I Was There; Pearl Harbor and Midway—Breaking the Secrets*, Old Saybrook, Connecticut: Konecky & Konecky, 1985

Linzey, Captain Stanford E., CHC, USN (Retired), *God Was At Midway*, Chula Vista, California: Black Forest Press, 1999 (reprinted 2004 as *The USS Yorktown at Midway*, Longwood, FL: Xulon Press)

Lord, Walter, *Incredible Victory*, New York: Harper & Rowe, 1967

Lundstrom, John B., *The First Team: Pacific Naval Air Combat From Pearl Harbor to Midway*, Annapolis, Maryland: Naval Institute Press, 1984

Morison, Samuel Eliot, *History of United States Naval Operations in World War II, Volume IV, Coral Sea, Midway, and Submarine Actions, May 1942-August 1942*; Edison, New Jersey: Castle Books, 2001

Parshall, Jonathan and Anthony Tully, *Shattered Sword: the Untold Story of the Battle of Midway*, Washington, D.C.: Potomac Books, 2005

Prange, Gordon W. with Donald M. Goldstein and Katherine V. Dillon, *Miracle at Midway*, New York: Penguin Books, 1982

Sherrod, Robert, *History of Marine Corps Aviation in World War II*, Washington, DC: Combat Forces Press, 1952

Stephan, John. J., *Hawaii Under the Rising Sun*, Honolulu: University of Hawaii Press, 1984

Weisheit, Bowen P., *The Last Flight of Ensign C. Markland Kelly, Junior, USNR* (Second Edition), Annapolis, Maryland: The Ensign C. Markland Kelly, Junior Memorial Foundation, Inc., 1996

ARTICLES:

Hannagan, Charles F. and Philip H. Jacobsen, "The 'In the Attic' Gang," *The Cryptolog*, Vol. 21 issue #4 (Fall 2000), pp. 9-10 and Vol. 22 issue #2 (Spring 2001), pp. 2 & 10.

Hill, Rear Admiral C. A., Jr., "Ready Room Reading: The Last Flight of Ensign C. Markland Kelly, Jr., USNR," *Wings of Gold*, Winter 1993, p. 54

Linder, Captain Bruce R., "Lost Letter of Midway," U.S. Naval Institute *Proceedings*, August 1999, pp. 29-35

DOCUMENTS:

Bombing Squadron Three, Report of Action, Period 4 June 1942 to 8 June 1942, Inclusive (Lt. D. H. Shumway)

Fisher, Clayton E., "The Battle of Midway; June 4, 5, and 6, 1942; U.S.S. *Hornet* Air Group Eight, Bombing Squadron Eight," 1979 (privately distributed by Fisher)

Jacobsen, Philip H., "Naval Cryptology and the Battle of Midway: Our Finest Hour" (text of speech to Naval Security Group Detachment, San Diego, 2000)

Mitscher, M.A., "Report of Action, 4-6 June 1942" (official *USS Hornet* after-action report of the Battle of Midway)

Office of Naval Intelligence (ONI), "The Japanese Story of the Battle of Midway" (OPNAV P32-1002), Washington, DC: U.S. Government Printing Office, 1947

Whitlock, Duane L., "And So Was I; a Gratuitous Supplement to *And I Was There*," 1986 (privately distributed by Whitlock; copy provided to the author by William H. Price)

INTERNET RESOURCES:

Barnett, William, "NAS Melbourne, Florida," http://www.nasmelbourne.freeservers.com/: 30 October 2005

Bowen, James K., "The Pacific War Historical Society," http://www.users.big-pond.com/pacificwar: 11 April 2005

Gay, Lieutenant George, USNR, "Oral History; Battle of Midway," http://www.history.navy.mil/faqs/faq81-8c.htm: 8 November 2005

Greaves, John, "John Greaves Art; a Gallery of Aviation, Marine, and Landscape Art," http://www.johngreavesart.com: 5 April 2005

Hawkinson, Christopher T., "Turning Point: the Battle of Midway, June 3-6, 1942," http://www.centurytel.net/midway, 23 March 2005

International Midway Memorial Foundation (IMMF), "In His Own Words: A Narrative From the IMMF 2001 Midway Veteran of the Month, LCDR Richard H. Best, USN (Ret.),"
http://www.immf-midway.com/narrative.html: 30 March 2005

Maryland State Bar Association, Inc., "The Plight of the Navigator," http://www.msba.org/departments/commpubl/publications/bar_bult/2005/feb05/weisheit.htm, 13 December 2005

Parker, Frederick D., "A Priceless Advantage: U.S. Navy Communications Intelligence and the Battles of Coral Sea, Midway, and the Aleutians," Center for Cryptologic History, http://www.ibiblio.org/hyperwar/PTO/Magic/COMINT-CoralSea/Forward.html: 31 July 2005

Naval Historical Center, http://www.history.navy.mil: 28 November 2005

Sinclair, Geoffrey, "JN-25 fact sheet, Version 1.1, September 2004," http://www.ibiblio.org/hyperwar/PTO/Magic/JN-25/JN-25.1.html: 4 August 2005

USS Enterprise CV-6 Association, "Battle of Midway-1942," http://www.cv6.org/1942/midway/default.htm: 14 November 2005

USS Enterprise CV-6 Association, "Bombing Squadron 6 Action Report, 4-6 June 1942," http://www.cv6.org/ship/logs/action19420604-vb6.htm: 3 April 2006

Appendix A
The Men of the Roundtable

Listed here are my coauthors, the veteran members of the Roundtable whose personal accounts of the Battle of Midway comprise this book's heart and its reason for being. The listing also includes those authors, historians, and others on the Roundtable who contributed additional material that in many cases helped to explain a concept, a veteran's story, or a certain segment of the battle. I thank them all once again for their willingness to share their memories, knowledge, and expertise.

*   *   *   *

Battle of Midway veteran*

*BERNSTEIN, Lt. George, USN-Ret
    Sea1/c, VT-8, USS *Hornet* (flight deck seaman)

*BOULIER, WO Kenneth A., USN-Ret
    Y1/c Combat Intelligence Unit, Melbourne, Australia (JN-25 cryptologist)

BOWEN, Mr. James
    Australian military archivist, webmaster for The Pacific War Historical Society

CAVALCANTE, Mr. Bernard C. "Cal"
    Archivist, U.S. Naval Historical Center, Washington, D.C.

*CHEEK, Cdr. Tom F., USN-Ret
  WO, VF-3/42, USS *Yorktown* (F4F pilot)

*CHILDERS, Lt. Col. Lloyd F., USMC-Ret
  ARM3/c, VT-3, USS *Yorktown* (TBD Devastator radioman-gunner)

CORIO, Mr. Paul L.
  Composer, screenwriter

*COTTON, FTC Bernard C., USN-Ret
  FC1/c, USS *Hornet* (Mk 37 fire control director)

*COTTON, Lt. Francis X. "FX", USN-Ret
  AOM1/c, VT-8, USS *Hornet* (TBD Devastator bombardier & ordnanceman)

CRESSMAN, Mr. Robert J.
  Author, historian, U.S. Naval Historical Center, Washington, D.C.

*CRISMAN, Mr. Bryan A.
  Ens., disbursing officer, USS *Yorktown*

*DELCHAMPS, AOCM Newton E., USN-Ret
  AOM3/c, USS *Yorktown* (bombsight shop)

DELORENZO, Capt. Frank L., USN-Ret
  PB2Y seaplane pilot (flew Adm. Nimitz to Pearl Harbor, 25 December 1941)

*DRAKE, Lt. Cdr. Donald J., JAGC, USNR-Ret
  PFC, Btry G, 6th Marine Defense Battalion, Midway

*EICHORN, Mr. Raymond "Jerry"
  BKR1/c, ship's galley, USS *Yorktown*

EVANS, Mr. Thomas F.
  Brother of VT-8 pilot Ens. William R. Evans

*FISHER, Cdr. Clayton E., USN-Ret
  Ens., VB-8, USS *Hornet* (SBD pilot)

*FOX, SFC Edward R., U.S. Army-Ret
  Pvt., 6th Marine Defense Battalion, Midway

*GARDNER, Mr. John V.
  Cpl., 6th Marine Defense Battalion, Midway

*GEE, Capt. Roy P., USN-Ret
  Ens., VB-8, USS *Hornet* (SBD pilot)

*GRAETZ, Mr. Ronald W.
  ARM3/c, VT-6, USS *Enterprise* (TBD Devastator radioman-gunner)

*GRIST, MSgt. Walter C., USMC-Ret
  PFC, Engineering Section, VMSB-241, Midway (aircraft mechanic)

GUILLORY, Jr., Mr. Troy T.
  Son of Ens. Troy T. Guillory, Sr., VB-8 pilot, USS ***Hornet***

HAMILTON, Mr. Daniel R.
  Attorney and scale model warship hobbyist

*HOPKINS, Rear Adm. Lewis A., USN-Ret
  Ens., VB-6, USS *Enterprise* (SBD pilot)

*HOUSER, Vice Adm. William D., USN-Ret
  Ens., USS *Nashville* (assistant gunnery officer)

*JACOBSEN, Lt. Cdr. Philip H., USN-Ret
  RM3/c, Station H, Hawaii (Japanese radio intercept operator)

*JONES, Mr. Elmer L.
  F1/c, USS *Hammann* (enlisted sailor, Engineering Department)

*KASEBERG, Mr. Willis D. (Dan)
  Y3/c, VT-3, USS *Yorktown* (squadron clerk)

*KELLEJIAN, Mr. John J.
    EM2/c, USS *Enterprise* (electrician's mate, E Division)

*KERNAN, Mr. Alvin B.
    AOM3/c, USS *Enterprise* (aviation ordnanceman, VT-6)

*KIGHT, Lt. Cdr. Otis G., USN-Ret
    Sea1/c, VF-42, USS *Yorktown* (flight deck seaman)

KRAVER, Mr. Theodore C..
    Aerospace software engineer, naval air model aircraft hobbyist

*LEONARD, Rear Adm. William N., USN-Ret
    Lt.(jg), VF-3/42, USS *Yorktown* (XO, F4F pilot)

*LINZEY, Capt. Stanford E., Jr., CHC, USN-Ret
    Mus2/c, ship's band, USS *Yorktown*. Subsequent career as a Navy chaplain.

*LUCIUS, Col. William R., USMC-Ret
    WO, Quartermaster, MAG-22, Midway

LUNDSTROM, Mr. John B.
    Historian, author, World War II naval aviation specialist

McDONALD, Mr. Donald C.
    Cryptologist, OP-20-G; National Security Agency (retired)

MOORE, Mr. Ivon Nigel
    Business consultant (United Kingdom)

*NEWBERG, Mr. Peter L.
    EM3/c, USS *Yorktown* (electrician's mate, E Division)

O'NEIL, Capt. William D., USNR-Ret
    Former USN amphibious warfare specialist

PARSHALL, Mr. Jonathan B.
Historian, author, Imperial Japanese Navy authority

PRICE, Mr. William H.
Retired communications security specialist; founder of the Roundtable

REECE, Jr., Mr. William M.
Research Technician, NC State University; aircraft scale modeler, SBD specialty

*ROY, Cdr. William G., USNR-Ret
PhoM2/c, USS *Yorktown* (ship's photographer)

*SHOWERS, Rear Adm. Donald M. "Mac", USN-Ret
Ens., Combat Intelligence Unit, Pearl Harbor (intelligence analyst)

*SURGI, Jr., AMM1 William F., USN-Ret
AMM3/c, VF-42, USS *Yorktown* (aviation mechanic)

*SWAN, Cdr. Robert A., USNR-Ret
Ens., VP-44, Midway (PBY pilot/navigator)

TILLMAN, Mr. Barrett
Historian, author, naval aviation specialist

*TREMBLAY, Lt. William H., USN-Ret
Y2/c, Combat Intelligence Unit, Melbourne, Australia (JN-25 cryptologist)

VICKREY, Mr. BILL K.
Private archivist, Battle of Midway specialist

WALSH, Sr., Lt. Cdr. George J., USNR-Ret
SB2C Helldiver pilot

*WILHELM, Cdr. Ralph V. "Kaiser", USN-Ret
Lt.(jg), USS *Portland* (SOC seaplane pilot)

*WOODSON, ATC Richard T., USN-Ret
   ARM2/c, VS-8, USS *Hornet* (SBD radioman-gunner)

*   *   *   *

The following Roundtable members, all Battle of Midway veterans, are also acknowledged. The fact that their contributions to the group's discussions over the years didn't make it into this book does not mean that their generous participation was not important and appreciated.

ADY, Jr., Capt. Howard P., USN-Ret: Lt., PBY pilot, VP-23
ANDERSON, Gen. Earl E., USMC-Ret: Capt., Marine Detachment, USS *Yorktown*
ARCHER, CPO Theodore R., USN-Ret: AMM1/c, V-1 Division, USS *Hornet*
BOUTERSE, Cdr. Matthew J, CHC, USN-Ret: Lt.(jg), Chaplain, USS *Astoria*
BROWN, Mr. Richard S.: RM2/c, CTF-17 staff, USS *Yorktown*
BURKEY, Cdr. Gale C., USN-Ret: Ens., PBY pilot, VP-23, Midway
CANNON, Lt. Cdr. William E., USNR-Ret: Ens., PBY pilot, VP-24, Midway
DAVIS, Cdr. Douglas C., USN-Ret: Lt.(jg), PBY pilot, VP-24, Midway
EARNEST, Capt. Albert K., USN-Ret: Ens., VT-8 (TBF detachment), Midway
EASON, CWO4 Joseph, USN-Ret: EM1/c, USS *Tamaha* (YNT-12), Midway
FERRIER, Cdr. Harry H., USN-Ret: RM3/c, VT-8 (TBF detachment), Midway
FORBES, Capt. James M., USN-Ret: Ens., VS-8, USS *Hornet*
HENDRICK, Mr. Robert E.: Cpl., 6th Marine Defense Battalion, Midway
HORNE, Lt. Cdr. Philip A. USN-Ret: Ens., SOC pilot, USS *New Orleans*
KAIT, Capt. H. Hart, USN-Ret: Lt., Gunnery Officer, USS *Monaghan*
LANE, Mr. David H.: ARM3/c, VT-3, USS *Yorktown*
LASER, Lt. Cdr. Sam, USNR-Ret: Y2/c, 6th Div., Gunnery Dept., USS *Yorktown*
MINICLIER, Col. John F., USMC-Ret: PFC, 6th Marine Defense Battalion, Midway
QUAM, Mr. Ellsworth R. "Bud": F3/c, USS *Yorktown*
PRIOR, Mr. Raymond H.: Cpl., 6th Marine Defense Battalion, Midway
SOBEL, Mr. Alvin A.: ARM1/c, VS-5, USS *Yorktown*
SPRINGER, ACC Wilbur S., USN-Ret: AMM3/c, USS *Enterprise*
WALKINSHAW, Capt. David J., USN-Ret: Ens., PBY pilot, VP-91, Kauai, Hawaii

Vintage and modern photos of many of the Roundtable's Battle of Midway veterans may be viewed on the association's Internet site at http://www.midway42.org.

Appendix B
Synopsis of the Battle of Midway

The Japanese Plan for Midway

The attack on Pearl Harbor on 7 December 1941 abruptly cast the United States into a war for which it was woefully unprepared. American military power, drawn down by the isolationism of the 1930s and the constraints of the Great Depression, was substantially inferior to that of its potential adversaries, Nazi Germany and Imperial Japan. While the Roosevelt administration could see war clouds on the horizon, its principal reaction was to beef up the ranks with personnel rather than what was truly needed: a major increase in both the quantity and quality of the weapon systems that those personnel were expected to employ in combat. Such shortcomings were especially felt in the U.S. Pacific Fleet, which was mainly based on an aging battleship force and an inadequate support structure that suffered further due to the buildup in the Atlantic. Assets that could have helped in the Pacific were retained on eastern shores in the face of a growing U-boat threat.

If anything remotely good can be said of the Pearl Harbor tragedy, it was the fact that the loss of nearly all Pacific Fleet battleships compelled the Navy to shift its fundamental strategy to its other available capital ships, the aircraft carriers, which Japan had already done all too well. Through a succession of small engagements early in 1942 and a costly but strategically successful major clash in the Coral Sea in May, the U.S. Navy established its carrier fleet as a force that could stand up to the Japanese when the odds were more or less equal. Unfortunately, equal odds were not a reasonable expectation in the first half of 1942. Japan had aggressively developed its navy in the 1930s, with the result that it had some of the best ships and naval aircraft in the world, more of them than nearly anyone else, and pilots and aircrews with training and combat experience that Japan's adversaries could only jealously admire.

The U.S. Navy had no shortage of courage among its sailors and airmen, but compared to the Japanese its fleet had too few ships, its combat aircraft were woefully inferior in all but one category, and its pilots were largely inexperienced, a great many having had little or no time in the air after flight training. The qualified success at Coral Sea was as much due to poor judgment on the part of the enemy fleet commander as it was to American valor and resolve. And the USN could not afford any more successes like Coral Sea, in which one precious fleet carrier was sunk and another badly damaged.

That was the situation in the spring of 1942 when Japanese Admiral Isoroku Yamamoto developed his plan for a final, crushing victory over the U.S. Navy in the Pacific: he would send an overwhelmingly powerful fleet to attack and invade tiny Midway Atoll, only 1100 miles from Pearl Harbor and a part of the Hawaiian Island chain itself. Yamamoto reasoned that the Americans would not stand for a Japanese bastion so close to Pearl Harbor and would throw everything they had at Midway's occupiers in order to retake the island. He would then destroy the few carriers that the U.S. could muster for such an operation, thus compelling a quick end to the Pacific war on Japan's terms.

A Lethal Advantage

Admiral Yamamoto never reckoned on America's intelligence operations as a lethal weapon against his navy, but that's exactly what the U.S. possessed with its superior codebreaking skills and resources, developed as far back as the 1920s. The Japanese assumed both before and throughout the war that the complexities of their language coupled with intricate encryption techniques would preclude successful interception of its radio message traffic. Consequently, they had few reservations about passing battle plans and schedules over the air.

But for all that it lacked in modern weaponry and aerial combat training, the U.S. Navy was unsurpassed in its ability to decipher the enemy's radio transmissions and thus discern their intent. Thanks to language and decryption skills that the Japanese never imagined, communications intelligence (ComInt) specialists in Hawaii, the Philippines, and Australia gradually developed an ability to read significant portions of the enemy's radio traffic almost as reliably as the Japanese radiomen themselves. That priceless advantage led to the successful intercept of the enemy's invasion fleet in the Coral Sea, but more importantly, it gave the Americans an advance look at Admiral Yamamoto's intentions for Midway. If the U.S. could somehow muster up enough battle-worthy ships and planes to spring an effective trap, it might just be possible to thwart the Midway invasion and thus prevent another calamity like Pearl Harbor.

Setting the Trap

Japanese strategy included a feint toward Alaska. A small force would invade a couple of inconsequential islands in the Aleutians just before the Midway strike, in order to disperse some of the American fleet away from Midway and, as a bonus, prevent any future U.S. operations toward Japan from Alaska. But the Navy's ComInt team saw that primarily as a diversion, recommending to Admiral Nimitz, the USN Pacific Fleet commander, that he focus on defending Midway. They underscored their suggestion by providing the admiral with the entire Japanese attack plan, including the very day and time that enemy planes could be expected over Midway atoll! All Nimitz had to do was position sufficient firepower on the island and aboard the Navy's ships, and Yamamoto's invincible armada could be in for a rueful surprise.

But sufficient firepower was a tall order for Nimitz. He did assign Midway's U.S. Marine defenders every available fighter and bomber not needed aboard the carriers, and the Army Air Force added as many B-17 and B-26 bombers as the island could support. But the Army planes had no track record of successfully attacking moving warships, and the Marines were shackled with mostly obsolete aircraft (woefully antiquated in the case of their fighters) and inadequately trained aircrews. As for the Navy's ships, only two undamaged carriers were at hand, the USS *Enterprise* and USS *Hornet*. A third carrier, the USS *Yorktown,* mauled at Coral Sea, could also join the fleet but with reduced capability due to battle damage. And again, too many of the naval aviators were minimally trained and had no combat experience.

Against that thrown-together defense, Yamamoto was sending four of his fleet carriers to Midway, veterans of the Pearl Harbor attack as well as successful campaigns against the British in the Indian Ocean. Backing them up were eleven battleships, sixteen cruisers, a whopping fifty-four destroyers, and twenty-two submarines. On paper at least, the Japanese were clearly bringing enough muscle to the fight to prevail in spite of the Americans' codebreaking advantage.

But Nimitz had little choice. Yamamoto was right in one key regard: the U.S. positively could not suffer a Japanese occupation of Midway. Two USN task forces, one centered on *Yorktown* and the other on *Enterprise* and *Hornet,* sortied from Pearl Harbor on the 28th and 30th of May to take up station northeast of the atoll. The enemy fleet was expected to appear not later than Thursday, June 4th, 1942.

Defending the Atoll

Commander Joseph Rochefort, mastermind of the Navy's ComInt team at Pearl Harbor, had gotten it right almost to the minute. In the very early morning hours of June 4th, the Japanese carrier force, *Kido Butai*, launched a massive air strike against Midway. The Japanese intention was to eliminate any air defense the island might put up, then conduct an amphibious invasion to secure the atoll and thus create the trap to which the American carriers would surely come.

But the Midway's defenders were forewarned by both search plane reports and radar, resulting in all serviceable aircraft on the island being in the air before the attackers arrived. The Japanese bombed the two islands more or less as planned, but caused only a handful of casualties among the Marine defenders and damage to the island's facilities that was visibly spectacular but strategically unimportant. And the Marines put up a stout defense, knocking down several of the enemy's planes and damaging a great many more. Those facts caused the Japanese strike commander to radio *Kido Butai* with unexpected news upon heading back to his carrier: "there is need for a second attack."

And that's the point at which things began to unravel for the invaders. Vice Admiral Nagumo, *Kido Butai*'s commander, had prepared his second wave of strike aircraft with anti-ship weapons rather than land bombs, in anticipation of dealing with any U.S. Navy vessels that might be in the area. The call for a second attack upon the atoll compelled him to start the tedious process of switching the ordnance on his planes from armor-piercing to high-explosive types, thus delaying any launch for at least forty-five minutes or more. And at almost that very moment, the U.S. Navy's strike aircraft from its three carriers began to appear on the horizon.

The Sacrifice of the Torpedo Squadrons

American naval air doctrine was rather unrefined that early in the war, resulting in uncoordinated attacks on the part of all three air groups. The USS *Yorktown* flyers, with more combat experience than the men from the *Enterprise* or *Hornet*, were perhaps the most successful of the three as a group, but on the whole the American effort suffered from numerous shortcomings. The most egregious of those was arguably the leadership of Commander Stanhope C. Ring, air group commander of the *Hornet*. Ring was an up-and-coming career naval officer, generally competent save for one key regard: he was not skilled as a warplane pilot or navigator. The course he determined his planes would fly upon launch from the *Hornet* had no chance of finding the enemy fleet, and at least one of his squadron commanders, Lieutenant Commander John C. Waldron of Torpedo Squadron 8 (VT-8), adamantly argued for a more logical plan. But Ring was not swayed by his subordinates' opinions that day. He ordered all four of his squadrons (VT-8, VB-8, VS-8, and VF-8) to follow him on his chosen course and would brook no further arguments.

Waldron played along for perhaps thirty minutes after launch, then veered away from Ring, taking his fifteen torpedo bombers on what he knew to be the proper track to the Japanese carriers. It was a bold, almost outrageous thing to do—defying his commander in wartime, taking his squadron away from the ordered course—but in the event, he turned out to be right and Ring turned out to be wrong. After about another hour, VT-8 spotted *Kido Butai* on the horizon and turned to engage. Waldron must have had mixed emotions at that point. He had proven the validity of his chosen course, but the *Hornet's* fighter escort was with Ring, not VT-8. The fifteen old, slow, and very vulnerable TBD Devastator torpedo bombers were on their own against a fatal encounter with swarming Japanese Zeros.

Kido Butai had defended itself from torpedo attacks launched from Midway only two hours before. Six TBF Avengers (detached from VT-8) plus four army B-26s had made a brave but fruitless strike, scoring no hits and losing seven of their ten aircraft. Now the Zeros turned to yet another torpedo bomber threat, jumping upon Waldron's charges with a ferocious zeal. The *Hornet* squadron suffered even worse than the Midway planes, losing all fifteen of their aircraft without a single hit on a Japanese ship. Only one pilot in Waldron's flight, Ensign George Gay, survived the attack. Waldron and the rest of his airmen were all killed.

But this action, like that of the Midway-based strike earlier, caused further consternation for Nagumo. With his carriers desperately zigzagging to avoid the much-feared aerial torpedo, no progress could be made on arming his strike planes and getting them spotted on his flight decks. Moreover, the presence of TBDs indicated that American carriers were nearby, compelling him to countermand his previous order to switch from anti-ship ordnance to land bombs. The hangar deck crews on the Japanese carriers worked furiously to swap their planes' bombs and torpedoes yet again, but that laborious task was made nearly impossible by the ships' frantic maneuvering during the VT-8 attack.

As the last of Waldron's planes sank beneath the waves, Nagumo was confounded to learn of a second flight of TBDs about to menace his fleet. An ill-advised launch scheme aboard the *Enterprise* (the same as employed by *Hornet*) indirectly caused that ship's torpedo squadron (VT-6), its two bombing squadrons, and its fighter squadron to all become separated from each other, with the result that the torpedomen of VT-6 were as unescorted and alone as Waldron had been. Their commander spotted smoke on the horizon—the end of *Kido Butai's* fight with VT-8—and turned to engage. Once again, Nagumo was facing a torpedo attack that interrupted his crew's abilities to prepare any sort of counterstrike. But the luck of VT-6 was only marginally better than VT-8's. Four of its fourteen planes survived the ordeal, but none of their torpedoes struck home.

Yet, Nagumo's nightmare was far from over. By sheer coincidence, the *Yorktown's* air group came upon his ships just as the last of VT-6's TBDs were escaping the fray. However, the Yorktowners had done a better job with their launch than either of the other two U.S. carriers, for their torpedo, dive bomber, and fighter squadrons all showed up over the Japanese fleet at about the same time. Nagumo now had a very potent attacking force to contend with, but he had no idea how critical his situation had become.

A gunner in the *Yorktown's* Torpedo Squadron 3 was first to spot smoke on the horizon from the Japanese ships. The squadron turned to engage, but once again the Zeros pounced upon the obsolete TBDs, assuring that VT-3's fate would be virtually identical to that of VT-8 and VT-6: no hits and only two surviving aircraft, both heavily damaged, and twenty-one of twenty-four pilots and gunners killed in action.

But yet again, Nagumo's carriers could not get their strike planes launched while dealing with VT-3. Nor would they, for Nagumo's luck was about to turn even worse.

Arashi Points the Way

The U.S. Navy had deployed nineteen submarines in the Midway area as another potential weapon against the enemy fleet. One of them, USS *Nautilus*, actually threatened Nagumo's carriers in the midst of the VT attacks, which drew the attention of Japanese destroyer *Arashi*. *Nautilus* broke off its attack under depth-charging from *Arashi*, running submerged toward the southwest with the Japanese ship in determined pursuit. *Arashi* continued the chase for about thirty minutes, finally giving up in order to return to *Kido Butai* and resume its proper defensive role.

And at that point, another sheer coincidence blessed the American cause. Two dive bomber squadrons from the *Enterprise* had fruitlessly searched for the enemy's carriers, flying ahead and well beyond Nagumo's track toward Midway. Their leader, Lieutenant Commander C. Wade McClusky, knew the Japanese could no longer be ahead of him, so he turned his formation to the north, thinking to search along the reciprocal of Nagumo's predicted course. But he held little hope for success because his planes were dangerously low on fuel. He quickly reached the point where he had to turn back toward the *Enterprise* or risk losing both squadrons in the ocean. He swung back around to the northeast—and spotted *Arashi* below him, charging at high speed back to the Japanese carriers. McClusky thought the destroyer might be bound for the fleet he couldn't find, so he altered his course in line with *Arashi's* heading and surged forward. Within a few minutes, *Kido Butai* lay before him.

A Fatal Five Minutes

Yet another improbable coincidence favored the American cause at that moment. Although *Enterprise* had launched its planes long before *Yorktown*, McClusky's circuitous route caused his two squadrons of SBD dive bombers to arrive high over *Kido Butai* at precisely the same time as the *Yorktown* SBDs of VB-3. And because of the incessant low level torpedo attacks with which the Japanese fighters had been forced to contend for the previous two hours, none of them were at high altitude when three squadrons of American dive bombers materialized directly over their carriers.

The one category of warplane in which the U.S. excelled over the Japanese was the Douglas Dauntless SBD dive bomber, generally acclaimed as the best such aircraft employed by any navy or air force in the entire war. In the hands of skilled pilots, the SBD was a lethal weapon, virtually an early-day cruise missile. With no high altitude opposition, *forty-eight* of them simultaneously peeled off against the Japanese carriers *Akagi, Kaga,* and *Soryu*. Within five minutes, all three were flaming wrecks, the victims not only of the SBDs but also of Nagumo's helter-skelter ordnance change orders, which had left bombs, torpedoes, and refueling hoses hazardously scattered about the Japanese hangar decks. The exploding weapons and gasoline turned each of the three ships into a hellish cauldron, eliminating not only themselves but more importantly, all three of their air groups from the war. The Battle of Midway was all but over.

The Loss of USS Yorktown

Nagumo's fourth carrier, the *Hiryu*, had escaped the SBDs' onslaught because the wild maneuvering to avoid the VT squadron attacks had caused it to stray several miles out of position. Thus *Hiryu* was undamaged, and Japanese scout planes had informed its commander of the location of at least one American carrier. *Hiryu* dive bombers and torpedo planes launched against the *Yorktown,* and in spite of that ship's aggressive antiaircraft and fighter defense, it was struck by three bombs and two torpedoes, severely damaging it for the second time in less than a month.

The joy aboard *Hiryu* was short-lived, for a second strike by SBDs launched from *Enterprise* delivered the same fate to it as had befallen its three sister ships earlier in the day. Thus, by sundown on the fourth of June, Vice Admiral Nagumo did not have a single aircraft left with which to attack Midway or defend his remaining fleet. On the American side, *Enterprise* and *Hornet* were unscratched, and it seemed as if the *Yorktown* once again could be saved. But the Imperial Japanese Navy was not through yet.

While salvage crews feverously worked to save the *Yorktown* and with success apparently at hand, a Japanese submarine managed to make its way inside the American destroyer screen and launch four torpedoes at the motionless carrier. Two struck dead center and a third sank the destroyer USS *Hammann*, tied alongside *Yorktown* to supply power to the salvage team. The great carrier, beloved by her crew, was now mortally wounded. It rolled over and sank the following morning. In small consolation, Marine and Navy bombers succeeded in sinking a fifth Japanese ship, the cruiser *Mikuma* at almost the same time *Yorktown* had been struck its fatal blow.

But the Midway operation was now a lost cause for the Japanese. With no air power and with the Americans not only in possession of Midway but with at least two of their carriers in the vicinity, Admiral Yamamoto had no choice but to recall his forces back to Japan. His great plan to destroy the U.S. Navy in the Pacific before the United States could adequately reinforce its fleet had failed, and he would never learn the reason why.

Midway's Incredible Victory

Walter Lord and Gordon Prange called it the "Incredible Victory" and the "Miracle at Midway," respectively, in their best-selling books. The reasons why the miracle was incredible are twofold: (1) the force brought to Midway by the Japanese was so overwhelming in firepower and numbers that they should have been able to prevail in spite of the U.S. codebreaking advantage. And (2), given that fact, the only way the Americans could have won is through a combination of unprecedented courage, superb skill, and especially unbelievable luck. And that's exactly what happened.

Virtually no postulating about alternative tactics by either side at Midway has produced a better scenario for the Americans than what actually occurred. Given the U.S. Navy's experience at Coral Sea, Admiral Nimitz had to expect that losses at Midway would be painful, worse than the earlier battle because of the more massive enemy force involved. Retention of the atoll in U.S. hands was by no means a safe bet on the third of June. Indeed, had anyone predicted that within seventy-two hours the Japanese would be down four fleet carriers and a heavy cruiser against one American carrier and a destroyer, he would have been admired for his positive outlook but scorned for his lack of practicality. No one on either side expected that anything remotely like that was in the cards.

Midway's Consequences

The consequences of victory at Midway were profound, not only for World War II in the Pacific but for the entire war itself as well as subsequent history. For it was victory at Midway that made follow-on operations in the South Pacific possible. A loss at Midway would have indefinitely postponed the Guadalcanal campaign launched only two months after the *Hiryu* went to the bottom. With a Japanese bastion on Guadalcanal, Allied operations in Australia would have been severely endangered. General MacArthur and his meager forces would have been at risk for capture, but more importantly, the Americans would not have been able to establish and sustain submarine bases on Australia's western coast. It was those Australian-based submarines that devastated enemy shipping in the succeeding years of the war, greatly contributing to Japan's collapse in 1945. No one believes that the Japanese would have ever won the war in the Pacific, but a loss at Midway undeniably would have afforded them the means to prolong it for untold months or years.

Japanese possession of Midway would have brought at least the threat of operations against Pearl Harbor, and they did have plans for a full-scale invasion and occupation of Hawaii. Whether they would have had the logistical resources to do that is debatable, but any sustained threat against Hawaii would have forced American strategists to divert some, and perhaps a lot of the forces destined for Europe to the west coast in order to counter the fear of a Hawaiian invasion or even Japanese carrier operations against west coast naval bases and shipyards. Any lessening of the resources deployed against the Germans would have resulted in one of two very unpleasant situations: (1) the invasion of Normandy and the western European campaign would have to have been postponed, giving Hitler enough time to mount a better defense on both of his fronts and thus perpetuating the Nazi horror in Europe for months, years, or even decades. Or alternately, (2) the lack of a maximum Allied effort in western Europe could have allowed the steamrolling Red Army to overrun all of Germany, not just the eastern third. A communist domination of most of Europe would then have been likely, bringing about dismal conditions at the outset of the Cold War. What would have transpired with the Soviet Union in control of the entire European continent is anyone's guess, but no positive images come to mind.

In considering the many vital engagements of the Second World War, Midway often loses out to other famous battles and campaigns like the Solomons, Philippine Sea, Normandy, and the crossing of the Rhine. Indeed, the relatively small quantity of men and military hardware involved at Midway is dwarfed by comparison to any of those other conflicts as well as a great many more. But without the "Incredible Victory," it is likely that those other battles would have occurred much later than they did, if at all, and that their outcome would probably have been far more costly to Allied forces. To that you can add the toll of bitter battles that were never fought in the central and eastern Pacific because the advance of the Japanese empire was abruptly stopped short only six months after the war began.

Clearly, the improbable American victory at Midway had consequences for the rest of World War II and beyond that were far out of proportion to the scope of the event itself.

Appendix C
The Battle of Midway:
Order of Battle

*   *   *   *

AMERICAN FORCES

TASK FORCE 17

USS *Yorktown* (CV-5)
Commander Carrier Striking Force, Rear Adm. Frank Jack Fletcher
Commander Task Force 17, Rear Adm. Frank Jack Fletcher
Capt. Elliott Buckmaster, CO, USS *Yorktown*
Lt. Cdr. Oscar Pederson, CYAG
VF-3, Lt. Cdr. John Thach (25 F4F-4)
VB-3, Lt. Cdr. Maxwell Leslie (18 SBD)
VS-5, Lt. Wallace Short, Jr. (19 SBD)
VT-3, Lt. Cdr. Lance Massey (13 TBD)

Task Group 17.2, Cruiser Group, Rear Adm. William Smith
USS *Astoria* (CA-34)
USS *Portland* (CA-33)

Task Group 17.4, Destroyer Screen, Capt. Gilbert Hoover, ComDesRon 2
USS *Hammann* (DD-412)
USS *Hughes* (DD-410)

USS *Morris* (DD-417)
USS *Anderson* (DD-411)
USS *Russell* (DD-414)
USS *Gwin* (DD-433)

TASK FORCE 16

USS *Enterprise* (CV-6)
Commander Task Force 16, Rear Adm. Raymond Spruance
Capt. George Murray, CO, USS *Enterprise*
Lt. Cdr. Clarence Wade McClusky, CEAG
VF-6, Lt. James Gray (27 F4F-4)
VB-6, Lt. Richard Best (19 SBD)
VS-6, Lt. Wilmer Gallaher (19 SBD)
VT-6, Lt. Cdr. Eugene Lindsey (14 TBD)

USS *Hornet* (CV-8)
Capt. Marc Mitscher, CO, USS *Hornet*
Cdr. Stanhope Ring, CHAG
VF-8, Lt. Cdr. Samuel Mitchell (27 F4F-4)
VB-8, Lt. Cdr. Robert Johnson (19 SBD)
VS-8, Lt. Cdr. Walter Rodee (18 SBD)
VT-8, Lt. Cdr. John Waldron (15 TBD)

Task Group 16.2, Cruiser Group, Rear Adm. Thomas Kinkaid, Com-CruDiv 6
USS *Vincennes* (CA-44)
USS *Northampton* (CA-26)
USS *Pensacola* (CA-24)
USS *New Orleans* (CA-32)
USS *Minneapolis* (CA-36)
USS *Atlanta* (CL-51)

Task Group 16.4, Destroyer Screen
Capt. Alexander Early, ComDesRon 1
USS *Phelps* (DD-360)
USS *Worden* (DD-352)
USS *Monaghan* (DD-354)

USS *Aylwin* (DD-355)
Capt. Edward Sauer, ComDesRon 6
USS *Balch* (DD-363)
USS *Conyngham* (DD-371)
USS *Benham* (DD-397)
USS *Ellet* (DD-398)
USS *Maury* (DD-401)

Oiler Group
USS *Cimarron* (AO-22)
USS *Platte* (AO-24)
USS *Dewey* (DD-349)
USS *Monssen* (DD-436)

SUBMARINES

Task Group 7.1, Midway Patrol Group
USS *Cachalot* (SS-170)
USS *Flying Fish* (SS-229)
USS *Tambor* (SS-198)
USS *Trout* (SS-202)
USS *Grayling* (SS-209)
USS *Nautilus* (SS-168)
USS *Grouper* (SS-214)
USS *Dolphin* (SS-169)
USS *Gato* (SS-212)
USS *Cuttlefish* (SS-171)
USS *Gudgeon* (SS-211)
USS *Grenadier* (SS-210)

Task Group 7.2, Roving Patrol
USS *Narwhal* (SS-167)
USS *Plunger* (SS-179)
USS *Trigger* (SS-237)
Task Group 7.3 (TG 7.3)

Task Group 7.3, North of Oahu Patrol
USS *Tarpon* (SS-175)

USS *Pike* (SS-173)
USS *Finback* (SS-230)
USS *Growler* (SS-215)

MIDWAY ATOLL

Naval Air Station Midway

Capt. Cyril Simard, CO, NAS Midway
VP-23 (14 PBY-5)
VP-24 (6 PBY-5A)
VP-44 (8 PBY-5A)
VP-51 (3 PBY-5A)
VT-8 Detachment (6 TBF)

Lt. Col. Ira Kimes, CO, Marine Air Group 22
VMF-221, Maj. Floyd Parks (20 F2A, 7 F4F-3)
VMSB-241, Maj. Lofton Henderson (16 SBD, 11 SB2U)

Lt. Clinton McKellar, Jr., Motor Torpedo Boat Squadron 1
7 PT boats

USS Tamaha (YNT-12) (harbor tugboat)

7th Army Air Force Detachment
4 B-26 (Capt. James F. Collins)
13 B-17 (Lt. Col. Walter C. Sweeny, Jr.)
6 B-17 (Maj. George A. Blakey)

Midway Defense Force
Col. Harold D. Shannon
6th Marine Defense Battalion (Reinforced)

Midway Refueling Unit
Cdr. Harry R. Thurber
USS *Guadalupe* (AO-32)
USS *Blue* (DD-387)
USS *Ralph Talbot* (DD-390)

OTHER DEPLOYMENTS

Kure Island
2 PT boats, 4 small patrol craft (part of MTB Squadron 1, Midway)

French Frigate Shoals
USS *Thornton* (AVD-11)
USS *Ballard* (AVD-10)
USS *Clark* (DD-361)
USS *Kaloli* (AOG-13)

Pearl and Hermes Reef
USS *Crystal* (PY-25)
USS *Vireo* (ATO-144)

Lisianski, Gardner Pinnacles, Laysan, and Necker
4 patrol boats

*   *   *   *

JAPANESE FORCES

FIRST MOBILE FORCE (*KIDO BUTAI*), VICE ADM. CHUICHI NAGUMO (IN *AKAGI*)

Carrier Divison 1

IJNS *Akagi* (CV)
21 A6M Zero (Zeke) fighters
21 Type 99 (Val) dive bombers
21 B5N2 (Kate) torpedo bombers

IJNS *Kaga* (CV)
30 A6M Zero (Zeke) fighters
23 Type 99 (Val) dive bombers
30 B5N2 (Kate) torpedo bombers

Carrier Division 2

IJNS *Hiryu* (CV)
21 A6M Zero (Zeke) fighters
21 Type 99 (Val) dive bombers
21 B5N2 (Kate) torpedo bombers

IJNS *Soryu* (CV)
21 A6M Zero (Zeke) fighters
21 Type 99 (Val) dive bombers
21 B5N2 (Kate) torpedo bombers

Support and Screen

IJNS *Tone, Chikuma* (CA); IJNS *Haruna, Kirishima* (BB); IJNS *Nagara* (CL)
IJNS *Nowaki, Arashi, Hagikaze, Maikaze, Kazagumo, Yugumo, Makegumo, Urakaze, Isokaze, Tanikaze, Hamakaze* (DD)

Supply Unit

4 "Maru" oilers plus IJNS *Akigumo* (DD)

MAIN BODY (FIRST FLEET), ADM. ISOROKU YAMAMOTO, CINC COMBINED FLEET (IN *YAMATO*)

IJNS *Yamato, Nagato, Mutsu*
IJNS *Hosho* (CVL) with 8 torpedo bomber
IJNS *Yukaze* (DD) (accompanying *Hosho*)
IJNS *Sendai* (CL)
IJNS *Fubuki, Hatsuyuki, Murakumo, Shirayuki, Ayanami,Isonami, Shikinami, Uranami, Amagiri, Asagiri, Yugiri, Shirokumo* (DD)
IJNS *Naruto* (oiler) plus 3 "Maru" oilers

MIDWAY OCCUPATION FORCE, VICE ADM. NOBUTAKE KONDO (IN *ATAGO*)

Covering Group

> IJNS *Atago* (flagship), *Chokai, Myoko, Haguro* (CA)
> IJNS *Kongo, Hiei* (BB)

Screen

> IJNS *Yura* (CL); IJNS *Asagumo, Harusame, Minegumo, Murasame, Natsugumo, Samidare, Yudachi* (DD)

Light Carrier Unit

> IJNS *Zuiho* (CVL)
> > 12 A6M Zero (Zeke) fighters
> > 11 Type 99 (Val) dive bomber
>
> IJNS *Mikazuki* (DD)

CLOSE SUPPORT GROUP, VICE ADM. TAKAO KURITA (IN *KUMANO*)

Cruiser Division 7

> IJNS *Kumano, Mikuma, Mogami, Suzuya* (CA); IJNS *Arashio, Asashio* (DD)

Oiler: *Nichiei Maru*

TRANSPORT GROUP, REAR ADM. RAIZO TANAKA (IN *JINTSU*)

Transports

> 12 troop transports, 1 oiler, 3 patrol boats

Screen

> IJNS *Jintsu* (CL, flagship), IJNS *Amatsukaze, Arare, Hatsukaze, Kagero, Kasumi, Kuroshio, Oyashio, Shiranuhi, Tokitsukaze, Yukikaze* (DD)

SEAPLANE GROUP

IJNS *Chitose*
20 observation seaplanes

Kamikawa Maru
8 observation seaplanes
Additional seaplane group intended for Kure Island

IJNS *Hayashio* (DD)

SUBMARINE GROUP

I-121, I-122, I-123, I-156, I-157, I-158, I-159, I-162, I-165, I-166, I-168, I-169, I-171, I-174, I-175

*   *   *   *

Note: the foregoing Order of Battle was adapted primarily from the Internet site of the U.S. Naval Historical Center. Not shown are the American and Japanese forces involved in the "Aleutians Diversion" nor some of the support and auxiliary vessels in the vast Japanese armada.

Appendix D
The Battle of Midway in the Media

Books, movies, magazine articles, and video productions on the Battle of Midway exist in great abundance. The following listing includes a critical review of those that have elicited the most comment over the years on the Battle of Midway Roundtable. The entries in each category appear in the order of their value as a Battle of Midway reference, as determined by feedback received from Roundtable members. Most of them are widely available from booksellers, video vendors, and auction sites.

Items marked by an asterisk are freely available for viewing and download on the Internet.

*   *   *   *

BOOKS

1: *A Glorious Page in Our History*
by Robert Cressman and several coauthors (1990)

A Glorious Page In Our History is considered by most members of the BOMRT to be the essential reference on the Battle of Midway. It was produced by a group of military historians who felt that nothing then available provided full and accurate coverage of all of the important elements of the battle. If you can only afford one book on the Battle of Midway, Roundtable members will tell you to get this one.

2: *Shattered Sword: the Untold Story of the Battle of Midway*
by Jonathan Parshall and Anthony Tully (2005)

The title of this book is a little misleading, for it's not another overall history of the battle. Instead, it is a definitive new work on the Imperial Japanese Navy (IJN) at Midway, compiled with a thoroughness of research, documentation, and perceptive analysis not previously seen. The graphics are outstanding, with computer-generated charts and diagrams that ably support and augment the text. *Shattered Sword* can justifiably be considered the essential resource on the Japanese side of the Battle of Midway, supplanting Fuchida & Okumiya's *Midway, the Battle That Doomed Japan* for that honor (see below). Indeed, Parshall and Tully demonstrate that many of the points made by Fuchida in his book were less than truthful, apparently tainted for the Japanese audience for whom the book was originally written.

3: *Incredible Victory*
by Walter Lord (1967)

Walter Lord's book is considered by most to be the classic account of the Battle of Midway. Virtually every known resource available to the public in both the U.S. and Japan was meticulously researched by the author, resulting in a superb and highly accurate accounting of the battle that reads like an entertaining novel. Its faults are few and minor, and can generally be attributed to the limits of known and unclassified information in 1967.

4: *And I Was There*
by Rear Admiral Edwin T. Layton (1985)

Layton was the Pacific Fleet Intelligence Officer throughout the war. His book is the whole story of U.S. communications intelligence accomplishments from Pearl Harbor to VJ Day. The successes (and some failures) of U.S. ComInt forces prior to Pearl Harbor, Coral Sea, Midway, and the interception of Admiral Yamamoto's flight in 1943 are detailed in depth. In particular, *And I Was There* thoroughly and accurately relates how ComInt was the cornerstone of the "Incredible Victory" at Midway. A few very minor points have been subject to correction or debate, but they do not measurably detract from the book's essential value.

5: *The First Team*
by John Lundstrom (1984, revised 1990)

The First Team is nearly 600 pages of amazingly detailed text, covering everything one might want to know about "Pacific Naval Air Combat from Pearl Harbor to Midway" (the subtitle). John Lundstrom knows this topic (U.S. naval aviation history) extremely well and his writing shows it. The general opinion on the Roundtable has been that his book is much more accurate than the better known works and best sellers by Lord and Prange. The only reason it is not higher on this list is because the Battle of Midway comprises just the last chapter of the book, about 140 pages. Nevertheless, its Midway segment is widely regarded as one of the most faithful accounts of the battle to be found anywhere.

6: *Marines at Midway**
by R. D. Heinl (1948)

Marines at Midway is a highly detailed account of the role played by the U.S. Marines in the base development and defense of Midway. Anyone desiring a thorough reference on the Corps at the BOM will probably have no need to look elsewhere.

7: *Miracle at Midway*
by Gordon W. Prange (1982)

This book has been the number one best seller among those that are exclusively focused on the Battle of Midway, although it is not technically nor historically the best of them. That explains its ranking well down this list. It does provide a good narrative description of the battle, reading more like an interesting novel than a history reference. Knowledgeable readers may determine that it contains a few minor points (and perhaps a couple of major ones) that are not an accurate rendition of events, but most will still find it highly interesting and a worthy addition to any Midway library. The "Chronology" (timeline) at the end of the book is a particularly useful resource.

8: *The Japanese Story of the Battle of Midway**
U.S. Navy publication OPNAV P32-1002 (1947)

While not exactly a book, this 68-page official U.S. Navy document deserves to be ranked with all other important references on the BOM, because it is unquestionably one of the most important of them. all. It is the official Japanese after-action report on the Battle of Midway as recorded by Vice Admiral Nagumo and his staff. It includes a detailed chronology of each event during the battle, and there is an abundance of supporting graphics, charts, and tables. Virtually any serious writing on the Battle of Midway will of necessity include frequent mention of and quotes from this important resource, including the book you're reading now.

9: *A Priceless Advantage**
by Frederick D. Parker (1993)

This is another case of a key resource on the BOM that isn't exactly a book (although it exists in very limited availability in book form), but should always be included in any list of important references on the battle. Its subtitle is "U.S. Navy Communications Intelligence at the Battles of Coral Sea, Midway, and the Aleutians," and it is perhaps the best treatment of that subject in relatively concise form.

10: *Double-Edged Secrets*
by Captain C. Jasper Holmes (1979)

This book nicely complements that of Edwin Layton (above), since Jasper Holmes was an insider in Cdr. Joseph Rochefort's Combat Intelligence Unit at Pearl Harbor before, during, and after the BOM. Holmes was the originator of the famous "water ruse" ploy detailed in Chapters 4 and 12.

11: *The Last Flight of C. Markland Kelly, Junior, USNR*
by Bowen P. Weisheit (1996)

Major Weisheit's research is the subject of and the fundamental source for Chapter 8 in this book. It is a compelling, fascinating study, culminating in a detailed chart showing the track of all USS *Hornet* squadrons on the morning of 4 June 1942. (The chart is the basis for Figure 2 in Chapter 8.) To someone whose only view of where the *Hornet* air group flew that day comes from the official record as related by Samuel Elliott Morison and repeated by other respected authors, *The Last flight of Ensign C. Markland Kelly* will be a stunning revelation.

12: *SBD-3 Dauntless; the Battle of Midway*
by Daniel Hernandez (2002)

This is a very unique and interesting book, published in Spain but readily available world wide on the Internet. The author, Daniel Hernandez, is a Spanish airline captain who happens to have an intense interest in the Battle of Midway and its principal weapon system, the SBD Dauntless dive bomber. The book's primary focus is the SBD itself, but it also provides an in-depth history of the plane's finest hour, the Battle of Midway.

First about the SBD: the diagrams and photographs are simply outstanding, and there seems to be no end to them. The see-through color line drawings are especially good. As for its level of detail: would you like to know the difference between the crankshaft bearings used in the SBD-3 vs. the SBD-2? Or the number of degrees that the trim tabs will move up and down? How about the amount of fluid required to charge the hydraulic system? Or the engine's compression ratio? The point is, the level of technical detail about the plane and its various component parts far exceeds anything else one is likely to find. You're almost led to believe that, using only this book as a guide, you could assemble an entire Dauntless yourself if you had all the parts and the necessary tools. In summary, if you want to dig very deeply into the nuts and bolts of the SBD (all of them!), this is a book you're going to want to have.

As for the Battle of Midway itself, this book does a reasonably good job of covering the essential details but its strongest feature is the color graphic set, which are simply outstanding. Also to its credit, it does not fall prey to some of the usual myths and errors found in other books. For example, the "Midway is short of water" ruse, commonly mistaken as an attempt to learn the meaning of "AF" in

Japanese ciphers, is correctly explained here. And when a book, movie, or video gets that part right, it's an indicator that the authors have done their homework and know what they're talking about. You get that feeling throughout this volume.

If the book has one noticeable flaw, it's the fact that its author wrote it in Spanish, then directly translated it into English rather than paraphrasing it into idiomatic English. The result is Spanish grammar and syntax using English words, and that can be a bit odd or cumbersome at times. But it's a relatively minor flaw that you can live with, particularly in view of the book's very fine quality in other regards.

13: *Sole Survivor*
by George Gay (1979)

George Gay was the only one of thirty TBD pilots and radioman/gunners who survived VT-8's attack upon the Japanese carriers. As such, he was both a participant and an eyewitness in one of the most daring, aggressive, and brutal combat actions in American military history.

It should be noted that Gay waited thirty-seven years to write his book, long after his recollection of the details could be considered fresh. Readers on the Roundtable have offered the opinion that, as a result, his text contains a number of factual errors and a few arguable conclusions. However, his perspective on his squadron's action was that of one who was there, and therein lies the value of the book. The last chapter, focusing entirely on John Waldron, is especially good.

14: *Midway: the Battle That Doomed Japan*
by Mitsuo Fuchida and Masatake Okumiya (1955)

Until the appearance of *Shattered Sword* (above), this work was long accepted as the fundamental resource on the Japanese side of the battle, since one of its authors (Fuchida) personally led the attack on Pearl Harbor and was present on the *Akagi* at Midway. Nevertheless, new revelations show that Fuchida embellished his tale significantly for the sake of his primary audience in Japan. But despite the book's several faults (as outlined in *Shattered Sword*), readers may still find it important for its first-person Japanese view of the battle, however inaccurate it may be in some of the details.

15: *That Gallant Ship*
by Robert Cressman (1985, revised 2000)

That Gallant Ship is the complete story of *USS Yorktown* (CV-5), from its launch in 1936 to its loss at the Battle of Midway in 1942. All of *Yorktown's* operations in the Atlantic, in the island raids of early 1942, at Coral Sea, and at Midway are thoroughly covered. The book is extensively illustrated with photographs. It has gone through four printings, and the fourth edition (February 2000) includes photos and text not included in the earlier ones.

16: *Combined Fleet Decoded*
by John Prados (1995)

Prados' book is a very highly regarded detailed treatise on both U.S. and Japanese communications intelligence during WWII, frequently cited by the ComInt veterans on the Roundtable.

17: *Return to Midway*
by Robert Ballard (1999)

Return to Midway mainly focuses on undersea explorer Ballard's search for the wrecks of *Yorktown* and *Kaga* during an expedition sponsored by the National Geographic Society. The images in the book, including closeup photos of the *Yorktown* as it sits on the ocean floor, are outstanding. See also the video version, below.

18: *Midway*
by Hugh Bicheno (2002)

Roundtable members report this book as a good general accounting of the BOM. It includes a listing of all ships engaged and their disposition after the battle, and goes into considerable detail on the differences between Japanese and American cultures, the intelligence resources of both sides, and their ships, planes and other military hardware. It includes colorful map graphics, although the placement of certain defenses on the atoll's two islands is not consistent with that remembered by the Roundtable's Marine Corps veterans.

19: *The Unknown Battle of Midway: the Destruction of the American Torpedo Squadrons*
by Alvin Kernan (2005)

Roundtable member and university professor Kernan's main focus in this book is the three torpedo squadrons at Midway, VT-8 from the *Hornet*, VT-6 from the *Enterprise*, and VT-3 from the *Yorktown*. Professor Kernan, who was an enlisted hangar-deck crewman with VT-6 during the battle, tells a gripping story from the perspective of one who was there at the time.

20: *The Big E*
by Edward P. Stafford (1960)

This is the whole story of the *USS Enterprise* in WWII, including thorough coverage of its vital role in the Battle of Midway. The book was very highly recommended by readers.

21: *God Was at Midway*
by Stanford E. Linzey (1999, re-released in 2005 as *The USS Yorktown at Midway*)

Many adhere to the belief that the "Incredible Victory" at Midway could only have happened as it did through some sort of supernatural or divine intervention. That theme is eloquently expressed by Navy chaplain Linzey, a survivor of the USS *Yorktown*. His harrowing tale of escape from the stricken vessel is typical of what a couple thousand of the ship's crew and air group experienced on the afternoon of 4 June 1942.

22: *A Battle History of the Imperial Japanese Navy*
by Paul Dull (1978)

Dull served in the Office of War Information during the war, and thereafter spent a number of years researching Japanese archives in order to get a view of the war as seen from the other side. The book covers the entire war through 1945, but the 1942-43 segments are particularly good. Approximately ten percent of the book (56 pages) is on the Battle of Midway.

23: *Sunburst*
by Mark Peattie (2002)

Subtitle: "The Rise of Japanese Naval Air Power, 1909-1941." This book is very interesting for its coverage of Japanese training and doctrine, and especially for its very comprehensive appendices, which are packed with extensive information on key IJN personnel, organizations, ships and planes, and much more.

24: *They Turned the War Around at Coral Sea and Midway*
by Stuart Ludlum (2000)

This is the story of *Yorktown's* air group, from Pearl Harbor to Midway. Readers have reported what they believe to be some notable factual errors, but they say the book still gets high marks for its first-person accounts from *Yorktown* aviators, particularly at the Battle of the Coral Sea.

25: *The Ship That Held the Line: the USS Hornet and the First Year of the Pacific War*
by Lisle A. Rose (1995)

This book is reported as being highly interesting and well-written, although its research appears to be faulty in spots. For example, VB-8 pilot Lt.(jg) Clayton Fisher is said to have been missing in action at the Battle of the Santa Cruz Islands, which was news to Fisher.

26: *The USS Enterprise*
by Steve Ewing (1982)

Subtitle: "The Most Decorated Ship of World War II, A Pictorial History." Another tribute to the Big E, with extensive photos. Reviewers rate it below Stafford's *The Big E*.

27: *Midway: Battle for the Pacific*
by Edmund L. Castillo (1968)

Said to be a tight, well-written book that covers all the basics. Includes many of the familiar black & white photographs.

28: *Midway 1942: Turning Point in the Pacific*
by Mark Healy (1993)

The main value of this book is its excellent illustrations of ships and aircraft. Modelers will find it particularly useful. Readers' opinions are less favorable in other regards.

-----

29. *The Battle of Midway: the Battle That Turned the Tide of the Pacific War*
by Peter C. Smith (1976, revised 1996)

British author Smith has produced a decent account of the battle that gets good reviews in Great Britain, but some readers on the Roundtable have citicized his book for what they view as anti-American undertones.

-----

30. *Climax at Midway*
by Thaddeus Tuleja (1960)

This book covers the basics of the battle well enough, but is very limited in value by the level of knowledge available when it was written, thus falling prey to some of the misconceptions cited in Chapter 12.

31: *Miracle at Midway*
by Charles Mercer (1942)

Don't confuse this one with the Gordon Prange book by the same title (see above). It first came out in 1942, and is therefore possibly the earliest general markets work on the battle. The copyright was renewed in 1977 at which time it was re-published. It is reported as written on a juvenile level.

Readers should expect significant factual errors, given the very limited knowledge about the battle available in 1942. For example, there should be *no* mention of anything related to communications intelligence (in the original edition, at least), which was the fundamental key to the victory. The 1942 edition is of interest for its contemporary view of the battle, factual errors and omissions notwithstanding.

Note: the following two books are fictional novels and are not ranked. They are included here because of their interest among Roundtable members and their relevance to the BOM.

Dauntless
by Barrett Tillman (1992)

Dauntless, by naval aviation expert Barrett Tillman, traces the fortunes of Lt.(jg) Philip "Buck" Rogers, a VB-3 SBD pilot, through Midway on the *Yorktown* and the Battle of the Eastern Solomons on the *Saratoga*. Other characters include Marine fighter pilot Captain Jim Carpenter and Flight Petty Officer Hiroyoshi Sakaida. Those familiar with the facts of the battle will find this book highly interesting and entertaining.

Love and Glory
by Alvin Kernan (2004)

Professor Kernan was an aviation ordnanceman (AOM3/c) aboard the *Enterprise* during the BOM. After the war he commenced a long career at both Yale and Princeton universities, and thus is uniquely qualified to write about the battle. *Love and Glory* tells the whole story of the first day of the battle, 4 June 1942, focusing mainly on the *Hornet* air group and the saga of Torpedo Squadron 8.

The book's protagonist is one Ensign Clay Hunt, a brand new naval aviator assigned to VT-8 aboard the *Hornet*. We follow the experiences of Ens. Hunt as he qualifies in the TBD and assimilates into the squadron, under the leadership of its colorful commander. We then ride with him as the air group launches on its errant course on the first day of the battle.

Kernan is unmerciful toward the *Hornet's* air group commander before, during, and especially after the battle. He also gives no slack to the ship's captain, having him deliberately conspire to falsify *Hornet's* after-action report in order to save his own hide as well as that of his buddy, the CHAG. This is the sort of thing that Roundtable members discussed for years, and it's highly interesting to see it played out in a novel.

MOVIES AND VIDEO PRODUCTIONS

For the most part, Roundtable members (especially the BOM veterans) are highly critical of movies and video productions about the Battle of Midway. As Otis Kight explained it, "you just can't beat the real thing with the original cast!" More specifically, though, their criticisms almost universally focus on the inevitable archival film clips of ships and planes that are mismatched for the event being shown. F6F Hellcats, SB2C Helldivers, F4U Corsairs, and *Essex*-class carriers in Battle of Midway scenes are the usual culprits. Of course, that's a fundamental weakness of all film productions prior to the modern era of computer-generated images of literally anything you want to see. Motion picture editors were limited to what was available and technically feasible in the way of film footage of the ships and planes they wanted to portray. Hence, they invariably would use whatever looked (to them) like the right sort of vessel or aircraft from whatever film clips they could find in their archives, with the result that movies about the Battle of Midway would inevitably include scenes of the wrong ships and planes. Of course, the average moviegoer doesn't know a Corsair from a crop duster, but to those who fought the battle and to others with only a modest awareness of World War II aircraft, a Corsair in a movie about the Battle of Midway is laughable.

The veterans were also hard on the tacky fictional love stories or other emotional dramatics injected in almost any war movie. However, such dramatizations have always been considered essential by Hollywood studios that have to market their expensive productions to the public. Presumably, a movie showing nothing more than charging ships and zooming planes won't score anywhere near the box office take as one with a juicy human drama thrown in.

Thus, there wasn't a whole lot of praise from Midway veterans for any theatrical motion picture about the BOM. Some of the short subjects and video productions got off easier, but they also had their problems. In any event, here are the Roundtable's impressions of the BOM films and videos available through 2005.

THEATRICAL MOVIES

1. *Midway*
starring Charlton Heston (1976)

Midway is the second of only two full-length Hollywood feature films that focus solely on the Battle of Midway. It is a lavish production, representing about the best that Hollywood could do given the resources and techniques available in 1976. Unfortunately, that did not include the realistic computer graphics appearing in later productions, which meant that *Midway's* producers had to resort to the familiar tactic of incorporating old combat footage, carefully spliced, edited, and colorized as best they could in order to convey a more or less authentic look. To the uninitiated moviegoer, the effect was very good: the scenes were dramatic and the audio (in theaters during the initial 1976 release) was positively awesome.

Besides the ubiquitous problem of mismatched ships and planes, the script suffers from a painfully inane soap opera subplot revolving around Charlton Heston's fictional character, a CINCPAC staff captain, and his fighter pilot son who has incomprehensibly fallen in love with a local Nisei girl in Honolulu. The girl's family is suffering through the persecution endured by Japanese-Americans in 1942, an obvious sop to the transformation of racial/ethnic sensitivities in American society during the 1960s and 1970s. If you're a fan of wartime history, you simply have to let that sort of silliness pass and focus on the majority of the film, which more or less adequately deals with things that really happened.

Roundtable members have generally echoed the above criticism (plus a few others: see Chapter 4), but many still give *Midway* high marks for at least bringing an awareness of the battle to the general public on a grand scale. And on balance, even with non-authentic ships and aircraft and the sappy love story fiction, it's still a very good production.

Interestingly, later releases of the film shown on cable TV channels include a lengthy segment on the Battle of the Coral Sea that was not included in the theatrical release.

2: *A Wing and a Prayer*
starring Don Ameche and Dana Andrews (1944)

A Wing and a Prayer is a wartime-produced version of the Battle of Midway and the only other one (besides the 1976 *Midway*) that is centered entirely on the battle. It is a very interesting film, although not for the reasons one might expect. As for accuracy in detail, it's actually much worse than the 1976 movie, with wrong planes, wrong attack scenes, and wrong, unidentified, or curiously missing ships (both U.S. and Japanese). Additionally, there are a lot more fictional characters than in *Midway*. But in 1944 the specifics of the BOM were still largely unknown to the general public (including movie producers), plus wartime security restrictions prevented revealing much of the detail we now take for granted, especially the names of the personalities. Consequently, when we see Hellcats, Avengers, and Helldivers from an Essex-class CV destroying only three Japanese carriers (*Akagi* is a no-show in the movie), and absolutely no mention of reading the Japanese naval code, perhaps we can understand.

But its production during the war itself is actually what makes this a great BOM movie, in spite of the usual complaints about mismatched film clips. You get the authentic feel of the times by watching rather good actors portray characters and events that, to them, are contemporary. There is no misrepresentation of wartime social or moral values that inevitably creeps into movies produced in other eras. You are watching scenes and hearing dialog that is as close to the real thing as you're likely to ever experience. This is a movie about the Battle of Midway that has most of the historic details quite wrong, but you definitely don't feel disappointed when it ends if you're not totally focused on historically correct ships and planes.

-----

3. *Task Force*
starring Gary Cooper (1949)

The BOM is only part of the tale in *Task Force*, which is the life story of a fictional naval aviator. It doesn't have quite the contemporary authenticity of *A Wing and a Prayer*, but its postwar production allowed for a much more factual portrayal, including a far better collection of background film clips (correct aircraft, etc.) than is usually seen.

MOTION PICTURE DOCUMENTARIES

1. *The Battle of Midway*
produced by John Ford (1942)

Famous Hollywood producer John Ford, equipped with a 16 mm. camera and color film, was dispatched by Admiral Nimitz to Midway just prior to the battle. He obtained remarkable footage of the Marines' preparations for the invasion plus amazing scenes of the Japanese air attack. Ford accomplished this at considerable danger to himself, but the results obtained are excellent: graphic, real, and professional, although a few non-authentic scenes (i.e., from film taken during the Pearl Harbor attack) were spliced in for the sake of continuity.

Segments from Ford's production have been included in a great many war movies. It is the only motion picture footage available showing a significant portion of the Battle of Midway from the actual scene. (Note: Ford's camera on Midway had no sound capability, so any audio that accompanies a showing of it has been inserted by the producers.)

-----

2. *Torpedo Squadron 8*
U.S. Navy (1942)

This official U.S. Navy short subject was produced as a tribute to VT-8 shortly after the battle. The loss of the entire squadron's aircraft and all but one of its men was an exceptionally emotional event for the Navy as well as the public in 1942, and you sense that emotion in watching this production. It was filmed aboard the *Hornet* in May as the ship was returning to Pearl Harbor in advance of the BOM. It opens with the fifteen pilots assembled for their group photo; the famous VT-8 portrait seen as a still photo in many sources, i.e. p. 91 of *A Glorious Page In Our History*. We then see closeups of the TBDs and clips of the aircraft taking off on a mission. The heart of the film is the man-by-man tribute to the aircrews: each pilot is seen with his R/G, preceded by a view of a memorial plaque bearing their two names.

For fans of wartime history and students of the Battle of Midway, watching this film is something of a poignant experience. You get to see the pilots and gunners of VT-8 up close and personal, in real life. It makes them much more than a grim statistic in a history book, and gives one pause to reflect upon who they really were and what they really did.

The original film is in color but without audio, and runs for only a few minutes.

VIDEO DOCUMENTARIES (TELEVISION AND DVD PRODUCTIONS)

1. *The Battle of Midway*
Discovery Channel documentary (Thomas H. Horton production, 1999)

As Battle of Midway documentaries intended for the general public go, this may be the best of them all. Some of our members were quick to point out the usual errors in archival film footage showing the wrong aircraft or ships, but as explained above, you nearly always get that in such productions. The Horton program stands out for its extensive use of the *correct* ships and planes, including many scenes of SBDs in action, and a few decent clips of TBDs. One movie clip even appears to show the listing *Yorktown* with the *Hammann* alongside.

From the standpoint of the Roundtable, the program is especially interesting for its extensive participation by three of its members: VF-3 pilot Tom Cheek, Midway Marine Bill Lucius, and VT-8 TBF radioman Harry Ferrier. Other BOM vets contributing to the program include VB-6 skipper Dick Best, VB-6 pilot Wilbur Roberts, John Snowden (VS-6 gunner with Lt.(jg) Kleiss), Donald Hoff (VS-6 gunner with Ens. Dexter), and Stuart Mason (VB-6 gunner with Lt.(jg) Anderson). Several Japanese vets were also interviewed, including Bill Surgi's friend and Kate crewman Taisuke Maruyama.

The program includes some simple computerized images showing the four Japanese carriers, and a very good map graphic that displayed the enemy's complex strategy for Midway and the Aleutians. The carrier images are a bit crude, but the map graphic is excellent for its clear explanation of Yamamoto's convoluted plan.

A couple of factual errors in the narration were noteworthy: the program repeated the myth that the Midway "water plant failure" ruse was an attempt to find out the meaning of the Japanese code symbol "AF." There was also a claim that Adm. Nimitz had made an on-the-spot decision to go after the *Hiryu* on the afternoon of June 4th. Historians generally agree that Nimitz was pretty much in the dark about the battle at that point, and that the *Hiryu* decision was more likely made by the on-scene commander, Rear Adm. Spruance.

But in summary, this is an excellent portrayal of the BOM, as good as you're going to get until someone decides to make a better one using modern computer imagery in order to show the correct ships and planes, and knowledgeable technical consultants in order to get every last factual detail right.

2. *War Stories with Oliver North: the Battle of Midway*
Fox News Channel documentary (2002)

This is one of the weekly documentaries presented on the Fox News Channel and hosted by Oliver North. It's a very good overall presentation of the Battle of Midway, ranking a very close second to the Thomas Horton *Battle of Midway* documentary (above). But it particularly excels in its coverage of the signal intelligence aspect of the American victory.

Roundtable members and Midway veterans Mac Showers, Lew Hopkins, and Bill Surgi are extensively interviewed in the program, as are members Mark Horan and Robert Cressman, two of the co-authors of *A Glorious Page In Our History.*

-----

3. *The Battle for Midway: Discovery of the USS Yorktown*
National Geographic documentary (1999)

The Battle for Midway is a special National Geographic production covering undersea explorer Dr. Robert Ballard's expedition to find and photograph the wrecks of the *Yorktown* and *Kaga* (see book version above). The video includes a lot of wartime footage, some from the John Ford film plus some of the usual non-authentic archival clips. But the main thrust of the production is the modern-day search for the two carriers, and it's a highly interesting quest.

Ballard took four Midway veterans with him on the expedition, including Roundtable members Harry Ferrier and Bill Surgi, plus two Japanese vets from the *Kaga*. The video also includes interviews of VT-3 gunner Lloyd Childers, VB-6 skipper Dick Best, and VT-8 TBF pilot Bert Ernest. The participation of these seven veterans is a key part of the production and adds greatly to its interest. The surround-sound audio on the DVD version is also excellent.

-----

4. *Battlefield: The Battle of Midway*
PBS telecast, 1994

Unlike the other listings in this appendix, this one does not appear to be readily available for purchase. That's unfortunate, because it is a rather good production that in some regards is even better than those of Thomas Horton and Oliver North (above). For example, there are plenty of scenes with F4Fs, SBDs, and TBDs, and nary a single Hellcat, Corsair, or Essex-class CV. Another plus: the program starts with a very good segment on the Coral Sea, including helpful map graphics. On the down side, it perpetuates some of the familiar myths about the battle, but on balance it's a worthy addition to anyone's BOM video library if a copy can be found.

-----

5. *The Search for the Japanese Fleet*
Discovery Channel documentary (2000)

Like the National Geographic expedition above, this is another search for the sunken ships of the Battle of Midway; the Japanese carrier *Kaga* in this case. The search team uses the recorded track of the submarine USS *Nautilus*, which had attacked the *Kaga* at a known position, to successfully plot the location of the sunken carrier. The sophisticated equipment aboard the research vessel first produces sonar images of the wreck, and eventually video of pieces of the carrier strewn about the sea floor.

The program gives a good overview of the battle itself, including good coverage on the signal intelligence aspect. However, it's somewhat disappointing in that, unlike Robert Ballard's search for the *Yorktown* in the National Geographic production, the *Kaga* itself is not found and photographed due to limitations in the research vessel's availability. Aside from that, this is a very well done documentary that anyone having a high interest in the Battle of Midway will want to see. Roundtable member and IJN authority Jon Parshall appears at the end of the program, aiding the team in determining exactly what pieces of the ship had been photographed.

-----

6. *F4F Wildcat*
DVD set by Aircraft Films, www.aircraftfilms.com (2003)

This two-disk set includes film and still photos of just about every F4F you'll ever want to see, including a lengthy segment on the magnificently restored Wildcat at the Naval Aviation Museum at Pensacola. But most of the photography is vintage, showing early development of the Wildcat (including its biplane predecessors) during the 1930s, a huge assortment of WWII combat film and stills, and interesting close-ups with Jimmy Thach and Butch O'Hare. There is also a lot of actual combat footage of the *Yorktown* at Midway, the *Enterprise* at Eastern Solomons, and the *Hornet* at Santa Cruz. And this isn't just a few grainy glimpses of carriers under attack as viewed from a distant destroyer. You are looking at film from the carriers themselves; some from a handheld camera and some from fixed cameras. In particular, the fixed cameras show gripping footage of the attacks on *Enterprise* and *Hornet*. Another plus: this set includes the John Ford *Battle of Midway* movie (see above).

Roundtable member and VF-3 pilot Tom Cheek is featured as the narrator on a couple of the segments, one of which shows his upside-down crash landing on the *Yorktown* during the BOM.

-----

7. *Command Decision: The Battle of Midway*
History Channel documentary (2004)

If you're interested enough in the BOM to digest the book you're reading now, viewing the *Command Decision* video might not be a rewarding use of your time. Its sequence number on this list should be "last" instead of seven, which sounds much too generous to this writer. Roundtable members unanimously lambasted it as the most dismally inept film or video production on the Battle of Midway ever foisted upon the public. It was their opinion that even a novice student of the battle would be dismayed by its treatment of the historical details.

Note: the following productions are not ranked. They were not released to the public in time for a critical review here, but I've included them in order to make this listing as complete as possible.

Days That Shook the World: the Battle of Midway
Lion Television (London, 2005)

The Roundtable had a small part in the development of this British documentary. I was contacted by an associate producer for help in getting the details right concerning a ready room scene on a BOM carrier. With the assistance of a couple of our Midway vets, I provided them some photos showing certain equipment in a squadron ready room that they particularly needed. That was our only involvement, though, so the quality of the production remains to be seen. The project was completed in June 2005 and aired by the BBC in England shortly thereafter. Its expected showing on American networks had not yet occurred by the time this book went to press.

The Pacific War
Gary Goetzman/Tom Hanks/Steven Spielberg production (2006)

This is an expansive historical drama covering all of World War II in the Pacific, produced by the same group as the acclaimed *Band of Brothers* television miniseries. The Battle of Midway comprises the second episode, and it has the potential for finally telling the story with accurate imagery and all the correct facts, thanks to the inclusion of Hugh Ambrose on the consulting team. Hugh, the son of author/producer Stephen Ambrose and a long-term member of the Roundtable, actively sought the advice of its BOM veterans on several issues in the early stages of the project, which should translate to a quality production. Don't look for Corsairs buzzing the *Akagi* or Rochefort puzzling over the meaning of "AF" in this one.

Appendix E
Exposing the Imposters

The following newspaper article, cited in Chapter 15 and written by George Walsh, Jr., appeared in the December 10, 2004 issue of *The Daily Gazette* of Schenectady, New York.

* * * *

ESAM SPEAKER'S PHONY WAR TALES ARE LATEST FABRICATIONS EXPOSED
By George M. Walsh, Gazette Day City Editor

Ed Holden thought he was doing the right thing lying about his exploits during World War II, contributing somehow to children's appreciation of the nation's combat veterans. "A lot of this is flight of the imagination," he said when confronted with discrepancies in the details of a speech he gave Sunday at the Empire State Aeroscience Museum. "I didn't think I was doing anything wrong." The story was dramatic, and ESAM officials later said they were taken in by dubious documentation of Holden's adventures. Bogus claims of heroics have been a constant problem in an era of easily available history and waning memories of the actual participants of America's wars. In his talk, Holden described in vivid detail strafing the deck of a Japanese aircraft carrier from his seat as rear gunner in a dive bomber during the Battle of Midway on June 4, 1942.

As he and his pilot flew away from the burning carrier *Soryu*, they were jumped by a Japanese Zero fighter and shot down, only to be rescued by a U.S.

submarine after a night in a life raft. His fire had been so effective, Holden claimed, that the second in command of his bomber group credited him with setting off munitions and fuel arrayed on the deck of the carrier, speeding its demise.

That was just one of the tales Holden spun for the audience at ESAM's opening of a World War II Navy exhibit on Sunday. The organizers of the event were happy to have the 80-year-old Rhode Island man as a speaker after they were shown a 2003 newspaper story about his experiences not only at Midway, but Iwo Jima, the Japanese surrender in Tokyo Bay, as a cargo plane pilot in the Berlin airlift and as a Navy combat diver during the Korean War, the abortive Bay of Pigs invasion in 1961 and in Vietnam. For his Midway heroics, Holden told the gathering of 45 children and adults, he was awarded a Distinguished Flying Cross and permission from Admiral Chester Nimitz, chief of the Pacific Fleet, to train—at just barely 18 years old—as a pilot. Time passed and he had many other adventures, meeting along the way some of the most famous figures in the war; Greg "Pappy" Boyington of Black Sheep Squadron fame, Bob Hope, and Winston Churchill among them.

As the pilot of a TBM Avenger torpedo bomber in 1945, Holden told his audience, he was shot down dropping napalm on Iwo Jima's Mount Suribachi, later the scene of what became the iconic flag raising by a group of victorious Marines. Safely ditching his plane and rescued yet again, Holden went on to say his experience was indeed similar to that of another Avenger pilot downed near Iwo Jima: President George H. W. Bush. "He played second base when I was playing third base," Holden told a Times Union reporter at the ESAM event. In fact, Bush had been shot down in 1944 raids near Iwo Jima, was sent home and was training other pilots in Virginia by the time Holden's tale put him in the combat zone as a pilot on the carrier U.S.S. Bon Homme Richard.

As for his Midway account, there is no record of Holden or the pilot he named, Bill Havron, on the rosters of any of the fighter, dive bomber, or torpedo squadrons that fought at Midway, the turning point of the Pacific war and one of the most decisive battles of World War II.

Based on his remarks, Holden's name should have turned up on the lists of Bombing 3, the Dauntless squadron attached to the U.S.S. Yorktown, the only American carrier sunk during a battle that saw four Japanese carriers destroyed by dive bombers.

In documents reviewed by The Daily Gazette, the last name "Holden" does show up on the roster of rear gunners in Bombing 6, embarked on U.S.S. Enterprise. That man, Glenn Lester Holden, was indeed shot down with his pilot at

Midway, initially declared missing and later rescued, according to Enterprise "after action" reports. The pilot of Glenn Holden's plane was Tony Schneider and they were rescued by a Navy patrol plane, not a submarine as described by Ed Holden. Glenn Holden was killed in a July 1942 accidental crash of a Dauntless, and nobody named Ed Holden or Bill Havron flew during the battle, according to a Midway archivist contacted by e-mail through the Midway Web site, *www.midway42.org*.

How did ESAM end up hosting a speaker with dubious credentials? "I was convinced mainly because he was written up by newspapers," said Rob Verbsky, the museum's interim curator, who said Holden's military records were not checked in advance. "We were working purely off of what we received, the Narragansett Times article." The Times is a twice-weekly newspaper that relied largely on Holden's own account of his personal history in its July 4, 2003 article. The museum trusted the sources of information they had on Holden, who was asked to speak after a local resident had befriended him through a Navy contact and passed his name to the museum, Verbsky said. In a statement Thursday, the museum said it "had no initial reason to doubt that the lecture Edwin Holden gave on Sunday, December 5th was fabricated. Mr. Holden volunteered to speak at the museum with what appeared to be a factual lecture with corroborating evidence." Holden was not paid for the talk. Explaining his actions, Holden said Thursday he has been speaking to schoolchildren for years on the subject of "Duty, Honor, Country." Over time, he wove in war stories and then gradually made them his own, putting himself in the place of the actual heroes. "Maybe kind of a legend" built over time, he said. "I thought these stories were good for the children and it got out of hand," Holden said. "I won't do it again."

Was he actually in the service? Holden says he did serve on four-engine Navy patrol aircraft doing anti-submarine duty in Iceland, Jacksonville and San Diego. "I'll destroy my notes and discontinue the practice of falsehood," Holden said. "I thought I was doing good."

Other cases of fabricated war records have been exposed in recent years. In April 2003, the first vice chairman of the Saratoga County Conservative Committee resigned his party post and withdrew from organizing pro-U.S. troop rallies after his admission that he lied about serving as a paratrooper during the Korean War.

Donald Neddo's confession and resignation came less than two weeks after he organized a pro-U.S. troop rally in Clifton Park that drew more than 5,000 spectators. At that rally, Neddo claimed he was a Korean War veteran. In June, Juanita Smith lost her job as director of the Topeka YWCA's teen pregnancy prevention program after she admitted lying about serving as a Navy nurse during World War II. That lie was exposed after readers questioned a Topeka Capital-Journal account of her surviving the infamous Bataan Death March in 1942. Smith told the Capital-Journal she made up the death-march story in the early 1990s to make an impression during a job interview. A newspaper managing editor resigned the same day Smith confessed, and the next day Smith resigned the YWCA position.

＊   ＊   ＊   ＊

Index

978-0-595-40511-4
0-595-40511-8